Convergence or Divergence in Europe?
Growth and Business Cycles in France, Germany and Italy

Olivier de Bandt
Heinz Herrmann · Giuseppe Parigi

Convergence or Divergence in Europe?

Growth and Business Cycles
in France, Germany and Italy

With 116 Figures and 80 Tables

 Springer

HF3556

Fc168.7

2006

Olivier de Bandt
46-1405 DGEI-DAMEP
Banque de France
39 rue Croix des Petits Champs
75049 Paris, France
olivier.debandt@banque-france.fr

Heinz Herrmann
Forschungszentrum
Deutsche Bundesbank
Wilhelm Epsteinstraße 14
60431 Frankfurt/Main, Germany
heinz.herrmann@bundesbank.de

Giuseppe Parigi
Servizio Studi
Amministrazione Centrale
Banca d'Italia
Via Nazionale 91
00184 Roma, Italia
giuseppe.parigi@bancaditalia.it

ISBN-10   3-540-32610-3 Springer Berlin Heidelberg New York
ISBN-13   978-3-540-32610-6 Springer Berlin Heidelberg New York

Cataloging-in-Publication Data
Library of Congress Control Number: 2006929199

Springer is a part of Springer Science+Business Media

springeronline.com

© Springer Berlin · Heidelberg 2006
Printed in Germany

SPIN 11678830   Printed on acid-free paper – 42/3100 – 5 4 3 2 1 0

Acknowledgements

The articles published in this book were discussed by academics and economists from central banks or international organisations during the Conference held in Paris on 22 and 23 June 2005. The authors wish to express their sincere appreciation to them. This includes, in alphabetical order:

Prof. A. Benassy-Quéré (CEPII and University Paris X-Nanterre), Prof. A. Brender (Dexia Bank and University Paris-Dauphine), G. Cette (Banque de France), P. Crowley (Suomen Panki, Helsinki), M. Diron (European Central Bank, Franfurt), E. Dubois (French Treasury), B. Enfrun (Banque de France) Prof. R. Faini (University of Rome - Tor Vergata), Prof. D. Giannone (Université Libre de Bruxelles), Prof. H. Kempf (University of Paris I-Sorbonne), B. Mojon (European Central Bank, Frankfurt), Prof. J. Pisani-Ferry (Bruegel Institute, Brussels, and University Paris-Dauphine), W. Röger (EU Commission), G. Rünstler (European Central Bank, Frankfurt), F. Sédillot (OECD), Prof. S. Schreiber (University of Frankfurt), H. Strauss (OECD), M.-O. Strauss-Kahn (Banque de France), J. Torres (Bank of Spain).

In addition, special thanks to C. Cahn (Banque de France) who, on top of contributing a paper, expertly assembled the different articles in LaTeX.

Preface

Against the background of the subdued recovery in the euro area and increasing disparities among member countries at the beginning of the new century, the objective of the book is to investigate the common features as well as the sources of differences in the performance of Germany, France and Italy, the three largest euro area countries, over the last 15 years. The book is a collection of papers written as part of a Joint Research Project carried out in the last two years by economists in the Bundesbank, Banque de France and Banca dItalia.

Two major changes characterise the period since the last decade of the twentieth century. The first concerns the technological paradigm on which production systems are based. Here a sort of revolution is taking place. The extensive use of information and communication technologies (ICT) is radically changing all production systems in a way not very dissimilar from what the electric engine did one century ago. The benefits of ICT for an economy depend however on three key conditions: a) all firms in the economy should apply them, not only the firms in the high-tech sectors; b) the human capital should be improved and enlarged according to the needs of the new paradigm; c) firms reorganize their productive structure in order to exploit all the advantages deriving from the use of ICT. All these factors are at the root of what has been defined as the New Economy and the European economy is far behind anglo-saxon economies in the adoption of the new paradigm.

The second major change is the appearance on the international markets of new and very aggressive competitors, mainly from Far East Asia. Actually, this is not a new event. In the last two centuries the same happened for the USA, Germany and Japan. The appearance of China and India on the international markets has wide-ranging effects on the industrial systems of the incumbent economies, especially for those countries which are most fragile and exposed to the international competition in mature industries. On this regard it is interesting to analyze the different reactions of the economies of

Germany, France and Italy during a period with a common currency so that exchange rate adjustments are no longer possible.

A central question is to assess the degree of comovement of the French, German and Italian economies or the lack thereof at particular occasions. Are they extraordinary events vis à vis a long term trend favouring convergence, or can we detect changes in the last few years?

The book endeavours to provide some explanations of the movements observed in the last years: in view of the major changes described above can they be ascribed to potential growth dynamics, are they associated with external trade performance, or more generally are they linked to a different behaviour of demand components?

In this respect divergences in the external positions of the three countries under consideration are remarkable and this volume tries to shed more light on this issue. A further point is to what extent the German unification is still playing a role when we compare the three economies today. A final important question is whether monetary union fosters convergence. Krugman (1993), in his work on the location of economic activities and agglomeration associated with increasing returns to scale, argued that as countries become more integrated they specialise in the production of goods and services for which they have a comparative advantage, hence they become less diversified and more subject to idiosyncratic shocks, what reduces the gains for monetary union. In response, Frankel and Rose (1998) stressed the endogeneous nature of an optimum currency area: trade integration associated with monetary union develops intra-industry trade, hence higher co-movement across the countries in the union. Empirical work has indeed shown that intra-industry trade has increased between European countries.

Although the book looks mainly at possible divergence between the three countries, one should not overemphasise the differences. It becomes clear that there are also many similarities. Furthermore, one should keep in mind that in a monetary union some disparities may always exist. In particular, it has been demonstrated that the growth differentials among the 12 euro area countries - measured by the standard deviation of euro area growth rates - is of the same order of magnitude as among the 51 American states, which benefit from much more powerful risk-sharing mechanisms like the US Federal Budget. What may appear to be new, however, is the widening differences across the more mature economies in the euro area, even if, in retrospect, to some extent this already occurred in the recent past.

The book is organised into six sections. An overview of the main findings of the papers is presented in Part I, recasting them in the perspective of the existing literature. The following four parts are designed to answer the questions presented above. They deal with measuring growth and cyclical asymmetries (Part II); assessing the role of supply side (Part III); studying the dynamics of demand components (Part IV); analysing the contribution of external trade (Part V).

The assessment of the book is that there is evidence of significant correlation in the short and medium run between the countries, while more significant differences appear in the long run, in terms of potential growth. Apart from demographic factors (the insufficient growth and the ageing of the population which may affect the overall growth rate of a country as well as its capacity to fund its welfare state) this may depend as well on the structural reforms, which have not made sufficient progress during the last few years. In this respect the delay with which the different features of the New Economy are having an impact in the different economies requires particular attention. This factor is also at the origins of the disappointing evolution of Total Factor Productivity in most European countries vis à vis the US economy. These asymmetries should therefore encourage more structural reforms in both the labour and product markets in order to facilitate and speed up the process of convergence towards more modern productive systems according to the new technological paradigm. This is why central bankers support structural reforms, even if it goes beyond monetary policy.

In view of these extraordinary challenges, one final question is whether the differences that are highlighted in the book (in particular higher GDP growth in France), although structural in nature, will be enduring if one projects these economies over the 15-year horizon. The better export performance of Germany, described in Part V of the book, may indicate that profound changes are currently at work.

First drafts of the papers were presented in a conference held at the end of June 2005 in Paris, introduced by Marc-Olivier Strauss-Kahn, Director General of Economics and International Relations at the Banque de France. Each paper was then individually discussed by experts from academia and other central banks, notably the European Central Bank. In the same conference a panel discussion was also organised among leading European experts, such as Anton Brender of Dexia Bank, Jean Pisani-Ferry of the Bruegel Institute in Bruxelles, R. Faini of the University of Rome (Tor Vergata) and Domenico Giannone from Université Libre de Bruxelles. Their contributions are also presented in Part I of the book.

The Joint Research Project was designed to reinforce convergence not only between the economies of France, Germany and Italy, but also between economists and researchers in the respective Central banks. This book may be interpreted as a sign of the success of this effort. Each national central bank contributed in each of the different parts of the book and common conclusions were jointly drafted.

Nevertheless, the articles express the opinion of the authors and do not necessarily reflect the position of the Bundesbank, the Banque de France, the Banca d'Italia, or the Eurosystem.

Olivier de Bandt, Banque de France
Heinz Herrmann, Bundesbank
Giuseppe Parigi, Banca dItalia

Contents

List of Contributors

Deutsche Bundesbank:
Jörg Doepke, Heinz Herrmann, Thomas Knetsch, Kerstin Stahn.
Contact : Deutsche Bundesbank, Economics Department and Research Centre, Wilhelm Epstein Strasse 14, 60014 Frankfurt am Main, Germany.

Banque de France:
Mustapha Baghli, Olivier de Bandt, Catherine Bruneau (and Université Paris X-Nanterre),
Christophe Cahn, Alexis Flageollet (and Université Paris X-Nanterre), Bertrand Pluyaud, Rémy Lecat, Jean-Pierre Villetelle.

Contact : Banque de France, 46-1405 DGEI-DAMEP, 39 rue Croix des Petits Champs, 75049 Paris Cedex 01, France.

Banca d'Italia:
Antonio Bassanetti, Guido Bulligan, Riccardo Cristadoro, Giuseppe Parigi, Alberto Felettigh, Roberto Tedeschi, Andrea Tiseno,
Roberto Torrini, Giovanni Veronese, Roberta Zizza, Francesco Zollino.
Contact : Banca d'Italia, Servizio Studi, Via Nazionale 91, 00184 Rome, Italy.

Part I

General Conclusions

Measuring Cyclical Comovements and Asymmetries in Growth and Business Cycles*

Olivier de Bandt

Banque de France, 46-1405 DAMEP, 39 rue Croix des Petits Champs, 75049 Paris Cedex 01, France olivier.debandt@banque-france.fr

1 Introduction

The succession of periods of short-lived recoveries of economic activity since 2001 and more significant divergence across the most mature economies in the euro area, in particular France, Germany and Italy have surprised many analysts. During that period, there were recurrent debates as to whether or not a recovery was under way, for examples in 2003Q3. Indeed, as indicated in Table 1, GDP growth, in volume terms, averaged between 2.0 and 2.2% in the three countries since the mid 1970s, but reached, since 2001Q4, 0.4% in Germany, 0.7% in Italy, and 1.1% in France. At the same time, beyond these recent growth disparities, Fig. 1 indicates that the business cycle was quite correlated, when measured by deviation from the trend derived with a HP filter.

Table 1. Average GDP growth, volume

	Germany	France	Italy
1975Q2-1981Q1	2.9	2.7	3.8
1981Q1-1993Q2	2.3	2.0	1.8
1993Q2-2001Q4	1.6	2.2	1.9
2001Q4-2005Q3	0.4	1.1	0.7
1975Q2-2005Q3	2.0	2.2	2.2

Source: Villetelle et al., 2005

NB: subperiods are determined by the Harding & Pagan algorithm applied jointly to the GDPs of the 3 countries, see 3.2.

* Contributions by S. Eickmeier, A. Flageollet, R. Cristadoro, J. Matheron, G. Veronese and J.-P. Villetelle, as well as comments by H. Herrmann are gratefully acknowledged.

Looking at overall growth performance, a first set of contributions to the Joint Research Project aimed at finding out whether the current disparities were "normal" or rather extraordinary, taking into account historical evidence as well as more recent events. The objective of the paper is to summarize available evidence on the degree of co-movement between the three countries, how it varied over time, and what are the factors driving these co-movements. We also consider whether periods of transitory divergence were mainly due to the asymmetric behaviour of some individual country, or whether all countries simultaneously diverge from the other two. Our assessment is based on both a survey of the recent literature on business cycle co-movements and asymmetries and their recent evolution, and findings of the papers published in Part II of this volume.

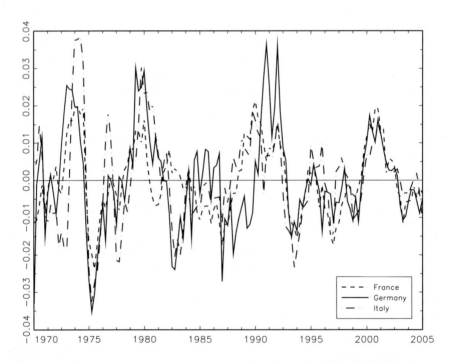

Fig. 1. Business cycles in France, Germany and Italy : deviation from HP trend on GDP

The main conclusions that emerge from the literature as well as from the work carried out in this volume from a large spectrum of methods, both univariate or multivariate, is that one should distinguish between business cycle fluctuations which have become more correlated over time, in particular in the 2000s, against the background of trade liberalisation and globalization, while countries may still exhibit differences in growth potential, measured by stochastic trends notably in GDP. Univariate methods conclude that GDP is correlated across the three countries at business cycle frequency after an episode of "correlation breakdown' in the 1980s (Flageollet, 2006; Cristadoro and Veronese, 2006, this volume). Such results are confirmed by multivariate approaches, which exploit more information and can capture co-movement along a broader set of macroeconomic variables.

Section 2 introduces a brief literature overview, before looking at univariate indicators in section 3 and multivariate results in section 4.

2 Literature overview

In the applied economic literature, the issue of business cycle co-movement recently met renewed interest with the simultaneous slowdown of activity in industrialized countries in 2001. The specific issue of business cycle co-movements in France, Germany and Italy had previously received more attention with the implementation of the Single Market in the 1990s and the introduction of the euro. A casual look at the economic literature indicates however that, in many instances, business cycle co-movements are taken for granted. In contrast, asymmetries come as a surprise. However, a deeper investigation into the empirical literature reveals more diverse conclusions. Obviously, the conclusions depend on the period considered and the method chosen.

Regarding the period chosen, authors diverge as to whether synchronization has indeed increased over time. In contrast, Bordo and Helbling (2003) document the secular increase in synchronization between core European countries. What emerges from the literature is that synchronization between the three countries was quite high in the 1970s, in particular due to the 1974 recession, consistently with the findings that synchronization is higher during periods of recession than during periods of recovery (Helbling and Bayoumi, 2003; Canova, Ciccarelli and Ortega, 2003). More divergence was then observed in the 1980s and in the early 1990s, in the wake of German reunification and turmoil in the EMS. Montfort et al. (2004) concluded that the post-reunification boom was country-specific in Germany. Indeed while Artis et Zhang (1999) argued that correlation among EU countries increased with the introduction of EMS, comparing the 1960-1979 period to the 1979-1997 period, Inklaar and de Haan (2001) noted that rather high correlation during the 1971-1979 was actually followed by significantly lower correlation during both the 1979-87 and 1987-97 periods. Perez, Osborn and Censier (2004), using 10 year- rolling windows, found similar conclusions with a decrease in the correlation of HP detrended GDP between France and Germany in the 1980s, followed by an increase afterwards. The period after 1992-1993 witnessed a deepening of European integration, hence closer business cycles. As indicated above, the increased correlation observed in the first half of the 2000s is usually attributed to the worldwide slowdown observed after

2001. However, analysts diverge as to the causes of such a phenomenon, between common shocks or increased spillovers. From that point of view the "re-synchronization" between the three countries would be part of a more global trend that took place in the second half of the 1980s and the 1990s according to Monfort et al (2004). Perez, Osborne and Artis (2003) concluded to the increased impact of US shocks. Canova, Ciccarelli and Ortega (2003) provided evidence in favour of the existence of a worldwide cycle and against a euro area business cycle. Camacho, Perez-Quiroz and Saiz (2005) even argued that synchronization among euro area countries had not increased over the last twenty years.

Conclusions also differ because of the methods used. A fruitful avenue is the decomposition of output in cycles of different frequencies. Croux, Forni and Reichlin (2001) showed that long cycles are usually well correlated within the euro area but some differences appear for business cycle frequencies, a conclusion also stressed by Helbling and Bayoumi (2003). Some analysts argued that only detrended output series, e. g. output gaps, should be used. Helbling and Bayoumi (2001) concluded that output gaps in Germany until 2001 were more correlated than Italy or France to "Anglo-Saxon" countries. Flaig and Sturm (2003) also found lower correlation of Germany with the rest of the euro area when difference from HP filter is used.

In order to illustrate these results we provide now a few univariate statistics before considering multivariate and factor methods.

3 Univariate indicators of synchronization

A first set of indicators deal with univariate statistics to shed light on the the comovement of the overall business cycles and their correlation across countries. We discuss first the correlation of the business cycle indicators, before looking at turning points indicators.

3.1 Correlation of business cycles

Several indicators are available to measure business cycles. Indicators like the Purchasing Manager Indexes (PMI) in the manufacturing industries and the services sector, based on surveys among companies, exhibit quite significant correlation over the whole 1998-2005 period (see Fig. 2 and bilateral correlation indicators in Table 2). However, one can also note that indicators on services -which include a more significant domestic component- are on average less correlated than the ones related to manufacturing industry in particular in the post 2001 period. Indeed, the correlation of industrial production between Germany and France is stable over sub-samples, while indicators for Italy with either Germany or France appear to be slightly more correlated in the latter part of the sample than over the whole sample. In addition, the correlation of PMI indicators for manufacturing industry are

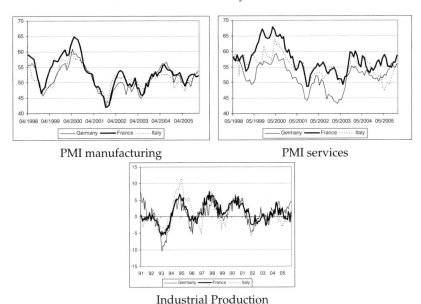

PMI manufacturing   PMI services

Industrial Production

Fig. 2. Macro-economic indicators

slightly lower for the 2002-2005 period -contradicting somewhat the previous remark on industrial production- while the decrease in correlation is is more pronounced for PMI indices in the services sector. The correlation for Italy and the other countries even becomes negative at the end of the sample.

Table 2. Correlation of macro-economic indicators

	1991-2005	1998-2005	2002-2003
Industrial Production			
DE/FR	0.69	0.68	0.67
DE/IT	0.65	0.77	0.77
FR/IT	0.67	0.73	0.76
PMI Manufacturing			
DE/FR	na	0.90	0.83
DE/IT	na	0.86	0.58
FR/IT	na	0.86	0.62
PMI Services			
DE/FR	na	0.77	0.67
DE/IT	na	0.60	−0.48
FR/IT	na	0.71	−0.66

monthly data, IPI: year-on year growth

More comprehensive data are National Account indicators, and in particular GDP (the components of GDP are examined in Part IV of the book). GDP data have the additional advantage of being available for a longer period, hence to allow an investigation of their correlation structure over time.

In order to concentrate on business cycle frequencies, the data are filtered. Due to the dependence on the method, the results of Cristadoro and Veronese (2006, this volume) as well as Flageollet (2006) are therefore based on several methods: Hodrick Prescott, Baxter and King and Christiano and Fitzgerald filters (respectively HP, as in Fig. 1, BK and CF, hereafter) applied to the GDP series in the three countries during the period 1970:1-2004:4.

Table 3. Correlation of business cycles as measured from filtered GDP

	France/Germany	*Italy/Germany*
	1970Q1-2004Q4	
correlation[1]	0.57	0.52
dynamic correlation[2]	0.59	0.62
	1970Q1-1979Q4	
correlation[1]	0.86	0.52
dynamic correlation[2]	0.69	0.52
	1980Q1-2004Q4	
correlation[1]	0.36	0.57
dynamic correlation[2]	0.49	0.48
	1980Q1-1991Q4	
correlation[1]	−0.05	0.49
dynamic correlation[2]	0.19	0.19
	1992Q1-2004Q4	
correlation[1]	0.85	0.80
dynamic correlation[2]	0.79	0.76

Source: Flageollet (2006), Cristadoro and Veronese (2006, this volume)
[1] corr. between business cycle fluct. from Christiano Fitzgerald filter
[2] dynamic correlation measured at business cycle frequencies

Table 3 displays the instantaneous cross-correlation of cyclical components on various subsamples. We also report the dynamic correlation at business cycle frequencies (i.e. for periodic movements between 8 and 32 quarters), introduced by Croux et al. (2001). The latter measure is totally nonparametric whereas the measure of dependence derived from the CF filter relies on the assumption that the underlying process is just a random walk.

Over the whole sample, the two measures provide close results: correlation between business cycle lies between 0.5 (Italy/Germany) and 0.7 (France/Germany). The results from subsamples exhibit a significant decrease during the 1980s, with a recovery afterwards (see section 1). From 1970Q1 to 1979Q4, we observe a large correlation between the French and

German GDP and between the French and Italian ones, whereas the relation of the cyclical component of Italy with Germany is weaker. During the 1980s, synchronization disappeared between France and the other two countries, while correlation between Germany and Italy always seems to remain close to 0.5. However if we consider dynamic correlation, the link between Germany and Italy is actually rather weak. These indicators cannot therefore explain which country was responsible for this "correlation breakdown".

Lead-lag correlation analysis between the three countries (figures not reported in Table 3) indicates that since the 1970s, business cycles of the three countries have tended to move closer.

3.2 Analysis of turning points

We now consider another type of analysis of the business cycle, namely the identification of turning points, as derived from the level of the variables.

In the terminology of business cycle analysis, we therefore look at 'classical cycles', i.e the identification of expansion and recession periods, or peaks and troughs on the level of the variables, as advocated by Harding and Pagan (2002).[2] Such an approach is opposed to the analysis of 'growth cycles' (ie deviation from a trend) as exhibited in Fig. 1 and envisioned again from a multivariate point of view in section 4.1.

The turning points are displayed in Figure 3. At least three different periods can be distinguished: 1974/1975, 1980/1981, 1992/1993. In addition, applying the method to the three countries uncovers a peak in 2001Q1 and a trough in 2001Q4. The number of turning points in France is much smaller than in the other two countries. In contrast, in Germany, the procedure identifies too many turning points. However, over the whole period, there is, a high degree of communality between the countries in terms of cycles. The concordance index on levels is above 0,8 (Villetelle, *op. cit.*) for all pairs formed by the countries. Such a high degree of concordance reveals long run movements. Indeed, while countries may belong to the same phase, they may exhibit very different behaviour at the business cycle frequency. In particular, according to Fig. 3, all three countries were in an expansionary period between 1980 and 1993, while according to Table 3, business cycles where uncorrelated.

Computing average GDP growth rate over country specific cycles, as in Table 4, offers the possibility to measure potential growth. In contrast to France and Italy, which experienced a slowdown in the 1980s, potential

---

[2] As indicated in Villetelle et al. (2005), A peak/trough is reached at t if the value of the series at date t is superior/inferior to previous k values and to the following k values, with k fixed *ex ante* ($k = 2$ or 2 on quarterly series). The first striking feature is that, for all countries, a peak is in general closer to the following trough than to the previous one. This gives an asymmetric view of the business cycle: the expansion phase from trough to peak is longer than the contraction phase, from this peak to the following trough.

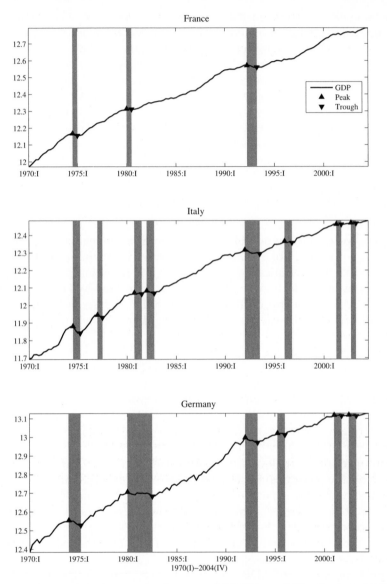

Fig. 3. Expansion and recession phases on GDP (Source: Villetelle et al., 2005)

growth remained quite robust until 1993, due to the reunification period. However, during the following period the slowdown was more pronounced in Germany, while France recovered slightly.

Table 4. Average GDP growth for country specific dating

Germany	*France*	*Italy*
		$1975 : 2 - 1977 : 3\ 3.6\%$
$1975 : 2 - 1982 : 3\ 3.1\%$	$1975 : 1 - 1980 : 3\ 2.7\%$	$1977 : 3 - 1981 : 3\ 3.4\%$
		$1981 : 3 - 1982 : 4\ -0.1\%$
$1982 : 3 - 1993 : 2\ 2.6\%$	$1980 : 3 - 1993 : 2\ 1.9\%$	$1982 : 4 - 1993 : 3\ 2.0\%$
$1993 : 2 - 1996 : 1\ 1.3\%$		$1993 : 3 - 1996 : 4\ 1.6\%$
$1996 : 1 - 2001 : 4\ 1.6\%$	$1993 : 2 - 2004 : 3\ 2.1\%$	
$2001 : 4 - 2003 : 2\ -0.1\%$		$1996 : 4 - 2004 : 2\ 1.5\%$
$2003 : 2 - 2004 : 3\ 0.9\%$		
$1975 : 2 - 2004 : 3\ 2.0\%$	$1975 : 1 - 2004 : 3\ 2.1\%$	$1975 : 2 - 2004 : 2\ 2.2\%$

Source: Villetelle et al. (2005)

The most recent period – the period 2003q1-2004q3, which does not correspond to a cycle – appears as a phase of slow recovery, with an average growth rate markedly below average in all countries.

4 Results from multivariate analysis

The correlation between the cycles in the variables displayed in Fig. 2 naturally leads to a more systematic investigation of such comovements. This is the intuition behind multivariate analysis and in particular of factor models, which exploit more information, hence tracks co-movements in aggregate variables and offer richer interpretations in terms of underlying economic behaviour. Two types of analysis have been carried out in the context of the Joint Research Project, in the stationary case : Cristadoro and Veronese, 2006, this volume) and in the non stationary case (Eickmeier, 2005, as well as de Bandt, Bruneau and Flageollet, 2006, this volume).

4.1 Comovements from factor analysis in a stationary environment

The paper by Cristadoro and Veronese (2006, this volume) constructs a set of monthly business (growth-) cycle indicators for Germany, France, Italy and for the Euro area that can be used not only for *ex post* characterization of the cyclical behaviour of these economies, but, most importantly, for short to a medium run assessment of their current overall economic outlook. The monthly cyclical indicators are constructed as the projection of quarterly national account aggregates on the space spanned by a suitable set of regressors i.e. the factors extracted from a large panel of monthly time series that comprises all sources of potentially useful cyclical information. To motivate this approach the authors show that, consistently with stylized facts, at business cycle periodicities the dynamics of the panel can be captured by few common shocks, responsible for the co-movements across series (see Fig. 3 in Cristadoro and Veronese, *op. cit.*). This approach improves on more traditional univariate methods of signal extraction along several dimensions spelled out in the paper.

Having a set of business cycle indicators for the major European economies the authors can address questions regarding the degree of co-movement and synchronization across these economies. They do it by first applying the Harding and Pagan (2002) methodology on growth-cycle and deriving a preliminary "eye-ball" indication of the degree of concordance of the cycles of different economies. The dating of the turning points shows that over the past two decades European economies experienced similar and rather synchronized episodes of acceleration and deceleration in growth. This evidence is further corroborated by testing explicitly the hypothesis that there is a significant degree of correlation among the cycles in the major euro area countries, along the lines of Pagan and Harding (2001).

The cyclical facts that emerge from the study of monthly indicators of GDP and its components for the 3 countries and the Euro area are consistent with the established view of the cycle gained with traditional univariate filtering techniques as surveyed in section 3 of the current paper (see also Tables 2 and 4 in in Cristadoro and Veronese, *op. cit.*)

4.2 Constructing indicators of euro area business cycles and stochastic trends

Two papers of the Joint Research Project addressed the issue of the construction of indicators of the euro area business cycles using a set of non stationary variables, on the basis of recent advances by Bai and Ng (2004).[3] Considering the stochastic trend in the panel and implementing the Bai and Ng (2004) methodology, they provide, beyond the analysis of cycles, an assessment of potential growth in the three countries.[4] Both papers use a large database of quarterly series assembled by Eickmeier (2005), while, selecting a different subset of variables and a different empirical strategy, they provide complementary views.

---

[3] References in this section are available in de Bandt et al, 2006, this volume.
[4] A more systematic analysis of potential growth and its explanatory factors is addressed in part 3 of this volume.

Eickmeier, 2005

The paper by Eickmeier (2005) uses data for a set of 7 "core" euro area countries (156 variables) observed between 1981Q1 and 2003Q4.[5] Using static PCA and the Bai and Ng's PANIC methodology, the paper estimates 5 factors which explain 32% of total variance, 81% of the variance of euro area GDP growth and 13% of changes in euro area inflation. Using Johansen cointegration tests, 4 common trends or non-stationary factors and 1 stationary factor are found.

Based on the idea that the factors are identified up to a rotation (i.e a linear combination of the factors), the author maximises the variance share of any of the 5 factors at or below business cycle frequencies in order to find a common euro area business cycle and a common euro area stochastic trend, respectively. The latter is highly correlated with EUROCOIN (correlation coefficient of 0.82) while the former moves in parallel with the HP trend of euro area GDP, after correction for the deterministic trend.

In addition, the author uses rotation techniques as well as uni- and multivariate correlation measures in order to interpret the different factors. It turns out that the fluctuations of common euro area factors mainly reflect variations of German and/or French real economic activity as well as prices, long-term interest rates and/or real effective exchange rates, and confidence indicators in various countries. Not surprisingly, national factors driving the economy of Germany and France are most highly correlated with the euro area factors; Italian factors exhibit a relatively low correlation.

Regarding the variables that are broadly "consistent" with the factors, it appears that the factors coincide more with real variables than prices. The factors are more highly correlated with GDP than with consumption which is consistent with previous empirical findings (e.g. Kose, Otrok and Whiteman, 2003) and the quantity anomaly puzzle (Backus, Kehoe and Kydland, 1992). The correlation is higher for producer prices than for consumer prices which is not surprising given that the basket for producer prices includes a much larger share of tradables than the basket for consumer prices. As concerns the transmission channels, trade, exchange rates and long-term interest rates are more highly correlated with the factors than stock prices. Of the global shock proxies, shocks to the US economy seem to be more strongly linked to the euro area factors than oil price shocks.

The paper also examines changes in correlation over time, and in particular whether the variance share explained by the euro area factors has increased over time, considering rolling 5-year samples. It concludes that there is evidence of overall convergence, but temporary real and nominal divergence. In addition, the results for individual countries are mixed. On the one hand, for Germany, there is evidence of real divergence in the first half of the 1990s in Germany, possibly due to reunification; the variance share explained

---

[5] The paper, prepared in the context of the Joint Research Project, is not included in this volume.

by the common factors is smaller at the end of the sample than at the beginning. On the other hand, real convergence in France and Italy is followed by a period of divergence.

De Bandt et al., 2006, this volume

The paper by de Bandt et al. (*op. cit.*) uses the same data source as S. Eickmeier (2005), but selects different variables. Data are also observed over the 1981Q1-2003Q4 period.

In particular all 12 euro area countries are included into the analysis (instead of 7 "core" countries). In addition, a pre-selection of the variables is made *ex ante* in order to keep an homogeneous database in terms of order of integration, retaining nevertheless about 220 series. The gain is that the estimated factor model is consistent with the one suggested by Bai (2003), for which statistical inference becomes possible on the factors. In addition the analysis is run on factors in levels, allowing to derive statistical indicators on the levels. As in Eickmeier (2005), the authors find 5 common factors, explaining 39% of total variance. Obviously, the factors are not the same as in the previous paper. Three out of 5 of the factors are persistent. In that case, all sources of non stationarity are therefore of common nature. The paper also shows that the first factor has a significant contribution to fluctuations of GDP at business cycle frequencies. It appears that Germany, France and Italy were commonly hit by the same negative shock in the early 2000s- representing the first common factor. As a consequence, it is suggested to use the first non stationary factor in order to build a coincident indicator of euro area stochastic trends and cycle.

The indicator summarizes the persistent shocks affecting equally all euro area countries. Such an indicator exhibits the following properties:

- it provides a convenient dating of "classical" cycles;
- it allows to distinguish between increasingly correlated business cycles and divergent long term growth : indeed all three countries are closely correlated with the first factor at the business cycle frequency, while at lower frequency, France outperforms the other countries over the second half of the sample period, pointing to a higher rate of potential growth;
- it is significantly correlated with euro area GDP, on the basis of Bai (2003) confidence band analysis;
- it is also correlated with US business cycle, what implies that the indicator also measures global shocks.

References

Angeloni, I., Dedola, F. (1999) From the ERM to the Euro. European Central Bank, Working paper

Altissimo, F., Bassanetti, A., Cristadoro, R., Forni, M., Lippi, M., Reichlin, L., Veronese, G. (2001), EuroCoin: A real time coincident indicator of the Euro Area business cycle, CEPR Working Paper No. 3108

Backus, D. K., P. Kehoe and F. E. Kydland (1992) International Business Cycles, Journal of Political Economy, 100 (4), 745-775.

Baffigi, A., Bassanetti, A. (2003) Turning point indicators from business surveys: real time detection for the euro area and its major member countries, Banca dItalia

Bordo, M., Helbling, T. (2003) Have national business cycles become more synchronized? NBER Working Paper, n 10310.

Buisse, A., Lefranc, S., Sagnes, N. (2003) L'écart de croissance France zone euro observe depuis 1998 va t-il perdurer?, Analyses Economiques, Direction de la Prévision, Minefi, december.

Camacho, M., Perez-Quiros, G., Saiz, L. (2005) Are European business cycles close enough to be just one?, CEPR Discussion Paper, n 4824.

Croux, C., Forni, M., Reichlin, L. (2001) A measure of comovement for economic variables: theory and empirics, The Review of Economics and Statistics, 83(2), 232-241.

Doyle, B.M., Faust, J.(2002), An investigation of comovements among the growth rates of the G-7 countries, Federal Reserve Bulletin, October, 427-437

Eickmeier, S. (2004), Business cycle transmission from the US to Germany - a structural factor approach, Bundesbank Discussion Paper 12/2004.

Eickmeier, S.(2005), Common Stationary and non stationary Factors in the euro area Analysed in a Large Scale Factor Model, Bundesbank Discussion Paper 2005/2.

Flageollet, A. (2006) Modèles factoriels dynamiques et analyse des cycles économiques, thèse pour le doctorat es Sciences Economiques, Université Paris X, forthcoming.

Flaig, G., Sturm, J.E., Woitek, U. (2003) Synchronisation of national business cycles in Europe, paper presented to the 4th Eurostat colloquium on Modern tools for business cycle analysis.

Inklaar, R., de Haan, J. (2001) Is there really a European business cycle? A comment, Oxford Economic Paper, 53, 215-220.

Kose, M., Otrok, C., Whiteman, C.H. (2003) International business cycles : world, regions and specific factors, American Economic Review, September 2003, 93 (4)

Lumdsdaine, R., Prasad, E.S. (2003) Identifying the common component of international economic fluctuations: a new approach, Economic Journal, 113, 101-127

Prasad, M., Terrones, E. (2003b), How does globalization affect the synchronization of business cycles?, American Economic Association Papers and Proceedings, May 2003, 93(2), 57-62

Perez, P.J., Osborn, D.R., Artis, M. (2003) The International Business Cycle in a changing world: volatility and the propagation of shocks;affiliations in the context of European integration, paper presented to the 4th Eurostat colloquium on Modern tools for business cycle analysis

Perez, P.J., Osborn, D.R., Sensier, M. (2003) Business cycle affiliations in the context of European integration, paper presented to the 4th Eurostat colloquium on Modern tools for business cycle analysis.

Stock, J.H., Watson, M.W. (1991) A Probability Model of the coincident economic indicator, in K. Lahiri and G. Moore (eds) Leading Economic Indicators: new approaches and forecasting records, Cambridge University Press, pp. 63-89.

Stock, J.H., Watson, M.W. (2003), Understanding changes in international business cycle dynamics, NBER Working Paper 9859

Schumacher, C., Dreger, C. (2004), Estimating large-scale factor models for economic activity in Germany: Do they outperform simpler models? Jahrbuecher für Nationaloekonomie und Statistik, forthcoming

Villetelle, J.-P., Golfier, C., Matheron, J. (2005) The structure of GDP growth in Germany, France and Italy: a statistical picture, paper presented to the JRP seminar in Rome, January

Supply-side Developments[*]

Heinz Herrmann and Jörg Döpke

Deutsche Bundesbank, Economics Department. Wilhelm-Epstein-Strasse 14, 60014 Frankfurt a. M., Germany. Heinz.Herrmann@bundesbank.de, joerg.doepke@bundesbank.de

The economic performances of European countries differed markedly in recent years, although the differences may be less pronounced than with respect to some other countries in Europe. Supply-side conditions explain some of the differences and the approach taken here is therefore to estimate potential GDP for the three countries under investigation. In addition, the results for the three countries are compared and some conclusions are drawn from these considerations.

Supply-side developments in Europe have been analysed extensively over the past few years, although the focus has differed. For example, some papers stressed the role of technical progress and ICT, in particular, whereas others concentrated more on the output gap and its use for policy purposes.[2] Also, methods used to analyse potential output have varied, ranging from purely statistical approaches - like trends and univariate filters - to methods which allow greater interpretation from an economic point of view. With an orientation on policy issues both papers included in part III of the book use a more economically oriented approach to estimate potential GDP, namely the calibrated production function on the one hand and the so-called non-parametric approach on the other hand. In fact, it is one aim of this project to use harmonized concepts in order to improve comparability among the three economies.

It must be kept in mind that the degree of uncertainty surrounding estimations of potential GDP growth is often too large for policy purposes, in particular, for calculating a reliable output gap. In the literature, the methods used here are criticized because they do not provide information on the degree of uncertainty. In addition, it has to be kept in mind that there are

---

[*] Useful comments and suggestions from A. Bassanetti, M. Baghli, C. Cahn, O. de Bandt, J.-P. Villetelle and R. Zizza are gratefully acknowledged. The opinions in the paper are those of the authors alone and do not necessarily reflect the views of the Deutsche Bundesbank.
[2] see Jorgenson (2005) and van Ark (2005).

Table 1. Potential GDP growth (1) - results from different sources

	France	Germany	Italy
JRP, non-parametric approach	1.9	0.8	1.1
JRP, calibrated production function, long-term	2.5	2.2	1.0
JRP, calibrated production function, medium term	2.2	1.5	1.2
OECD	1.9	1.3	1.1
IMF	2.0	1.5	1.2
EU	2.3	1.1	1.4

Note: Data from non-parametric approach refer to 2004, data from calibrated production function refer to 2003. Source: Baghli et. al. (2006), Bassanetti et al. (2006), OECD (2005).

other problems. In particular, the non-availability of "real-time" estimates that would have been relevant for current policy decisions has to be considered.[3] However, even after taking into account these caveats, we may conclude that, according to the obtained results, the main stylised facts of the growth process in the three countries, namely, those referring to the question of whether potential GDP growth has accelerated or decelerated, are relatively robust with regard to the choice of the method used. Nevertheless, looking into the various factors explaining growth, the two articles do not always come to identical conclusions.

Baghli, Cahn and Villetelle (2006, this volume) discuss the supply conditions defining the potential GDP growth estimated by the production function approach for France, Germany and Italy. The authors maintain a consistent framework as regards national accounts terminology related to institutional sector classification and treat the three countries homogenously, especially regarding the model specification and the construction of certain variables such as the capital stock series.

In order to estimate potential output, Baghli et al.(*op. cit.*) assume that the production technology of the productive sector can be represented by a Cobb-Douglas function which takes the real value added as a combination of the stock of *productive* capital, the labour input in the productive sector (measured in hours worked) and the Total Factor Productivity (TFP).

In order to get an estimate of potential output for the whole economy, the other components of GDP, namely the value added of households, non-profit institutions serving households, public administrations and institutions and the indirect taxes, net of subsidies are filtered (Hodrick-Prescott) and added to the potential growth in the production sector. A two-step approach is adopted. First, the labour share is calibrated as equal to its average level over the sample so that the Solow residual can be deduced from the

---

[3] see Orphanides and van Norden (2002).

Cobb-Douglas production function. Then, the Solow residual is regressed on a time trend (defining the TFP trend) and the difference of both the capacity utilisation rate and the age of the capital stock of equipment to their corresponding average levels. The paper uses two different approaches: a medium run approach and a long run approach. In the medium-run approach, potential output depends on the actual capital stock, the TFP trend and the smoothed component of the labour input. In the long run, it is often supposed that the capital stock growth is equal to the growth rate of the economy and, hence, the capital/output ratio is constant, as the economy remains on a balanced growth path. This hypothesis is relevant insofar as the actual capital/output ratio is roughly stable. In France, a quick look at the data indicates that this requirement is not fulfilled: the productivity of capital is strongly downward-sloping. However, the capital/output ratio in value terms is much more stable over the sample, indicating that the drift in relative prices between the value added deflator and the investment deflator becomes a determinant of the long-run growth.

A shift in relative prices was observed during the 20th century: until the mid-20th century, when the economic structures shifted from agriculture to industry. Today, the rise of ICT could be the source of the difference observed between the value added deflator and the investment deflator. Nevertheless, it cannot be entirely ruled out that the split between volumes and prices as regards the value added on the one hand and the investment deflator on the other hand is merely a statistical problem.

According to the medium-run estimates average potential growth in France and Germany was about 2 percent, whereas in Italy the average growth rate was somewhat lower. In Italy and Germany the potential growth rate declined since the middle of the nineties while in France potential growth was somewhat higher in the new century compared to the decade before. This picture is more or less confirmed by the long-term approach: while in Germany and Italy potential growth became lower in the second half of the 1990s, it was rather stable in France. With respect to the contributions of the different factors to potential growth the paper identifies remarkable differences between the three countries. In Germany and Italy the development of labour had a negative effect on potential growth, the contribution of Total Factor Productivity was strongest in Germany, being twice as high as in France and four times as high as in Italy.

The second paper in Part III of the book, Bassanetti, Döpke, Torrini and Zizza (2006), analyses the development of potential GDP growth and its components in the 1982-2004 period. To this end, it relies on a non-parametric approach which has the advantage of not requiring any assumption about the specific functional form of the production technology. Compared with the paper summarised above, it allows a flexible output/labour elasticity over time. Moreover, the relative ease of computation associated with this method facilitates the update of quarterly estimates. This usefully complements the analyst's toolkit for a real-time assessment of economic performance.

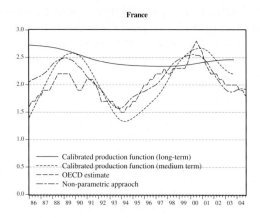

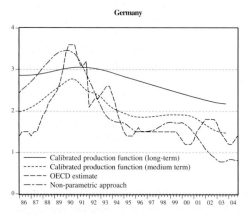

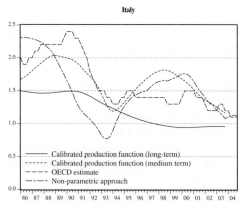

Note: quarterly rates. Source: Baghli et al. (2006), Bassanetti et al. (2006), OECD (2005a).

Fig. 1. Potential GDP growth

The approach adopted by the paper is fundamentally based on the growth accounting identity.[4] This renders it possible to quantify the contributions of the primary inputs of production and of productivity to the dynamics of potential GDP, which have been particularly weak in recent years.

Table 2. Results from growth accounting

	In terms of the number of full time equivalent employed				In terms of hours worked			
	Contribution of				VA(1)	Contribution of		
	Capital	Labour	TFP	POT(2)	Capital	Labour	TFP	Other
Bassanetti et al. (2006), 2001-2004								
France	0.5	0.5	0.5	1.5	(−)	(−)	(−)	(−)
Germany	0.4	−0.1	0.6	0.5	0.4	−0.4	0.8	(−)
Italy	0.7	0.7	−0.3	1.1	0.7	0.5	−0.3	(−)
Baghli et al. (2006), 2001-2003								
France	(−)	(−)	(−)	2.5	0.5	0.3	1.0	0.8
Germany	(−)	(−)	(−)	1.7	0.2	−0.4	1.4	0.5
Italy	(−)	(−)	(−)	1.6	0.7	−0.1	0.3	0.8

Note: percentage points. (1) VA: Value added, total economy, Bassanetti et al. (2006) (2): POT: Potential GDP, whole economy, Baghli et al. (2006).
Source: Bassanetti et al. (2006) and Baghli et al. (2006).

The paper also provides estimates of the non-accelerating inflation rate of unemployment (NAIRU), based on an unobserved component approach. The authors show that the long-run labour market developments differed among the three countries under investigation. In France and Italy, the NAIRU grew constantly from the 1980s, peaked in the mid-1990s and declined thereafter. This development reflects, in part, successful labour market policies adopted in the two countries since the early 1990s. In Italy, the unemployment rate and the NAIRU kept falling until recently, while in France the recent economic slowdown has contributed to increased unemployment.

The picture for Germany is worse: coming from a much lower level of unemployment historically, the NAIRU increased considerably and continuously in the post-reunification growth period, reaching levels close to those of France and Italy. In 2004, the NAIRU rose to 9.4 per cent, its peak value in the period under investigation.

Notwithstanding these differences, the paper documents the adverse role played by both the high levels of the NAIRU in all of the three countries (despite the improvements seen in Italy and, to a much lesser extent, in France

---

[4] For another example of a growth accounting exercise see Musso and Westermann (2005) which look at the aggregated output growth in the euro area.

since the mid-1990s) and by the marked deceleration of Total Factor Productivity (which affected Italy the most). In this respect, the two papers differ since in Baghli et al. (*op. cit.*) the contribution of TFP in Italy and Germany is assumed to be constant, whereas it varies slightly in France. The findings of Bassanetti et al. (*op. cit.*) point to an increasing difficulty to improve the efficiency of the combination of factors of production. According to these results the reduced potential growth is also due to the sizeable slowdown in the accumulation of capital stock, despite increased investment in information and communication technologies. The overall evidence is further confirmed by the outcomes of a simple growth accounting exercise, which shows that labour productivity is less supported by capital deepening and Total Factor Productivity.

While the two factors explaining the deceleration of potential GDP, namely the high NAIRU and the lower TFP growth, have been widely addressed by the empirical literature, the slowdown in capital accumulation in the three countries deserves more attention than what it has attracted until now. One possible explanation, given by Bassanetti et al. (*op. cit.*), though certainly not the only one, may be seen in the process of potential labour to capital substitution, induced by their relative prices in the past 15 years. This argument applies quite well to France and Italy, with significant wage moderation until the early 2000s. In contrast, in Germany, the significant wage increase after reunification was only partially offset by a lower growth of unit labour costs than in the other two countries since the end of the 1990s. There is overall evidence of more general difficulties in deploying factors of production.

Some tentative policy conclusions might be drawn from the the two papers. First, the recent differences in the economic performance of the three countries seem to have a supply-side counterpart. Estimation of potential GDP growth suggests that the differences are, to a considerable extent, driven by supply-side developments resulting in a weak trend growth. Second, while the competing methods of estimating potential GDP have their respective merits and weaknesses and the discussion on this issue is undoubtedly important, the main conclusions concerning the pace of the underlying growth remain unaffected by such considerations. In particular, starting from a phase of virtually equal trend growth in the mid-1990s, potential GDP picks up in France and slows down in Germany; in Italy, it remained more or less unchanged until the end of the 1990s, and has declined in more recent years. Third, one suspect for explaining this difference is the strongly diverging development in the labour markets. However, it must be kept in mind that the differences across the three countries appear to be relatively small when compared with the more dynamic countries within the OECD (See Fig. 2).

While, in France and Italy, labour contributes positively using growth accounting approaches, the opposite does hold for Germany. This result is further supported by an analysis of the NAIRU's in the three countries. In the second half of the 1990s, the NAIRU declined in France and Italy, getting back to their early-1990s levels at the end of the decade. This contrasts with

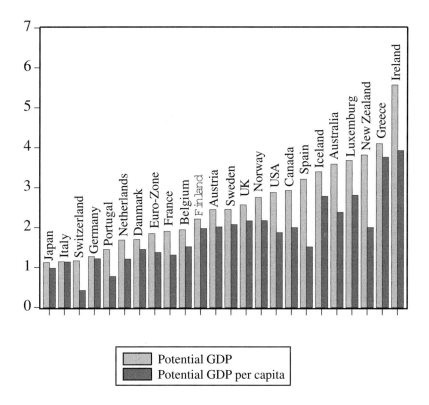

Note: Change over previous year.
Source: OECD (2005a)

Fig. 2. Potential GDP growth and potential GDP per capita growth in selected OECD countries in 2004

Germany, where the NAIRU has been increasing towards a value well above its 1991 level. More recently, the NAIRU declined in Italy, increased in Germany, and remained flat in France.

Taking the results of the Part III in a broader perspective, it should also be mentioned that the differences in the level of per capita potential GDP reflect diverging productivity levels, but also diverging trends in labour force participation. In particular, hours worked per worker are much lower in most of the European countries than in the US. However, the underlying reason for this empirical fact is still under heavy debate. While Blanchard (2004) argues that at least a considerable part of the gap might be due to diverging preferences in leisure and, therefore, not necessarily a matter of concern for economic policy, Prescott (2004) sees the main reasons for the lower number of hours worked in Europe in the distorting taxation of labour. Alesina et al. (2005) argue that labour market regulations, that have been advocated mainly by trade unions along the motto of "work less, work all" may explain a large part of the difference between the US and Europe.

All in all, seen from the supply side, we do observe more significant differences across the three countries in the first half of the 2000s, even if the similarities are clearly more important than the differences. It remains also to be seen whether the differences will endure. Accordingly, the policy recommendations by international organisations for the three countries read quite similarly and point to the need for a higher labour utilisation as the key measure for closing the per capita income gap with respect to to the US (see, for example, OECD, 2005b). Furthermore, additional reforms are necessary also to promote the diffusion of new technologies and foster TFP growth. Such reforms may include removing remaining product markets rigidities and, in particular, making the labour markets more flexible. Some of the reforms already have been implemented, though the process certainly remains to be completed (see Blanchard, 2005).

References

Alesina, A., E. Glaeser and B. Sacerdote (2005), "Work and leisure in the U.S. and europe: Why so different?", *NBER Working Paper* No. 11278. Cambridge MA.

Baghli, M., C. Cahn and J.-P. Villetelle (2006), "Estimating Potential Output with a Production Function for France, Germany, and Italy", in this volume.

Bassanetti, A., J. Döpke, R. Torrini and R. Zizza (2006), "Capital, Labour and Productivity: What Role do They Play in the Potential GDP Weakness of France, Germany and Italy?", in this volume.

Blanchard, O.J. (2005), "European unemployment: the evolution of facts and ideas", MIT, *Department of Economics Working Paper Series*, No. 05-24.

Blanchard, O.J. (2004), "The Economic furture of Europe", Journal of Economic Perspectives, 18, 3-26.

Cotis, J. P., J. Elmeskov and A. Mourougane (2005). "Estimates of Potential Output: Benefits and Pitfalls from a Policy Perspective." In: Reichlin (ed.). *The Euro Area Business Cycle: Stylized Facts and Measurement Issues*. London.

EU (2005), "AMECO data base", Brussels.

IMF (2005), "Data base to the World Economic Outlook", available at : http://www.imf.org/external/pubs/ft/weo/2005/02/data/index.htm.

Jorgenson, D.W. (2005), "Information technology and the G7 economies". *Revista di Politica Economica*, 95, 25-56.

Musso, A. and T. Westermann (2005). "Assessing Potential Output Growth in the Euro Area - A Growth Accounting Perspective." *ECB Occasional Paper* No. 22. Frankfurt a.M.

OECD(2005a), "Economic Outlook", Paris.

OECD(2005b), "Going for Growth", Paris.

Orphanides, A. and Van Norden, S. (2002). "The unreliability of output-gap estimates in real time". *The Review of Economics and Statistics*, 84, 569-583

Prescott, E.C. (2004), "Why do Americans work so much more than Europeans?", *Federal Reserve Bank of Minneapolis Quaterly Review*, 28, 2-13.

van Ark, B. (2005),"Does the European Union needs to revive productivity growth?" *Groningen Growth and Development Centre Research Memorandum GD-75.* Groningen.

Cyclical Patterns in Main Components of Aggregate Demand[*]

Francesco Zollino

Bank of Italy, Research Department, V. Nazionale 91, 00184 Rome, Italy
francesco.zollino@bancaditalia.it

1 Introduction

Since the beginning of the years 2000, the average growth performance in the euro area as a whole has been subdued, in comparison with both more dynamic behaviour in previous years and the buoyant trend in world output. The slowdown of GDP between 2000 and 2005 as opposed to the sustained growth over the second half of the nineties may be attributable to a lower stimulus coming from gross exports, together with the deceleration in domestic demand, checked by a very moderate capital accumulation and the prolonged weakness in private consumption. Developments in both GDP and demand components have been pretty different across the main economies, with Germany and Italy performing worse than France, respectively because of a sluggish domestic demand and a dramatic loss in export competitiveness (Figure 1).

Understanding the structural and the cyclical factors determining the developments in the three economies in isolation and the scope for their synchronization is a key input in order to gauge the way and the timing to overcome the current, prolonged phase of sluggish growth. This is the basic aim of the research conducted in Part IV of the book, which deals with the short and long run features of demand components. In the first place, the paper by Bulligan (2006, this volume) investigates the degree of synchronization of demand components across countries by adopting a variety of methodologies identified in the recent literature in order to check for robustness in results. Interestingly, evidence based on individual series is compared with a common factor analysis, which helps assessing if an European cycle is at work. In the second place, the paper by Knetsch (2006, this volume) mainly analyses

[*] Useful comments and suggestions by Olivier de Bandt, Jean-Pierre Villetelle, Giovanni Veronese are gratefully acknowledged. The author is sole responsible for all remaining errors. The paper expresses the author's personal opinion which does not necessarily reflect the views of the Bank of Italy.

28   Francesco Zollino

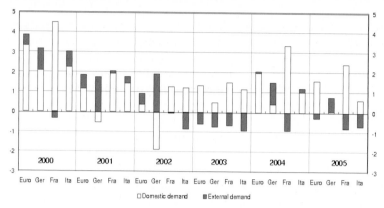

Fig. 1. Contributions to GDP growth in the euro area (%)

within country comovements among GDP and largest demand components;
it also contributes in assessing robustness in cross countries comovements
by computing confidence intervals around point estimates of some measure
of synchronization. As in the first paper, attention focuses on a robust measurement of synchronization across the largest economies in the euro area,
while possible determinants are not fully adressed. In contrast, the purpose
of the paper by Tiseno (2006, this volume), is to understand the mechanism
driving cyclical comovement. A variety of simulations based on the macro-
econometric models developed within the national central banks are implemented. Its objective, in particular, is to disentangle the respective role of
idiosyncratic shocks *versus* different reactions to common shocks in shaping
the recent cyclical divergence of main economies in the euro area. In this respect, the paper sheds light on the degree of similarity in responses of GDP
and main demand components to selected exogenous shocks.

After sketching a statistical picture of the different cycles that may be
identified in France, Germany and Italy since the middle of the seventies,
in this section we briefly review the main results obtained in Part IV. They
can be summarized as follows: i) the structure of demand seems different
between Germany - which turned increasingly centred on net trade since
the middle of the nineties - and France, where consumption and, to a lower
extent, investment keep driving GDP growth; in Italy a shift has recently occurred from net trade to domestic demand; ii) over the full time horizon,
synchronization across main countries proves high at the business cycle frequencies under different statistical measures; it proves stronger for imports,
GDP, investment and export, by far lower for consumption; for the latter aggregate, however, a sizeable gain in comovement is found since the nineties
compared with the previous two decades; moreover, at lower frequencies
synchronization is high, to pretty similar extents, for all demand components; iii) long run comovements within countries show similar patterns in

France and Germany, where evidence supports a dual development between a stochastic trend driving internal components and a different one driving the external components; the picture is much less clear-cut in Italy, amid both a weak evidence of co-integration found for consumption, investment and GDP, and signs of instability in the long run relation between imports and exports; iv) at the cyclical frequencies, in all countries business investment data show, as expected, the highest volatility and GDP the smallest; the standard deviation of cyclical component of consumption lies in the middle; persistence in cyclical components proves higher in France than in Germany and Italy for all main demand aggregates; v) with the caveat that results may be affected by differences in underlying macro-econometric models for each economy in addition to differences in the national economic structures, the pattern of responses to a shock to world demand over the last five years proves pretty similar across countries for GDP and main demand aggregates, while sizeable differences arise in case of shocks to exchange rate, with Germany proving more responsive than France and, even more Italy; shocks to government spending in Germany and Italy, aimed at equalizing the expenditure actually observed in France, do not cause important changes with respect to historical developments in the two countries.

2 Demand components in GDP cycles

By adopting the dating suggested by Harding and Pagan (2002), over the different cycles identifiable for Germany, France and Italy in isolation consumption growth uniformly contributes the most to GDP growth; [2] it comes with no surprise considering that household demand is by large the most important component in aggregate demand. On the contrary, the contribution coming from gross fixed capital formation is negligible. Interestingly, net exports and inventories changes provided a positive contribution only in Germany, against a virtually nil role played on average in France and Italy. The picture looks like more fragmented if distinction is made across cycles and countries. The impulse coming from private consumption is much more unstable in Germany and, even more, in Italy than in France. Two further peculiarities of the French economy are the following: i) investment expenditure never dragged GDP growth, whereas it was the case for Germany (in three different cycles since the nineties) and in Italy (only in the cycle at the beginning of the eighties); ii) net exports never provide a substantial support in France in constrast to Germany (to increasing extents since the middle nineties) and Italy (over the three cycles running between 1981/Q1 and 1996/Q4).

Focusing on the latest years, a cyclical trough can be identified only for Germany (at 2003/Q2) while its dating is controversial for the other two

---

[2] This section heavily relies on Villetelle et al. (2005), who identify five country specific cycles for Germany, three for France and six for Italy.

economies; it is however hardly disputable that all the three main economies in the euro area have been far away from a cyclical peak over the last three years. Over this period, stagnating domestic demand in Germany, induced by sluggish consumption and declining investment, contrasts with more dynamic development in France and Italy. This stands as an important innovation for Italy, where the average GDP growth rate is rather similar to the previous cycle, but the structure of demand has shifted from net exports to private consumption; the picture is less clear in France, due to a more controversial dating of latest cycle.

If we shift to common cycles, for the three economies a peak would have been reached in 2003/Q1 and developments since then can be compared with the same phases of previous cycles: a general feature in the last two cycles is that GDP was flat for some quarters before starting a moderate growth (Villetelle et al., 2005). In the latest cycle, the increase after ten quarters proves marginally higher in France than in Germany and Italy; in the latter country, volatility was higher, with deep contractions in the last quarter in 2004 and the first in 2005 virtually recovered by a rebound in the following six months. As for demand developments, in Germany exports and, partly interrelated, imports were by large the most dynamic components, against a prolonged weakness in both investment and household consumption (Figure 2).

The picture proves relatively more balanced in France and Italy. Differently from Germany, in the former country surging imports were apparently driven more by autonomous components in domestic demand, in particular by investment expenditure, than by exports, which show a smooth improvement over time. Against disappointing developments in exports, Italian economy shares a weak capital formation as in Germany, while consumption performed better, albeit slower than in France, thanks to the stimulus coming from employment creation. Accordingly, the general picture shows that the three largest economies in the euro area reveal important differences in the demand development underlying the pretty similar GDP changes, implying differrent balances of risks in the way towards a solid recovery.

3 Cross countries comovements in GDP and main demand components

Focusing on business cycles, by usual assumption identified by fluctuations with a period between 1.5 and 8 years, a first indicator of synchronisation along the lines of the Harding and Pagan (2002) methodology (hereafter "H&P") measures the length of time two variables spend in the same cyclical positions (expansion and recession). Accordingly, it reflects the similarity in the sequence of turning points (troughs and peaks).

Based on this measure, in the paper by Bulligan (*op. cit.*) GDP cycles prove generally significantly and positively correlated, with similar intensity between Italy and either Germany or France, to a lower extent between the

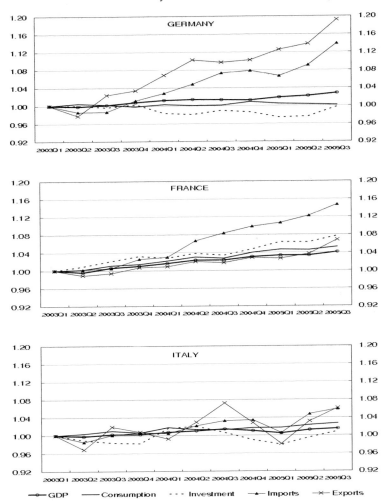

Fig. 2. Changes in GDP and demand components after the cyclical peak in 2003Q1 (Index, 2003Q1 = 1)

latter two. Looking at demand components, synchronisation is rejected for private consumption (CON), while it is generally high for private non residential investment (INV), and gross trade flows. By averaging across all possible pairs within the three largest economies in the euro area, correlation proves the strongest for GDP and imports (IMP), marginally weaker for other components with the exception of a low value found for consumption (column "H&P" in Table 1).

A second measure of comovements focuses on the similarity of the shocks affecting the three economies and on their propagation at different time horizons. In order to isolate the shocks to a single demand component, country pair-wise vector auto regression (VAR) models have been estimated; as the resulting forecast errors can be reasonably interpreted as innovations or shocks to each variable in the VAR, synchronisation at the business cycle horizon (32 quarters) can be properly assessed. In this case average results point to a stronger correlation for both GDP and demand components than in the previous exercise (column VAR in table 1). Interestingly, synchronization for consumption turns sizeable, but, here again, lower with respect to GDP and imports. Like for exports, comovements in consumption is checked by a scant commonality between Germany and Italy at the business cycle frequency. At a lower frequency (within a quarter), VAR forecast errors generally point to a very low correlation: idiosyncratic shocks start very differently across the largest economies in the euro area, and gains in comovements over time are mainly driven by the propagation mechanisms.

Table 1. Average correlation between business cycles

	H&P	VAR*	CFR	ComFac
GDP	0.5	0.7	0.3	0.4
CON	0.1	0.5	0.2	0.2
INV	0.4	0.6	0.2	0.3
EXP	0.4	0.4	0.3	0.3
IMP	0.5	0.7	0.3	0.1

* For 32 quarter ahead projections.
Source: Bulligan (2006).

A third measure of synchronisation considered in the paper is the dynamic correlation and its extension to the multivariate case, in line with the cohesion statistics put forward by Croux, Forni and Reichlin (2001). The two indexes are defined on the frequency domain and allow for selecting the band (and therefore the periodicity) of interest in the analysis. Focusing again on business cycle fluctuations, results prove in a middle range with respect to the previous two measures (column CFR in Table 1). On average point estimates of cohesion are not very different across GDP and main demand components. Consumption synchronization is confirmed as being the lowest, mainly because Italian households expenditure scarcely comoves with developments in France and Germany.

By extending the analysis to long run properties, the most interesting finding is that cohesion across countries is high and fairly similar for single expenditure aggregates, suggesting that the consumption puzzle, longly stressed in the open economy literature (Backus, Kehoe and Kydland, 1992), could prove strictly a business cycle phenomenon for the largest euro area countries.

Having evaluated the degree of comovement between GDP cycles as well as expenditure aggregates, Bulligan (*op. cit.*) adopts an unobserved component model to extract a common European cycle and to assess its importance in explaining the observed variability in national series. The exercise finds evidence of a common cycle, with a much lower explanatory power for consumption than for GDP (respectively 20 and 40 per cent of the observed variability in the quarterly rate of growth). The analysis also confirms that national idiosyncratic factors may play a leading role in the short run fluctuations, to larger extents for main demand components.

An interesting point finally raised in the paper concerns the possibility that the intensity in business cycle synchronisation has been changing over time. By replicating the cohesion estimate for three different sub periods, it actually turns out that the three economies have become more synchronised since the middle of the nineties. For GDP and consumption the result is even stronger if the comparison is made between the periods 1970-90 and 1999-2004, signalling that the start of Monetary Union might have spurred cyclical similarities across main countries. As domestic financial markets keep integrating and enlarging, a deeper risk sharing and income insurance would improve consumption smoothing across countries, supporting the argument for an endogenous convergence of European countries towards sounder condition for an optimal currency area (Sorensen and Yosha, 1998). However evidence found in Bulligan's paper is very preliminary and needs to pass the test of statistical significance as the short time span for latest years presumably affects the accuracy of estimates. Still, significant differences remain in the level of correlation between GDP and trade variables on one side and consumption and investment on the other, which confirms much lower than it is generally found for USA (Krueger and Perri, 2002).

4 Comovements within countries and more on cross-country synchronization

In the second paper in Part IV, Knetsch (*op. cit.*) deals with developments of demand components within countries and across countries, addressing main properties and similarities in both the short and the long run. At the same time it provides a helpful contribution in statistical methods as for detrending procedure, which preserves empirical features of GDP and its main demand components, and for the significance detection by parametrically bootstrapping.

In the first place, under the reasonable tenet of within-country co-integration, a trend-cycle decomposition is achieved based on a fully specified vector error correction model, or the associated common trend representation. As for the long run properties, the main results point to distinct patterns between France and Germany on one side and Italy on the other. In particular, in the first two countries evidence supports a dual development between a stochastic trend driving internal components and a different one driving the external components, both exports and imports; analysis of long run residuals shows a pretty similar pattern, in duration, volatility and cyclical phases, as for the investment-output relation, a much weaker similarity as for the consumption-output one and no commonality as for the export and import equilibrium.

The picture is much less clear-cut in Italy, amid both a weak evidence of co-integration found for consumption, investment and GDP, and signs of instability in the long run relation between imports and exports. As a distinct feature in the Italian data, imports seem to significantly affect investment, likely because of the higher dependence of the national industry form energy and raw materials purchased abroad, and the pattern of Italian specialization, more centred on the supply of consumer goods.

As for the cyclical properties, in all countries business investment data show, as expected, the highest volatility and GDP the smallest; the standard deviation of cyclical component of consumption lies in the middle. While exports are more volatile than imports in Germany, the contrary holds true in both France and Italy. Persistence in cyclical components - as proxied by first order autocorrelation - proves higher in France than in Germany and Italy for all demand components, with a close similarity between the latter two countries for non-residential business investment and between France and Germany for consumption and GDP. As a general result, important differences in the national cyclical patterns arise when we extend analysis from GDP to the main components of demand. In this respect, progress towards a more disaggregated and harmonized dataset would be very welcome in view of a better understanding of both cyclical and long run developments of the main economies in the euro area.

In the second place, comovements across the three countries are explored in a dynamic setting according to a cohesion measure, much alike the approach implemented by Bulligan. An important difference relates to the identification of cycles components, which in Knetsch' paper is based on cointegration analysis rather than on more usual filtering techniques. It turns out that point estimates for cohesion in the business cycle frequencies are now lower for GDP and trade flows, marginally higher for investment expenditure, with a virtually the same low level for consumption (Table 2). On the positive side, these findings basically confirm the picture found in the previous paper, which proves more robust from a methodolology standpoint. On the negative side, bootstrapped confidence intervals detect high sampling variability and uncertainty from model specification and estimation, resulting in loss of significance in the point estimate of cohesion for all individual aggregates. This raises additional concern as for the actual strength in co-cyclicality across the core countries of a monetary union. As already mentioned, the result could suffer from the low level of disaggregation in demand components considered in the research, which in turn is mainly due to the reasonable requirement of data harmonization across countries over a long time horizon. Grouping across components in order to mitigate the variation bands, the identification of synchronization confirms controversial for external demand, while proving sounder for internal demand, for which a larger set of components is available at the start. Only when all aggregates, including GDP, are grouped together, cohesion in the cyclical frequencies turns out statistically significant.

Table 2. Cohesion between reference cycles

	GDP	CON	INV	IMP	EXP
Bulligan (2006)*	0.3	0.2	0.2	0.3	0.3
Knetsch (2006)**	0.1	0.2	0.4	0.2	-0.1

* Cycles based on Baxter-King filter
** Cycles based on VECM representation

By first differencing the trend component in order to assess comovements in the long run, the cohesion point estimates for single aggregates are again not very accurate. However, the hypothesis of co-trending across countries cannot be rejected not only by overall grouping, like for co-cycling, but also by grouping only consumption, investment and GDP. Moreover, cohesion point estimates for this group prove higher than for external demand, delivering a possible interpretation that technical progress spillovers across euro area are significant, whereas the national patterns differ significantly regarding external trade.

5 Synchronization in response to exogenous shocks

In view of the preliminary evidence of co-cyclicality, albeit moderate, found in the first two papers, the final contribution in the demand section investigates to which extent the three largest economies in the euro area may follow a common response to a variety of exogenous shocks. From this standpoint, by controlling for homogenous impulses the paper by Tiseno (*op. cit.*) sheds some light on both the features of the progagation mechanisms at work in each of the three largest economies in the euro area and the way they contribute to determine cross country comovements at the business cycle frequency.

5.1 The simulation design

For this purpose, a set of simulations for each economy is run based on a linear approximation of the dynamic elasticities of endogenous variables with respect to exogenous variables as retrieved from the macro-econometric models of the national central banks of France, Italy and Germany under the harmonized assumptions and shocks agreed within the Inflation Persitence Network of the European System of Central Banks. In particular the paper develops two classes of exercises. In the first one, the degree of synchronization is tested against the response patterns of main demand components to purely hypothetical shocks, that hit the three countries at the same time at the bussines cycle frequency. Three types of exogenous shocks are considered: i) shock to the balanced growth rate of world demand; ii) shock to the steady state of the euro exchange rate; iii) shock centred on growth rate of government consumption. The exercise aims at addressing similarities in dynamic responses to exogenous common shocks at the business cycle frequency. In this respect, the results allow for assessing the role of pure systematic differences in the propagation mechanisms of common impulses in determining the degree of co-cyclicity of the three countries. In the second class of experiments, the exogenous shocks are designed in a way to offset the cyclical components which have been observed in main exogenous variables over the period 1998Q4-2003Q4. This period likely defines a full cycle in the three exogenous variables considered in the first exercise. The purpose is to figure out to what extent the cycle in GDP and main components over the same period has been driven by the cycle in the selected exogenous variables. In other terms, comparing counterfactual histories of GDP and its main components in the three countries allows for gauging how smoother their cyclical developments would have been with no fluctuations in the exogenous "world" and whether it would have increased synchronization.

The counterfactual shocks apply again to world demand, exchange rate and government consumption, in particular: i) a cyclical shock (lasting five years) that would make world demand grow constantly at the average rate of 6.8% per year; ii) a cyclical currency shock that would cause a zero appreciation of the euro with respect to all other currencies; iii) a growth rate of government consumption in Germany and Italy as countercyclical as that observed in France. A controversial point in the full exercise relates ex post to the selection of the time horizon, since it is disputable nowadays that a full cycle in GDP has been completed in the three economies, whereas it is less problematic for world demand and exchange rate movements. In this respect, the three economies can still be in a different cyclical position even if they have been hit by the same shock in recent years, and the exercise misses part of the joint dynamics in the national economic systems.

5.2 The main results

As a preliminary step in reviewing main results, it must be kept in mind that the classes of exercise hinge on macro-econometric models that each individual central banks developed following different strategies. It is therefore not an easy task to disentangle how much reported results reflect differences in the economies and how much they respond to differences in the modelling strategies. This caveat applies in particular to the results of the currency shock experiment, which may depend on a priori modelling considerations while evidence found in Part V of this volume indicates that structural differences may have changed over time.

In the Tiseno's paper, the response patterns to hypothetical shocks show a high degree of synchronization across the three economies when they are hit by an exogenous shock to world demand, both for GDP and main components. In this case, the reaction is larger for German exports, imports, GDP and investment expenditure, followed by France and Italy; as predicted by the life cycle theory, the response of consumption is negligible for all three economies. Synchronicity is scant for GDP reaction to a shock to the euro exchange rate; the German economy appears to be the most responsive, although the swing of its GDP growth rate is slower than that of France; the GDP growth of the Italian economy has a very slow reaction, plausibly because of the very rapid adjustment of prices in the Bank of Italy macromodel. Also aggregate demand components react at different times and with different strength to the external stimulus. Consumption remains almost flat in Germany, while moving counter cyclically to the shock in the other two economies. Investment has very different behaviour across the three countries, with the Italian one going into a very long cycle. As for exports, the growth rate of the French ones responds the most and the quickest. Imports move opposite to exports as one would expect.

As for world demand, the three economies respond synchronously to shocks to government consumption, but with negligible differences in the amplitude of the response. The impact is very small on consumption as well as on exports, while different behaviours occur for investment and imports. While in Italy government consumption activates a long and large cycle in the growth rate of investment, this does not happen for the other two countries where investments react quite regularly and in line with the exogenous shock. In France the largest impact of the government consumption cycle is on imports, which respond synchronously and with a large swing, much larger than in the other two countries.

In the counterfactual experiment of a flat growth rate of world demand all three economies would have followed a smoother growth path for GDP than actually observed, with likely gains in welfare. Again consumption would have not changed much, while import and export would have obviously accounted for a large part of the difference.

By comparing average growth rates between the first and the second half of the period as a rough measure of how much of the cycle (both in GDP growth and in the growth of its components) can be accounted for by the shock in world demand growth, it turns out clearly that the effects seems negligible for GDP, with the exception of France, and for consumption; a sizeable effect arises for the cycle of investment growth, particularly for Italy, and for imports and exports, in which France would see a particularly strong reduction in the cycle under the counterfactual scenario.

In the counterfactual experiment of a flat euro, according to the underlying country model specification France would have had a negligible cycle in GDP, while Germany would have gone expansively; the difference with actual cycle is not significant for Italy. Consumption takes a big stake in changing the history of the cycle, even if in Italy an offsetting swing comes from investment. The growth rate differential in exports is obviously large in all countries, but the effect on imports is more moderate. For both France and Italy, the counterfactual history would bring about a stronger cycle in consumption growth, while Germany would see a dampening of the cycle. While there is no doubt that the cycle in French and German investment growth would be reduced by the counterfactual history, this does not seem to be true for Italy. The counterfactual history would definitely reduce the cycle in export growth in Italy, and, to a larger extent, in Germany. Vice-versa, the French cycle would be reversed. The cycle in import growth would be amplified for all three countries, particularly for France.

Finally the counterfactual experiment to replicate for Germany and Italy the same growth rate of French government expenditure shows negligible changes in the two countries both for GDP and main demand components growth rates; also the cyclical patterns would remain virtually the same as actually observed.

References

Backus DK, Kehoe PJ, Kydland FE (1992) International real business cycles The Journal of Political Economy 100:745–775

Bulligan G (2006) Synchronization of cycles: a demand perspective. In this volume

Croux C, Forni M, Reichlin L (2001)A measure of comovement for economic variables: theory and empirics. The Review of Economics and Statistics 83:232–241

Harding D, Pagan A (2002) Synchronization of cycles. Melbourne Istitute of Applied Economic and Social Research, mimeo

Knetsch TA (2006) Short run and long run comovement of GDP and some expenditure aggregates in Germany, France and Italy. In this volume

Krueger D and Perri F (2002) Does income inequality lead to consumption inequality? NBER Working Paper 9202

Sorensen BE and Yosha O (1998) International risk sharing and European monetary unification. Journal of International Economics 45:211–238

Tiseno A (2006) Cross-country synchronization of aggregate demand responses to exogenous cyclical shocks: what central banks' macro models have to say about the recent experience of France, Germany and Italy. In this volume

Villetelle JP, Golfier C, Matheron J (2005) The structure of GDP growth in Germany, France and Italy: a statistical picture. Banque de France note DEER-SEMEP m05-001-DCONJ-SSC 04-295

Convergence and Divergence in External Trade*

Olivier de Bandt and Jean-Pierre Villetelle

Banque de France, 46-1405 DAMEP, 39 rue Croix des Petits Champs, 75049 Paris
Cedex 01, France olivier.debandt@banque-france.fr,
jean-pierre.villetelle@banque-france.fr

1 Introduction

The evolution of external trade over the last few years has exhibited quite
different patterns across Germany, France and Italy. From that point of view,
it certainly constitutes one source of asymmetry between the three countries. Over the 2000-2005 period the average annual growth rate of exports
of goods and services in value was 5.5 % in Germany, but only 3.0 % in Italy
and 1.5 % in France. In real terms and over the same period, exports grew
by 5.6 % annually in Germany, 1.5 % in France and remained constant in
Italy. After German reunification and weak export performance in Germany
in the early 1990s, the 2nd part of the 1990s witnessed a recovery of German
trade performance, which accelerated at the beginning of the 2000s, a move-
ment going beyond a simple catching-up process. Conversely, Italian trade
performance, in strong progression in the first half of the 1990s, has eroded
since the mid-1990s and stabilised only recently. The recent good external
performance of Germany has been partly offset by weak domestic demand
(see Part 4 on demand side), resulting in GDP growth below the other two
countries.[2] Nevertheless, it may have structural implications. The question
is therefore whether Germany is returning to a development pattern which
is mainly export-driven, as already observed in the 1980s, or whether we are
observing a different international division of industrial activities among the
three countries on top of changes in the distribution between the euro area
and the rest of the world in terms of relocation of stages of production.

Several explanations have been put forward to explain the most recent
German performance and, in contrast, the mediocre external results experienced by France and Italy. A preliminary remark is, however, necessary: one

---

* Comments by H. Herrmann, B. Pluyaud and K. Stahn are gratefully acknowledged
[2] Had Germany experienced the same progression of domestic demand as in France,
its net external trade surplus would have turned into a net deficit in value terms,
see also Artus et al. (2006)

should distinguish between the current specialisation structure in terms of market shares at the country or sector level – which results from past decisions – and the performance achieved, i.e. the ability to defend or even increase market shares in that context. Obviously, the euro appreciation in 2002-2004 may partially explain some subsequent losses in market shares for the euro area with respect to the rest of the world during that period. However, it cannot explain the divergence between the three countries. We survey here the conclusions gathered from the economic literature as well as the papers in Part 5 of the book along different lines:

- the evolution of price competitiveness;
- the impact of geographic and sectoral specialisation;
- the contribution of non-price competitiveness.

The general conclusion is that the usual determinants of export performance, namely the first two items listed above, fail to account fully for the recent poor export performance, at least for France and, to a smaller extent, for Italy.

Table 1. Average export growth, volume (%)

	Germany	France	Italy
In volume terms:			
1995-2000	9.0	10.3	4.0
2000-2005	5.6	1.5	0.0
In value terms:			
1995-2000	9.2	8.6	5.7
2000-2005	5.5	1.5	3.0

Source: Eurostat.

2 Price competitiveness

Felettigh, Lecat, Pluyaud et Tedeschi (2006, this volume), hereafter FLPT, show that both export and producer prices in Italy suffered significant losses in competitiveness, as compared to the other two countries since the mid 1990s. The impact of price competitiveness is all the more acute that Italian exports are more sensitive to price evolutions. Comparing France and Germany, however, FLPT note that price competitiveness indicators cannot explain the better performance of Germany in the years 2000. L'Angevin and Seravalle (2005) note that Germany improved competitiveness substantially since 2000. Cheptea, Gaulier and Zignago (2004) using detailed export data also show that German exporters reduced prices during the depreciation of the euro until 2002, while French exporters increased their margins. The latter behaviour was also observed for Italy.

Pluyaud (2006, this volume) for France as well as Stahn (2006, this volume) for Germany estimate trade equations distinguishing between intra and extra euro area trade. The first paper estimates both export and import equations, while the second one concentrate on exports. Pluyaud (*op. cit.*) highlights that price competitiveness matters more significantly for intra-trade than for extra-trade, while for Stahn (*op. cit.*), there is evidence pointing in that direction, although it is still tentative. These equations are not, strictly speaking, fully comparable since the long run elasticity of exports to world demand and imports to domestic demand is constrained to one in the first paper and not not in the second paper. However, such a result might be the consequence of trade in more homogeneous products within the euro area than outside the area. In addition, in a large integrated market as the euro area, monopoly rents based on differentiated products are more difficult to extract. For export equations in Germany, the evolution of the product-mix traded by Germany may also have contributed to these results. Indeed, it is often argued that the higher quality of German exports is responsible for the lower price elasticity of its exports (see Jarvis and Prais, 1997). A substantial caveat is that, apparently, the two countries exhibited divergent behaviour more, recently, with a lower impact of competitiveness on exports for Germany, while France has been experiencing a higher sensitivity to price competitiveness : according to Stahn (*op. cit.*) price elasticities for the short sample starting in 1993 is lower than in the long sample starting in 1980. The shift to less price-elastic products, increasing globalisation, the establishment of the euro area, the enlargement of the EU, the increase in intra-firm trade, the growing share of inputs purchased from abroad may all have played a role. These results are consistent with the observation that the latest appreciation of the euro has so far had relatively little adverse impact on German exports to many observers a surprising outcome. Regarding France, on the other hand, Nivat and Villetelle (2006) estimating an export equation for goods in volume, indicate that the long run price elasticity jumps from 0.6 to 1.2 when a regime shift is allowed as from 2001. This may imply that French exports are more likely to be substituted away, or equivalently, of poorer relative quality. More research should be devoted to understanding such a phenomenon in the explanation of the evolution of external trade.

3 Geographic and sectoral specialisation

Geographic and sectoral specialisation are often mentioned as possible factors explaining the divergence between the three countries, but it appears that they offer only partial explanation, as opposed to questions on country's export performance that are covered in section 4.

3.1 Geographic specialisation

First of all, as indicated in FLPT, external demand addressed to each of the three countries exhibited different patterns: Germany enjoyed more dynamic external demand partly due to higher growth of domestic demand in France. Such a feature was compounded in terms of contribution to GDP growth by the higher share of exports in German GDP. Secondly, France is more specialised on euro area markets; conversely, Germany and Italy appear to be specialised in world regions where demand is more dynamic. However, FLPT, as well as Deruennes (2005), stress that the appearance of emerging countries as exporters induces a structural change in external demand and question the traditional measures of external demand. Overall, there is an agreement that geographic specialisation only explains roughly around 10% of the export differential between France and Germany over the last few years.

Thus, according to Pluyaud (*op. it.*) the slowdown in French exports to the *extra* euro area between 2000 and 2003 may be explained by the joint decrease in the contributions of demand and price competitiveness. In particular, the contribution of price competitiveness becomes negative after 2002, as a consequence of the appreciation of the euro, but also due to cost developments. In 2004, extra euro area exports were still hampered by losses in price competitiveness, but benefited from a much more favorable demand growth, due to the general upturn outside the euro area. According to Pluyaud (*op. it.*), the recent evolution of intra euro area exports in France is in line with the evolution of demand and price competitiveness since 2002, but from 1998 to 2001, the model tends to overpredict intra euro area exports on the basis of its usual determinants in terms of demand and price competitiveness. The latter result is consistent with a break in the French performance in the early 2000s, as considered in section 4.

Another contribution highlighting the role of geographic specialisation is Boulhol and Maillard (2005). Using the OECD STAN database, the authors conclude that geographic specialisation tends to differ between France and Germany since 1991, but less significantly so with respect to Italy. The more significant reliance of Germany on trade with the new EU member states is in particular highlighted by the authors. A further argument is the FDI activities of German firms in Eastern European Countries, which may have positive effects on German exports (ECB, 2005).

3.2 Product specialisation

According to FLPT, using the CHELEM database, the product specialisation structures of Italy and France are, for opposite reasons, not as favourable as the German one. A high specialisation in low-technology, labour intensive products exposes Italy to the competition of emerging Asian countries at the lowest end of the quality scale. France tends to be specialised in high tech products, but this specialisation is weak in extent and rely mainly on a single sector, aeronautics, which is a source of fragility. On the contrary, German product specialisation includes many capital goods, whose demand tends to pick up strongly during the first phase of a cycle.

4 Export performance

FLPT stress that initial geographic specialisation in itself is not sufficient to explain the export performance, since whatever the regions, exports have been growing since 2000 more rapidly in Germany than in other European countries. Comparing France and Germany on the 2000-2003 period, L'Angevin and Serravalle (*op. cit.*) indicate that German exports increased faster than in France particularly in the EU15, the new EU Member States, the US and China. In the latter case, the authors argue in particular that France, contrarily to Germany, failed to accompany the broadening of Chinese domestic demand by developing intra-industry trades. Nivat and Villetelle (*op. cit.*, look at the geographic structure of exports by France, as compared to its main partners on the period 2001-2004. They conclude that 80% of the export differential in value terms between Germany and France is explained by a lack of performance of French exports and not by the specialisation structure. The same conclusion is reached fot Italy, although the export growth differential is four times lower, as indicated in the lower panel of table 1.

Regarding sectoral specialisation of exports, Boulhol and Maillard (*op. cit.*) challenge the idea that the sectoral specialisation differ between France and Germany. According to their analysis, the actual evolution of external trade in France is, however, affected to a significant extent, over the 1998-2003 period, by poor performance in a certain number of sectors like pharmaceutical products, telecommunication equipments, office machinery and computers. L'Angevin and Serravalle (*op. cit.*) also using the OECD STAN database show that France lost market shares vis-à-vis Germany in all manufacturing sectors over the 2000-2003 periods, but that they were particularly pronounced in machines and equipment as well as transport equipments, both being sectors with a high technological content. Non-price competitiveness indicators, such as R&D spendings and education level, show a clear lead of Germany, which may also be at the root of its better trade performance than the other two countries.

References

Artus, P., Boyer, S., Maillard, L., Silipo, L. (2006) 'Qu'y a t-il de différent entre l'Allemagne, d'une part, la France et l'Italie d'autre part." Flash, CDC-IXIS, 2006-25.

Boulhol, H., Maillard, L. (2005) Une analyse descriptive du décrochage récent des exportations francaises CDC-IXIS, Etude, 2005-02.

Cheptea, A., Gaulier, G., Zignago, S. (2004) Marché mondial: positions acquises et performances, La lettre du Cepii, février, n231.

Crozet, M., Erkel-Rousse, H. (2003) Trade performance, Product quality perceptions and the Estimation of Trade Price Elasticity, Review of International Economics, 12(1), 109-129.

Deruennes, A. (2005) Quelle lecture faire de lévolution récente des exportations franaises, Ministère de lEconomie et des Finances, DPAE, n70, avril.

ECB (2005) Competitiveness and the export performance of the Euro Area, European Central Bank, Occasional Paper 30, June 2005.

Jarvis, V., Prais, S. (1997) The quality of manufactured goods in Britain and Germany, International Review of Applied Economics, vol. 11.

L'Angevin, C., Serravalle, S. (2005) Performances l'exportation de la France et de l'Allemagne: une analyse par secteur et destination géographique, Insee, Document de Travail, G2005-05.

Nivat, D., Villetelle, J.-P. (2006) "Les mauvaises performances du commerce extrieur de la France sont elles lies un problme de demande?", Bulletin Mensuel de la Banque de France, February.

Panel Discussion

Anton Brender[1], Jean Pisani-Ferry[2], Domenico Giannone[3], and Riccardo Faini[4]

[1] Dexia Bank and University Paris-Dauphine, anton.brender@dexia-am.com
[2] Bruegel Institute, Brussels, and University Paris-Dauphine, jpf@bruegel.org
[3] ECARES, Université Libre de Bruxelles; CP 114, Av. F.D. Roosevelt, 50, B-1050 Brussels, Belgium dgiannon@ulb.ac.be
[4] Università di Roma Tor Vergata, CEPR and IZA, faini@economia.uniroma2.it

1 Comments by Anton Brender

I will make only two remarks on the research conducted within the Joint Project. But first, I have to say how much I appreciated not only the technical virtuosity but also the clarity of most of the papers, which has been of great help for the discussants. This being said, I would like in my comment to broaden the perspective of the papers. The objective of the project was clearly to help those in charge of economic policy to see what measures could be taken to avoid, in the future, the kind of economic slump the euro area went through during the first half of this decade. The conclusion reached, sometimes a bit hastily, is that it is urgent to reduce the rigidities crippling the supply side of our economies, in particular their labour markets. This, I think, deserves to be discussed, since the papers that study the demand side have, in my view, two important weaknesses.

First, the conclusion pushed forward gives the impression that the cyclical character of demand is a fatality. Cycles are caused by exogenous factors and nothing can or should be done to help counter them. A counter-factual simulation exercise would, nevertheless, have been interesting: what would activity in the euro area have been if fiscal policy in the three countries here under study had followed the logic of the Stability and Growth Pact, that is if they had moved to a restrictive stance during the last part of the nineties, and to an expansionary one after 2001? Would such a policy have helped absorb the shocks of the beginning of the decade?

Second, a component of domestic demand is, surprisingly, absent from the various demand side papers: residential investment. This component is either left aside - only non-residential investment is looked at - or included in total investment. But it never appears as such. This is regrettable since residential investment played a key role in insulating the US economy from many demand shocks since the Asian crisis. Its role after the bursting of the stock market bubble, in particular, has been crucial. While firms were trying hard, from 2001 on, to reduce their indebtedness, households accelerated their borrowing: residential investment strongly picked-up while non-residential investment faltered. By not looking at residential investment as a key demand component, one misses the opportunity to observe the working of this potentially powerful shock-absorbing mechanism: following a negative demand shock, long term interest rates tend to weaken and household borrowing and spending tend to increase, helping stabilize activity (and vice versa if activity is booming...). By not isolating residential investment, the studies cannot discuss the consequences of European national financial systems remaining deeply different as regards households borrowing conditions and this, despite currency unification. This is regrettable since those financial rigidities also deserve the attention of the national central banks in the euro area, the more so since these rigidities directly affect the transmission channels of monetary policy.

2 Comments by Jean Pisani-Ferry

The papers presented in this volume address an issue whose importance for research and policy is increasingly recognised. The choice to limit the scope of investigation to France, Germany and Italy makes possible to investigate the extent and sources of divergence in a much more systematic way than can be done in comparisons involving the entire euro area. This is what distinguishes this research and gives it value in comparison to various other publications on the same topic.

The analysis presented draws on a variety of methodologies and gives a complex picture of the situation. The role of the panel is to summarise the evidence, thereby making a multifaceted story somewhat simpler, and then to discuss the policy conclusions that may be drawn from it. Let me start with the evidence, before turning to possible conclusions.

The research by the three national central banks first documents the very high degree of cyclical convergence of certain components of GDP that has been reached in the euro area. In manufacturing and to a lesser extent in services, there is now a common euro area business cycle. While it can be pointed out that such comovements existed in the 1970s, at that time they owed much to major common external shocks. The fact that they have been observable in the relatively quiet environment of the 2000s probably indicates a higher degree of underlying synchronisation. This is obviously good news for the common monetary policy of the ECB as it diminishes the risk that it becomes out of tune with some national cyclical developments.

Two qualifications should nevertheless be kept in mind. National idiosyncrasies continue, as could be expected, to play a larger role in consumption. One should add differences in residential investment behaviour, which as already noted was not directly covered in the papers. Furthermore, due to limitations to the observation period, the diagnosis on convergence at lower frequencies must remain guarded: especially, we do not know yet to what extent asymmetric boom-and-bust housing cycles have the potential of triggering serious divergence within the euro area.

The main message in this volume, however, is that growth and price divergence within the euro area tends to be persistent and must be related to supply rather than demand factors. In this respect, the papers document asymmetric changes in potential output growth (down in Germany and Italy, up in France) and in the NAIRU (down in Italy and France, up in Germany). The papers on foreign trade also documents the contrasting external performance of the three countries: in recent years, Germany has recovered its role as major world exporter while France, and even more Italy, have been losing ground.

Monetary Union is thus confronted with an unexpected situation which combines the faster-than-expected emergence of a common business cycle and the more-pronounced-than-expected re-emergence of a series of lasting divergences which are linked to structural factors (and, potentially, to boom-and-bust asset price cycles).

This brings us to the policy discussion. The questions to be investigated are, how well has EMU performed in coping with these shocks and, what remedies should policymakers contemplate to make it work better?

In a nutshell, what the central banks' research tells us about the period since monetary union was initiated is that in comparison to the other two countries,

1. France has experienced both a rise in its potential output and a decline in the world demand for its products;
2. Germany has experienced a decline in its potential output and a rise in the world demand for its products;
3. Italy has experienced ambiguous potential output developments and a sharp decline in the world demand for its products.

The normal response to those shocks should have been a real depreciation in France and Italy and a real appreciation in Germany. Such developments would have brought aggregate demand in line with potential supply. What about facts? From 1999-Q1 to 2005-Q3, average growth has been 1.2% per annum in Germany and Italy and 2.1% in France. From 1999 to 2005, unemployment has decreased by 3.8 percentage points in Italy and 0.8 in France, but has increased by 1.8 percentage points in Germany. Finally, average consumer price inflation has been 1.4% in Germany, 1.8% in France and 2.3% in Italy.

While developments in output growth and unemployment are roughly consistent with the characterisation of shocks given in this volume, price developments are certainly not. If anything, they have moved in the opposite direction to what could be deemed desirable. The country facing excess foreign demand has experienced a real depreciation while those in the opposite situation have experienced an appreciation.

Reasons for this paradox have to do with initial conditions, which could certainly not be characterised as an equilibrium, but also with the collapse of German domestic demand, which contributed to increasing the outward orientation of German industry. Confronted with the absence of any growth in domestic demand, German producers have slashed prices on export markets, while their French and Italian counterparts have continued increasing them. In other words, partially policy-induced developments in domestic demand have acted as a break on required price adjustments.

We can therefore understand what has happened but this does not mean we should consider it appropriate.

Instead of addressing without delay the consequences of the shocks experienced in the early years of the single currency, policymakers in the EMU have mainly contributed to postponing the adjustments, thereby amplifying their magnitude. The required real exchange rate correction now risk to be long and painful.

This observation certainly calls for the reinforcement of the competitiveness channel, i.e. for a higher sensitivity of prices and wages to market conditions. But it also calls for a more targeted approach of divergence within the euro area. The lesson from this early experience is that policymakers cannot refrain from establishing a shared diagnosis on the factors explaining observed divergence in macroeconomic developments and from deciding on appropriate responses.

3 Comments by Domenico Giannone

In my comments, the issue I wish to address is whether one should really care about output synchronisation.[5]

Arguably, in the recent past, the policy discussion has focused on heterogeneity of economic performance of countries in the European Monetary Union (EMU). The mechanisms through which the lack of flexibility based on national exchange rate and monetary policy may exacerbate the effect of shocks is well known (see Mundell, 1961, and subsequent literature) and the potential effect of common monetary policy on increasing divergence of economic performance between countries belonging to the union have been widely debated in the late nineties. Now, six years after the establishment of the monetary union, with some real observations to analyze and with the euro area facing unsatisfactory growth performance, the debate is having a second life. The book focuses indeed on growth and cyclical asymmetries among the three largest countries of the euro area.

Most of the studies on real asymmetries focus on the analysis of output and look at changes in growth and business cycles characteristics during the

---

[5] This contribution is an extract from Giannone and Reichlin (2005).

process of European integration and the establishment of the Euro. In fact, in terms of output there is no clear sign, or at least not yet, of changes in the cyclical characteristics of the euro area (see Giannone and Reichlin, 2005, for a survey). However, what matters for welfare is consumption rather than output. In principle, financial market integration, should make it easier for consumers, to insure against income risk through borrowing, lending and cross-country ownership of financial assets. Sorense and Yosha (1998) found that less risk is shared in Europe than in the US while Kalemli-Ozcan et al. (2004) found that risk sharing through financial market has increased in the last decade thanks to financial integration.

A measure of risk sharing can be obtained following Asdrubali et al. (1996), ASY from now on. We ask how much variance of output is smoothed by consumption via risk sharing at each period of time, i.e. how much the cross-country variance of consumption conditional on output has decreased over time. We consider the sample 1970-2004 and redo some of ASY's calculations on our data.

Let us define c_t^i and y_t^i as the log $\times 100$ of real individual consumption and output per capita, respectively, of country i in year t. We estimate (by OLS) the regression:

$$\Delta_h(c_t^i - c_t^{EU}) = \alpha_t + \beta_t \Delta_h(y_t^i - y_t^{EU}) + v_t$$

where Δ_h denotes the h-th differences $(1 - L^h)$ and the superscript EU indicates consumption and output per-capita in the euro area. The regression coefficient β_t is interpreted as the amount of risk not insured, i.e. the fraction of the variance of GDP that is not smoothed out through capital market, credit market and other channels.

Fig. 1 plots a smooth version of β_t in time and for the EU12 countries, excluding Luxemburg defined as $\tilde{\beta}_t$:

$$\tilde{\beta}_t = \frac{1}{2m+1} \sum_{j=-m}^{m} \left(1 - \frac{|j|}{2m+1}\right) \beta_{t+j}$$

and $m = 5$ years.

Results show that the ability of sharing risk among European countries goes up in the early 1990's when capital and good market integration has significantly accelerated in Europe.

Although the previous calculations provide an interesting rough descriptive statistics, a better measure of risk sharing should control for country heterogeneity in response to common, area-wide shocks and for the effect of relative prices. The heterogeneity of the responses of countries output and consumption to common shocks could emerge in case of imperfect risk sharing. In addition, relative prices fluctuations, whose nature has changed significantly with EMU, could have provided an automatic smoothing of the

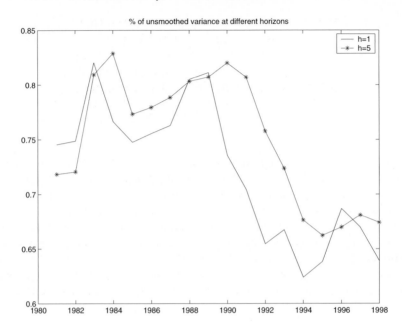

Fig. 1. Risk not shared over time

effect of country specific shocks (see for example Obstfeld (1994) and Hoffman (2004)).

To this end, we estimate the following panel regression for the whole sample and three sub-samples:

$$\Delta_h(c_t^i - c_t^{EU}) = \alpha_i + \beta_h \Delta_h(y_t^i - y_t^{EU}) + \gamma_i^c \Delta_h c_t^{EU} + \gamma_i^y \Delta_h y_t^{EU} + \gamma_i^R \Delta_h R_t^{i,EU} + v_t^i$$

where $R_t^{i,EU}$ is the real exchange rate between country i and the euro area as a whole[6] and Euro-area wide consumption is included as a regressor to control for common taste shocks.

We follow ASY and estimate it using weighted least square so as to downweight countries with a larger idiosyncratic component. We run the regression on all euro area countries, excluding Luxembourg. As an alternative, we also estimate the coefficients including in our panel only the six largest euro area countries (Germany, France, Italy, Spain, Netherlands and Belgium). Table 1 reports results.

Results from the simple measure of risk sharing are confirmed: risk sharing has increased in the last decade. The result is particularly robust at long

---

[6] $R_t^{EU,i} = P_t^{\$EU} - P_t^{\$i}$ where $P_t^{\$i} = \log\{C_t^{n,i}/C_t^{r,i}\} \times 100$, and $C_t^{r,i}$ and $C_t^{n,i}$ are the nominal consumption and the real consumption, respectively, in country i expressed in US dollars.

Table 1. Panel estimates of β_h for selected subsamples

	EU 12 (excl. LU)		EU (Largest 6)	
	h=1	h=5	h=1	h=5
1970-2003	0.75 (0.05)	0.77 (0.03)	0.83 (0.07)	0.94 (0.04)
1970-1989	0.80 (0.08)	0.87 (0.04)	0.86 (0.09)	0.91 (0.05)
1990-2003	0.65 (0.07)	0.59 (0.03)	0.70 (0.10)	0.65 (0.08)
1993-2003	0.76 (0.10)	0.59 (0.03)	0.77 (0.12)	0.63 (0.15)

horizons, indicating that the increased ability of countries to smooth is particularly significant in response to persistent shocks to output. We should also stress that long horizons results should be more robust to endogeneity issues that may affect these types of reduced form regressions.

We take the results above as an indication that EMU, and more generally European integration, seems to have worked in the right direction and we should worry less than before about asymmetries in output. Obviously, whether this process will eventually lead to higher growth in the aggregate is still unclear, but the understanding of this link should be in the research agenda.

4 Comments by Riccardo Faini

In my comments I would like to return to the issue of trade performance and stress some basic considerations on the link between trade, human capital, and growth. Greater openness to trade and investment flows in EU countries means that their economic performance is increasingly a function of the external environment and their ability to exploit the opportunities stemming from larger and more integrated global markets.

Countries may be relatively well placed to profit from globalization. A key question in this respect is whether the pattern of trade specialization matters. Take a standard macroeconomic approach, where growth in world demand is supposed to boost exports and contribute to rising GDP. In this context, the pattern of export specialization will matter for the very simple reason that if a country's sectoral (and geographical) export specialization is biased toward slowly growing sectors (and markets), then exports will tend to grow at a slower pace, with (presumably) a negative impact on GDP growth. Trade theorists would make a perhaps somewhat more elaborate argument by noting that an unfavourable pattern of export specialization will be reflected in a terms of trade deterioration (prices would typically tend to fall if world demand for a given commodity grows at a relatively slow pace). In turn, the decline in the terms of trade would result in a drop of measured GDP (at world prices) and in economic welfare.

The overview paper by de Bandt and Villetelle (2006, this volume) offers a very interesting comparison between France, Germany, and Italy. They show that both geographical and especially sectoral specialization is likely to have played a crucial role. The figures are quite stark. In volume terms, average annual export growth between 2000 and 2004 was 5.4% in Germany, 2.3% in France and close to nil in Italy. Further insights in this respect come from Table 2 below, which computes the hypothetical growth rate of exports for the three countries over different time periods under the assumption that the country's sectoral exports had increased at the same rate as world exports in that sector. In "shift-share" jargon, this is called the structural effect.[7] Two facts stand out. First, the pattern of export specialization is a key factor in determining export performance. This is mostly visible for Italy, where the structural effect shifted from strongly positive in the late eighties to negative in the late nineties, and for Germany, where the structural effects went from strongly negative to strongly positive. For France, there is no major change between the two periods, but the structural effect contributed positively to export growth in both sub-periods. Clearly enough, Germany and also France have benefited from their sectoral pattern of exports, while sectoral specialization appears to be a crucial determinant of Italy's poor export performance. Secondly, there is no great difference, both across countries and over time, in the behaviour of the structural component for manufacturing and total exports, suggesting that the former keeps playing a relevant role in determining the overall export performance.

Table 2. The role of sector composition in export growth

	Total manufacturing (percentage growth)			
	1987-92	1997-02	1987-92	1997-02
France	2.43	1.72	3.18	2.13
Germany	-1.89	2.46	-0.49	3.68
Italy	2.61	-0.89	2.92	-0.63

Source: Faini and Sapir (2005)

So far for the aggregate export performance. Trade economists however tend to delve deeper and look for the determinants of a given pattern of trade. Well established theories suggest that the pattern of comparative advantage is to a significant extent determined by the endowment of (immobile) factors. Capital however is regarded as increasingly mobile. Accordingly, in most empirical analyses, trade is supposed to be determined by the relative endowment across countries of skilled and unskilled labour. In what follows I rely on the OECD STAN data set and measure skilled intensity as

---

[7] The residual, i.e. the difference with actual export growth, is by definition equal to that part of export growth which is not accounted by structural effects. It is labelled the competitiveness effect.

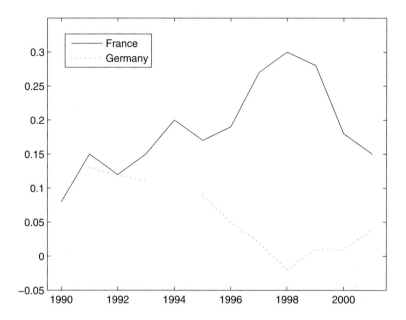

Fig. 2. Comparative advantage in skilled intensive sectors (correlation coefficient between RCA and skill intensity)

the share of R&D personnel in total employment.[8] This is likely to be a fairly imperfect measure of skill intensities, as skilled workers will typically take up mansions also in non R&D tasks. Yet, it provides one of the few truly internationally comparable measure of sectoral skilled intensities. As a second step, I look at the correlation between this measure of skilled intensities and the revealed comparative advantage (RCA) developed by Balassa.[9] Two main facts emerge. First, the correlation between skill intensities and RCA is positive for Germany and even more for France (Fig. 2), presumably as a reflection of Germany's specialization in middle technology exports. Secondly, Italy's exports are strongly concentrated in low skill sectors, as shown by the negative correlation coefficient between skill intensities and export specialization (Fig. 3). Quite strikingly, the bias in Italy's pattern of trade has grown stronger over time, as shown by the fact that the correlation coefficient

---

[8] In what follows I draw freely from a joint paper with André Sapir (Faini and Sapir, 2005).

[9] The Balassa indicator for sector i, noted B_i, is simply defined as the ratio between a country's share in world exports of sector i and its aggregate share in total world exports. If B_i is greater than one, then the country is deemed to have a (revealed) comparative advantage in sector i. See also Felettigh (2006, this volume).

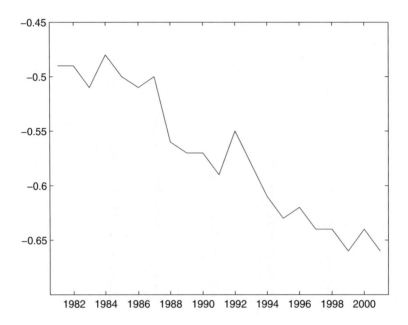

Fig. 3. Italy's polarized pattern of comparative advantage (correlation coefficient between RCA and skilled intensities)

becomes increasingly negative. The same pattern emerges if we focus on individual sectors and trace the value of the Balassa's indicator over time. In Faini and Sapir (2005) we show how Italy's comparative advantage in traditional sectors (textiles, furniture, apparel, and shoes) strengthened over time, while the size of the country's comparative disadvantage in more high tech sectors (cars, office equipment, electrical equipment, telecom equipments) rose substantially. In sharp contrast, in France, specialization shifted away from traditional sectors toward the more high tech sectors.

Italy's pattern of comparative advantage is not surprising in light of the country's relative factor endowment. From Table 3, we see how the average number of years of schooling has always been substantially lower in Italy than in France and Germany, with little or no indication of a closing of the gap. Interestingly enough, Germany's educational achievements seem to outperform those of France, a fact apparently at odds with the finding that France has a stronger comparative advantage in high skilled sectors. However, if we focus on tertiary education, we find that Germany performance is somewhat below that of France (Fig. 4).

The analysis so far has eschewed a key question, namely whether there are reason to be concerned about the pattern of trade specialization. Simple trade theory would suggest that all countries will benefit from trade, with the

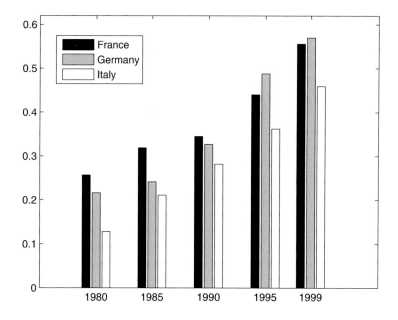

Fig. 4. Average number of years of tertiary education

Table 3. Average number of schooling

	1970	1975	1980	1985	1990	1995	1999
France	5.9	6.1	6.8	7.3	7.6	7.9	8.4
Germany	8.3	7.7	8.4	8.9	9.1	9.6	9.7
Italy	5.2	5.3	5.3	5.8	6.2	6.6	7.0

Source: Barro and Lee (2003)

gains from trade increasing with the degree of specialization among countries. Accordingly, Italy should benefit relatively more from an increasingly polarized and differentiated pattern of trade! Yet, this line of reasoning overlooks the fact that Italy has suffered more than Germany and France from the emergence of new protagonists in the world trade arena, most of which are specialized precisely in those commodities where Italy's comparative advantage lies. Put differently, Italy's has for long enjoyed a 'rent', to the extent that liberalization in world trade involved mainly industrial countries and, among this restricted group, Italy benefited from a fairly distinct pattern of comparative advantage. The 'flip' side of the coin is that Italy was more vulnerable to emerging markets competition. There are, nonetheless, a few facts that need to be explained. If emerging market competition was the whole story we would expect Italy to suffer from a deterioration in its terms of

58   A. Brender, J. Pisani-Ferry, D. Giannone, and R. Faini

trade. This is not the case, however, as shown by de Bandt and Villetelle (*op. cit*). Export prices rose much more rapidly for Italy (+3.3%) than for France (-0.3%) and Germany (-0.3%). There are two competing explanations to this finding. First, rising export prices may reflect the effort by Italian firms to upgrade their product quality so as to better face emerging markets competition. Secondly, rising prices may instead result from falling productivity and rising costs. Clearly, these two interpretations, while not necessarily mutually exclusive, have a totally different implications for the country's medium term prospects.

This may not be the end of the story. There is indeed a burgeoning literature on the effect of human capital on growth,[10] with both theoretical and empirical ramifications. One of the key issues here is the way human capital affects growth. First, it may do so through a traditional Solow effect, i.e. through the accumulation of a production factor along side the growth of the labour force and investment in physical capital. Secondly, there may be also a level effect, as suggested by some of the theoretical literature, where a substantial endowment of human capital will foster both technological innovation and technological adoption with a positive effect on growth. Presumably, the latter effect on growth may have become more relevant in the light of the ITC revolution, where technological innovations are no longer simply incorporated in new equipments but require substantial changes in the way the firm is organized and, hence, significant skills to this effect.

To sum up, the endowment of human capital may play a treble role. First, it will affect the pattern of export specialization and, as a result, the country's exposure to emerging market competition. Secondly, it will influence growth through the traditional accumulation effect. Thirdly, and perhaps more importantly, it will facilitate both the development and the adoption of new technologies and, through this channel, foster long run growth. Countries would then be advised to ensure that adequate resources are channelled to their education sector and, even more crucially, that such resources are profitably invested.

References

Asdrubali, P., Sorense, B.E., Yosha, O. (1996) Channels of Interstate Risk Sharing: United States 1963-1990, The Quarterly Journal of Economics 111:1081–1110

Barro, R., Lee, J. (2000), International data on educational attainment, NBER working paper n. 7911, updated at www.cid.harvard.edu.

Cohen, D., Soto, M. (2001), Growth and human capital: good data, good results, CEPR DP n. 3025, CEPR, London.

---

[10] See Temple (2001) for an overview and Cohen and Soto (2001) for a relatively recent empirical analysis.

Faini, R., Sapir, A. (2005), Un modello obsoleto? In T. Boeri et al. (eds), Oltre il declino, il Mulino, Bologna.

Giannone, D., Reichlin, L. (2005) Trends and cycles in the Euro Area: how much heterogeneity and should we worry about it? ECB Working paper, forthcoming.

Hoffman, M. (2004) International Prices and Consumption Risk Sharing, Manuscript, University of Dortmund.

Kalemli-Ozcan, S., Sorense, B.E., Yosha, O. (2004) Asymmetric Shocks and Risk Sharing in a Monetary Union: Updated Evidence and Policy Implications for Europe CEPR Discussion Paper n.4463

Mundell, R.A. (1961) A Theory of Optimum Currency Areas, American Economic Review, Vol. 51, 509-517.

Obstfeld, M. (1994) Are Industrial-Country Consumption Risks Globally Diversified?, NBER Working Paper.

Sorense, B.E., Yosha, O. (1998) International risk sharing and European monetary unification, Journal of International Economics 45:211–238

Temple, J. (2001), Growth effects of education and social capital in the OECD countries, OECD Economic Studies, 33, 2001.

Part II

Measuring Cycles

Tracking the Economy in the Largest Euro Area Countries: a Large Datasets Approach*

Riccardo Cristadoro and Giovanni Veronese

Servizio Studi, Banca d'Italia, riccardo.cristadoro@bancaditalia.it, giovanni.veronese@bancaditalia.it

Summary. The paper proposes a set of monthly business (growth-) cycle indicators for Germany, France, Italy and the euro area useful for *ex post* characterization of the cycle, and, most importantly, to assess the current economic outlook. These indicators are projections of quarterly aggregates on the space spanned by a set of regressors extracted from a large panel of monthly series. Being based on static linear combinations of monthly series, they do not suffer from the end-of-sample problem associated with traditional bilateral filters (HP filter). The indicators are used to: (1) study the degree of co-movement and synchronization across economies; (2) derive a dating of the cycle; (3) obtain the 'stylized' cyclical facts; (4) assess the predictive content of the panel for GDP growth. The monthly indicators are good forecasters of GDP performing often better than other simple methods. As expected, since the growth cycle indicator is a 'smoothed' estimate of the GDP growth, the best forecasts are obtained in terms of year-on-year (rather than quarter-on-quarter) GDP growth.

Keywords: Business cycle, dynamic factor model, business cycle filters, GDP forecast.
JEL classification C33, C51, E32.

1 Introduction

A well known and documented feature of decentralized market economies is that they experience recurrent fluctuations in economic activity, by which it is meant that, in a more or less regular fashion, periods of relative prosperity are followed by times of sluggish or declining activity (stagnations or recessions). In a much cited pioneering study of the business cycle in the US

* The authors wish to thank Olivier de Bandt, Sandra Eickmeier, Heinz Herrmann, the discussants and the participants of the conference held in Paris for their helpful comments. Many ideas presented here were first developed in collaboration with Filippo Altissimo, Antonio Bassanetti, Mario Forni, Marco Lippi and Lucrezia Reichlin in a joint research that led to the construction of the euro area business cycle indicator *Eurocoin*, currently published each month by the CEPR. The usual disclaimer applies.

economy, Burns and Mitchell describe with these words the phenomenon they are examining:

> *Business cycles are a type of fluctuation found in the aggregate eco-*
> *nomic activity of nations that organize their work mainly in business en-*
> *terprises: a cycle consists of expansions occurring at about the same time in*
> *many economic activities, followed by similarly general recessions, ... this*
> *sequence of changes is recurrent but not periodic. In durations business cy-*
> *cles vary from more than one year to ten or twelve years; they are not divis-*
> *ible into shorter cycles of similar character with amplitudes approximating*
> *their own.* (Burns and Mitchell, 1946)

Empirical and theoretical literature on the business cycle experienced a resurgence since the early seventies and the question of *"Why is it that in capitalist economies aggregate variables undergo repeated fluctuations about trend, all of essentially the same character?"* (Lucas, 1977) became a central issue of modern macroeconomics. The study of the business cycle has followed two parallel routes: on the one hand a huge amount of empirical evidence has been accumulated since the seminal work of Burns and Mitchell at the NBER. The "NBER approach" has led to the construction of various indicators aimed at capturing the essentials of the business cycle in a given country, and, possibly, to anticipate its developments. On the other hand an increasing body of the literature has tried to rationalize this evidence with microfounded models. These theoretical, stylized macro models, although based on a parsimonious parametrization, giving rise to simple shock and propagation mechanism, proved capable of delivering fluctuations of the same periodicity and magnitude as observed in the data (see the seminal paper of Kydland and Prescott, 1982).

It is beyond the scope of this work to survey this huge and growing body of empirical and theoretical literature, yet some of the main insights derived from it can guide our analysis:

1. the chief aspect of the business cycle is the comovement of macroeconomic time series.
2. the behaviour of macro variables during expansion and contractions tends to be similar across countries.
3. given this evidence, it is natural to assume that few common shocks should be at the origin of the cyclical behaviour of macro time series

The US is by far the most studied economy and comprehensive analyses have been published concerning: (i) the collection of stylized facts in terms of variability, comovements and persistence of cyclical fluctuation of macro variables (see among others Stock and Watson, 1999), (ii) the dating of the business cycle and the early detection of turning points, (iii) the development of business cycle coincident and leading indicators (among which an example is the Conference Board index for the US economy).

In comparison relatively little is known for the euro area economy as a whole. To our knowledge, a comprehensive study of the business cycle characteristics of the major EMU economies, performed in an homogenous and coherent setting, is still missing.

Official dating of the business cycle in the United States has a long standing tradition, tracing back to the contributions of Burns and Mitchell, and which lives through in the Business Cycle Dating Committee of the National Bureau of Economic Research (NBER).[2] The dating of the cycle in the euro area is still at an early stage; even among euro area countries an established official dating of national business cycles does not always exists (for a notable exception see Altissimo et al., 2000).

In 2003 the Centre for Economic Policy Research (CEPR) created a committee to date the euro area business cycle, in the same spirit of the NBER.[3] As in the NBER case, the CEPR committee decided to leave an important room to the judgemental evaluation of the evidence. In particular, it did not constrain its decisions on particular dating algorithms, or to particular statistical-econometric models of the euro area economy.

In this work we study the business cycle behaviour of the euro area and its three major economies and we address some of the issues raised in the literature on business cycles. We base our approach on the theoretical insight provided by microfounded equilibrium models: few 'fundamental' shocks can produce fluctuations in line with those observed in the data.

We first characterize the business cycle behaviour of the euro area and of its largest economies by extracting and studying the cyclical component of their GDPs and of the main components of aggregate demand using 'traditional' univariate techniques. We compare the results thus obtained with known and established facts for the US economy. This collection of facts will be later used to validate an alternative way of extracting the business cycle component from quarterly national account (NA) data that improves on univariate techniques in many respects.

The core of this paper is the construction of a set of monthly business cycle indicators for Germany, France, Italy and for the euro area that can be used not only for the *ex post* characterization of the cyclical behaviour of these economies, but also for short to medium run assessment of their current economic outlook. The business cycle facts implied by our monthly

---

[2] The NBER Dating Committee spells out the definition of a recession as, *a significant decline in economic activity spread across the economy, lasting more than a few months, normally visible in Real GDP, real income, employment, industrial production, and wholesale-retail sales* (see NBER, 2003).

[3] The CEPR Committee defines a recession as a *significant decline in the level of economic activity, spread across the economy in the euro area, usually visible in two or more consecutive quarters of negative growth in GDP, employment and other measures of aggregate economic activity for the euro area a whole, and reflecting similar developments in most countries* (CEPR 2003).

indicators are broadly in line with those obtained through more traditional signal extraction methods. But we improve on the traditional methods in several respects.

We obtain the cyclical components of the quarterly variables through an *appropriate static linear combination* of the series contained in a large set of monthly variables, exploiting the rich dynamic relations that exist among them (in particular, the leading information contained in the panel).

We can summarise our approach as follows: we estimate the common factors in a large dataset of euro area variables finding that at business cycle periodicities the dynamics of the panel can be captured by a small number of factors (or common shocks), that are responsible for the comovements across series, coherently with our a priori knowledge based on the results of the real business cycle literature and the evidence collected in other empirical studies. The modelling framework that embeds this idea is given by the dynamic factor model (as in Forni et al., 2002, Altissimo et al., 2001). The model is estimated on a panel of roughly 300 *monthly* time series that comprises both nominal and real variables of the euro area and its largest economies.[4]

The monthly cyclical indicators are constructed as the projection of quarterly NA aggregates on the space spanned by the monthly factors extracted from the panel. These indicators provide a basis to address a wide array of interesting questions: the degree of comovement and synchronization across major EMU countries, dating and identification of turning points, the reliability of the estimates of the cyclical components when the panel of time series on which they are based is only partly updated.

We apply an algorithm for the automatic dating and identification of turning points (see Bry and Boschan, 1971) deriving a preliminary 'eye-ball' indication of the degree of concordance of the cycles of different economies. The dating of the turning points shows that over the past two decades European economies experienced similar and rather synchronized episodes of acceleration and deceleration in growth.

This evidence is further explored by testing explicitly the hypothesis that there is a significant degree of correlation among the cycles in the major euro area countries, along the lines of Harding and Pagan (2001).

We assess the reliability of the estimates of the cyclical components by tracking the revision errors of the cyclical components estimated considering varying degrees of delay in the updates. The signals extracted with our method do not undergo major revision errors and can be used for an early assessment of the business cycle situation.

The paper is ogranised as follows. Section 2 describes the main characteristics (stylized facts) of the European business cycle and compares it with the US. The empirical results are introduced by a discussion concerning the filtering procedures that can be used to isolate the cyclical component of a time series and the robustness of inferences based on different filters. Section 3 de-

---

[4] We also included some world series, like oil prices, and few US and UK variables.

scribes the comovements among European economies through spectral techniques and can be seen as a prelude to the estimation of the dynamic factor model. This is taken up in the following section, where first we describe the method and then we report the main results in terms of number of common shocks, estimation of monthly indicators for the cyclical components on NA aggregates in the different countries and dating of their respective cycles. In the fifth section we present an analysis of revison errors and short term forecasting performance of the monthly indicators. We also insist on the fact that the business cycle component of the quarterly series that we extract should *not* be interpreted as an early estimate of the quarter on quarter growth rate of the corresponding series. The sixth section concludes.[5]

2 Business cycle behavior of main variables

2.1 Detrending and business cycle facts

It is customary to begin papers on business cycle analysis with the observation that there are well established characteristics of the cycle that the theory should explain or reproduce (see Kydland and Prescott, 1982, Backus and Kehoe, 1992, and Baxter, 1995). A collection of such cyclical features is usually obtained computing the second moments of the business cycle components of the main macroeconomic series such as GDP, consumption, investment, and so forth. Most of these time series exhibit a clear trending behaviour and since trend and cyclical components are not directly observed one has to make identifying assumptions in order to disentangle them. Most often this issue is set aside and the series are simply filtered with one particular method to obtain a stationary cycle (the Hodrick-Prescott filter is a prominent example). Unfortunately, as shown in Canova (1998), different filtering procedures induce different properties in the second moments of the cyclical components of the observed series and this in turn sheds doubts on the robustness of the so called 'stylized facts' of the business cycle.

Since the 'cycle' is an unobserved component of a given series there is no external validation for the method adopted to estimate it.[6] With a very useful metaphor one can say that different filters are different windows through which we look at time series, hence we must carefully assess the characteristics of the filter to know what exactly we are trying to look at. This is best done by analysing the gain of the filter in spectral domain.

---

[5] An appendix with a description of data, sources and data treatment is available upon request from the authors.

[6] It is worth noting that in the literature the operation of detrending a time series (i.e. making it stationary) is often confused with the extraction of a business cycle component through filtering which is conceptually and statistically a different operation (isolating fluctuations within a given periodicity range).

A time series in frequency domain is represented as a sum of an infinite number of waves of different periodicity. Filtering a time series x_t with a linear filter $b(L) = \sum_{j=-m}^{r} b_j L^j$ transforms the population (pseudo)spectrum of the series $s_x(\omega)$ into $s_y(\omega) = \left\| b\left(e^{i\omega}\right) \right\|^2 s_x(\omega)$ where $y_t = b(L)x_t$. Plotting the function $\left\| b\left(e^{i\omega}\right) \right\|^2$, the squared gain of the filter, over the interval $[0, \pi]$ gives a clear picture of the effect of filtering on waves of different length. In other words the plot illustrates how the linear filter affects oscillations of different periodicity.

In what follows we will examine the cyclical behaviour of euro area macroeconomic time series along with those of its main constituent economies (Germany, France and Italy) and compare it with US data. We will assess the robustness of the results using different filtering procedures.

Traditionally, trend removal was performed by regressing a time series x_t on a polynomial in time and the 'cycle' was identified by the residual. Following the seminal work of Nelson and Plosser (1982) this approach has been progressively abandoned in favour of methods consistent with the stochastic nature of the trending process as it emerged from the unit root tests conducted on US macroeconomic time series.[7] The simplest way to remove the stochastic nonstationarity from an integrated time series is to take differences ($\Delta - filter$) of the appropriate order. A shortcoming of this detrending procedure when applied to business cycle analysis is given by the amplification of the high frequency variations in the resulting detrended series.

By far the most popular choice in business cycle literature to isolate the stationary component of macro series is the Hodrick-Prescott filter ($HP - filter$).[8] As an alternative to the $HP - filter$, Baxter and King (1999) propose an approximation to the ideal two-sided band pass filter (see Sargent, 1987), which eliminates all the waves whose frequency is outside a given band $[\omega_1, \omega_2]$. In the case of the approximated band pass filter ($BK - filter$) the key parameter is the truncation lag of the filter which in most application on quarterly data is set equal to 12 based on the evidence presented in the original paper. One can thus estimate a smooth business cycle component for any given quarterly time series, but at the end of the sample the filter as it is cannot be applied and one therefore loses 3 years of data.

A further refinement of the filter has been studied by Christiano and Fitzgerald (2003). The basic idea of this modified band pass ($CF - filter$) is to take into account the nature of the time series at hand when deriving the weights of the approximated filter.

This procedure has the further advantage of an in-built 'unilateralization' algorithm (as it is the case for the HP-filter) so that the cyclical component can be computed till the end of the sample. This algorithm can be interpreted

---

[7] The Beveridge and Nelson decomposition is an example of this new detrending approach.

[8] See Hodrick and Prescott (1997) and for application to business cycle Kydland and Prescott (1982) or Backus et al. (1994).

as a way of extrapolating from the past of the series the missing future observations as is more often done by using direct forecasts of the series (say with ARIMA model) to obtained a filtered variable up to the end of the sample. Obviously, as new data become available, these preliminary estimates are subject to possibly large revisions.[9]

2.2 Filtering and the business cycle behaviour of the main macro variables

In the following we will compare the results obtained applying different signal extraction methods to the main macroeconomic variables of the euro area, Germany, France and Italy. As a benchmark we will also consider the United States, to compare results for European economies with with well established evidence concerning the US. All variables are log transformed, so that their movements can be interpreted in terms of percentage changes of the original time series.

Overall the results confirm stylized facts already documented for the US economy. Nonetheless some differences among euro area countries and between the euro area and US do emerge.

No matter what filtering technique is used (HP, BP or CF) the business cycle *within each country* presents similar characteristics. GDP standard deviation is about 1% over the sample period considered (1980Q1 - 2004Q4).[10] Investment is about three times more volatile than output, the exact magnitude shows little variation across filtering methods (in Germany and in the euro area investment appears less volatile: the ratio of its standard deviation to that of output is close to two, see Table 1). Consumption relative volatility is about 0.9 with the exception of Italy where the standard deviation is higher for households expenditures than for output (once again these results are robust across filtering procedures). Industrial production relative standard deviation (at quarterly frequency) ranges from little more then 1.5 to 2.5, exhibiting the highest variability with respect to GDP in Italy. Among expenditure components, investment is, in general, the most correlated with output over the cycle. In Italy and Germany the contemporaneous correlation of the investment cycles with GDP is lower (around 0.8 against 0.9 for France, the euro area and the US). As expected, given the importance of fluctuations in manufacturing production over the cycle, also the industrial production is

---

[9] Recently other methods to characterize the 'business cycle' (BC) that do not entail the extraction of a BC component have been proposed by Harding and Pagan (see Harding and Pagan, 2002). They offer the advantage of not taking a stance as to what is the cyclical component of the series, on the other hand, those method are useful to describe the cycle and not to construct indicators. Given that the latter is the main purpose of the paper and that the bulk of the literature on business cycle has considered "parametric" methods, we do not develop this point any further.

[10] It is worth noting that after filtering 12 observations are lost at both ends of the series so that the statistics are computed on the shorter span 1983Q1 - 2001Q4.

highly correlated with GDP at business cycle frequencies for all countries examined and across all filtering methods. Notwithstanding its higher weight over GDP, consumption is less correlated with output, coherently with the permanent income hypothesis.

Considering now the *international cyclical comovements*, European variables are only weakly correlated with the corresponding US ones (Table 2). The instantaneous correlation coefficient of the business cycle component of the euro area GDP with respect to US output ranges from 0.2 to 0.3 depending on the filter one uses. Interestingly the UK economy is more correlated to the US (0.3-0.5 in terms of GDP) than with the euro area (0.2). The well known fact that consumption correlation across countries is lower than that of output (the so called *consumption puzzle*, see Obstfeldt and Rogoff, 2000) emerges irrespective of the filtering technique adopted. Comovements across the Atlantic are higher if we consider trade (export in particular) and the industrial production cycle. For investment correlation is close to zero except when one uses a $CF - filter$ in which case it raises to 0.2 - 0.3.

Among European economies the degree of comovement is much higher. With respect to the area average, Germany, France and Italy show a very high correlation at business cycle frequences for all variables considered, only for government purchases there is some evidence of lower correlation over the cycle. Considering Germany as a benchmark, rather than the area, Italy and France have cyclical contemporaneous correlations with output of about 0.5, and an even higher one for investment and industrial production. It is once again worth noting that the UK displays a similar correlation pattern with respect to the US economy, while the comovements with the euro area and with Germany are much lower.

3 Describing the comovement across countries

The previous section found a significant degree of comovement between the three largest euro area countries using the notion of cross-correlation between filtered series. In this section we further investigate the extent of their comovement, resorting to the *cohesion* measure introduced by Croux et al. (2001), which is defined in the frequency domain. Next we use a factor model to examine the extent to which the comovements can be attributed to a small set of common driving forces.

3.1 Multidimensional measurement of the comovements: Coherence

Croux et al. (2000) propose a generalization of the correlation coefficient among two series to a panel of data, i.e. to a dynamic, multivariate context. Recall that considering two time series x and y, their dynamic correlation, at frequency ω, is defined as

$$\rho_{xy}(\omega) = \frac{C_{xy}(\omega)}{\sqrt{S_x(\omega)S_y(\omega)}} \tag{1}$$

where $C_{xy}(\omega)$ is the co-spectrum between x and y and $S_j(\omega)$ is the spectrum of series j, where $0 \leq \omega \leq \pi$. It can be shown that dynamic correlation, as its static counterpart, is bounded by -1 and 1.[11] Dynamic correlation can be defined on a frequency band $\Omega_+ = [\omega_1, \omega_2]$ as

$$\rho_{xy}(\Omega_+) = \frac{\int_{\Omega_+} C_{xy}(\omega)d\omega}{\int_{\Omega_+} \sqrt{S_x(\omega)S_y(\omega)}d\omega}. \tag{2}$$

In this case it can be shown that the static correlation between the two *band-passed* variables , coincides with the dynamic correlation if the same frequency band Ω_+ is considered.

Cohesion is the multivariate extension of dynamic correlation: given a vector of time series, $x_t = (x_{1t}, \dots, x_{nt})$, we construct a weighted average of the dynamic correlations, defined in (1), between all possible pairs of series

$$coh_x(\omega) = \frac{\sum_{i \neq j} w_i w_j \rho_{xy}(\omega)}{\sum_{i \neq j} w_i w_j}, \tag{3}$$

where w_i is the weight assigned to series i in vector x_t. Cohesion, as the dynamic correlation, is defined for every frequency point.[12]

We examine the cohesion in three stages. First, we consider the cohesion among all the quarterly variables in the panel (GDP, Consumption, Investment, Exports, Imports, Government Consumption and Net Exports) in all countries. The top-left panel of Fig. 1 shows that the cohesion among these variables is very small, concentrated at low frequencies (1.6 in the horizontal axis corresponds to periodicities of approximately one year).

Second, when we consider the cohesion across countries for each variable, the comovement is much stronger (see, second panel of Figure 1). Gross trade flows (Exports and Imports) display the greatest co-movement across countries ($> .3$ in the cyclical band), followed by GDP and Investment ($> .2$ in the cyclical band). As pointed out in the previous section, the consumption-output puzzle emerges also in this case, with Consumption exhibiting a lower cohesion than GDP. Net trade and Government Consumption display the smallest degree of comovement across all countries. Third, we gauge the existence of an euro area cycle by examining cohesion among its 3 largest countries (lower-left panel). As a reference we also consider the same measures among three other non euro area countries, the US, UK and Canada (lower-right panel). As expected, when focusing only on more homogenous

---

[11] Its relationship with coherency and squared-coherency is detailed in Croux et al. 2000.

[12] Weights are set to unity for all variables.

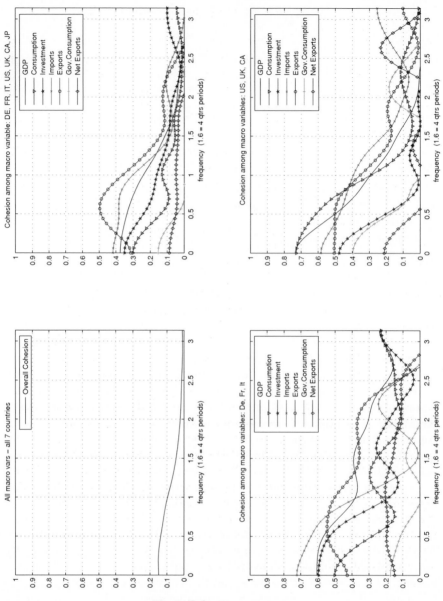

Fig. 1. Cohesion measures

subgroups, the cohesion substantially increases, especially for the non-trade variables (for which it almost doubles). For GDP and Consumption the degree comovement is found to be higher within the US-UK-CA group, while there exist a stronger comovement between investment cycles in the main euro area countries.

3.2 Dynamic factors and the number of driving forces in the panel

We proceed now to inquire whether the comovements within the euro area macroeconomic variables can be attributed to a small set of common driving forces. To address this question we assume that a parsimonious representation of the data, in the form of a *generalized dynamic factor model*, holds (see Forni et al. 2005a, 2005b). Under this assumption we can compute the share of the overall panel variance explained by the common factors, as well as the *commonality* of each variable with respect to the panel.

We examine a large panel dataset of monthly macroeconomic variables that comprises almost 300 time series including aggregate euro area and national statistics (for the 3 largest euro area countries) as well as sectoral data, spanning the Jan. 1987 - Oct. 2004 period. This analysis is not unrelated with the one performed on NA aggregates since all these variables tend to co-move at 'business cycle' (BC) frequencies (as will be shown below); furthermore, many of the monthly series are directly or indirectly used by National Statistical Institutes to build quarterly aggregates (e.g. monthly retail sales are used to compute Consumption).[13]

The estimation of the generalized dynamic factor model uses principal components analysis on the spectral matrix estimated on the panel of monthly series.[14]

Figure 2 displays the share of the first four dynamic principal components to the panel variability at each frequency (Brillinger, 1981). For example, the bottom line represents the variance explained by the first common factor at each frequency between 0 and π, the second line from the bottom the variance explained by the first two common factors and so on: the explanatory power is greater at frequencies below $\frac{\pi}{6}$, to the left of the vertical grid line (the $\frac{\pi}{6}$ frequency in the graph represents periodicities of 12 months).

Focusing on the monthly activity variables (e.g. overall industrial production in each country, and retail sales), we find that 4 common factors explain more than 70% of their overall variability; furthermore in the medium/long run, i.e. at periodicities longer than one year, the variance explained increases to almost 90%. In other terms industrial production (and retail sales) in the 3 largest countries of the euro area have a high degree of "commonality": the common factors account for a large share of their variability and this property is concentrated in the medium/long run.

---

[13] As a result our data set comes close to the type of information set that is nowadays available to central banks or other international institutions. In particular, it contains most of the variables that are routinely reviewed by central banks in the Eurosystem, when assessing the outlook for activity in each country.

[14] The data have been transformed to achieve stationarity as demanded for the estimation of the factor model. Information on the data set and the data treatment is available upon request.

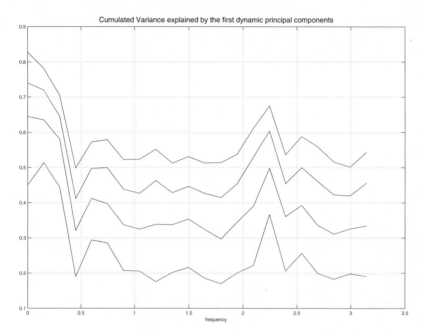

Fig. 2. Dynamic principal components

4 The monthly indicators of activity

4.1 The econometric method

The estimation of the monthly business cycle indicators relies on a specification of the factor model which closely follows the one first used in a similar context in Altissimo et al. (2001) and Cristadoro et al. (2001).

Let $x_t = (x_{1t}\ x_{2t}\ \cdots\ x_{nt})'$ be the vector of monthly series and let's assume that each variable x_{jt}, $j = 1, \ldots, n$, can be represented as the sum of two stationary, mutually orthogonal, unobservable components: the 'common component', call it χ_{jt}, and the 'idiosyncratic component', ξ_{jt}. The χ_{jt} component is driven by a small number q of common 'factors' or common shocks u_{ht}, $h = 1, \ldots, q$ (in our case $q = 4$, as argued in the previous section), while the 'idiosyncratic component' is driven by variable specific shocks. Formally, we have

$$x_{jt} = \chi_{jt} + \xi_{jt} = \sum_{h=1}^{q} \sum_{k=0}^{s} b_{jhk}\, u_{ht-k} + \xi_{jt} \tag{4}$$

where s is the maximum lag considered (i.e. 'loaded' into the series). If we could observe it, monthly GDP would then be treated as any other variable in the panel (say $x_{1t} = \Delta(log(GDP))$) and represented as in equation (4).

Established that, its monthly common component (χ_{1t}) could then be further decomposed in the sum of two unobserved series: a cyclical signal C_{1t} and a signal that captures short-run dynamics of no interest for business cycle analysis:[15]

$$x_{1t} = \chi_{1t} + \xi_{1t} = C_{1t} + \chi^S_{1t} + \xi_{1t}$$

The ultimate goal of our procedure will be to estimate C_{1t}, i.e. the common cyclical component of monthly GDP growth.

In the first step, we estimate the covariance structure of the common component in the monthly dataset (say $\Gamma_\chi(k)$ for each lag k using a dynamic factor approach. In the second step we find a consistent one-sided estimate of the space spanned by the common shocks (u_h) by solving a generalized principal component problem involving the matrices $\Gamma_{\chi(0)}$ and $\Gamma_{\xi(0)}$ (see Forni et al. 2005b). From the eigenvectors corresponding to the $r = q \times (s + 1)$ largest generalized eigenvalues we construct the factors F_t (in our case $r = 24$) that provide a basis for the linear space of common shocks. Finally, we obtain in a consistent way the unobserved monthly indicator for the cyclical component of GDP, C_{1t}, by projecting it on the space spanned by F_t. While GDP (and other NA variables) are available only at quarterly frequency, an estimate of the projection of its unobserved monthly cyclical component C_{1t} on the monthly factors can be recovered.[16]

An important feature of the resulting indicator is that it is derived from a *static* linear combination of the monthly series in the dataset (at time t the projection is on variables at t). This implies that, unlike other methods, no end-of-sample problems arise. In principle any quarterly NA series can be *projected* on our monthly dataset. Here we will focus on GDP, Consumption and Investment and proceed to construct their corresponding monthly indicators.

It is important to select r, the number of static factors, so that the common correlation structure of the panel, as expressed in the sum of past and present dynamic shocks (see eq. 4) is preserved. To illustrate this point we perform the following exercise. First, we estimate a set of 24 static factors on the full sample. Second, we consider 24 successive projections of the euro area GDP on an increasing subset of them (with the first projection using only the first factor,..., the last corresponding to the full set of 24 factors). The four panels in Fig. 3 display the projection of euro area GDP on 1, 6, 18 and 24 static factors.

As more factors are considered, the cyclical signal shifts in time as becomes manifest in the shifts in dating and shaded areas (see the *dating* of peaks and troughs reported on the time axis). What is happening is that the

---

[15] Just like any other stationary variable, the common component of GDP can be decomposed into the sum of waves of different periodicity, the so-called 'spectral decomposition' (Brockwell and Davis 1987, Chap. 4).

[16] The projection matrices can be obtained using the proper variance and covariance between the (quarterly) GDP and the (monthly) factors.

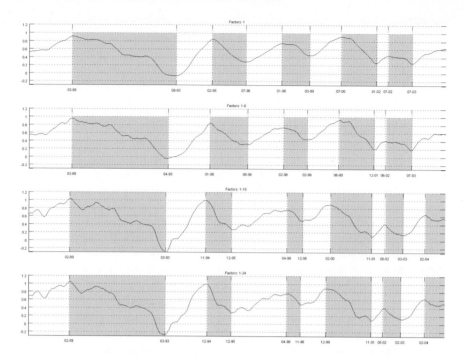

Fig. 3. Projection on an expanding set of factors

lagging and (most of all) the leading information contained in the panel is progressively captured producing an indicator that anticipates the turning points of those constructed in the previous steps and still based on an insufficient number of static factors.

4.2 Description of comovements and dating

Our approach uses the concept of *growth cycle* according to which the cycle is identified with deviations of activity from its long run trend. Peaks (troughs) have to be interpreted as periods of maximal (minimal) growth that are followed by a deceleration (acceleration) in overall activity. While this concept already existed in the traditional literature, it should be stressed that the procedures embodied in the original NBER methodology were based on the 'classical cycle' concept, which focuses instead on fluctuations in the absolute level of activity.

There is a large econometric literature that attempted to engineer a time series method capable of replicating the dates chosen by the Dating Committee of the NBER. The most famous of these is the Bry-Boschan algorithm (hereafter BB) (1971), which can be shown to successfully replicate the official US dates, as well as, with a minor modification, the more recent euro area dating established by the CEPR (see Monch and Uhlig, 2004). We use a mechanical dating algorithm for monthly series analogous to the BB routine and define a corresponding set of binary variables S_t^j indicating the (acceleration/deceleration) state for each indicator j.

As described in Harding and Pagan (2002a), at the center of the BB identification of turning points is the definition of a local peak (trough) in the *level* of a time series y_t as occurring at time t whenever $y_t > (<)y_{t\pm k}$, $k = 1, ..., K$ where K is set to five for monthly data.

As a first check we compare the growth cycle dating obtained with the monthly euro area GDP cyclical component with the Eurocoin turning points released by the CEPR (see Fig. 4).

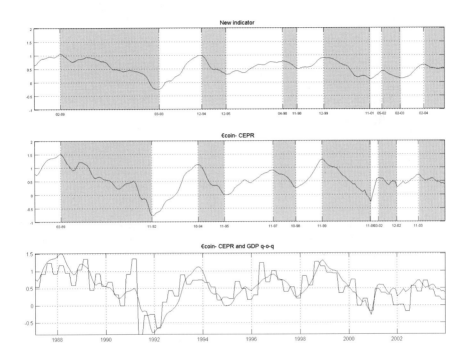

Fig. 4. Comparison of dating in Eurocoin and new indicator

There is a close match in the cyclical phases identified by the two indexes. They both isolate 5 'recessions' (in the broad sense) in the 1987-2003 period. The turning points are at most a few months apart between the two. The depth of recessions and the height of the peaks are substantially the same. The rightmost shaded area in the graph would point to a sixth recession in 2004, but this should only be taken with extreme caution since it is based on data that cannot be considered final in a sense that will be made precise in what follows.[17]

In the next graphs (see Fig. 5-7) the same exercise is repeated for the major expenditure components of GDP in Germany, France and Italy.

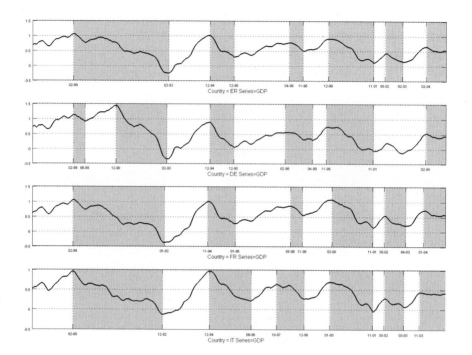

Fig. 5. Dating of GDP monthly indicators

Overall, the turning points seem to be common in all countries for each component. On the other hand, some differences emerge across components, so we can provisionally conclude that consumption and investment cycles tend to be common across countries but present some specificities when compared with GDP.

To measure synchronization between any two series x and y we define two regimes dummies, S_t^x and S_t^y (one for each series) where $S_t = 0$ during recession and $= 1$ during expansions and the we compute the concordance index as:

---

[17] The shaded areas adjacent to the end of the sample are only preliminary and may be subject to revisions as more observations are obtained. In this respect we depart from the Bry-Boschan algorithm which disergards any peak/trouhg found at the end of the sample.

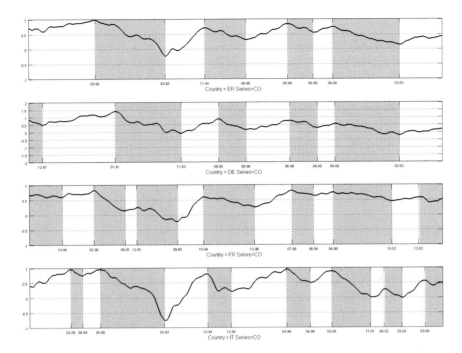

Fig. 6. Dating of consumption monthly indicators

$$Conc_{x,y} = \frac{1}{T}\left(\sum_{t=1}^{T} S_t^x S_t^y + \sum_{t=1}^{T}(1 - S_t^x)(1 - S_t^y)\right)$$

which measure the proportion of times the two variables are in the same state. We also compute the correlation coefficient ρ_{S_x,S_y} between the two state dummines S_t^x, S_t^y, which conveys similar information, but can also be used to test the significance of the degree of synchronization between the two series.[18] Results are presented in Table 3.

The concordance statistic $Conc_{x,y}$ is reported above the diagonal, while ρ_{S_x,S_y} is below the diagonal. In the case of GDP the values of $Conc_{x,y}$ are all larger than .5 suggesting that the monthly indicators of GDP in the euro area countries spend much of the time in the same state of the growth cycle. The pairwise correlations ρ_{S_x,S_y} are all smaller, and are found to be statistically significant only in a subset of cases.[19] The degree of comovement between the

---

[18] The test is carried out computing a t-statistic of the null of no correlation, corrected to take into account for the substantial autocorrelation in the state variables (with a HAC estimator for their covariance matrix).

[19] The concordance index depends also on the mean, μ_{S^j} and the standard deviation, σ_{S^j}, of the binary variables S^j, as $Conc_{x,y} = 1 + 2\rho_{S^x,S^y}\sigma_{S^x}\sigma_{S^y} + 2\mu_{S^x}\mu_{S^y} -$

	HP filter						BK filter						CF filter					
	US	ER	DE	FR	IT	UK	US	ER	DE	FR	IT	UK	US	ER	DE	FR	IT	UK
Volatility (% per quarter)																		
GDP	1.09	0.89	1.21	1.00	0.92	1.19	1.07	0.83	1.10	0.91	0.86	1.08	0.99	0.67	1.05	0.71	0.78	0.88
Consumption	0.81	0.84	1.10	0.86	1.22	1.49	0.77	0.79	0.93	0.78	1.15	1.37	0.68	0.48	0.78	0.58	0.86	1.07
Investment	3.72	2.54	2.78	3.15	3.11	4.09	3.80	2.35	2.26	2.99	2.93	3.69	3.43	1.58	2.00	2.17	2.51	3.30
Export	3.27	2.55	4.57	2.97	3.55	2.29	3.33	2.37	4.14	2.82	2.79	2.07	2.66	2.37	4.27	2.67	2.96	1.93
Import	3.65	2.81	3.53	3.09	4.09	2.99	3.50	2.68	3.30	2.94	3.73	2.82	3.23	2.10	3.09	2.48	3.39	2.56
Government Consumption	1.14	0.59	1.24	0.80	0.85	1.02	1.11	0.54	1.03	0.80	0.92	0.81	0.97	0.49	1.05	0.67	0.74	0.76
Industrial Production	2.11	2.02	2.63	1.73	2.35	1.78	2.11	1.92	2.50	1.62	2.20	1.60	1.87	1.75	2.43	1.40	2.02	1.51
Volatility with respect to own country GDP																		
GDP	1.00	1.00	1.00	1.00	1.00	1.00	1.00	1.00	1.00	1.00	1.00	1.00	1.00	1.00	1.00	1.00	1.00	1.00
Consumption	0.74	0.95	0.90	0.86	1.33	1.25	0.72	0.95	0.85	0.86	1.34	1.27	0.69	0.72	0.74	0.81	1.11	1.21
Investment	3.42	2.87	2.29	3.15	3.38	3.43	3.56	2.84	2.07	3.28	3.42	3.42	3.49	2.37	1.90	3.04	3.23	3.75
Export	3.00	2.88	3.76	2.98	3.87	1.92	3.12	2.86	3.78	3.09	3.25	1.92	2.70	3.56	4.05	3.74	3.81	2.20
Import	3.35	3.17	2.90	3.10	4.45	2.50	3.28	3.24	3.01	3.23	4.34	2.61	3.28	3.15	2.94	3.47	4.36	2.91
Government Consumption	1.05	0.66	1.02	0.80	0.93	0.85	1.04	0.65	0.94	0.87	1.08	0.75	0.99	0.74	0.99	0.94	0.96	0.87
Industrial Production	1.94	2.28	2.16	1.74	2.56	1.50	1.98	2.33	2.28	1.78	2.56	1.48	1.90	2.64	2.31	1.97	2.61	1.71
Correlation with own country GDP																		
GDP	1.00	1.00	1.00	1.00	1.00	1.00	1.00	1.00	1.00	1.00	1.00	1.00	1.00	1.00	1.00	1.00	1.00	1.00
Consumption	0.82	0.79	0.63	0.77	0.67	0.88	0.85	0.81	0.70	0.76	0.71	0.89	0.84	0.61	0.63	0.58	0.53	0.86
Investment	0.92	0.91	0.81	0.92	0.78	0.68	0.93	0.92	0.83	0.93	0.83	0.73	0.97	0.88	0.78	0.89	0.78	0.66
Export	0.54	0.77	0.81	0.72	0.34	0.40	0.50	0.77	0.86	0.70	0.46	0.39	0.55	0.88	0.90	0.74	0.63	0.19
Import	0.84	0.90	0.82	0.83	0.60	0.64	0.87	0.92	0.90	0.85	0.72	0.68	0.89	0.88	0.92	0.82	0.64	0.62
Government Consumption	0.05	-0.16	0.03	-0.48	-0.04	-0.42	-0.02	-0.14	0.13	-0.52	-0.05	-0.50	-0.19	-0.41	0.11	-0.62	-0.32	-0.39
Industrial Production	0.88	0.88	0.84	0.84	0.85	0.90	0.88	0.92	0.89	0.85	0.89	0.90	0.88	0.93	0.92	0.87	0.90	0.91

Table 1. Business cycle volatilities: quarterly indicators. Sample: 1980Q1-2004Q4

	HP Filter						BK Filter						CF Filter					
	US	ER	DE	FR	IT	UK	US	ER	DE	FR	IT	UK	US	ER	DE	FR	IT	UK
Correlation with the corresponding variable in the US																		
GDP	1.00	0.20	-0.03	0.19	0.29	0.48	1.00	0.24	-0.01	0.24	0.34	0.52	1.00	0.27	0.12	0.31	0.21	0.34
Consumption	1.00	0.01	-0.11	0.13	0.04	0.51	1.00	-0.02	-0.19	0.15	0.03	0.58	1.00	-0.08	-0.13	0.16	-0.19	0.51
Investment	1.00	0.01	0.01	0.07	-0.01	0.47	1.00	0.02	0.00	0.08	0.00	0.52	1.00	0.18	0.28	0.28	-0.02	0.52
Export	1.00	0.52	0.32	0.56	0.23	0.50	1.00	0.56	0.34	0.58	0.42	0.55	1.00	0.59	0.36	0.64	0.46	0.59
Import	1.00	0.24	0.14	0.22	0.32	0.40	1.00	0.27	0.19	0.27	0.32	0.49	1.00	0.43	0.35	0.32	0.42	0.47
Government Consumption	1.00	0.09	0.13	-0.25	-0.06	0.11	1.00	0.15	0.08	-0.19	0.09	0.26	1.00	0.14	0.25	-0.27	-0.31	0.42
Industrial Production	1.00	0.31	0.07	0.40	0.50	0.45	1.00	0.34	0.08	0.44	0.50	0.47	1.00	0.28	0.02	0.36	0.38	0.35
Correlation with the corresponding variable in the euro area																		
GDP	0.20	1.00	0.80	0.88	0.79	0.22	0.24	1.00	0.82	0.89	0.86	0.26	0.27	1.00	0.83	0.79	0.86	0.24
Consumption	0.01	1.00	0.77	0.83	0.80	0.20	-0.02	1.00	0.83	0.82	0.84	0.19	-0.08	1.00	0.80	0.60	0.72	-0.36
Investment	0.01	1.00	0.74	0.92	0.81	0.33	0.02	1.00	0.81	0.95	0.83	0.28	0.18	1.00	0.82	0.87	0.73	0.02
Export	0.52	1.00	0.83	0.87	0.61	0.41	0.56	1.00	0.83	0.91	0.68	0.53	0.59	1.00	0.82	0.91	0.76	0.64
Import	0.24	1.00	0.81	0.91	0.85	0.34	0.27	1.00	0.85	0.93	0.87	0.29	0.43	1.00	0.84	0.88	0.85	0.09
Government Consumption	0.09	1.00	0.80	0.45	0.57	0.16	0.15	1.00	0.75	0.49	0.65	0.27	0.14	1.00	0.84	0.41	0.58	0.07
Industrial Production	0.31	1.00	0.79	0.89	0.69	0.15	0.34	1.00	0.81	0.92	0.77	0.21	0.28	1.00	0.77	0.90	0.79	0.21
Correlation with the corresponding variable in Germany																		
GDP	-0.03	0.80	1.00	0.52	0.46	-0.25	-0.01	0.82	1.00	0.54	0.56	-0.23	0.12	0.83	1.00	0.36	0.57	-0.21
Consumption	-0.11	0.77	1.00	0.55	0.45	-0.15	-0.19	0.83	1.00	0.57	0.58	-0.17	-0.13	0.80	1.00	0.27	0.44	-0.52
Investment	0.01	0.74	1.00	0.57	0.53	-0.06	0.00	0.81	1.00	0.69	0.62	-0.11	0.28	0.82	1.00	0.56	0.54	-0.19
Export	0.32	0.83	1.00	0.62	0.25	0.24	0.34	0.83	1.00	0.63	0.30	0.34	0.36	0.82	1.00	0.59	0.36	0.52
Import	0.14	0.81	1.00	0.62	0.69	-0.04	0.19	0.85	1.00	0.68	0.76	-0.08	0.35	0.84	1.00	0.55	0.75	-0.20
Government Consumption	0.13	0.80	1.00	0.15	0.18	0.14	0.08	0.75	1.00	0.14	0.20	0.27	0.25	0.84	1.00	0.09	0.26	0.26
Industrial Productio	0.07	0.79	1.00	0.65	0.39	-0.08	0.08	0.81	1.00	0.68	0.49	-0.05	0.02	0.77	1.00	0.59	0.43	-0.13

Table 2. Business cycle comovements: quarterly indicators. Sample: 1980Q1-2004Q4

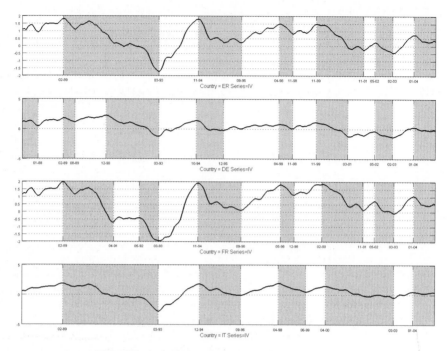

Fig. 7. Dating of investment monthly indicators

GDP of the 3 largest euro area countries is comparable to the one found for the UK-US-CA group. For Consumption correlations in the regimes identified by our dating exercise are statically significant but of smaller magnitude compared to the UK-US-CA group. For investment results are somewhat in between, with Italy and France displaying a comovement similar to the one observed between the US and Canada. The comovement of French and Italian investment with the German aggregate is quite low, of the same magnitude of the one observed in the consumption series. This results reinforce the analysis of the previous section, where it was shown that cohesion among the euro area countries was greater for GDP than for Consumption and Investment, mainly due to the high comovement in Exports and Imports.

4.3 Stylized business cycle facts revisited

Before turning to an analysis of the performance of the monthly indicators in terms of reliability of the signal (revision errors), and forecasting performance, we repeat the analysis of the stylized facts of the business cycle as

---

$\mu_{S^x} - \mu^{S_y}$. High values of this indicator therefore may just depend on acceleration/deceleration phases lasting for long periods of time relative to the sample.

they emerge from the second moments of our indexes and compare them with those obtained before with univariate filtering (HP, BK and CF) of quarterly NA series.

The picture of the business cycle properties of the main macro variables in the euro area is confirmed when using our alternative "filtering technique". On the other hand, we obtain an estimate of the cycle for the entire sample period, unlike univariate methods which cannot be performed on the tails of the sample.

Table 3. Concordance indexes and correlations in cycles

	GDP						
	US	ER	DE	FR	IT	UK	CA
US		0.62	0.5	0.62	0.63	0.91	0.93
ER	0.24		0.84	0.95	0.89	0.64	0.63
DE	0.02	**0.69**		0.8	0.76	0.54	0.51
FR	0.24	**0.91**	**0.61**		0.9	0.63	0.63
IT	0.24	**0.78**	**0.57**	**0.8**		0.64	0.62
UK	**0.81**	**0.28**	0.09	0.26	0.27		0.93
CA	**0.87**	0.26	0.03	0.26	0.23	**0.87**	

	Consumption						
	US	ER	DE	FR	IT	UK	CA
US		0.35	0.28	0.51	0.43	0.94	0.9
ER	-0.3		0.83	0.75	0.81	0.34	0.35
DE	-0.43	**0.66**		0.71	0.67	0.28	0.26
FR	0.01	**0.51**	0.44		0.65	0.54	0.5
IT	-0.13	**0.62**	**0.34**	**0.32**		0.39	0.49
UK	**0.88**	-0.31	-0.44	0.05	-0.21		0.86
CA	**0.8**	-0.29	-0.48	-0.02	-0.03	**0.72**	

	Investment						
	US	ER	DE	FR	IT	UK	CA
US		0.58	0.6	0.61	0.48	0.77	0.88
ER	0.14		0.8	0.91	0.91	0.76	0.54
DE	0.21	**0.62**		0.71	0.71	0.7	0.59
FR	0.22	**0.83**	**0.43**		0.86	0.81	0.57
IT	-0.06	**0.81**	**0.44**	**0.74**		0.69	0.45
UK	**0.55**	**0.53**	**0.4**	**0.61**	**0.38**		0.71
CA	**0.75**	0.06	0.2	0.14	-0.12	**0.41**	

Concordance Indexes in the upper diagonal part, correlations in the lower diagonal part; in boldface if the correlation coefficient is found to be statistically significant at 5% level.

The relative volatility results (Table 4) show that consumption is less volatile than output, with the notable exception of Italy, and that investment is about 3 times more volatile than GDP, with a somewhat smoother series for Germany and the euro area average.

Table 4. Business cycle volatilities: quarterly indicators

	Euro	Germany	France	Italy
	Volatility (% per month)			
GDP	0.29	0.39	0.32	0.25
Consumption	0.26	0.37	0.24	0.36
Investment	0.75	0.87	0.94	0.95
Export	0.90	1.15	1.06	1.20
Import	1.04	1.13	1.16	1.42
Government Consumption	0.18	0.26	0.26	0.31
	Volatility relative to own country GDP			
GDP	1.00	1.00	1.00	1.00
Consumption	0.90	0.94	0.75	1.41
Investment	2.64	2.20	2.92	3.74
Export	3.15	2.93	3.28	4.73
Import	3.64	2.87	3.59	5.61
Government Consumption	0.63	0.67	0.80	1.24
	Correlation with own country GDP			
GDP	1.00	1.00	1.00	1.00
Consumption	0.87	0.79	0.79	0.82
Investment	0.97	0.94	0.96	0.87
Export	0.80	0.76	0.78	0.63
Import	0.93	0.81	0.89	0.90
Government Consumption	-0.11	0.34	-0.59	-0.31
	Correlation with same euro area variable			
GDP	1.00	0.85	0.94	0.92
Consumption	1.00	0.81	0.73	0.90
Investment	1.00	0.75	0.93	0.93
Export	1.00	0.88	0.98	0.77
Import	1.00	0.94	0.97	0.97
Government Consumption	1.00	0.76	0.69	0.78

Within each country the correlation with the monthly GDP indicator is very high for investment and imports (in the first case it is close to one) while it is slightly lower for consumption and (generally) negative for government spending, likely as a consequence of the in-built countercyclical nature of many expenditure items and deliberate active government policies.

Not surprisingly, cross-country correlations within the euro area are higher than those measured with univariate filters. In particular, investment and GDP have contemporaneous correlation close to 1. A little lower is the correlation among consumption expenditures, private and (expecially) public, across countries.

We can conclude that our monthly cyclical components of NA series give a picture that is coherent with the received view about the business cycle, and has the advantage of producing an estimate of the cyclical components also at the end of the sample. We now turn to the issue of the reliability of the monthly BC indicators at the end of the sample.

5 Tracking activity in the euro area with monthly indicators: revision errors, nowcasting and forecasting

We want to answer the following question, that we believe is of key importance when building a business cycle indicator: how well does the proposed estimator of the cyclical component scores in terms of *timeliness, reliability, interpretability* and usefulness of the signal?

In other words we want to analyse the indicators in terms of:

1. how long is the lag between current period and the reference period of the last estimate of the indicator? (The **timeliness** of the signal)
2. how long has one to wait until the estimates of the cyclical signal can be considered 'stable' or final? (i.e. how large and how persistent is the **revision error** process)
3. how can we read the cyclical component *vis-à-vis* the original series? (The **interpretability** of the signal)
4. how can we complement our assessment of the economic outlook using these indicators? (What are their properties in terms of detection of **turning points** and **anticipation** the developments in the relevant macroeconomic variables?)

In what follows we make these requirements more precise and to provide an assessment of the indicators according to them.

5.1 Timeliness of the signal

National accounts (NA) figures in the euro area are usually available with a 3 to 4 months delay (the lag is a little shorter if one considers the preliminary estimates of GDP): for example, data for the first quarter of a given year are usually not available until the end of the following quarter (June). Central banks and professional forecasters usually construct early estimates of these figures either in a formal or in a judgemental way by looking at more readily available monthly statistics (as industrial production, surveys, sales, etc.).[20]

Our method does exactly this in a statistically rigorous way. First, it pools all the available monthly frequency information, then it finds the "best" estimate of the cyclical component of the quarterly series. In this way the figures for, say, GDP, can be produced with a much shorter delay. In practice, though, a problem arises. Since monthly data become available with varying delays if we were to wait for a complete set of statistics covering an entire quarter before producing an estimate of the cyclical components of GDP, consumption (CO), investment (IV), etc. for that quarter, we would have gained very little in terms of timeliness. Our method allows for staggered data releases so

---

[20] For the use of econometric models (the so called bridge models) in the forecasting of quarterly NA figures on the basis of monthly indicators as surveys of industrial production see Baffigi, Golinelli and Parigi, 2002.

that we can use monthly data as they arrive, taking into account the different timeliness of the updates and thus working with only partial information for a given quarter. [21] Following this procedure we can have an early estimate of the cyclical signal in real time. One can also push the approach a little forward and use the rich correlation structure of the panel to extrapolate our projection beyond the sample thus forecasting the cyclical component for a quarter without having any information directly related to that quarter. Of course each of these steps comes at a cost in terms of the precision and reliability of the signal. In what follows we address this issue.

5.2 Revision errors

Every signal extraction procedure is subject to revisions as a result of the updates of earlier estimates as more information becomes available. This is common to unobserved components extracted with a Kalman filter (see Stock and Watson, 1989) where we can immediately appreciate the errors (in sample) by comparing the filter with the smoother. Similarly, with model-based seasonal adjustment techniques (or, more generally, with any bilateral filtering), even if models and parameters are held constant, at the end of the sample the extraction is based on 'provisional' (forecast) data. Our method of extracting unobserved components is no exception in this regard, even though, being based on cross sectional, known information, rather than on future unknown data, we can anticipate that large and persistent revisions should not affect our provisional estimates.

The problem of revisions can be cast in the following terms. Let's call $C_t = C_{t/\infty}$ the **final estimate** of the cyclical component of a given series at time t and $C_{t/t}$ the estimate obtained with information up to time t (the **concurrent estimate**).[22] As information is updated we can form **revised estimates** of the unobserved component at time t, let us call them $C_{t/t+k}$ where $t + k$ indexes the time up to which information is available. [23]

For $k \to \infty$ we obtain the final estimate. In a finite sample this will never happen but for k large enough (say $k = \bar{k}$) one can regard the estimate as final in the sense that new information will not affect it in a detectable way. We can thus define the revision error as the difference between the final value $C_t = C_{t/t+\bar{k}}$ and the revised estimate of the component as of time $t + k$

$$r_{t/t+k} = C_t - C_{t/t+k}$$

---

[21] For a method to deal with the end of sample unbalances which is consistent with our approach, see Altissimo et al. (2001).

[22] For a similar analysis in the context of model based (ARIMA) methods see Kaiser and Maravall (2001).

[23] For example we can form a concurrent estimate of first quarter GDP as we have information up to that quarter, then, month after month we can update it obtaining a sequence of revised estimates of the cyclical component of GDP as of time t.

for $k \in [0, \bar{k}]$. We can then evaluate the reliability of early estimates of the cycle by considering two quantities:

1. the **magnitude** of the revision error: $r_{t/t} = C_t - C_{t/t}$ (i.e. the error made when considering the concurrent estimate instead of the final)
2. the **duration** of the revison error: i.e. the value of k for which the error is small enough to be considered negligible. One way of assessing the duration is to consider k large enough when the ratio between the MSE of the revised estimate and that of the concurrent estimate is less than a given threshold.

For each country and each indicator we choose a value of $\bar{k} = 24$, and we estimate the cyclical signal for a span of 36 months (from January 2000 to December 2002) considering for each of the 36 months the errors $r_{t/t+k}$ with k ranging 0 to 24.[24]

Results are reported in Table 5 only for GDP's and show revision errors of magnitutes ranging from 0.09 (Italy) to 0.16 (Germany).[25]

Table 5. GDP revision errors: $r_{t/t+k}$

k	Euro	Germany	France	Italy
0	0.139	0.162	0.145	0.091
3	0.109	0.124	0.114	0.076
6	0.079	0.086	0.087	0.059
9	0.061	0.068	0.068	0.048
12	0.046	0.053	0.055	0.038
15	0.040	0.046	0.049	0.034
18	0.033	0.044	0.040	0.028
21	0.018	0.024	0.023	0.015
24	0.000	0.000	0.000	0.000

Each column reports the revision error for the GDPs of the country indicated after k months, $r_{t/t+k} = C_t - C_{t/t+k}$ where $C_t = C_{t/t+\bar{k}}$ and $\bar{k} = 24$

For euro area GDP the error declines rather sharply and becomes negligible after about one year: in twelve months almost 70% of the overall magnitude of the error disappears

We can conclude by saying that early estimates of the unobserved cyclical components are reasonably precise and their reliability increases rapidly as the information set becomes larger.

---

[24] We also experimented with $\bar{k} = 36$, but the results convinced us that $\bar{k} = 24$ is more than sufficient to assess the reliability of early signals.

[25] A complete set of results is available upon request.

5.3 Nowcasting and forecasting

A related question concerns the reliability of the estimates of, say, GDP growth, produced when not all information for a given month (or quarter) is available. This can be thought of as a form of *nowcasting* where the target variable Y_t (quarterly GDP growth) is not yet available but we have some higher frequency related information. Formally, let us call

$$E\left(C_t/I_t^m, I_{t-3}^q\right)$$

the forecast of C_t based on monthly information up to time t and quarterly information up to time $t - 3$, C_t being the cyclical component of Y_t (GDP growth). We can evaluate the reliability of our nowcast computing:

$$RMSFE = \left\{ \frac{1}{T_Q} \sum_{t \in T_Q} \left[Y_t - E\left(C_t/I_t^m, I_{t-3}^q\right) \right]^2 \right\}^{\frac{1}{2}}$$

where T_Q is the range of the out of sample simulation exercise. As shown in the first row of Table 6, for quarterly growth rate of euro area GDP the RMSFE is 0.27, the errors are slightly larger for Italy and Germany (0.33 and 0.36 respectively) almost twice as large for France (0.48). This result should come as no surprise, since the euro area data can be considered an 'average' of country rates of growth, and therefore are smoother (the standard deviation of quarterly growth rates is 0.42 for the area, while ranges form 0.5 to 0.6 for the other three countries). For consumption the overall pattern is similar, but errors are slightly higher both for the area and for the countries. The worst performance is obtained when one considers investment, RMSFE are close to 1, for Italy is bigger than 2.

Table 6. RMSFE of monthly GDP w.r.t different targets

GDP	Euro	Germany	France	Italy
$(1 - L)log(GDP_t)$	0.273	0.362	0.484	0.329
$(1 - L^4)log(GDP_t)$	0.195	0.225	0.204	0.226
$(1 - L^4)log(GDP_{t+1})$	0.165	0.187	0.185	0.186
$(1 - L^4)log(GDP_{t+2})$	0.195	0.214	0.225	0.165
$(1 - L^4)log(GDP_{t+3})$	0.259	0.286	0.294	0.187
$(1 - L^4)log(GDP_{t+4})$	0.32	0.338	0.362	0.241

Each row reports the RMSFE of the monthly indicator for GDP growth, C_t, in each country with respect to the measure indicated in each row. For example the last row reports the RMSFE of C_t with respect to the year-on-year growth rate of GDP four periods ahead, $(1 - L^4)log(GDP_{t+4})$

Our indicators are smoothed estimates of the growth rates of GDP, consumption, investment and so on, or, more precisely, they are estimates of the cyclical components of these series. It is then natural to associate them

Table 7. RMSFE of monthly Consumption w.r.t different targets

Consumption	Euro	Germany	France	Italy
$(1 - L)log(CO_t)$	0.337	0.597	0.443	0.459
$(1 - L^4)log(CO_t)$	0.151	0.288	0.113	0.247
$(1 - L^4)log(CO_{t+1})$	0.178	0.333	0.112	0.223
$(1 - L^4)log(CO_{t+2})$	0.215	0.387	0.133	0.26
$(1 - L^4)log(CO_{t+3})$	0.253	0.448	0.163	0.312
$(1 - L^4)log(CO_{t+4})$	0.277	0.482	0.164	0.369

Each row reports the RMSFE of the monthly indicator for consumption growth, C_t, in each country with respect to the measure indicated in each row. For example the last row reports the RMSFE of C_t with respect to the year-on-year growth rate of consumption four periods ahead, $(1 - L^4)log(CO_{t+4})$

not to the quarter-on-quarter percentage changes in actual GDP, but with a longer term measure of GDP growth. To convey this idea we compared our monthly indicators in March, June, September and December with alternative measures of present and future year on year GDP growth, i.e. our target variable Y_t is the $RMSFE$ formula above is $(1 - L^4)log(GDP_t)$. This second type of exercise, which considers futures (i.e. beyond t) growth rates is a *forecasting* experiment. If the monthly data in the dataset contain enough *leading* information for GDP then our indicators may turn out to be good forecasters of year-on-year GDP growth.

For year-on-year figures the $RMSFE$ is about two thirds of the $RMSFE$ computed for quarter-on-quarter changes, as expected. In the case of consumption the reduction is even sharper. There is also some evidence that the indicators lead the year on year growth by about three to six months.[26]

We can now better motivate the claim made in the introduction that one should not interpret the indicators as early estimates of quarter-on-quarter growth. Even though the errors are not larger than those obtained in the literature on nowcasting, with methods targeted to that end, it would be an inappropriate use of the indicators as such.[27] A better way of interpreting the indicators is to consider the information they covey as medium term growth of the respective variables. Their primary purpose is the early detection of cyclical downturns and upturns. In this respect the revision errors, as illustrated in the previous section, are rather small and the proposed indicators could therefore be used as a reliable synthetic measure of business cycle behaviour of the key macro variables.

---

[26] In this case the $RMSFE$ are very close to those obtained for contemporaneous yearly changes, and therefore the differences are not statistically significant.

[27] Nothing prevents us to use the indicators in econometric models to enhance the forecast of quarter-on-quarter growth of variables of interest. We have not investigated this issue in the present paper.

6 Conclusions

This study has analyzed the business cycle behavior of the three largest countries in the euro area by means of a factor model that uses the information from a large dataset of macroeconomic time series. This framework has allowed us to investigate simultaneously the degree of comovement in these economies and to develop a set of monthly indicators for tracking economic activity in real-time.

The general finding is that in the last twenty years fluctuations of economic activity in these countries have been highly synchronized. In line with the tenets of most recent macroeconomic literature, we also show that business cycles in these countries are driven by a small set of common factors.

Having proved that there is strong comovement in the main macro variablesin the euro area, using both standard univariate filters and multivariate filters obtained from our factor model, we constructed a set of monthly indicators able to track, in real-time, the developments of economic activity in each country, as well as in the euro area as a whole. These indicators are developed for GDP and the main demand components of GDP, which are usually available to the policy maker only at a quarterly frequency, and with a considerable delay.

Our indicators are smoothed estimates of the monthly growth rates of GDP, Consumption, Investment and so on, or, more precisely, they are estimates of the cyclical components of these series. The estimation problem we tackle is therefore akin to standard signal extraction where the signal is the cyclical component of an (unobserved) monthly variable. These results are obtained with a method that improves on traditional filtering techniques by extracting smooth cyclical components till the end of the sample.

The stylized facts of the cycle, as they emerge from our monthly indicators are coherent with the results obtained through traditional univariate filters and with established evidence discussed in the literature. In particular, for European economies, investment and industrial production are about three times more volatile than output; cyclical correlations with own country GDP are positive and strong for all main components of aggregate demand (with the exception of public expenditure, which is counter-cyclical). The cross-country correlation of national components is stronger for output and investment, somewhat weaker for consumption.

We assess the performance of our monthly indicators in two respects: first, in the amount of revisions which they undergo as more information becomes available; second, in their ability to track the (observed) current and future growth rates in their corresponding target.

The preliminary evidence points to good performance of the monthly indicators in tracking the reference quarterly variable, both in terms of in sample performance, and in *pseudo* out-of-sample exercises. The revisions of the signal are small and after a period of 6 to 12 months revised estimates can be regarded as "final". Finally, the ability of producing forecast of quarterly series through the indicators needs further investigation, even though the preliminary evidence contained in the paper suggests that the monthly cyclical components contain indeed valuable information not for quarter on quarter growh rates but for a smoother longer term concept, as can be captured by future year on year growth.

References

Altissimo, F., Bassanetti, A., Cristadoro, R., Forni, M., Lippi, M., Reichlin, L. and Veronese, G. (2001) A real time coincident indicator for the euro area business cycle , *Working paper*, CEPR.

Altissimo, F., Marchetti, D. and Oneto, G. (2000) The italian business cycle: Coincident and leading indicators and some stylized facts , *Temi di discussione*, Banca d'Italia.

Backus, D. and Kehoe, P. (1992) International evidence on the historical properties of business cycles , *American Economic Review* **82**(4),864-888.

Baffigi, A., Golinelli, C. and Parigi, G. (2002) Euro area bridge models , *Temi di discussione*, Banca d'Italia.

Baxter, A. and King, R.G. (1999) Measuring business cycles approximate band-pass filters for economic time series , *Review of Economics and Statistics* **81**(4),575-593.

Baxter, M. (1995), International Trade and Business Cycles, p.1801-1864, in Handbook of International Economics, vol.3, Grossman, G and Rogoff, K. editors, North Holland.

Bruno, G. and Otranto, E. (2004) Dating the italian business cycle: a comparison of procedures. , *Working Paper 41*, ISAE.

Brillinger, D.R. (1981), Time Series Data Analysis and Theory, Holden Day, San Francisco.

Bry, G. and Boschan, C. (1971) Cyclical analysis of time series: Selected procedures and computer programs , *Technical Working Paper 20*, NBER.

Burns, A.F. and Mitchell, W.G. 1946, Measuring Business Cycles, NBER, New York.

Burnside, C. (1998) Detrending and business cycle facts: a comment , *Journal of Monetary Economics* **41**,513-532.

Canova, F. (1994) Detrending and turning points , *European Economic Review* **38**,614-623.

Canova, F. (1999) Does detrending matter for the determination of the reference cycle and the selection of turning points , *Economic Journal* **49**,126-149.

Christiano, L. and Fitzgerald, J. (2003) The band pass filter , *International Economic Review* **44**,435-465.

Cristadoro, R., Forni, M., Reichlin, L. and Veronese, G. (2005) A core inflation indicator for the euro area , *Journal of Money Credit and Banking* **37**(3),539-560.

92   Riccardo Cristadoro and Giovanni Veronese

Croux, C., , Forni, M. and Reichlin, L. (1998) A measure of comovement for economic variables: Theory and empirics , *Review of Economics and Statistics* **83**(2),232-241.

Eickmeier, S. (2005) Common stationary and non-stationary factors in the euro area analyzed in large-scale factor model , *mimeo*, Bundesbank.

Forni, M., Hallin, M., Lippi, M. and Reichlin, L. (2005a) The generalized factor model: identification and estimation , *The Review of Economics and Statistics* **82**,550-554.

Forni, M., Hallin, M., Lippi, M. and Reichlin, L. (2005b) The generalized factor model: One-sided estimation and forecasting , *Journal of the American Statistical Association* .

Hodrick, R. and Prescott, E. (1997) Post war us business cycles: an empirical investigation , *Journal of Money, Credit and Banking* **29**,1-16.

Kaiser, R. and Maravall, A. 2001, Measuring Business Cycles In Economic Time Series, Springer Verlag.

Kydland, F. and Prescott, E. (1982) Time to build and aggregate fluctuations , *Econometrica* **50**,1345-1370.

Lucas, R.E. (1977) understanding Business Cycles, *Carnegie - Rochester Conference Series on Public Policy* **5**,7-30.

Matheron, J. (2004) Business Cyle Datation in France, Germany and Italy , *mimeo*, Banque de France.

Monch, E. and Uhlig, H. (1999) Towards a monthly business cycle chronology for the euro area , *mimeo*, Humboldt University,Berlin.

Nelson, C. and Plosser, C. (1982) Trends and random walks in macroeconomic time series , *Journal of Monetary Economics* **10**,139-162.

Obstfeldt, M. and Rogoff, K. (2000) The six major puzzles of international macroeconomics: is there a common cause? , In: NBER Macro Annual, MIT Press,

Harding, D. and Pagan, A. (2001) Rejoinder to James Hamilton, *mimeo*, Australian National University.

Harding, D. and Pagan, A. (2002a) Dissecting the cycle: a methodological investigation , *Journal of Monetary Economics* **49**,365-381.

Harding, D. and Pagan, A. (2002b) Synchronization of cycles , *Working paper*, Australian National University.

Monch E. and Uhlig, H. (2004), Towards a Monthly Business Cycle Chronology for the Euro Area .

Ravn, M. and Uhlig, H. (2001) On adjusting the hp-filter for the frequency of observations , *Discussion Paper 40*, CEPR.

Sargent, T., 1987, Macroeconomic Theory, 2nd Edition, Academic Press, London.

Stock, J. and Watson, M. (1989) New Indexes of Coincident and Leading Economic Indicators, in NBER Macroeconomics Annual.

Stock, J. and Watson, M. (1999) Business Cycle Fluctuations in U.S. Macroeconomic Time Series , *Handbook of Macroeconomics*, Vol. 1A, North Holland,3-64.

Stock, J. and Watson, M. (2002) Macroeconomic forecasting using diffusion indexes , *Journal of Business and Economic Statistics* **20**(2),147-162.

Assessing Aggregate Comovements in France, Germany and Italy Using a Non Stationary Factor Model of the Euro Area[*]

Olivier de Bandt[1], Catherine Bruneau[2], and Alexis Flageollet[2]

[1] Banque de France, 46-1405 DAMEP, 39 rue Croix des Petits Champs, 75049 Paris Cedex 01, France olivier.debandt@banque-france.fr
[2] University of Paris X, Thema, 200 avenue de la République, 92000 Nanterre, France cbruneau@u-paris10.fr, alexisflageollet@yahoo.fr

Summary. The objective of the paper is to investigate to what extent business cycles co-move in Germany, France and Italy. We use a large-scale database of non-stationary series for the euro area in order to assess the effect of common versus idiosyncratic shocks, as well as transitory versus permanent shocks, across countries over the 1980:Q1 to 2003:Q4 period. We apply the methodology proposed by Bai (2004) and Bai and Ng (2004) to construct a coincident indicator of the euro area business cycle to which national developments appear to be increasingly correlated at business cycle frequencies, while more significant differences appear at lower frequencies which measures potential growth. The indicator is also shown to be related to extra euro area economic developments.

Keywords: factor models, non-stationary panel data models, euro area business cycles.
JEL classification: C12, C22.

1 Introduction

The objective of the paper is to investigate to what extent business cycles co-move in Germany, France and Italy, using a large database for the euro area on the 1980Q1 to 2003Q4 period. We construct a Business Cycle Index (BCI) to which the three countries cycles are compared, in order to determine how important are common versus specific shocks, and whether individual countries' business cycles have become more correlated within the euro area.

Against a general trend towards more synchronisation between euro area countries, triggered by the 1979 European Monetary System, the 1992 Internal Market programme and the 1999 European Monetary Union -although

---

[*] Comments by D. Giannone, S. Eickmeier and H. Herrmann are gratefully acknowledged. The authors are solely responsible for all remaining errors.

authors disagree on the direction of causality- Germany, France and Italy have regularly experienced periods of divergence. For example, the 1980s and some portion of the 1990s were periods of higher divergence. On the contrary, the simultaneity of the world slowdown in 2001 surprised observers. The three countries have, since then, exhibited more significant asymmetries. To assess these comovements, or the lack thereof, one needs a common benchmark and a simple reference indicator.

First, regarding the common benchmark against which each country's cyclical position can be compared, Germany has often been seen as the obvious choice (see e.g. Artis and Zhang, 1999, or Angeloni and Dedola, 1999), although there was evidence that Germany was more correlated with 'Anglosaxon' countries than France and Italy (Helbling and Bayoumi, 2003). Within the Single Currency Area, the sole reference to Germany is no longer warranted.

Second, with respect to the reference indicator to analyze cyclical features, it is usual to focus on a set of macroeconomic series, to filter them so as to extract its cyclical component, then to examine the correlations of the cyclical components across countries, taken contemporaneously or with lags or leads.

Such an approach usually requires to focus on a limited number of series, while many authors point out that a better representation of the cyclical movements can be captured from a large number of economic series. The idea is behind the methodology developed by the National Bureau of Economic Research (NBER) in the US, as described in the seminal book of Burns and Mitchell (1946) and since then widely used (Zarnowitz, 1992). The goal is to convert complex economic dynamics into one-dimensional figures, which leads to construct a BCI.

We adopt a multivariate approach with a view to characterizing the common part of the national economic dynamics. This is already the approach adopted in the literature which uses dynamic factor models. Recent examples are Stock and Watson (1998, 2002), Forni et al (2000) and Forni and Lippi (2001), Canova et al. (2004).

The paper is an additional contribution to this literature but the main difference with respect to previous studies stems from the choice we make to work with the levels of the series.

Hence, we implement a principal component analysis using the factor model introduced by Stock & Watson (1998) and largely developed by Bai & Ng (2004) and Bai (2004) for the non-stationary case. Moreover, the inference is proved to be complete, thanks to the large panel and time dimensions, which is a major improvement in the BCI literature in comparison with previous factor models.

Working with levels has distinctive advantages: it permits to extract the long run trend associated with the persistent effect of shocks and to derive useful statistical indicators associated with the levels of the variables, like turning points in the tradition of the classical cycles as recently advocated by Harding and Pagan (2002).

Moreover, this framework allows to examine whether the sources of similarities are transitory or permanent and more particularly whether the determinants of potential growth -associated with the permanent component-are pervasive or country-specific. The analysis uncovers three non-stationary factors, but we give more emphasis to the first factor as a source of potential growth, since it weights equally all these macroeconomic variables and captures the overall trend embedded in them.

The paper is therefore close to the one carried out by Eickmeier (2005), who also contributes to the literature on BCIs, by building such an indicator, studying cycles and trends based on stationary and non stationary factors. However, there are several differences. First of all, Eickmeier (2005) proposes a benchmark indicator based on "core" euro area countries while we consider all euro area countries. Second, using a different database, we manage to avoid differentiation of the variables before running the principal component analysis. In the end, not only do we get a different BCI, but also we perform a different identification of the factors. We use the Bai (2004) and Bai and Ng (2004) criteria to assess the number of non stationary factors, while she uses the Johansen test. She puts a lot of emphasis on comparing various variables to linear combinations of the factors (i.e. rotations), while we show, using the confidence interval derived by Bai (2004), that our first factor is close to euro area aggregate GDP in the 1990s.

We identify a small set of relevant factors to explain the fluctuations of GDP at business cycle frequencies in the different countries under study. We suggest therefore a useful decomposition of each GDP series -taken in levels-into three parts: a common persistent part, obtained by projection onto the common non-stationary factors, a common transitory part (obtained by projection onto the common stationary factor) and an idiosyncratic (stationary and hence) transitory part. In order to focus on the business cycle, these three components are filtered and we only keep the business cycle frequencies. Such results are comparable to the ones obtained by applying DFA as developed by Forni and Lippi (1998), but we do not identify the dynamic factors from a spectral analysis like these authors.

The real benefit of the application of the Bai and Ng methodology appears for the construction of our BCI from the first factor. We derive confidence band around the projection of euro area GDP on the indicator. We show, on the one hand, that the correlation of the cyclical components of the three largest euro area countries with the indicator has increased from the mid 1990s, indicating higher correlation of business cycle components On the other hand, long run components, expressing potential growth remain different. We also show that the indicator is well correlated with the lagged US indicator constructed according to the same methodology. This provides evidence, consistently with the analysis of Artis et al. (2004) and Montfort et al. (2004), that our euro area indicator is actually correlated with worldwide cycles in the context of globalization.

The paper is organized as follows. In section 2 we extract the common factors from the database in level, using the PANIC methodology. In section 3 we decompose GDP business cycles in three components. In section 4, we construct our euro area indicator and interpret it.

2 Extracting factors from a large-scale database: the PANIC approach

The goal of this section is to extract common trends from a large panel of non-stationary macroeconomic variables for the euro area. We identify trend components by referring to a non-stationary factor model and by using the PANIC (Panel Analysis of Non-stationarity in the Idiosyncratic and Common components) statistical procedure, recently developed by Bai and Ng (2004).

When the dimension of the panel (N) and the number of observation (T) both tend to infinity, approximate factor models are very convenient as the error term is allowed to be weakly cross-correlated across N as well across T and as consistent estimation of the space spanned by the common factors can be achieved by implementing a principal component analysis (PCA).

Accordingly, the estimation of such factor models involves a lower computational cost than the one of the Kalman filter, which is actually unfeasible as N and T are both large.

In the non-stationary case, the procedure of estimation is fairly the same as in the more common stationary case (Stock and Watson, 1998; Bai, 2003) and remains simple. Bai (2004) proves that a consistent estimator of factors obtains with the series in level even if they are integrated of order one, provided that the specific component is I(0) (see equation (5) below). Under these assumptions, he proves more precisely that the estimators of the common factors (or stochastic trends) are uniformly consistent when N is sufficiently large relative to T (see proposition 1 in Bai, 2004).

As it can be seen from the Monte Carlo simulations in Bai and Ng (2004), the estimated factor space is far from the true one when the errors e_{it} are I(1). Hence the estimation of the factor using the data in level is not always consistent. This is the reason why Bai and Ng (2004) have proposed a machinery named PANIC in order to test whether the idiosyncratic part is I(0) or equivalently whether the source of non-stationarity is of common nature. Moreover, the PANIC methodoly provides estimates of the factors obtained by extracting principal components from the first differenced data.

However, when the errors are found to be I(0), the estimators of the factors obtained by using data in levels, are proved to be more efficient than the ones based upon first differencing and, in this case, one can straightforwardly assess the number of common trends.

In what follows, we first implement PANIC and we validate the stationarity of the idiosyncratic components, as estimated from the first differences of the series. Thus, we estimate the common trends by using the level of the data.

2.1 Data

We consider a database of 220 quarterly macroeconomic series for all euro area countries.

The data were initially compiled and described by Eickmeier (2005). They include data on national accounts GDP components, industrial production, employment, prices and wages, money and finance (share prices and interest rates) on the 12 euro area member countries (See Annex A). No euro area aggregate is icluded in the database. Data are quarterly and the period we consider is from 1980Q1 to 2003Q4. Hence the individual dimension is $N = 220$ and the time dimension T is equal to 91. The period is long enough to cover at least two entire business cycles. However, contrary to Eickmeier (2005), we consider all 12 euro area countries and not only the core set of 7 countries. In addition, we select the series that look sufficiently persistent in order to be I(1), while Eickmeier uses a mixture of I(0) and I(1) series. Such an exogenous and initial selection of our dataset explains that the factors we extract have different properties.

2.2 The factor model in the PANIC approach (Bai and Ng, 2004)

Let X be our (N, T) panel of quarterly macroeconomic variables. We assume that each variable X_{it} for $i = 1, ..., N$ depends on a few undelying factors F_t, either stationary or non stationary.

The model is the following:

$$X_{it} = c_i + \beta_i t + \lambda_i' F_t + e_{it} \tag{1}$$

$$(1 - L)F_t = \alpha + C(L)u_t \tag{2}$$

$$(1 - \rho_i L)e_{it} = D_i(L)\varepsilon_{it} \tag{3}$$

with $C(L) = \sum_{j=0}^{\infty} C_j L^j$ and $D_i(L) = \sum_{j=0}^{\infty} D_{i,j} L^j$, $\mathbf{F}_t = (F_{1t}, F_{2t}, \ldots, F_{kt})'$ and $\lambda_i' = (\lambda_1, \lambda_2, \ldots, \lambda_k)$. The u_t's and ε_t's are white noise.

The factors may contribute to the deterministic trend in the DGP through α but this parameter cannot be identified; indeed, in PANIC, the principal component method is applied to the differenced and demeaned data. So the specification of the deterministic component has no impact on the estimation of the factors and loadings.

The model allows r_0 stationary factors and r_1 common trends with $r = r_0 + r_1$. Equivalently, the rank of $C(1)$ is equal to r_1.

The idiosyncratic e_{it} is $I(1)$ if $\rho_i = 1$ and is stationary if $\rho_i < 1$.

The factors F_{jt}, $1 \leq j \leq r$, and the idiosyncratic components e_{it} may be either I(1) or I(0) and can even be integrated at different order[3]. When the dataset $\mathbf{X}_t$ encompasses I(1)-series only and when the idiosyncratic components (the e_i's) are I(0), one can conclude that the source of nonstationarity of variables is of common nature.

The processes $\eta_t = C(L)u_t$ and therefore the F_t's may contribute to the common "business cycle" component. This is the reason why we apply classical business cycle filters to the non-stationary factors in Section 3, when we examine the different sources of business cycle fluctuations.

2.3 Estimation and test

We turn now to the estimation and test procedures as proposed by Bai (2004) and Bai and Ng (2004).

When the residuals e_{it} are $I(0)$, it is possible to get consistent estimates of the factors and loadings $\mathbf{F}_t$, λ_i, respectively (Bai, 2004).

When it is not the case, - e_{it} are $I(1)$-, it is not longer true and Bai and Ng(2004) propose to run the principal component analysis on the first differenced series, specified as:

$$\Delta x_{it} = \beta_i + \lambda_i' \eta_t + \Delta e_{it}. \tag{4}$$

The estimates of $\mathbf{F}_t$ and e_{it} from (1) are thus obtained for $t = 2, \ldots, T$ and $i = 1, \ldots, N$ as:[4]

$$\widehat{F_{kt}} = \sum_{s=2}^{t} \widehat{\eta}_{ks} \tag{5}$$

$$\widehat{e}_{it} = \sum_{s=2}^{t} \widehat{\Delta e}_{is}, \tag{6}$$

Bai and Ng (2004) show that $\widehat{\mathbf{F}}_t$ and $\widehat{e}_{it}$ are consistent for $\mathbf{F}_t$ and e_{it}, respectively (see Lemma 2). Once the factors have been extracted, it is possible to identify the source of nonstationarity of the series.

First of all, one focuses on the idiosyncratic components $\widehat{e}_{it}$, as the inference procedure crucially depends on their stationarity.

Indeed, as recalled before, if they are found to be $I(0)$, according to Bai (2004), it is possible and more efficient to extract the factors directly from the levels of the variables.

---

[3] It must be emphasized that a regression of x_{it} on $\mathbf{F}_t$ is spurious when e_{it} has a unit root, even if $\mathbf{F}_t$ is observed. The estimates of λ_i' and thus of e_{it} will not be consistent.

[4] Notice that one observation is lost due to the first differencing of data.

So, one first runs the standard univariate $ADF_{\widehat{e}(i)}$ (Augmented Dickey-Fuller) for each idiosyncratic component e_{it}:

$$H_0 : d_{i0} = 0; H_1 : d_{i0} < 0 \tag{7}$$

where $\Delta\widehat{e}_{it} = d_{i0}\widehat{e}_{it-1} + d_{i1}$ and $\Delta\widehat{e}_{it-1} + \cdots + d_{ip}\Delta\widehat{e}_{it-p} + \xi_t$

It is worth noting that the distribution does not coincide with the one of Dickey Fuller (DF),[5] because of the linear trend in the data (see Bai and Ng (2004) for more details).

Then, one implements a pooled test procedure, in order to increase the power of the test:[6]

$$H_0 : \forall i, d_{i0} = 0, H_1 : \exists i, s.t. d_{i0} < 0 \tag{8}$$

Pooling is achieved in the lines of Choi (2001) for $N \rightarrow \infty$. If $p_{\widehat{e}}^c(i)$[7] denotes the p-value associated with $ADF_{\widehat{e}(i)}$, the test statistics is:

$$P_{\widehat{e}}^c = \frac{-2\sum_{i=1}^{N} \log p_{\widehat{e}}^c(i) - 2N}{\sqrt{4N}} \tag{9}$$

which is proved to be asymptotically distributed as $N(0,1)$, provided that the idiosyncratic components e_i are independent.

In what follows, we will show that the idiosyncratic components $\widehat{e}_i$ can be considered as stationary according to a low value of the pooled P-value $P_{\widehat{e}}^c$.

Thus there are necessarily non-stationary factors, as the series are $I(1)$. In order to identify the number r_1 of common trends - that is non-stationary factors- Bai and Ng propose modified variants MQ of Stock and Watson's Q statistics, designed to test the number of common trends in a non-stationary multivariate dynamics.[8] However, the procedure supposes that the total number r of factors is known. [9] r is identified, by using information criteria proposed by Bai and Ng (2002) for the first-differenced series.

---

[5] In fact, the ADF based upon an augmented autoregression has the same limiting distribution as the DF distribution if the number of lags is chosen such as $p^3/\min[N,T]$ (see Said and Dickey (1984) or Bai and Ng (2004)).

[6] Such a pooling test is known as being more efficient than a procedure using separately the series $\widehat{e}_i$. However, the gain of efficiency is effective only if there is no cross-section for the series of interest. Bai and Ng (2004) argue that a pooled test based upon $\widehat{e}_{it}$ is more appropriate than upon X_{it}, as long as the original series embody common components and thus are related to each other.

[7] The individual p-values $p_{\widehat{e}}^c(i)$ are obtained by simulation

[8] There are two Q statistics respectively associated with the cases where the non-stationary components of F_t are finite-order autoregressive processes and are more general processes including moving-average errors.

[9] This test involves a sequential procedure where, in the first step, m is fixed equal to r with a one unit decrease when the null hypothesis is rejected, i.e. $H_0 : r_1 = m$ against $H_1 : r_1 < m$. The critical values associated with these statistics are tabulated by Bai and Ng (2004) and are available from one to six factors.

Before presenting the results, it is worth recalling that confidence intervals can be computed around any (true) underlying factor (or any linear combination of the factors) at each date t. For example, for the non-stationary factors, Bai (2004) proves that under the assumptions of absence of cross-section correlation for idiosyncratic errors, as $N, T \to \infty$ with $N/T^3 \to 0$:[10]

$$\frac{\sqrt{N\left(\widehat{\delta}'\widehat{\mathbf{F}}_t - Y_t\right)}}{\left[\widehat{\delta}'V_{NT}^{-1}\left(\frac{1}{N}\sum_{i=1}^{N}\widehat{e}_{it}^2\widehat{\lambda}_i\widehat{\lambda}_i'\right)' V_{NT}^{-1}\widehat{\delta}\right]^{\frac{1}{2}}} \to N(0,1) \tag{10}$$

where Y_t is the variable of interest, for example the GDP series, the parameter $\widehat{\delta}'$ rescales $\widehat{\mathbf{F}}_t$ toward Y_t via the following regression:

$$Y_t = \widehat{\delta}'\widehat{\mathbf{F}}_t + error \tag{11}$$

with $\widehat{e}_{it}^2$ denoting the estimated residuals $X_{ij} - \widehat{\lambda}_i'\widehat{\mathbf{F}}_t$ and V_{NT} is a diagonal matrix consisting of the first r largest eigenvalues of XX'/T^2N.

Such confidence intervals allow to assess, at each date t, how well a (true) factor component - that is an element of the space spanned by all factors F_t- can be approximated by an observed series Y_t.

2.4 Assessing common and idiosyncratic components

First, we run a principal analysis on the first differenced data and use the information criteria PC_2 and IC_2 proposed in Bai and Ng (2004) to determine the total number of factors. The former depends on an initial maximun number of factors, whereas the latter is invariant to this parameter. We choose these criteria since they prove to be more robust than the others, initially suggested by Bai and Ng (2002), when the residuals have serial-correlation.These criteria indicate that there are five factors which summarize the common information within data. The pooled test statistic ($P_{\widehat{e}}^c$) is equal to 3.13 with the associated p-value of 0.00; the assumption of $I(1)$-residuals is thus strongly rejected.

The existence of more than one non-stationary factor might be seen as a surprizing result from a Real Business Cycle point of view, for which technology is the sole driving factor of the economy. Here we observe additional persistent shocks that can be viewed as demand shocks, or shocks that appear as non-stationary on the sample period considered.

Before extracting the common trends, we can summarize these preliminary results as following:

---

[10] The previous results can be extended to the case where there are cross correlations in the residuals. The idea is to apply a White-type correction to consistently estimate the asymptotic variance matrix.

- *the data obey a factor structure which embodies a total number of 5 factors;*
- *the factors explain 39% of total variance of the database;*
- *the source of nonstationarity is not idiosyncratic, the forces driving trends in the Euro Area are only of common nature.*

An outstanding result concerns the loadings of all variables with respect to the first factor. By computing these loadings, one observes that the first non-stationary factor contributes to each of the 220 series with an almost constant loading (see Fig. 9 in Annex A). All the variables excluding interest rates contribute positively.[11] Apart from the German interest rates, the absolute value of the loadings of the variables range from 0.4% to 0.6%. The long term and short term German interest rates have the respective weights of -0.57% and -0.44% .

According to the fact that it represents an equally weighted average of the variables, we conclude that this unobservable variable is a synthetic variable which is a good candidate for a Business Cycle Index, in the lines, for example, of the US Conference Board index. It is therefore expected to provide a reliable synthesis of the economic fluctuations, as it can be seen in Marcellino (2005).

Being so comprehensive in nature, the first factor expresses the most persistent component included in the series. The negative loadings on interest rates only reflects the negative trend on interest rates, but it should be kept in mind that the total contribution of interest variables to factor 1 is less than 10%. The method, however, is not able to provide a really structural interpretation of the driving forces behind factor 1, similarly to the balance growth models where the main driving force results from a mixture of supply and demand shocks.[12]

The second factor opposes the real variables -except GDPs- to the nominal ones (CPIs, ULCs,...) (See Fig. 10 in Annex A).

Regarding the third factor, it generally opposes employment variables, private fixed capital formation and interest rates to the production variables. In that case, notice that the German long and short run interest rates highly contribute to the third factor, with 16.2% and 7.1%, hence a total of 23.3%,

---

[11] In the Figures displayed in Annex 2, variables are ranked on the x-axis in alphabetical order of the country, starting with Austria (AT) and finishing with Spain (SP), slight disadjustment were introduced to improve readability. The y-axis correspond to the loading in %, note that if all variables had the same weight, it would amount to 1/220, which is around 0.5%.

[12] Indeed, factors are linear combinations of the variables in the database, so that particular structural shocks on the variables have effects on the factors, and one may wish to assess whether shocks to the factors may be correlated to underlying structural shocks, i.e. whether they represent, e. g. monetary policy shocks, or supply shocks, etc. However, such an analysis would require either to have access to an exogenous indicator of the shock (e.g. an index of monetary policy shocks, or technological shocks, etc.), or to run a full impulse response analysis. This is beyond the scope of the paper.

whereas the contributions of the other variables are at most 3.5%. To get a clearer picture, the German interest rate is excluded from Fig. 11 in Annex A.

Then we try to distinguish between persistent and stationary factors. In order to estimate the number of common trends, we compute two of the three criteria proposed by Bai (2004). From our dataset, we obtain three non-stationary factors. The other two common factors are therefore stationary.

We can summarize these additional results as following:

- *among the 5 common factors, 3 are non-stationary.*

3 The source of business cycle fluctuations

Referring to the 5 common factors we have identified, we now examine more closely the main sources of business cycle fluctuations. For that purpose, starting from our factor decomposition in level as given by equation (1), we look for a decomposition of each country business cycle along the different factors. In order to focus on the business cycle frequencies we apply the Christiano and Fitzgerald filter which is a linear filter and remove the highest and lowest frequencies. Empirical studies tend to prove that such a filter is closer to the ideal filter which perfectly retain the desired frequencies. Moreover with this filter, truncation appears to have a lower impact than the usual filters (HP, Baxter and King, 1995), provided the assumed underlying DGP (i.e. a random walk in our case) is correct (Christiano and Fitzgerald, 1999, Fournier, 2000). In contrast to first-differencing, this allows to retain as much information as possible. We decompose GDP in the various countries into the common and the idiosyncratic components. We end up measuring the contribution to the business cycle from (1) the common non-stationary factors ; (2) the common stationary factors ; (3) the idiosyncratic components.

For each variable X in country i, one can extract its cyclical component, $\widetilde{CX}_{it}$, by applying the Christiano and Fitzgerald filter onto the common and idiosyncratic components.[13] Let $\widetilde{CF}_{kt}$ be the cyclical components of factor k, by extracting the periodic movements between 8 and 32 quarters, and $\widetilde{CE}_{it}$ cyclical components of the idiosyncratic component of variables i. Since the filter is linear, $\widetilde{CX}_{it}$ can be decomposed according to:

$$\widetilde{CX}_{it} = \sigma_{X_i} * \left(\sum_{k=1}^{5} \lambda_{ik} * \widetilde{CF}_{kt} + \widetilde{CE}_{it} \right) \tag{12}$$

where σ_{X_i} has to be considered as a scaling factor.

---

[13] The same analysis could have been carried out with another filter like the Hodrick-Prescott Filter.

The method proposed here is straightforward and consistent with the usual practice of identifying the business cycle from deviation to HP filtered-GDP for example.[14]

As usual, we are thus able to compute the share of the common/specific components in the business cycle. We can rewrite (12) as:

$$\widetilde{CX}_{it} = \widetilde{\Phi}_{i1t} + \widetilde{\Phi}_{i2t} + \widetilde{\Phi}_{i3t} + \widetilde{\Phi}_{i4t} + \widetilde{\Phi}_{i5t} + \widetilde{\xi}_{it} \qquad (13)$$

where $\widetilde{\Phi}_{ikt} = \sigma_{X_i} * \lambda_{ik} * \widetilde{CF}_{kt}$ ($k = 1, \ldots, 5$) are the common components of the variable i and $\widetilde{\xi}_i = \sigma_{X_i} * \widetilde{CE}_{it}$ the idiosyncratic one.

Furthermore, in computing the contribution of each common or idiosyncratic component $\widetilde{y}_{it} \in \left\{ \widetilde{\Phi}_{i1t}, \widetilde{\Phi}_{i2t}, \widetilde{\Phi}_{i3t}, \widetilde{\Phi}_{i4t}, \widetilde{\Phi}_{i5t}, \widetilde{\xi}_{it} \right\}$ to the cyclical part $\widetilde{CX}_{it}$ of X_{it}, we only take into account the influence of $\widetilde{y}_{it}$ when $\widetilde{y}_{it}$ and $\widetilde{CX}_{it}$ have the same sign (i.e. both components point in the same direction, namely peaks or troughs). This a sort of generalisation of concordance indicator. Accordingly, at each date t, the contribution $A_{ikt}(\widetilde{y})$ is characterized, after normalization, as:

$$A_{ikt}(\widetilde{y}) = \frac{1_{sign(\widetilde{y}_{it})} \cdot \widetilde{y}_{it}}{\sum_{k=1}^{5} 1_{sign(\widetilde{\Phi}_{ikt})} \cdot \widetilde{\Phi}_{ikt} + 1_{sign(\widetilde{\xi}_{it})} \cdot \widetilde{\xi}_{it}}, \qquad (14)$$

$1_{sign(\widetilde{y}_{it})} = 1$ if $\widetilde{y}_{it}$ and $\widetilde{CX}_{it}$ have the same sign and $1_{sign(\widetilde{y}_{it})} = 0$ otherwise.

Thus we can decompose the fluctuations of the variables i into common and specific fluctuations whose contributions depend on the cyclical economic situation. Fig. 1 displays for France, Germany and Italy the cumulative contribution of each common factors and the idiosyncratic component to the cyclical part of the corresponding GDP ($X_i = GDP_i$ in equ. 12 and 13), that add-up to the business cycle component of GDP. In the previous section we pointed out that the first non-stationary factor offers a quite good description of the random walk component underlying, in particular, the German, French and Italian GDPs. In this section, we also notice that, at least for the GDPs, the first non stationarity factor is generally the main source of the common cyclical variation. In Germany, however, the third factor also plays a significant role.

In tables reported B1 and B2 in appendix B, one can read the shares of the common *versus* specific contributions to the business fluctuations for each of the 12 countries studied here, as summarized by the GDP. The same kind of analysis could also by applied to other variables, like total employment. We have computed theses contributions over two sub-periods before and after 1992 in order to shed light on the convergence process.

---

[14] The method that we implement assumes the constancy of the factor loadings over the sample period. According to Canova et al. (2004) this is not a too strong assumption, since, allowing for time-varying factor loadings in the analysis of the transmission of shocks in the euro area, the authors find that factor loadings turn out to be almost constant.

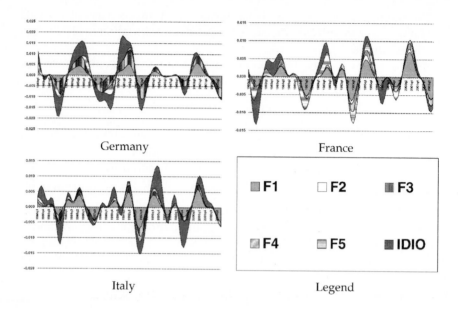

Fig. 1. Contribution to concordance of business cycles

We observe that the idiosyncratic part of the national business cycle is, in average, lower after 1993 than before. This is also the case for Germany, characterised as indicated before by a strong contribution of the third factor, as well as by the shock of German reunification in the first period. Specific-country cyclical movements remain also important, even over the most recent period, for Italy. It is interesting to note that the contribution of the first three non-stationary factors is the largest one, especially for the core countries in the European Union. This highlights the importance to take into account the common trend comovements in the characterization of the business cycle and in studying the convergence process.

We have also computed the shares of the different contributions over the last year 2003, in order to give an example of how to use the statistical procedure we propose to analyze current economic situation of the Euro area.

To summarize, it appears that the first factor is dominant. It explains a significant proportion of the variance of GDP for each of the three countries under study. Moreover its contribution is increasing over time. In the next section we therefore concentrate on the first non-stationary factor, that we use to build a coincident indicator of activity for the euro area.

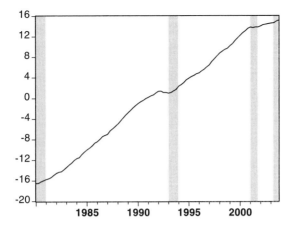

Fig. 2. First common factor and peak/troughs derived from euro area GDP

4 Constructing a coincident indicator for the euro area

In the lines of the literature on the BCIs derived from factor models, we now use the first common factor to construct a new coincident indicator of the Euro area GDP. We first compare this indicator with the other indicators that are available. Then, following Bai (2004) and using the confidence interval around the factor, we test more rigorously its information content by examining whether different variables belong or not to the corresponding confidence interval. Stability over time and existence of correlation with external variables are finally considered.

4.1 A coincident indicator of GDP: descriptive analysis

In this subsection, we illustrate the ability of the first factor to reproduce the main features of euro area business cycles.

Fig. 2 displays the factor together with the expansion/recession periods derived from "classical business cycle" analysis in the line of Harding and Pagan (2002). It appears that indeed the 1993 recession and the early 2001 slowdown are well captured by the indicator.

Looking more precisely at the business cycle frequencies in Fig. 3, namely $\widetilde{CGDP}_i$ (with $i = FR, DE, IT$) and $\widetilde{CF}_1$, using the same notations as in section 3,[15] we observe that the indicator reproduces the main cycles of the three countries GDP. The dotted line is factor 1, while the solid line is the country GDP. The two troughs that appear in early 1980s and in 1993 are consistent

---

[15] $\widetilde{CX}$ is the series X observed at its business cycle frequencies (i.e. for periodic movements btween 8 and 32 quarters).

with the Euro Area Business Cycle Dating Committee. However additional troughs appear also in 1987 as well as in 2002-2003.The main peaks appear during 1985, 1991, at the beginning of 1995 and in 2000.

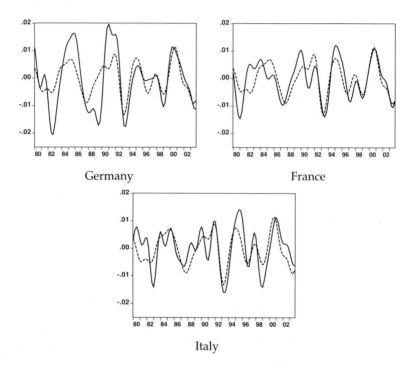

Germany   France

Italy

Fig. 3. First common factor and GDP at business cycle frequencies

Finally, as a complement to the previous analysis of the business cycle, it is also useful to consider the lowest frequencies, namely the component of F_1 and GDP_i with periodic movements above 32 quarters, which provides a measure of euro area potential growth. As indicated in Table 1, performance differentials measured at long run frequencies have tended to increase. Indeed, potential growth was in average very similar across countries in the 1980s, between 2.1 % and 2.3 %, while the range has increased in the 1990s and early 2000's, between 1.4 and 1.8 %, with France tending to outperform the other three countries as from the second half of the 1990s. In addition, as shown in Fig. 4, there remains substantial differences in the cyclical pattern of potential growth, especially when compared to the first factor.

The conclusion of the section is that the first factor allows to distinguish between correlation of business cycles and growth differentials in the long run.

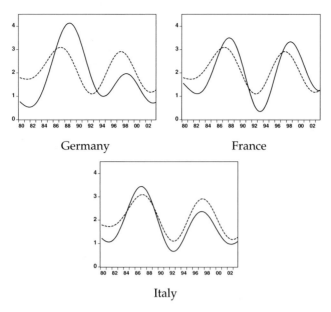

Germany   France

Italy

Fig. 4. First common factor and GDP at long run frequencies

Table 1. Potential growth from long run frequencies

Country	1980Q1-1991Q4		1992Q1-2003Q4	
	mean	std dev.	mean	std dev.
France	2.1	0.9	1.8	1
Germany	2.3	1.4	1.4	0.4
Italy	2.1	1.4	1.5	0.6
F1	2.3	0.9	1.9	0.7

(*) periodic movements above 32 quarters

4.2 Interpreting the factor

Fig 2 showed that the trend in factor 1 was close to that of euro area GDP. We now examine more precisely such an hypothesis. As explained in section 2, one can use confidence intervals around any (true) factor component to assess how well it is approximated by an observed series, at each date t.

We can test, for example, whether the aggregate Euro Area GDP, GDP_{euro}, is close to a linear combination of the nonstationary factors. Indeed, comparing the first common factor (as exhibited in Fig. 2) and GDP_{euro}, it is easy to construct a 95% confidence interval for the linear combination $\delta' F_t$ which rescales F_t toward $GDP_{euro,t}$.

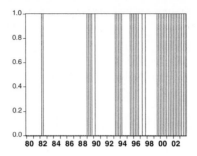

Fig. 5. Periods when Euro Area GDP belongs to Conf. Interval around Factor 1

Fig. 5 displays the correspondance between Euro Area GDP and the first common factor. A vertical line at a given quarter indicates that euro area GDP belongs to the confidence interval.

The aggregate Euro Area GDP is often outside the 95% confidence interval around the trend: on average during the whole period it is within the band 40 percent of the time (4 quarters out of 10). However, the correspondence between the first factor and euro area GDP is increasing over time, as revealed in the more dense grid from 1992 onwards. In addition, the correspondance is very good since mid 1999.

4.3 Assessing stability over time

When looking at the intertemporal correlation of the first common factor with GDP in France, Germany and Italy, one can confirm the conclusion that it is a contemporaneous indicator. In addition, it is increasing when comparing the two subperiods.

For this purpose, we estimate the factors, and in particular factor 1, on the whole period, but we compare it to country GDPs for two subsamples : 1980-1991 and 1992-2003. We follow Stock and Watson (1999) by computing the instantaneous, lag and lead cross-correlations between the cyclical component of the first factor ($\widetilde{CF}_1$) and the country GDP ($\widetilde{CGDP}_i$). Fig. 6 displays $corr(\widetilde{CGDP}_{i,t}, \widetilde{CF}_{1,t+h})$ for each subsamples and for German, French and Italian business cycles. A maximum correlation at $h = 0$ indicates that the common cyclical component and business cycle of the country i tends to be synchronous, whereas a maximum correlation at , for example, $h = +1$, indicates that the cyclical component of the country i tends to lead the common cyclical component by one quarter.

Strikingly, we can clearly notice an increasing correlation between the first and the second subsample (1992-2003): while contemporaneous correlation is between 0.5 and 0.7 during the first period, it increases to around 0.9

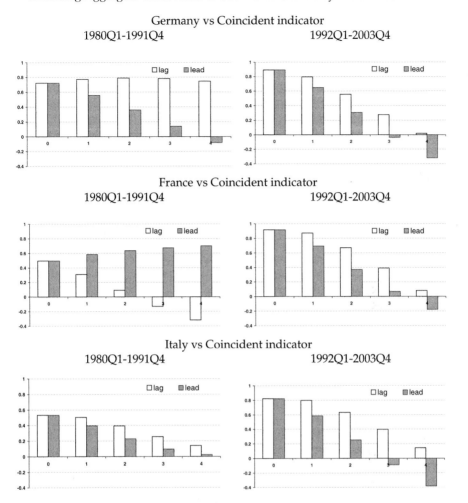

Fig. 6. Correlation of national GDPs with factor 1 at bus. cycle frequency

in the second period.[16] Moreover, we can observe that, for one or two quarters, both the leads and the lags become correlated during the second period, while only leads or lags are correlated during the first period. Finally, the patterns of correlation are almost the same for each countries in the second subsample, whereas no common features appear from the first period. We interpret such a result of stronger dependence as a larger contribution of the CCI to national business cycles of each countries. In other words, countries

---

[16] We focus here on lead/lag correlations up to 4 quarters since above one year, correlation is likely to be spurious: with cycles of short duartion, long leads/lags may capture correlation with the following/previous cycle.

have become more sensitive to the euro area shocks than before, what it is consistent with the convergence process occurring in the 1990s.

4.4 Comparing euro area and global business cycles

Finally, we consider non Euro area variables and investigate their correlation with our Euro area coincident indicator. When looking at US GDP at business cycle frequencies, there is evidence of significant correlation. Actually, Fig. 7 indicates that especially for the second subperiod, US GDP is rather leading the euro area (lead correlation is marked with dark boxes).

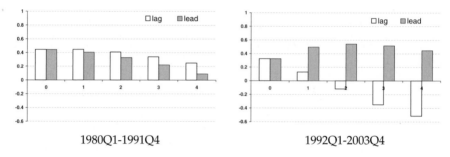

Fig. 7. Correlation between US GDP and fact. 1 at business cycle frequency

Fig. 8 below displays the dynamics of the filtered US GDP - shifted two quarters backwards- and the one of the Euro area coincident indicator over the second period. To compare the two series, we have used two different vertical scales and the origin of the scale is centered at two different levels, the top series (right-hand scale) is the common factor, while the bottom series (left-hand scale) is the business cycle component of GDP. The left figure corresponds to the Euro area GDP and the right figure to the US. While, obviously, the Euro area business cycle is close to factor one, as already discussed for the three main Euro area countries in Fig. 3 and 6, the largest fluctuations of the US GDP are also correlated with the common factor derived from the 220 euro area series, once moved forward by two quarters.

Similarly to what we did in section 3, it is possible to project any series outside the database on the five euro area factors and to compute the contributions of each of these factors. In table 2, we concentrate on our coincident indicator, which is the first common factor, and report its contributions only to filtered US and Euro area GDP. Consistently with the findings that the US GDP leads the euro area by two quarters, the coincident indicator has been moved forward by two quarters to compare it to the US. The coincident indicator appears to explain most of US GDP in the early 2000s (95% in 2003, as indicated in the table below).

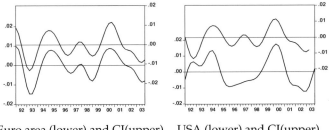

Euro area (lower) and CI(upper)   USA (lower) and CI(upper)

Fig. 8. GDP and fact. 1 at business cycle frequency (US moved forward by two quarters)

Table 2. Shares of business cycle explained by factor 1

Country	Period	Coincident Indicator
Euro Area	1993Q1-2003Q4	53%
	over 2003	71%
United-States[1]	1993Q1-2003Q4	49%
	over 2003	95%

(1) the coincident indicator (first common factor) has been shifted forward by two quarters to be compared to the US case

All these results tend to prove the existence of common world shocks and corroborate the conclusions obtained by Artis et al. (2004) and Montfort et al. (2004), regarding the correlation of business cycles in the US and the Euro area.

5 Conclusion

In the paper we apply a large-scale factor model recently developed by Bai (2003 and 2004) and Bai and Ng (2004) to extract common stationary and non-stationary factors in the euro area. It turns out that we are in the right case where the factors can be extracted from the database in levels, as the idiosyncratic component identified according to the PANIC methodology are found to be stationary. We find that the euro area economies share three common non-stationary factors. The first one is close to the Euro area aggregate GDP in the second part of the sample. We suggest a way to decompose the cyclical fluctuations of each of the three countries under study, by filtering the different components - the non-stationary common one, the stationary common one and the idiosyncratic one- using the Christiano Fitzgerald filter.[17] We also use the first common factor to build a coincident indicator of the euro area that constitutes a benchmark against which country developments can be compared. We show that the common persistent movements significantly contribute to the common cyclical fluctuations, especially since the 1990's, pointing to increasing comovements. At the same time, the low frequency components -that can be associated with potential growth- exhibit more significant differences. In particular the first factor allows to distinguish between correlated business cycles and growth differentials in the long run.

These features could not have been pointed out if one had worked with the first differences series directly. This is the main advantage of using dynamic factor models estimated from a large non-stationary data set. More generally, the statistical tool we use appears to be useful to compare the behavior of the different countries over different periods and for various key macroeconomic variables, allowing for an economic interpretation of what is common/versus specific in the behavior of a European country, and what has a permanent/versus transitory effect.

Regarding further research, notice, that we have just focused on the analysis of activity, as summarized by GDP series. One way forward is obviously to implement the same kind of analysis by decomposing other types of series : employment, industrial production indexes and so on. (See table A3 for example). This gives interesting results to identify the sources of specific/versus common behavior for each European country vis-à-vis a common benchmark.

References

Angeloni I, Dedola F (1999) From the ERM to the Euro. European Central Bank, Working paper

Artis M, Osborn D, Perez-Vazquez P (2004) The International Business Cycle in a Changing World: Volatility and the Propagation of Shocks in the G-7. CEPRCentre for Economic Policy Research) Discussion Paper 4652

Artis M, Zhang M (1999) Further evidence on the international business cycle and the ERM. Oxford Economic Papers, 51:120–132

Bai J (2003) Inference in Factor Models of Large Dimensions. Econometrica 71:135–171.

Bai J (2004) Estimating Cross-Section Common Stochastic Trends in Non-stationary Panel Data. Journal of Econometrics, 122(1), 137-184.

Bai J and Ng S (2002) Determining the Number of Factors in Approximate Factor Models. Econometrica 70:191–221.

Bai J, Ng S (2003) A PANIC Attack of Unit Root and Cointegration, Econometrica

---

[17] In order to assess the impact of the factors to business cycles, as implemented in section 3, a further refinement has been to restrict the analysis to cycles of significant magnitude.

Baxter M, King RG (1995) Measuring Business Cycles Approximate Band-Pass Filters for Economic Time Series. NBER Working Paper, 5022

Burns AM, Mitchell WC (1946) Measuring Business Cycles. NBER, New York

Canova F, Ciccarelli M, Ortega E (2004) Similarities and Convergence in G7 Cycles. CEPR Discussion Paper, 4534

Choi I (2002) Combination of Unit Root Tests for Cross-Sectionally Correlated Panels. Mimeo, Kong Kong University of Science and Technology

Christiano LJ, Fitzgerald TJ (1999) The Band Pass Filter. NBER Working Paper, 7257.

Eickmeier S (2005) Common stationary and non-stationary factors in the Euro Area analyzed in a large-scale factor model. Mimeo, Deutsche Bundesbank, Economic Research Center

Forni M, Hallin M, Lippi M, Reichlin, L (2000) The generalized dynamic-factor model : identification and estimation. The Review of Economics and Statistics, 82(4):540–554

Forni M, Lippi M (2001) The Generalized Factor Model: Representation Theory. Econometric Theory, 17:1113–41.

Fournier JY (2000) L'approximation du filtre passe-bande propos[ ]ee par Christiano et Fitzgerald. INSEE Working Paper

Giannone D, Reichlin L, Sala L (2002) Tracking Greenspan: Systematic and Unsystematic Monetary Policy Revisited. CEPR Discussion Paper, 3550

Harding and Pagan (2002) Synchronisation of cycles, Melbourne Institute of Applied and Social Research,

Helbling T, Bayoumi T (2003) Are they all in the same boat? the 2000-2001 Growth Slowdown and the G7 cycle linkages. IMF Working Paper, 46

Hodrick RJ, Prescott E (1980) Post-war U.S. Business Cycles: An Empirical Investigation. Working Paper, Carnegie-Mellon University

Marcellino M (2005) Leading Indicators: What Have We Learned? CEPR Discussion Paper, 4977

Monfort A, Renne J, Rüffer R, Vitale G (2003) Is Economic Activity in the G7 Synchronized? Common Shocks versus Spillover Effects. CEPR Discussion Paper, 4119

Stock JH, Watson, M (1988) Testing for Common Trends. Journal of American Statistical Association, 83:1097–1107.

Stock JH, Watson M (1998). Diffusion Indexes, NBER Working Paper, 6072

Stock JH and Watson M (1999) Business Cycle Fluctuations in US Macroeconomic Time Series. In: Rautenstrauch C, Seelmann-Eggebert R, Turowski K (eds) Handbook of Macroeconomics. Springer, Berlin Heidelberg New York

Stock JH and Watson M (2002) Macroeconomic forecasting using diffusion indexes. Journal of Business and Economic Statistics 20(2):147–162.

Zarnovitz M (1992) Business cycles: Theory, History, Indicators and Forecasting. Springer, Berlin Heidelberg New York

A Data and factor loadings

Table A1 : Mnemonics of the variables in the database

Mnemonics	Type of Variables
	National Accounts
gdp	*GDP, volume*
ge	*Government Consumption, volume*
exp	*Exports of goods and services, volume*
imp	*Imports of goods and services, volume*
pcfe	*Personal Consumer Expenditure, volume*
pnrfcf	*Private-sector non-residential Investment, volume*
ptfcf	*Private Total Fixed Capital Formation, volume*
tde	*Total domestic expenditure, volume*
	Employment
demp	*Total Employees*
temp	*Whole economy employment*
	Prices and Wages
cpi	*Consumer price, harmonized*
gdpd	*Gross domestic product, deflator, market prices*
comp	*Compensation to Employees, total*
ulc	*Unit Labour Cost*
	Production Index
ip	*Industrial production*
ipc	*IIP Consumer Durable*
ipm	*IIP Manufacturing*
ppi	*PPI Manufacturing Industry Index*
	Money and Finance
lti	*Long-term interest rate on government bonds*
sti	*Short-term interest rate*
m1	*M1 aggregate*
m3	*M3 aggregate*
mst	*Share Price*

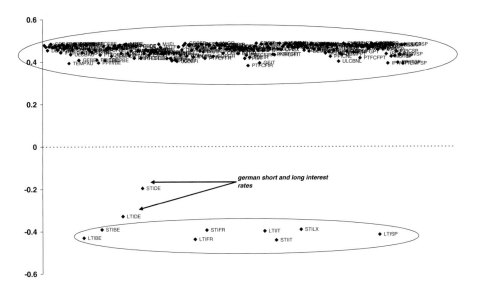

Fig. 9. Contribution of variables to first common factor (%)

Table A2 : Mnemonics of the countries
in the database

Mnemonics	Country
AU	Austria
BE	Belgium
FI	Finland
FR	France
DE	Germany
GR	Greece
IR	Ireland
IT	Italy
LX	Luxembourg
NL	Netherlands
PT	Portugal
SP	Spain

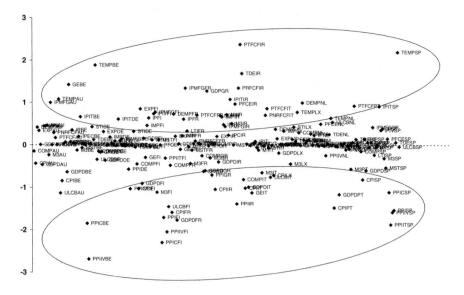

Fig. 10. Contribution of variables to second common factor (%)

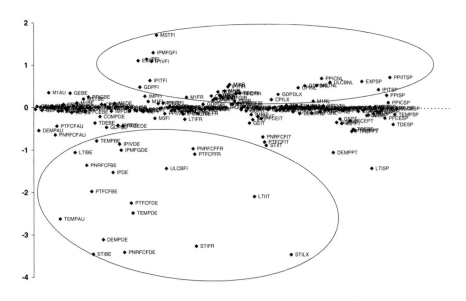

Fig. 11. Contribution of variables to third common factor (%)

B Contributions of factors to GDP at business cycle frequency

Table B1: Shares of business cycle explained by common and specific component[a,b]

Country	Period	Common					Specific
		F1	F2	F3	F4	F5	e_i
	1980Q1-1992Q4	32%	2%	14%	4%	7%	42%
AUSTRIA	1993Q1-2003Q4	43%	4%	14%	2%	6%	32%
	over 2003	▽75%	1%	21%	1%	2%	0%
	1980Q1-1992Q4	33%	6%	13%	2%	5%	40%
BELGIUM	1993Q1-2003Q4	35%	8%	11%	1%	3%	41%
	over 2003	▽53%	3%	15%	2%	0%	26%
	1980Q1-1992Q4	10%	1%	13%	21%	28%	27%
FINLAND	1993Q1-2003Q4	17%	6%	6%	20%	28%	23%
	over 2003	–54%	5%	8%	12%	8%	13%
	1980Q1-1992Q4	28%	2%	11%	0%	23%	36%
FRANCE	1993Q1-2003Q4	40%	6%	13%	0%	14%	27%
	over 2003	▽62%	2%	17%	0%	1%	17%
	1980Q1-1992Q4	20%	0%	26%	5%	12%	37%
GERMANY	1993Q1-2003Q4	35%	1%	32%	6%	9%	17%
	over 2003	▽45%	0%	35%	1%	3%	2%
	1980Q1-1992Q4	15%	12%	2%	4%	22%	47%
GREECE	1993Q1-2003Q4	8%	12%	6%	4%	24%	46%
	over 2003	△0%	0%	13%	3%	4%	80%

[a] Business cycles extracted from GDP

[b] Symbols, $\nabla, \triangle, -$ refer to a negative, positive, null output gap respectively

Table B2: Shares of business cycle explained by
common and specific component (end)[a,b]

Country	Period	Common					Specific
		F1	F2	F3	F4	F5	e_i
	1980Q1-1992Q4	26%	14%	10%	7%	16%	26%
IRELAND	1993Q1-2003Q4	25%	19%	3%	7%	17%	29%
	over 2003	▽66%	13%	0%	1%	1%	19%
	1980Q1-1992Q4	30%	0%	15%	7%	4%	43%
ITALY	1993Q1-2003Q4	32%	1%	11%	4%	1%	50%
	over 2003	▽74%	0%	21%	4%	1%	0%
	1980Q1-1992Q4	30%	3%	12%	3%	13%	39%
LUXEMBOURG	1993Q1-2003Q4	34%	6%	8%	3%	12%	38%
	over 2003	▽66%	2%	18%	1%	2%	11%
	1980Q1-1992Q4	26%	6%	4%	5%	16%	42%
NETHERLANDS	1993Q1-2003Q4	44%	14%	4%	4%	15%	19%
	over 2003	▽52%	4%	4%	0%	3%	37%
	1980Q1-1992Q4	14%	0%	15%	2%	6%	62%
PORTUGAL	1993Q1-2003Q4	23%	3%	23%	2%	4%	45%
	over 2003	▽57%	2%	38%	0%	2%	0%
	1980Q1-1992Q4	36%	5%	14%	0%	5%	40%
SPAIN	1993Q1-2003Q4	52%	11%	19%	0%	9%	9%
	over 2003	▽76%	4%	20%	0%	0%	0%

[a] Business cycles extracted from GDP

[b] Symbols, ▽, △, − refer to a negative, positive, null output gap respectively

Part III

Supply Side

Capital, Labour and Productivity: What Role Do They Play in the Potential GDP Weakness of France, Germany and Italy?*

Antonio Bassanetti[1], Jörg Döpke[2], Roberto Torrini[1], and Roberta Zizza[1]

[1] Banca d'Italia, Research Department, Via Nazionale 91, 00184 Rome, Italy.
antonio.bassanetti@bancaditalia.it,
roberto.torrini@bancaditalia.it, roberta.zizza@bancaditalia.it
[2] Deutsche Bundesbank, Economics Department. Wilhelm-Epstein-Strasse 14, 60014
Frankfurt a. M., Germany. joerg.doepke@bundesbank.de

Summary. The paper analyses the recent supply side developments in France, Germany, and Italy by employing a non-parametric approach to estimate potential GDP. The analysis reveals marked heterogeneity among the three countries with regard to the contribution of labour input. Similarities can be found, however, in the slowdown of capital accumulation and in the pronounced worsening of Total Factor Productivity growth. The paper is complemented by estimates of some measures of wage pressures and profitability in order to assess the role played by the movements of relative input prices in the intensity of use of primary factors in the production process.

JEL classification: O47, O52, E32.
Keywords: Potential output, growth accounting, productivity, NAIRU, factor shares.

1 Introduction

In recent years the economic debate has frequently focused on the widening gap between GDP growth in the U.S., on the one hand, and the euro area, on the other hand. The slowdown of the largest European countries, in particular, launched a major wave of empirical research seeking to understand its determinants. Although some consensus emerged regarding a few of them, mainly concerning the marked deceleration of total factor (and labour) productivity and the relatively poor performance of the labour market, much still remains to be uncovered and properly understood.

* We thank Heinz Herrmann, Franck Sédillot, Karl-Heinz Tödter, Michael Dear and participants in the seminar held at the Minda de Gunzburg Center for European Studies at Harvard University (Cambridge, MA, 14 December 2005). All remaining errors are ours. The opinions expressed in the paper are those of the authors and do not necessarily reflect the views of the institutions with which they are affiliated.

The present paper concentrates on the supply-side conditions in France, Germany and Italy; in particular, it analyses the development of potential GDP growth and its components in the 1982-2004 period. In doing so, we rely on a non-parametric approach that has the advantage of not requiring any assumption about the specific functional form of the production technology (section 2).

Though the supply-side focus certainly limits the scope of the research, the fact that the approach is fundamentally based on the growth accounting identity enables us to evaluate the contributions of the primary factor inputs and of productivity to the slowdown of potential GDP growth in recent years.

We uncover the adverse role played both by the high levels of the Non-Accelerating Inflation Rate of Unemployment (NAIRU) in all of the three countries (despite the improvements seen in Italy and, to a much lesser extent, in France since the mid-1990s) and by the marked deceleration of Total Factor Productivity (TFP), which is indicative of a diffuse and increasingly serious lack of efficiency (section 3). The reduced potential growth is also attributable to the sizeable slowdown in the accumulation of capital stock, despite increased investment in information and communications technologies (ICT). The overall evidence is further confirmed by the outcomes of a simple growth accounting exercise that indicates that labour productivity receives a diminishing support from capital deepening and, to a greater extent, from Total Factor Productivity (section 4).

While the first two determinants of the decelerating potential GDP have been widely addressed in the empirical literature, the slowdown of capital accumulation in the three countries deserves more attention than it has attracted until now. We focus on one possible explanation, though certainly not the only one, which deals with the process of substituting labour for capital that would have been induced by their relative prices in the last decade, characterised by a steep decrease in labour shares (section 5). While this argument applies quite well to France and Italy, where wage moderation has been substantial until the early years 2000 and real producers's labour costs have grown more slowly than labour productivity, for the case of Germany the interpretation is more problematic; here the overall evidence seems to point to more general difficulties in deploying both factors of production profitably since reunification in the early 1990s.

A brief summary of our results is reported in the last section of the paper.

2 Estimating potential growth: a non-parametric approach

In order to estimate potential output, we refer to the non-parametric approach proposed by Tödter and von Thadden (2001): although founded on the theory of production, it has the advantage, beyond its simplicity, of not requiring any assumption about the specific functional form of the production technology.

A quick sketch of the method may start with the production function $Y_t = A_t F(K_t, L_t)$, where $F(K_t, L_t)$ is assumed to be continuous and differentiable and A_t is the Hicks-neutral technical progress; in the following analysis we will also adopt the standard assumptions of constant returns to scale and of perfect competition. Taking logs and differentiating leads to the growth accounting equation:[3]

$$\Delta y_t = \alpha_{kt}\Delta k_t + \alpha_{lt}\Delta l_t + a_t; \quad \alpha_{kt} + \alpha_{lt} = 1 \qquad (1)$$

The growth rate of output (Δy_t) is equal to the sum of the growth rates of the factors of production (Δk_t and Δl_t), weighted by the corresponding output elasticities (α_{it}), plus Total Factor Productivity growth (a_t).

On the basis of the assumptions made,[4] the unobservable output elasticities are equal to the observable factor shares, given by the ratio of the cost of each input to the value of output; factor shares sum up to unity.[5]

Taking this as a starting point, the aggregate potential output y_t^* can be obtained very simply, by: 1) calculating Total Factor Productivity growth (a_t); 2) estimating trend (potential) growth of TFP (a_t^*) and the labour input (l_t^*);[6] 3) substituting them into the growth accounting equation, together with an appropriate initial value for y_0^*, and solving for y_t^* recursively.

Before reviewing these three steps in greater detail, it is worth mentioning some caveats about the standard growth accounting exercise that, for pragmatic reasons, we use in this paper. Specifically, beside the already mentioned assumptions, we use the official capital stock and employment data as input measures and therefore we disregard the possibility of estimating the actual flow of services released by the productive factors.[7] This would

---

[3] The natural logarithm of a variable X is indicated using lower-case letters (i.e. $x = ln(X)$) and its changes over time (differences) with the symbol Δ (i.e. $\Delta x_t = x_t - x_{t-1}$).

[4] Though quite common in the literature, the assumptions are undoubtedly restrictive and their failure invalidates the identity of TFP and technological progress. However, it has been noted that the resulting growth accounting allows useful analysis even when they are not fully satisfied (see, for example, Barro, 1999; Basu and Fernald, 2002).

[5] In this framework the factor shares are allowed to vary over time.

[6] It should be noted that, considering the cyclical fluctuations in the use of capital input (proxied by the degree of capacity utilisation), a distinction may also be made between the potential and actual capital stock. Anyway, following the procedure adopted by the OECD and the European Commission, we preferred to make no distinction and to use the actual capital stock in the third step of the procedure.

[7] The only exception is for France, for which we use a measure of the *productive* capital stock provided by the Banque de France. See also Baghli et al. (2006, this volume).

require us to take into consideration the potentially different marginal pro-
ductivities of different types of both capital goods and workers through the
correction of capital stock for its efficiency loss due to depletion and of employment by means, for example, of educational attainments. All of this may
translate into some imprecision in the measures of the factor contributions
to economic growth and, therefore, of TFP. However, since the aim of the
research was not a detailed growth accounting analysis, we preferred to remain within a simple framework; moreover, we think that the sharpness of
the stylised facts that emerge from our exercise makes the findings quite robust to more sophisticated settings. Finally, we remind the reader that we do
not use harmonised data and that, therefore, the potential differences in the
procedures adopted by national statistical institutes may have a (hopefully
minor) effect on international comparisons.

First step

Total Factor Productivity is the only unknown in the growth accounting
equation and can be calculated as a Solow residual on the basis of the historical data:

$$a_t = \Delta y_t - \alpha_{lt}\Delta l_t - (1 - \alpha_{lt})\Delta k_t \qquad (2)$$

Specifically in our exercise we focused on the quarterly sample ranging
from 1982 Q1 to 2004 Q4; this frequency was chosen with the aim of providing potential GDP estimates to be compared with the corresponding actual
releases of national accounts, allowing a "real-time" economic analysis. In
this context, y_t is the log of GDP evaluated at constant prices and l_t is the log
of total employment.[8] Statistical institutes release capital stock data (whose
log in real terms is k_t) at only an annual frequency; we obtained quarterly
estimates to be inserted in equation (2) through interpolation.[9] As regards
the output elasticity a_{lt}, we used the adjusted wage shares released regularly
by the European Commission.[10]

Second step

Smoothing TFP. Calculated as a residual, the TFP shows highly pro-
cyclical fluctuations that need to be eliminated to assess its contribution to

---

[8] In the context of a growth accounting analysis, the value added at basic prices
would be a better measure of aggregate activity; the choice of GDP at market
prices, due to the fact that we are targeting potential growth (possibly comparable
with actual GDP to get an assessment of the output gap), may be reflected in the
estimates of TFP. However we think that the impact on the trend of productivity,
obtained in the second step through a smoothing procedure, is indeed minor.

[9] For Germany we used quadratic interpolation; for Italy we recurred to a Chow-Lin
procedure exploiting the dynamics of a quarterly estimate of the stock of capital
available at the Banca d'Italia; for France, as already mentioned, we adopted a
quarterly measure of *productive* capital stock provided by the Banque de France.

[10] Also in this case we obtained quarterly series by quadratic interpolation of annual
data; moreover, a_{lt} is the two-period average of the wage share.

France

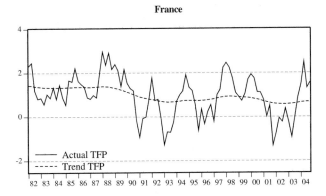

Germany

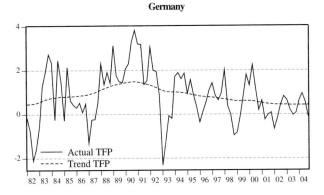

Italy

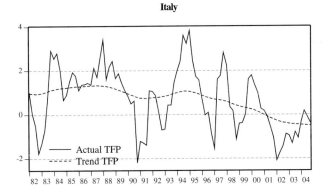

Note: quarterly year-on-year rates of growth. The three figures have the same scale to facilitate comparison.

Source: elaborations on national statistics.

Fig. 1. Total Factor Productivity: actual and trend values

potential output. Its trend (a_t^*) can be obtained in various ways: for example, by using simple moving averages, or by recurring to widely used univariate filters such as the Hodrick-Prescott (HP)[11] or the exponential smoothing filter. In this paper we follow the original contribution by Tödter and von Thadden, resorting to the extended exponential smoothing (EES) approach advocated by Tödter (2002). Like the HP filter, the EES implies revisions of the estimated trend values as new observations become available.[12] However, according to Tödter, the EES distributes them more evenly across all trend values, whereas the HP concentrates their impact at the very end of the sample.[13] The outcomes of the filtering procedure are shown in Figure 1 in which the quarterly TFP is compared with its trend;[14] we will return to them in the next section.

Smoothing labour input. Since the number of employed persons can be expressed as

$$L_t = LF_t(1 - u_t) \qquad (3)$$

where LF_t is the labour force and u_t is the unemployment rate, we need to estimate the 'natural' rate of unemployment (u_t^*) and substitute it into equation (3) to get the trend (potential) level of employment (L_t^*).

The same methods available to estimate the TFP trend (a_t^*) could also be adopted for smoothing the labour input. However for our purposes we preferred to rely on recent research carried out at the Banca d'Italia, focusing on the estimation of the NAIRU through the unobserved component method.[15] This approach allows to decompose the unemployment rate (u_t) into a cycle and a trend component; the last one is interpreted as the measure of the NAIRU (u_t^*) we are looking for.[16] The attractiveness of the unobserved component method lies in the fact that it combines positive aspects of purely statistical and purely structural frameworks yet implying a low burden in terms of data requirements.[17]

---

[11] See Hodrick and Prescott (1997).

[12] Both filters, in fact, are symmetrical for central observations and become increasingly asymmetrical towards the tails of the sample.

[13] To see how the EES extends the original exponential smoothing filter and for further comparison with the HP filter, the reader is referred to Tödter (2002).

[14] It has to be said that, for the sake of robustness of our final results, we also calculated potential GDP relying on HP-filtered TFP; our findings were revealed to be consistent with those described in the rest of the paper.

[15] In order to obtain smoother estimates of the potential employment L^*, the labour force LF has been filtered as well, using the HP technique.

[16] It can be added that this approach 'encompasses' the HP technique, since under particular conditions the trends stemming from the two methods are equivalent (Harvey and Jaeger, 1993).

[17] Moreover, since it derives optimal asymmetric weighting schemes at the tails of the series (see Harvey and Timbur, 2003), it produces reliable estimates at the end

Referring to Appendix 1 and to Zizza (2005, 2006) for methodological details, we just recall that, for the sake of robustness, two unobserved component models have been estimated for each country: a univariate model for the unemployment rate and a bivariate model with unemployment and GDP, embedding Okun's Law.[18] In each case our best estimates of u_t^* - in terms of both precision and smoothness - derived from the bivariate specification.[19]

As shown by Figure 2, the long-run labour market developments have been quite different among the three major euro-area members.[20] In France and Italy the NAIRU grew constantly in the first part of the sample, climbing up to 11.1 and 10.6 per cent, respectively, in 1994 and 1996. This was followed by a reduction, which was much faster in the Italian economy than in France, as a result of the labour market policies adopted in the two countries since the early 1990s (which we will revisit in the next section). In the current decade, whereas in Italy the unemployment rate and the NAIRU kept falling, dropping to 8 per cent in spite of a very weak cyclical phase, in France the economic slowdown contributed to increased unemployment, which in 2004 rose to 10 per cent; for the moment, however, this worsening did not imply an increase in the NAIRU as well.

The picture for Germany is quite different: although the level of unemployment has been historically much lower, it underwent sustained post-reunification growth in both actual and potential terms, reaching levels close to those of France and Italy.[21] In 2004 the NAIRU rose to 9.4 per cent, its peak value in the period under investigation.

Third step

The trend values for total factor productivity (a_t^*) and potential labour input (l_t^*) are inserted into the growth accounting equation:

---

of the sample, thus reducing the uncertainty regarding the current level of the NAIRU.

[18] This law holds that there exists a link between cyclical fluctuations of output and unemployment. See Apel and Jansson (1999); Fabiani and Mestre (2001) and Runstler (2002).

[19] This is not surprising since multivariate unobserved component models usually improve upon univariate specifications enhancing the accuracy of the estimates, allowing consistency with the underlying economic theory to be achieved and reducing the revisions between real-time and final estimates (see, for example, Runstler, 2002 and Camba-Mendez and Rodriguez-Palanzuela, 2003). In our exercise, the univariate models produced measures of the NAIRU that were substantially equal to the unemployment rate itself; in other words, they were not able to identify a significant cyclical component. This is also the reason why we did not use this method for filtering the TFP.

[20] Alternative measures, either coming from *ad hoc* filtering techniques, such as the HP or the EES filters, or provided by international institutions such as the OECD and the European Commission, are broadly in line with our estimates.

[21] When estimating the NAIRU, the break due to the reunification has been modelled explicitly by including a dummy to account for the level shift.

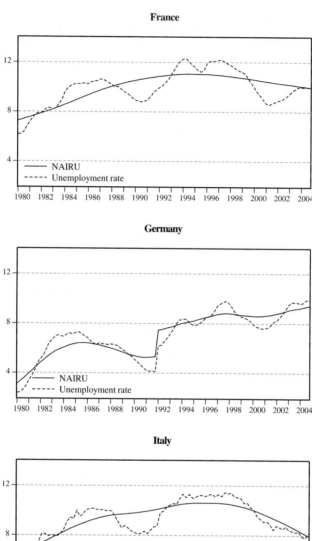

Note: quarterly rates. The three figures have the same scale to facilitate comparison.
Source: elaborations on national statistics.

Fig. 2. Unemployment rate and NAIRU

$$y_t^* = y_{t-1}^* + a_t^* + \alpha_{lt}\Delta l_t^* + (1 - \alpha_{lt})\Delta k_t \qquad (4)$$

In order to obtain the level of potential output, a starting y_0^* can be freely selected.[22] In the following, however, our results will be shown only in terms of year-on-year quarterly rates of growth, Δy_t^*, which are the sum of the contributions given by trend TFP (a_t^*), capital $(1 - \alpha_{lt})\Delta k_t$ and labour ($\alpha_{lt}\Delta l_t^*$). These determinants can be used to interpret the main driving forces behind the evolution of the supply side of the economy.

3 Evidence on potential growth and its determinants

Meagre performance.

The main results stemming from the non-parametric approach are shown in Figure 3. Since 2000 potential GDP growth has been decreasing in all of the three countries. In Germany and, to a lesser extent Italy, this evidence seems part of the negative trend characterising a large fraction of the sample, while in France it follows a series of growth rates fluctuating around fairly low levels.[23]

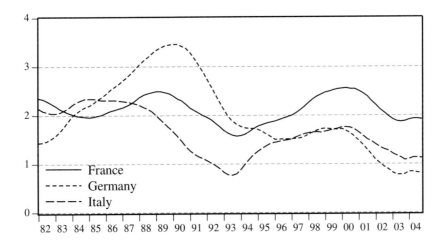

Note: quarterly year-on-year rates of growth.
Source: elaborations on national statistics.

Fig. 3. Potential GDP growth

---

[22] Tödter and von Thadden suggest choosing y_0^* such that the output gap in the reference period assumes the average value of zero.

[23] For Germany, see also Deutsche Bundesbank (2003).

Our estimates give broadly the same picture as those released by the OECD and the European Commission; moreover, the longer time span available from these institutions allows us to emphasise that the decrease of potential growth is a long-standing feature of these economies. Actually it was much steeper in the past decades: according to the European Commission,[24] in the mid-1960s potential output was growing at a yearly rate of close to 5 per cent both in France and in Italy and 4 per cent in Germany; ten years later the rate decreased to about 3 per cent and 2 per cent respectively. Finally, in the mid-1980s French and Italian potential GDP growth had also fallen to only slightly above 2 per cent, whereas in Germany it remained stable at that rate for about ten years, undergoing a brief, though marked, acceleration in the second part of the decade, prior to German reunification.[25]

Although one can think that a relatively low rate of output growth is a typical characteristic of well developed and advanced economies, nonetheless the very recent performance of the three largest euro-area members has been somewhat meagre even in comparison with other European countries. As an example, the potential growth rates of Spain, Sweden and the U.K. have been on a mildly positive trend since the mid-1980s, and in 2004 they were slightly above those estimated for France, Germany and Italy.[26] According to the OECD, U.S. performance has been even better: since 1975 its potential GDP growth has fluctuated only slightly around a flat trend of around 3 per cent, which is also the estimated rate for 2004.

The overall picture drawn by these developments requires an attempt to understand their determinants.

The role of labour.

A sharp heterogeneity among the three countries emerges when focusing on the contribution of the labour input to potential output, in terms of its levels and fluctuations (Figure 4). Since the mid-1990s, France and, in particular, Italy have managed to reverse the long-term trend of labour's small or even negative support to potential growth. Nothing of this sort can be observed for Germany: its labour contribution shows a marked decline characterising the post-reunification years and a stabilisation at low levels thereafter.

To shed some light on this evidence, we should recall that the contribution of labour is given by the rate of growth of potential employment, Δl_t^*, weighted by the labour share α_{lt}: namely $\alpha_{lt}\Delta l_t^*$. While postponing the discussion about factor shares to section 5, at this stage we simply emphasise that, in the time range considered, the labour share α_{lt} markedly declined in all three countries, thus adversely affecting the respective labour contri-

---

[24] The potential output estimates of the European Commission are available in the AMECO database.

[25] This overall evidence emerges also from the potential output estimates of the OECD.

[26] On the basis of the estimates of the European Commission, in 2004 potential growth in Spain, Sweden and the U.K. was, respectively, 2.9, 2.1 and 2.6 per cent.

France

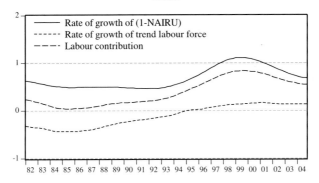

Germany

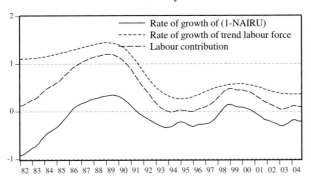

Italy

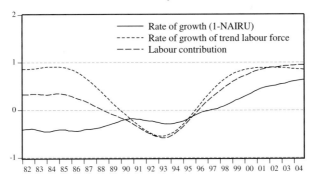

Note: percentage points. The three figures have the same scale to facilitate comparison.

Source: elaborations on national statistics.

Fig. 4. Labour contribution to potential GDP growth

butions. Nevertheless the dynamics of potential employment l_t^* explains the higher labour contribution in France and in Italy. According to equation (3), Δl_t^* can be decomposed into two parts: the rate of growth of the labour force and the complement to 1 of the NAIRU (1-NAIRU). From Figure 4 it emerges that in the second half of the 1990s the increase of Δl_t^* in France and Italy (and therefore the rise of the labour contribution as well) reflected both the reduction in the natural rate of unemployment (see previous section) and, to a larger extent, the marked acceleration of the labour force. In turn, this caused a sizeable increase in the employment rate, which in 2004 reached 62.8 and 57.5 per cent in France and Italy, respectively, from the low levels of 59.6 and 51.8 per cent in 1995.

The good labour market performance in these two countries is even more striking considering that the contemporaneous cyclical upturn was not particularly intense with respect to previous expansionary phases and that, nonetheless, the acceleration in job creation was driven in both cases by the business sector.[27] Actually, the results also reflect the labour market policies adopted in the early 1990s,[28] which, in both countries, were aimed at wage moderation and, more generally, at restraining labour costs (through cuts in employer social security contributions in France and a new bargaining system in Italy),[29] while at the same time enhancing flexibility in the use of labour input (relaxing the restrictions on taking up part-time work and on non-standard and fixed-term contracts).[30] The outcome has been actual labour cost moderation: as we will see in section 5, since the early 1990s labour cost growth in both France and Italy has been substantially slower than that of labour productivity. These developments probably induced an important change in the relative prices of inputs and, presumably, a shift in the factor composition of the production technology in favour of the more intensive use of labour emphasised by Figure 4. Evidence of this also can be found when analysing the role of capital, as will soon be clearer.

The situation in Germany has been quite different: labour's contribution to potential output growth did not benefit from either an increase in the labour force, whose growth has been substantially stable after the post-reunification slowdown, nor from the evolution of the NAIRU which, in fact, has increased sharply since 1992, emphasising the inability of the economy to exploit cyclical expansions in order to reintegrate the unemployed population into labour activity. Recent developments in wage bargaining outcomes

---

[27] In the 1996-2000 period the average yearly rate of GDP growth in France and Italy was 2.8 and 1.9 per cent respectively.

[28] For a detailed analysis, see Pisani-Ferry (2003) and Estevao and Nargis (2005) for France and Brandolini et al. (2005) and Torrini (2005 a, b) for Italy.

[29] Certainly the French labour market dynamics have been influenced also by the reduction in the work week to 35 hours; the extent of its effect, however, is still controversial.

[30] The increased adoption of non-standard and fixed-term contracts also contributed to moderate labour costs.

and the adoption by the Federal Government of new labour market policies are designed to address these issues.[31] As was the case for France and Italy, some of these policies were implemented in order to reduce labour costs and increase flexibility in the use of labour input through the easing of the tax and social contribution burden for part-time jobs and for the low-wage sector; furthermore a greater use of temporary jobs has been promoted, together with improved incentives for self-employment. It is, however, too early to assess their impact on the labour market.

In recent years the labour contribution stood at relatively high levels (close to 1 percentage point) only in Italy, where the labour force continued to increase at a fairly healthy rate and the unemployment rate kept decreasing despite the country's very poor overall economic performance. While in Germany the labour contribution remained substantially flat at around 0.1 percentage point, in France the peak recorded in 2000 has been partly cancelled out by the decline that occurred during the latest economic slowdown, when the NAIRU no longer decreased and the labour force decelerated markedly. Despite these heterogeneities, potential GDP growth in the three countries is still constrained by high unemployment and, above all, by its structural component. The literature has sought to uncover its main determinants;[32] and a relative consensus has emerged, as reflected in the policies implemented in the last decade. Still, however, an additional effort is needed to understand what undermines the incentives for a more intensive participation of the labour input in the production process.

The role of capital

As could be expected, in the period under investigation the amplitude of variations of the capital contribution to potential output growth is much lower than the labour input. Nonetheless, a few heterogeneities emerge among the three countries (Figure 5): while the French and Italian contributions are fairly synchronised, with a recovery in the second half of the 1990s that partially offset the decrease in the first part of the decade, the support from capital has shown a steep downward path in Germany since 1992. It reveals a pronounced restructuring process that appears not to be over yet: by 2004 German capital's contribution had been halved (0.3 percentage point) with respect to the early 1990s and was smaller than in France and in Italy (each 0.7 percentage points); even in these two countries, however, it started to decline since the beginning of the new century.

A deeper look at the data reveals that, in all three countries, the contribution of capital, given by $\alpha_{kt}\Delta k_t$, was strongly supported by the stable rise, in the whole sample, of the capital share α_{kt}.[33] As we did for the labour input, we shall leave aside for the time being any consideration about what

---

[31] In this respect, an important stimulus came from the proposals of the "Hartz Commission"; for a discussion of these issues, see Deutsche Bundesbank (2004).

[32] See, for example, Blanchard (2005).

[33] Proxied by $(1-\alpha_{lt})$ on the basis of the assumptions made in the present exercise.

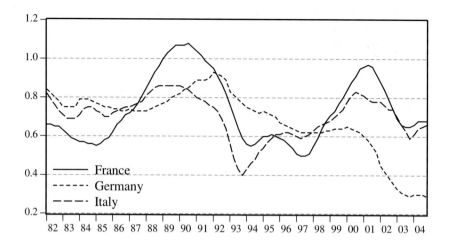

Note: percentage points.
Source: elaborations on national statistics.

Fig. 5. Capital contribution to potential GDP growth

this means in terms of profitability for firms (the issue will be addressed in section 5) and focus on Δk_t. Though characterised by relatively small cyclical fluctuations, the rate of increase of the capital stock in the three countries slowed down: on average for the 1980s it was equal to 2.7, 2.6 and 2.7 per cent in France, Germany and Italy respectively;[34] in the following thirteen years (1991-2003), the yearly rates decreased to 2.1 per cent in the first two countries and 2.0 per cent in Italy.

Combining these dynamics with those from the labour market and with the reduction in the labour costs recorded in France and Italy[35] provides further evidence in favour of interpreting the developments in the 1990s in these two countries as being characterised by a process of partial substitution of labour for capital. This seems to be confirmed by the deceleration of their capital-labour ratio (Figure 6). It can also help to explain why, despite the recovery in the second part of the last decade, the contribution from capital remained at relatively low levels.[36]

Once again, the outlook seems quite different for Germany: in line with a less favourable development of the cost of labour, its capital-labour ratio

---

[34] For Germany, gross capital stock since the net one is available only starting in 1991.

[35] In section 5 we will show that in France, in the second half of the 1990s, the labour cost per efficiency unit fell (followed by a slight recovery); the decrease was even sharper in Italy where, in 2001, the cost was about 10 per cent lower than in 1991.

[36] The increase in the French ratio in recent years is mainly due to the sharp deceleration of employment.

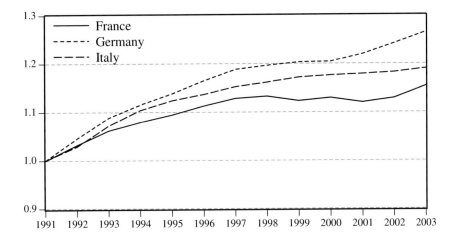

Note: index 1991=1. Net capital stock divided by labour measured in terms of number of employed persons.
Source: elaborations on national statistics.

Fig. 6. Capital-Labour ratio

increased much faster than in the other two countries, which means that factor substitution cannot be blamed for the slowdown in capital accumulation in this country. In fact, the declining contribution of capital to potential output, in conjunction with a similarly sluggish employment growth, seems to reflect a lower efficiency in the combination of factors of production.

The role of TFP

Finally, we consider the role played by the Total Factor Productivity trend growth (a_t^*): the developments shown in Figure 7 depict an extremely negative picture. In the last fifteen years in Germany the growth rate of trend TFP steadily dropped from 1.5 per cent in 1990 to 0.4 per cent in 2004. In Italy the decrease is even more pronounced: since 2001 TFP growth has entered negative territory, approaching -0.5 in 2004. In France the reduction has been less severe thanks to the brief stabilisation in the late 1990s; nonetheless this country has also experienced a decreasing rate of productivity growth since 1999, to 0.7 per cent per year in 2004.

A comparison with some other European economies aggravates the picture: according to European Commission estimates, in the 1995-2004 period Total Factor Productivity increased at an average annual rate of 1.4 and 1.9 per cent in the U.K. and Sweden, respectively, with signs of accelerations in recent years.[37]

---

[37] On the other hand, Spain performed the worst, with an average rate of 0.1.

Such a disappointing outlook deserved a huge effort by empirical re-searchers, focusing on the dynamics of TFP at the industry level and on their respective contributions to overall productivity. Since a disaggregated analy-sis is beyond the scope of this paper, we draw from some results of previous work to gain insights into recent developments.

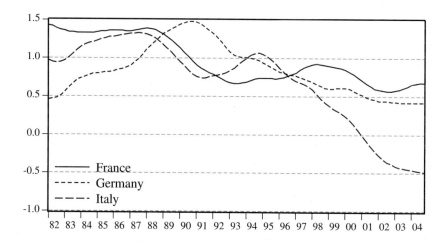

Note: percentage points.
Source: elaborations on national statistics.

Fig. 7. Trend TFP contribution to potential GDP growth

Among the three countries, in the second half of the 1990s some relevant heterogeneities emerged in the manufacturing sector: while in Germany and, above all, in France, Total Factor Productivity kept growing at a relatively fast pace (thanks also to the good performance of ICT manufacturers),[38] in Italy it stalled, with a sharp and sudden slowdown relative to the previous periods.[39] The deceleration, which was particularly severe for non-durables industries, came in anticipation of an even worse development that led to Italian manufacturing TFP undergoing a marked generalised decline in the current decade. The available evidence on the service sector appears much more homogeneous: since the mid-1990s all of the three countries under-went increasingly extreme TFP slowdowns. In a marked departure from the experience of the U.S., the U.K. and the Northern European countries, the poor productivity performance has been particularly pronounced with re-

---

[38] See, for example, Inklaar et al. (2003).
[39] See Bassanetti et al. (2004).

spect to ICT-using industries, such as wholesale and retail trade.[40] This fact has raised questions about the role that could have been played by higher levels of ICT capital stock in France, Germany and Italy: in fact, despite the substantial increase during the late 1990s, ICT share of total gross fixed capital formation and, more generally, the adoption of new technologies are still lagging behind the evidence available for the U.S., the U.K. and the Scandinavian countries.[41] However, although one can certainly think of possible positive network effects to enhance productive efficiency, the link between ICTs and TFP is still the object of research in the empirical literature. Much effort has also been devoted to investigating the possible relationship between the product market regulatory settings and the dynamics of productivity, arguing that a higher degree of competition and lower administrative burdens tend to improve the efficiency of the economic system and TFP growth.[42] In any case, our reading of recent developments implies a broad definition of TFP, according to which its decline might suggest that France, Germany and Italy still have possibilities of stimulating potential GDP growth by improving the environmental and institutional factors, both internal and external to the firms, through the removal of rigidities and the introduction of innovative organisational forms. At this juncture it is worth mentioning the possibility that, particularly in France and in Italy, the relatively easy and increased use of low-cost part-time and fixed-term contracts, quite often for unskilled work, may have reduced the stimulus to undertake deeper and efficient re-organisational processes during the last ten years. This is an issue that certainly deserves a place on the agenda for future research.

4 A growth accounting exercise

To complete the analysis and gain further insights, we applied the same growth accounting framework described in section 2 to annual data;[43] this

---

[40] As regards financial intermediation, another well-performing ICT-using industry in the U.S., the decreasing TFP contribution in the French economy has coincided with the recovery in Germany and in Italy (Inklaar et al., 2003; Bassanetti, 2004). In the latter country the result was supported by the extensive re-organisational process that took place in the last decade, allowing matching efficiency gains; however in the 2000-2003 period this sector was also caught up in the general Italian productivity slump (see Daveri and Jona-Lasino, 2005, for most recent Italian updates).

[41] See, for example, Colecchia and Schreyer (2002).

[42] See, for example, Nicoletti and Scarpetta (2003) Further, a number of studies tried to investigate the possible relationships between product market reforms and labour market performances, and also the impact of employment protection on innovative activity (see, for example, Nicoletti et al., 2001); results, however, are not always clear cut.

[43] We adopted the same standard assumptions described in the potential output methodology and keep on using the wage shares available in the European Commission's AMECO database.

time, however, we do not filter out any cyclical fluctuation from the determinants of growth. We used value added at basic prices as a measure of aggregate output and net capital stock data from the national statistical institutes.[44] As for labour input, we used both the number of full time equivalent employed[45] and the hours worked. Unfortunately, however, in the case of France we were able to find hours worked only with reference to the business sector; therefore for this country we limit the exercise to the use of the first measure of labour input.

Bearing in mind the caveats mentioned in section 2 about the growth accounting framework adopted, we present the results in Table 1.

The left panel of the table broadly confirms the findings that emerged in the context of the potential output estimation. These include: the substantially stable contribution from capital over the last twenty years (which we now know is the result of an increasing capital share and a decelerating capital stock); the recovery of labour's contribution since the mid-1990s in France and especially Italy (coinciding with a sharp decline in wage shares) and the contemporaneous relatively poor performance of the German labour market; the pronounced worsening of TFP in the recent period, common to all of the three countries but particularly marked in Italy, where it did not recover even during a cyclical expansion, as transpired in the second half of the past decade.

In Italy the same results are found when measuring the labour input recurring to the hours worked (right-hand panel of the table). In Germany, instead, the contribution by labour has sizeable differences with respect to the exercise based on the number of employed persons, though the alternation of downturns and recoveries is substantially the same; this is also reflected in the estimates of TFP. This result is due to a large extent to the changed institutional setting in the German labour market: several laws have promoted the development of "mini-jobs", especially since the second half of the 1990s. Moreover, reductions in working hours were a long-standing goal pursued by Germany's trade unions. Last, there was a substantial increase in part-time work during the sample. All this has contributed to the fact that the employment measured in terms of the number of persons looks somewhat more favourable than employment measured in hours.

By subtracting Δl_t from both sides of equation (1), the growth accounting exercise can be easily modified to assess the dynamics of labour productivity, which is composed of the contribution by capital deepening and TFP.

From Table 2 it emerges that, since the mid 1990s, labour productivity markedly decelerated in France, Germany and Italy, with a further worsen-

---

[44] For Germany the net capital stock at constant prices has been available only from 1991 on; for previous periods, therefore, we had to use the dynamics of the gross capital stock.

[45] With the exception of Germany, where only data on the number of employed persons are available.

Table 1. Results from growth accounting

Period	In terms of the number of full time equivalent employed[1]			In terms of hours worked			
	Contribution of			Value added	Contribution of		
	Capital[2]	Labour	TFP		Capital[1]	Labour	TFP
	France						
1981 − 1985	0.7	−0.3	1.4	1.8	(−)	(−)	(−)
1986 − 1990	0.8	1.0	0.9	2.8	(−)	(−)	(−)
1991 − 1995	0.8	−0.3	0.8	1.2	(−)	(−)	(−)
1996 − 2000	0.7	0.8	1.3	2.8	(−)	(−)	(−)
2001 − 2004	0.5	0.5	0.5	1.5	(−)	(−)	(−)
	Germany						
1981 − 1985	0.8	0.1	0.5	1.2	0.8	−0.6	1.1
1986 − 1990	0.8	1.3	1.4	3.4	0.8	0.5	2.2
1991 − 1995	0.9	0.0	1.2	2.0	0.9	−0.4	1.6
1996 − 2000	0.7	0.5	1.0	1.8	0.7	0.0	1.6
2001 − 2004	0.4	−0.1	0.6	0.5	0.4	−0.4	0.8
	Italy						
1981 − 1985	0.8	0.3	0.7	1.8	0.8	0.3	0.7
1986 − 1990	0.8	0.5	1.5	2.8	0.8	0.8	1.2
1991 − 1995	0.6	−0.5	1.2	1.3	0.6	−0.5	1.2
1996 − 2000	0.7	0.5	0.7	1.9	0.7	0.5	0.7
2001 − 2004	0.7	0.7	−0.3	1.1	0.7	0.5	−0.3

Note: percentage points. (1) For Germany, number of persons employed. (2) For Germany, gross capital stock for 1980-1990; net capital stock from 1991 onwards.
Source: elaborations on national statistics.

ing occurring during the current decade, when Italian growth stalled.[46] The labour productivity developments reflect, to a very large extent, those of the TFP, which we already described in the previous section, both at the aggregate and at the industry level.

It has to be added, however, that the slowdown in the second half of the last decade has been also the consequence of the strong reduction of the contribution of capital deepening, reflecting the capital-labour deceleration shown in Figure 6. This is true not only for France and Italy, but also for Germany. Whereas in France and Italy the small support from capital deepening also continued in recent years, its small rise in Germany is due to the wors-

---

[46] For productivity developments in Germany, see also Deutsche Bundesbank (2002).

Table 2. Labour productivity and its determinants

Period	In terms of the number of full time equivalent employed (1)			In terms of hours worked		
	Labour productivity	Capital (2) deepening	TFP	Labour productivity	Capital (2) deepening	TFP
France						
1981 – 1985	2.2	0.8	1.4	(−)	(−)	(−)
1986 – 1990	1.3	0.3	0.9	(−)	(−)	(−)
1991 – 1995	1.7	0.9	0.8	(−)	(−)	(−)
1996 – 2000	1.5	0.3	1.3	(−)	(−)	(−)
2001 – 2004	0.8	0.3	0.5	(−)	(−)	(−)
Germany						
1981 – 1985	1.3	0.8	0.5	2.2	1.0	1.1
1986 – 1990	1.6	0.2	1.4	2.7	0.5	2.2
1991 – 1995	2.1	0.8	1.2	2.7	1.0	1.6
1996 – 2000	1.4	0.4	1.0	2.2	0.7	1.6
2001 – 2004	1.1	0.5	0.6	1.4	0.6	0.8
Italy						
1981 – 1985	1.3	0.6	0.7	1.4	0.7	0.7
1986 – 1990	2.1	0.6	1.5	1.6	0.4	1.2
1991 – 1995	2.1	0.8	1.2	2.1	0.8	1.2
1996 – 2000	1.1	0.4	0.7	1.1	0.4	0.7
2001 – 2004	0.0	0.3	−0.3	0.2	0.4	−0.3

Note: percentage points. (1) For Germany, number of persons employed. (2) For Germany, gross capital stock for 1980-1990; net capital stock from 1991 onwards.
Source: elaborations on national statistics.

ening of the employment situation rather than to increased accumulation; in fact, during this period the rate of growth of the German capital stock further decelerated.

Once again, a disaggregated analysis is left for further research: the assessment of the capital deepening dynamics for different kinds of capital goods and in different sectors would probably help to shed some light on the issue. As an example, Daveri and Jona-Lasino (2005) argue that in Italy, once buildings are netted out, capital accumulation actually resembled TFP growth;[47] Inklaar et al. (2003) argue that in France and in Germany the de-

---

[47] It has to be said, however, that they use the OECD database; the same argument should be checked on the basis of the official data released by the Italian national statistical institute.

clining contribution of non-ICT capital deepening in 1995-2000 can explain a large percentage of the labour productivity slowdown with respect to the 1979-1995 period, pointing, as we also do, to movements in relative factor prices as a possible explanation of these developments.

5 Evidence from some measures of profitability and wage pressure

In the previous sections, labour market performance was found to be markedly heterogeneous in the three countries under analysis, possibly reflecting differences in the corresponding wage setting mechanisms and in regulations. We now present some measures of profitability and wage pressure in order to assess the role of the wage dynamics in the economic performance of France, Germany and Italy.

We first consider the evolution of the labour share: though not completely satisfactory either as a measure of profitability or of wage pressure, it nevertheless allows to detect changes in the labour market equilibrium after adding other indicators. As observed in the literature, factor shares showed large fluctuations during the 1970s and 1980s in most developed countries, the most pronounced being in continental Europe. These fluctuations were related to the wage push of the 1970s, which would have initially prompted a rise in the labour share, followed by a reversal during the 1980s when firms adjusted their capital stock substituting capital for labour, reducing labour demand and inducing a slowdown in real wage dynamics (Blanchard 1997, 2000).

By using data from the OECD STAN database and focusing on the 1980-2003 period, we compute the labour share correcting for self-employment income at the industry level, namely by attributing to self-employed workers the same remuneration as employees working in the same industry.[48] Specifically the share (WS) is given by:

$$WS = \frac{1}{Y} \sum_i W_i (L_i/E_i) \tag{5}$$

---

[48] Unlike what we did in the non-parametric estimation of potential output and in the growth accounting exercise, in the present section we chose the OECD STAN over the more up-to-date European Commission AMECO database. The choice is due to the fact that STAN provides greater detail regarding sectors, allowing us to single out a measure for the business sector. Moreover it enables us to get rid of the real estate sector, whose output (rents) mostly consists of the services provided by the housing stock; as a consequence, variations in the price of housing services affects the weights of the real estate sector on aggregate value added, changing the aggregate wage share irrespective of any change in wage dynamics.

where Y is total value added whereas W_i, L_i and E_i stand, respectively, for compensation of employees, total employment and employees in industry i.

Consistently with previous findings, our measure of the labour share declined in the 1980s in all of the three countries,[49] offsetting the 1970s rise; in the 1990s, it continued to decline at a slower pace in France and unified Germany, and plummeted in Italy (see Table A1 in Appendix 2).[50]

Limiting the analysis to the business sector and excluding real estate, similar results are found in France and in Italy; in Germany, on the other hand, the labour share in the total economy net of real estate increased during the 1990s, while remaining fairly stable in the business sector (Figure 8). As a result, in 2002 the labour share in the German business sector was 3.8 and 8.2 percentage points higher than in France and Italy respectively; a decade earlier, in 1991, in Germany and in France it was virtually the same, while in Italy it was less than 3 percentage points lower than in the other two countries.

The picture shown in Figure 8 is part of the evidence of the change in the relative price of inputs that took place in France and in Italy in the second half of the 1990s. The cheaper cost of labour induced the process of substitution of labour for capital that we described in section 3. In this respect, further confirmation emerges from Figure 9, where we report the developments of labour productivity and of the real producer labour cost (measured by the ratio of compensation per employee to the value added deflator) in the business sector net of real estate.

The increase in German labour productivity, the largest among the three economies, was matched by a similar rise in real compensation per employee; in France, by contrast, productivity improvement was lower, but the real cost of labour lagged even behind, as it did to a greater extent in Italy.

Similar signals can be deduced from the analysis of the developments of the labour cost per efficiency unit of labour, proposed by Blanchard as a measure of wage pressure (Figure 10; see Appendix 3 for its calculation).[51]

---

[49] Data for Germany refer to West Germany only.

[50] A tax reform in 1998 explains part of the decline of labour share in Italy in the late 1990s. A new tax on value added (IRAP) was introduced, substituting for some payroll taxes. This reform reduced total compensation of employees while leaving the value added measured at basic prices unchanged, as this includes taxes levied on production. As a consequence of this reform the wage share of value added dropped, although firms profitability was not affected. To evaluate the impact of this reform we have computed a corrected labour share, by applying to total compensation of employees the dynamics observed for wages and salaries, which were not affected by the introduction of this new tax. It turns out that the introduction of IRAP accounts for a drop in the labour share of roughly 1 percentage point (see Table A1 in Appendix 2).

[51] In a balanced growth path, if wages grow at the same pace as labour efficiency, the ratio of capital to labour in efficiency unit should remain constant. This is not the

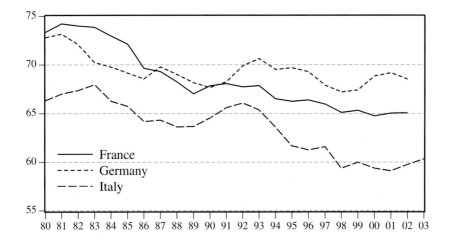

Note: percentage points, business sector net of real estate.
Source: elaborations on OECD STAN data.

Fig. 8. Wage shares

In Italy the decline in this indicator and the contemporaneous drop in the labour share point to a reduction in wage pressure beginning in the early 1990s. Although this did not immediately translate into a rise in employment,[52] it set the stage for the rapid recovery starting in the mid-1990s and continued in the first half of the 2000s. In France there is similar, although less pronounced, evidence for wage moderation, whereas in Germany, consistently with the evolution of the labour share, real wages per efficiency unit displayed greater dynamics, remaining well above their starting levels of 1991.

With regard to profitability, we constructed a measure of the return on capital stock as the ratio of the value added net of labour costs to the capital stock at substitution prices (Table A2 in Appendix 2).[53] In the business sector

---

case if wages grow at the same pace as labour productivity, which also depends on capital deepening. In fact if workers appropriate productivity gains due to capital deepening, this could prompt a further rise in the capital-labour ratio, and a reduction in labour demand.

[52] Actually, during the recession in the early 1990s employment dropped for the first time in thirty years, due to the drastic restructuring of private and state-owned companies and to the stop imposed by budget constraints to public employment growth (Torrini, 2005a).

[53] In order to calculate the rate of return on capital, we computed the capital stock at substitution prices applying to the capital stock at 1995 prices the deflator of capital formation.

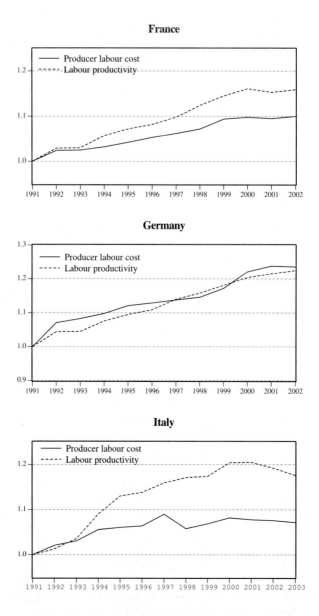

Note: index 1991=1; business sector net of real estate; labour measured in terms of employed persons. Producer labour cost in real terms. The three figures have the same scale to facilitate comparison.
Source: elaborations on OECD STAN data.

Fig. 9. Labour productivity and producer labour cost

net of dwellings, the rate of return has been rising in France since the mid-1990s, while remaining fairly stable in Germany and in Italy (Figure 11).

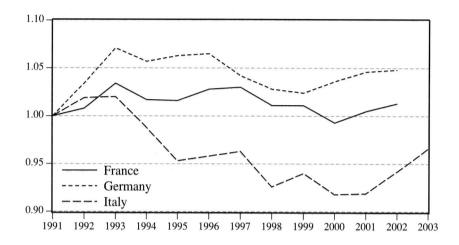

Note: index 1991=1.
Source: elaborations on OECD STAN data.

Fig. 10. Cost of labour per efficiency unit

Considering the drop in real interest rates, we can argue that in all three countries the return on capital with respect to its user cost increased during the last decade, though the development was most pronounced in France.[54] This further rises the puzzle of the slowdown of capital accumulation described in section 3. Though the developments of relative input prices can contribute to the explanation, there remains much to be understood.

Finally, focusing on the manufacturing industry, whereas in France the rate of return followed the same pattern as the entire business sector, in Italy and to some extent in Germany it was much less favourable (Table A2 in Appendix 2). Part of the better performance observed in France was due to the fact that in the business sector the capital deflator grew less quickly than the value added deflator, and in the manufacturing sector labour efficiency grew much faster than in the other countries.

Overall, the measures of wage pressure and profitability depict, for France and Italy, a more favourable context for employment growth than for Germany, helping to explain the largest labour contribution resulting from previous sections.

---

[54] Comparing the levels of the rate of return, France's was highest, followed by Italy and Germany.

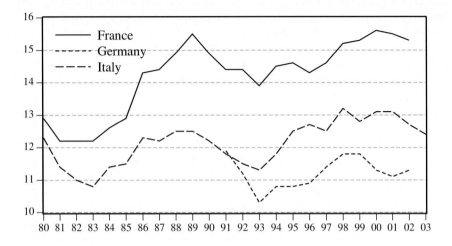

Note: business sector net of real estate.
Source: elaborations on OECD STAN data.

Fig. 11. Returns on gross capital stock

6 Conclusions

The paper analyses recent supply side conditions in France, Germany and Italy by estimating their respective potential GDP growth. The adoption of a non-parametric framework, fundamentally based on a growth accounting setting, allows us to decompose the potential output dynamics into contributions by long-term developments in employment, capital and total factor productivity.

We find that, since 2000, potential growth has been sharply decreasing in all three countries; in Germany and in Italy the same findings also characterised most of the 1990s. These performances was revealed to be relatively poor not only in comparison with the U.S., but also with other European countries such as Spain, Sweden and the U.K..

Despite the fact that the three economies we examine share a meagre rate of growth, relevant heterogeneities are at the basis of their recent developments, especially concerning the contribution of labour input. While in France and, above all, in Italy it recovered significantly since the mid-1990s, triggered by the restraint of labour costs induced by the policies adopted in the last decade, in Germany it decreased in the post-reunification period and subsequently stabilised at low levels. All three countries, however, still share a high level of unemployment and of its structural component.

The change in relative input prices induced by the wage moderation observed in France and in Italy also contributed to a process of substitution of capital with labour, inducing a slowdown in the accumulation activity and limiting its support of growth. However, additional research would be necessary to understand the further elements that underpin the incentives for more intensive investment in capital goods. In the German case, the relative price movements seem less relevant, in particular because the wage shock that followed reunification was only partially offset by lower growth of unit labour costs than in the two other countries since the end of the 1990s. A more general difficulty of harnessing both factors of production profitably seem to characterise the last fifteen years.

Total Factor Productivity contribution to economic growth declined in the three countries, particularly in Italy. This points to the need of enhancing the institutional environments in which firms operate and of deep reorganisation of the production systems.

A large part of the recent economic debate focused on the need for structural reforms, mainly in the product and labour markets. Some of them have been implemented, though the process certainly remains to be completed. In the past few years a strand of literature highlighted the existence of a trade-off between efficiency-improving reforms and the degree of employment security and equity. While completing the process in order to adapt the institutional framework to increased global competition, the trade-off related issues should be addressed as well, with the goal of dealing with the possibility of an adverse impact on household incomes, in this way also expanding the political consensus on the reform process.

References

Apel, M. and Jansson, P. (1999), "A theory-consistent system approach for estimating potential output and the NAIRU", *Economics Letters*, 64, pp. 271-275.

Barro, R. (1999), "Notes on Growth accounting", *Journal of Economic Growth*, Vol. 4, No. 2, pp. 119-137.

Bassanetti, A., Iommi, M., Jona-Lasinio, C. and Zollino, F. (2004), "La crescita dell'economia italiana negli anni novanta tra ritardo tecnologico e rallentamento della produttività", Banca d'Italia, *Temi di discussione*, No. 539.

Basu, S. and Fernald, J. G. (2002), "Aggregate Productivity and Aggregate Technology", *European Economic Review*, Vol. 46, No. 6, pp. 963-991.

Blanchard, O.J. (1997), "The medium run", *Brooking Papers on Economic Activity*, No. 2, pp. 89-158.

Blanchard, O.J. (2000), "The economics of unemployment. Shocks, institutions, and interactions", Lionel Robbins Lecture, MIT mimeo.

Blanchard, O.J. (2005), "European unemployment: the evolution of facts and ideas", MIT, *Department of Economics Working Paper Series*, No. 05-24.

Brandolini, A., Casadio, P., Cipollone, P., Magnani, M., Rosolia, A. and Torrini, R. (2005), "Employment growth in Italy in the 1990s: institutional ar-
rangements and market forces", Banca d'Italia, mimeo.

Camba-Mendez, G. and Rodriguez-Palenzuela, D. (2003), "Assessment criteria for output gap estimates", *Economic Modelling*, 20, pp. 529-562.

Colecchia, A. and Schreyer, P. (2002), "The contribution of information and
communication technologies to economic growth in nine OECD countries", *OECD Economic Studies*, No. 34.

Daveri, F. and Jona-Lasino, C. (2005), "Italy's decline : getting the facts right",
mimeo.

Deutsche Bundesbank (2002), "Productivity developments in Germany",
Monthly Report, September, pp. 47-61.

Deutsche Bundesbank (2003), "The development of production potential in
Germany", *Monthly Report*, March, pp. 41-52.

Deutsche Bundesbank (2004), "Greater flexibility on the German labour market", *Monthly Report*, September, pp. 43-57.

Estevao, M. and Nargis, N. (2005), "Structural labor market changes in
France", *IZA Discussion Paper Series*, No. 1621, Bonn.

Fabiani, S. and Mestre, R. (2001), "A system approach for measuring the euro
area NAIRU", *ECB Working Paper Series*, No. 65.

Harvey, A.C. (1989), "Forecasting, structural time series models and the
Kalman filter", Cambridge University Press.

Harvey, A.C. and Jaeger, A. (1993), "Detrending, stylised facts and the business cycle", *Journal of Applied Econometrics*, Vol. 8, pp. 231-247.

Harvey, A.C. and Trimbur, T.M. (2003), "General model-based filters for extracting cycles and trends in economic time series", *The Review of Economics
and Statistics*, Vol. 85, pp. 244-255.

Hodrick, R.J. and Prescott, E.C. (1997), "Postwar US business cycles: an empirical investigation", *Journal of Money, Credit, and Banking*, Vol. 29, pp. 1-16.

Inklaar, R., O'Mahony, M. and Timmer, M. (2003), "ICT and Europe's productivity performance. Industry-level growth account comparisons with the
United States", *Groningen Growth and Development Centre, Research Memorandum* GD-68.

Nicoletti, G., Bassanini, A., Ernst, E., Jean, S., Santiago, P. and Swaim, P.
(2001), "Product and labour markets interactions in OECD countries",
OECD Economics Department Working Papers, No. 312.

Nicoletti, G. and Scarpetta, S. (2003), "Regulation, productivity and growth:
OECD evidence", *OECD Economics Department Working Papers*, No. 347.

Pisani-Ferry, J. (2003), "The surprising French employment performance:
what lessons?", University Paris-Dauphine, mimeo.

Runstler, G. (2002), "The information content of real-time output gap estimates: an application to the euro area", *ECB Working Paper Series*, No. 182.

Tödter, K.-H. (2002), "Exponential smoothing as an alternative to the
Hodrick-Prescott filter?", in Mittnik, S. and Klein, I. (eds.), *Contributions*

to modern econometrics - From data analysis to economic policy, Kluwer Academic Publishers, Dordrecht, Boston, London, pp. 223-237.

Tödter, K.-H. and L. von Thadden (2001), "A non-parametric framework for potential output in Germany". Deutsche Bundesbank, mimeo.

Torrini R. (2005a) "Profit share and returns to capital in Italy: the role of privatisations behind the rise of the 1990s", *CEP Working Paper*.

Torrini, R. (2005b) "Quota dei profitti e redditività del capitale in Italia: un tentativo di interpretazione", *Banca d'Italia, Temi di discussione*, No. 551.

Zizza, R. (2005), "A measure of Nairu for France, Germany and Italy: an unobserved component approach", Banca d'Italia, mimeo.

Zizza, R. (2006), "A measure of output gap for Italy through unobserved component models", *Journal of Applied Statistics*, forthcoming.

A Appendix

A.1 Estimating the NAIRU: the unobserved component approach

In a *structural* time series framework, a variable of interest y (in our case, the unemployment rate) can be decomposed into two components: one accounting for the trend - μ_t (*permanent component*) - and the other - ϕ_t (*transitory component*) - for the cycle, plus a disturbance term (ε_t)

$$y_t = \mu_t + \phi_t + \varepsilon_t, \quad t = 1, ..., T$$

The two parts are modelled separately. Usually, the permanent component is taken to be a local linear trend (LLT), where both the level (μ) and the slope (β) are stochastic and evolve as random walks; moreover it is supposed to be affected by two shocks, one (η) hitting its level, the other (ζ) its slope.

$$\mu_t = \mu_{t-1} + \beta_{t-1} + \eta_t \quad \eta \sim NID(0, \Sigma_\eta)$$

$$\beta_t = \beta_{t-1} + \zeta_t \quad \zeta \sim NID(0, \Sigma_\zeta)$$

The transitory component can be either modelled as an autoregressive process or, more generally, as a stochastic cycle, according to the following specification:

$$\begin{bmatrix} \phi_t \\ \phi_t^* \end{bmatrix} = \rho \begin{bmatrix} \cos \lambda_c \sin \lambda_c \\ -\sin \lambda_c \cos \lambda_c \end{bmatrix} \begin{bmatrix} \phi_{t-1} \\ \phi_{t-1}^* \end{bmatrix} + \begin{bmatrix} \kappa_t \\ \kappa_t^* \end{bmatrix}$$

where ρ is a damping factor and $0 < \lambda_c \leq \pi$ the frequency of the cycle in radians; $\kappa_t \approx NID(0, \sigma_\kappa^2)$ and $\kappa_t^* \approx NID(0, \sigma_{\kappa^*}^2)$ are mutually independent.[55]

This structural model can be cast in a state space form (SSF):

---

[55] Note that ϕ_t^* is introduced only to allow ϕ_t to be generated iteratively in the state space form, with no intrinsic relevance.

$$y_t = Z_t \alpha_t + \varepsilon_t \quad \alpha_1 \sim N(0, P)$$

$$\alpha_{t+1} = T_t \alpha_t + \xi_t$$

The first equation is the measurement equation, linking the observable variables to the state vector $\alpha_t = (\mu_t, \beta_t, \varphi_t, \varphi_t^*)'$ The second is the transition equation, describing the dynamics of the state vector, where $\xi_t = (\eta_t, \zeta_t, \kappa_t, \kappa_t^*)'$. The system matrices are $Z_t = [1, 0, 1, 0]$ and

$$T = \begin{bmatrix} 1 & 1 & 0 & 0 \\ 0 & 1 & 0 & 0 \\ 0 & 0 & \rho \cos \lambda_c & \rho \sin \lambda_c \\ 0 & 0 & -\rho \sin \lambda_c & \rho \cos \lambda_c \end{bmatrix}$$

Once the model is in SSF, the application of the Kalman filter (a recursive algorithm) allows us to obtain the optimal (MMSE) estimate of the state vector based on past and current observations, given the initial values. In practice, parameters are unknown and need to be estimated by maximising a likelihood function (Harvey, 1989). The framework can be easily generalised to a bivariate case, considering output and the unemployment rate as variables of interest. Specifically, let denote the log transformation of real GDP and u the unemployment rate. Both potential output (the GDP permanent component) and the NAIRU are assumed to be characterised by stochastic trends: potential output (μ) is modelled as a random walk with drift (β), whereas the NAIRU (u^*) follows a pure random walk. Accordingly, the model becomes

$$y_t = \mu_t + \varphi_t + \varepsilon_t^Y$$

$$u_t = u_t^* + \varphi_t + \varepsilon_t^U$$

$$\mu_t = \beta_t + \mu_{t-1} + \varepsilon_t^\mu$$

$$u_t^* = u_{t-1}^* + \varepsilon_t^N$$

where φ is the common (stochastic) cycle. Once it is translated in SSF, the state vector is $\alpha_t = (\mu_t, u_t^*, \varphi_t, \varphi^*)'$.

The system matrices are

$$Z = \begin{bmatrix} 1 & 0 & 1 & 0 \\ 0 & 1 & 1 & 0 \end{bmatrix}$$

and

$$T = \begin{bmatrix} 1 & 0 & 0 & 0 \\ 0 & 1 & 0 & 0 \\ 0 & 0 & \rho \cos \lambda_c & \rho \sin \lambda_c \\ 0 & 0 & -\rho \sin \lambda_c & \rho \cos \lambda_c \end{bmatrix}$$

The vector $c = (\beta, 0, 0, 0)'$ must be finally added to the right-hand side of the transition equation. The same considerations relative to the estimation in the univariate framework apply here as well.

A.2 Tables

Appendix Table A1: Wage shares

Year	Total Economy	Total economy net of real estate	Business sector	Business sector net of real estate	Business sector net of real estate and agr.	Business sector net of real estate, agr., and manuf.
			France			
1980	69.9	76.4	65.6	73.3	73.0	73.1
1981	70.4	77.1	66.1	74.2	73.9	74.2
1982	70.4	77.0	66.0	74.0	74.2	73.7
1983	70.0	76.7	65.7	73.9	73.6	73.3
1984	69.1	75.9	64.7	73.0	72.4	72.4
1985	68.5	75.3	63.8	72.1	71.7	72.0
1986	66.2	72.9	61.5	69.6	69.3	68.6
1987	65.4	72.2	60.9	69.3	68.9	68.0
1988	64.1	71.0	59.8	68.2	67.7	67.6
1989	63.1	70.1	58.6	67.0	66.8	66.7
1990	63.5	70.6	59.2	67.8	67.8	67.7
1991	63.5	70.9	59.1	68.1	67.9	67.4
1992	63.1	70.8	58.4	67.7	67.8	67.7
1993	63.0	70.9	58.0	67.9	67.9	67.5
1994	62.0	69.8	56.8	66.5	67.0	66.8
1995	62.0	69.9	56.5	66.2	66.9	67.4
1996	62.1	70.1	56.5	66.4	67.1	67.3
1997	61.8	69.8	56.1	66.0	66.9	67.7
1998	61.3	69.2	55.4	65.1	66.2	67.5
1999	61.6	69.5	55.7	65.3	66.3	67.5
2000	61.4	69.0	55.4	64.7	65.5	66.7
2001	61.7	69.3	55.8	65.0	65.8	67.3
2002	61.7	69.3	55.6	65.1	65.7	67.3

Note: percentage points. Source: elaborations on OECD STAN data.

Appendix Table A1: Wage shares, continued

Year	Total Economy	Total economy net of real estate	Business sector	Business sector net of real estate	Business sector net of real estate and agr.	Business sector net of real estate, agr., and manuf.
			West Germany			
1980	68.9	74.5	65.9	72.8	71.0	69.6
1981	68.8	74.7	65.9	73.2	71.5	69.5
1982	67.8	74.0	64.6	72.1	70.8	68.8
1983	66.0	72.4	62.5	70.2	68.7	66.8
1984	65.3	71.9	61.8	69.8	68.4	66.3
1985	64.9	71.5	61.2	69.1	67.7	66.0
1986	64.5	71.1	60.6	68.6	67.2	66.1
1987	65.3	72.1	61.4	69.8	68.4	66.1
1988	64.5	71.4	60.7	69.0	67.9	66.1
1989	63.7	70.6	59.9	68.1	67.3	65.3
1990	63.2	70.1	59.5	67.7	66.9	64.3
1991	63.2	70.0	59.3	67.5	66.6	63.3
			Germany			
1991	64.3	70.6	60.3	68.3	66.5	61.6
1992	65.2	71.9	61.4	69.9	68.3	63.1
1993	65.5	72.8	61.6	70.6	69.1	63.7
1994	64.5	72.0	60.4	69.5	68.1	63.2
1995	64.5	72.4	60.2	69.7	68.4	63.3
1996	64.0	72.3	59.4	69.3	68.2	63.4
1997	63.0	71.3	58.2	67.9	67.0	62.2
1998	62.6	70.8	57.8	67.2	66.3	61.8
1999	63.0	71.2	58.0	67.4	66.5	62.0
2000	64.0	72.4	59.3	68.8	68.0	63.7
2001	64.1	72.7	59.4	69.2	68.5	64.2
2002	63.5	72.2	58.6	68.5	67.8	63.9
2003	63.3		58.0			

Note: percentage points.
Source: elaborations on OECD STAN data.

Appendix Table A1: Wage shares, continued

Year	Total Economy	Total economy net of real estate	Business sector	Business sector net of real estate	Business sector net of real estate and agr.	Business sector net of real estate, agr., and manuf.
Italy						
1980	66.6	70.4	62.1	66.3	65.3	65.1
1981	67.6	71.3	62.7	67.0	66.1	66.0
1982	67.8	71.6	63.0	67.4	66.8	66.7
1983	67.9	71.9	63.3	68.0	67.1	66.5
1984	66.3	70.8	61.2	66.3	65.3	65.1
1985	65.8	70.2	60.7	65.7	64.8	64.6
1986	64.3	68.8	59.0	64.1	63.4	62.8
1987	64.1	68.8	58.9	64.3	63.6	63.3
1988	63.6	68.3	58.2	63.6	62.8	62.2
1989	63.5	68.3	58.2	63.7	63.2	62.2
1990	64.4	69.4	58.7	64.5	64.1	62.2
1991	65.1	70.4	59.4	65.6	65.5	63.1
1992	64.8	70.6	59.3	66.1	65.9	63.6
1993	63.9	70.1	58.2	65.4	65.2	62.7
1994	62.1	68.5	56.2	63.6	63.6	61.3
1995	60.3	66.8	54.3	61.7	61.9	59.8
1996	59.9	66.6	53.6	61.2	61.6	58.8
1997	60.3	67.0	53.9	61.6	62.0	58.8
1998	57.9	64.3	52.0	59.4	59.8	56.7
1999	58.2	64.8	52.4	60.0	60.6	57.5
2000	57.8	64.3	52.0	59.4	59.9	56.9
2001	57.6	64.0	51.7	59.1	59.6	56.7
2002	57.8	64.5	52.0	59.8	60.3	57.2
2003	58.1	65.0	52.3	60.3	60.9	57.4
Corrected for the impact of the tax reform of 1998						
1998	58.9	65.4	52.8	60.2	60.6	57.3
1999	59.2	65.9	53.1	60.8	61.4	58.2
2000	58.8	65.4	52.7	60.2	60.7	57.5
2001	58.5	65.1	52.4	59.9	60.4	57.3
2002	58.8	65.6	52.7	60.6	61.1	57.8
2003	59.1	66.2	53.0	61.2	61.7	58.0

Note: percentage points.
Source: elaborations on OECD STAN data.

Appendix Table A2: Returns on gross capital stock

Year	Total Economy	Total economy net of real estate	Business sector	Business sector net of real estate	Business sector net of real estate and agr.	Business sector net of real estate, agr., and manuf.
			France			
1980	6.0	8.8	6.7	12.9	13.7	12.7
1981	5.8	8.5	6.5	12.2	13.0	12.0
1982	5.8	8.5	6.5	12.2	12.7	12.2
1983	6.0	8.6	6.6	12.2	13.0	12.5
1984	6.2	9.0	6.8	12.6	13.5	12.9
1985	6.3	9.2	7.0	12.9	13.8	13.1
1986	7.0	10.3	7.7	14.3	15.3	15.3
1987	7.2	10.6	7.9	14.4	15.3	15.7
1988	7.6	11.1	8.2	14.9	16.0	16.2
1989	8.0	11.5	8.7	15.5	16.4	16.6
1990	7.9	11.3	8.6	14.9	15.7	16.2
1991	7.7	11.0	8.3	14.4	15.2	16.1
1992	7.9	11.0	8.5	14.4	15.1	15.9
1993	7.8	10.8	8.4	13.9	14.7	15.7
1994	8.1	11.2	8.7	14.5	15.0	15.8
1995	8.1	11.2	8.7	14.6	15.0	15.3
1996	8.0	10.9	8.6	14.3	14.6	15.1
1997	8.1	11.1	8.7	14.6	14.8	15.0
1998	8.3	11.5	9.0	15.2	15.5	15.4
1999	8.4	11.5	9.2	15.3	15.6	15.6
2000	8.4	11.7	9.3	15.6	16.0	16.1
2001	8.4	11.6	9.2	15.5	15.9	15.8
2002	8.3	11.6	9.1	15.3	15.8	15.7

Note: percentage points.
Source: elaborations on OECD STAN data.

Appendix Table A2: Returns on gross capital stock, continued

Year	Total Economy	Total economy net of real estate	Business sector	Business sector net of real estate	Business sector net of real estate and agr.	Business sector net of real estate, agr., and manuf.
				Germany		
1991	7.0	9.1	7.8	11.9	13.6	14.1
1992	6.9	8.7	7.6	11.2	12.6	13.7
1993	6.6	8.1	7.2	10.3	11.6	13.2
1994	6.8	8.4	7.5	10.8	12.1	13.4
1995	6.8	8.3	7.5	10.8	11.9	13.3
1996	6.8	8.3	7.6	10.9	11.9	13.2
1997	7.0	8.6	7.8	11.4	12.5	13.5
1998	7.1	8.9	7.9	11.8	12.9	13.7
1999	7.1	8.8	7.8	11.8	12.9	13.8
2000	6.8	8.5	7.6	11.3	12.2	12.9
2001	6.8	8.3	7.5	11.1	12.0	12.6
2002	6.9	8.5	7.6	11.3	12.2	12.7
2003	7.0		7.8			

Note: percentage points.
Source: elaborations on OECD STAN data.

Appendix Table A2: Returns on gross capital stock, continued

Year	Total Economy	Total economy net of real estate	Business sector	Business sector net of real estate	Business sector net of real estate and agr.	Business sector net of real estate, agr., and manuf.
				Italy		
1980	6.7	9.2	7.8	12.3	13.6	13.6
1981	6.2	8.5	7.2	11.4	12.6	12.8
1982	6.0	8.3	7.0	11.0	12.1	12.4
1983	6.0	8.2	6.9	10.8	11.9	12.7
1984	6.4	8.6	7.4	11.4	12.6	13.3
1985	6.5	8.7	7.5	11.5	12.7	13.5
1986	7.0	9.4	8.0	12.3	13.6	14.6
1987	7.1	9.4	8.0	12.2	13.4	14.3
1988	7.2	9.6	8.2	12.5	13.8	14.7
1989	7.3	9.6	8.3	12.5	13.7	14.7
1990	7.1	9.4	8.1	12.2	13.4	15.0
1991	6.9	9.0	7.9	11.8	12.8	14.5
1992	6.9	8.8	7.8	11.5	12.5	14.2
1993	6.8	8.6	7.8	11.3	12.2	14.1
1994	7.2	9.0	8.2	11.8	12.7	14.4
1995	7.6	9.5	8.7	12.5	13.4	14.8
1996	7.8	9.7	8.9	12.7	13.5	15.3
1997	7.7	9.5	8.8	12.5	13.2	15.1
1998	8.1	10.3	9.1	13.2	14.0	15.8
1999	8.0	10.0	9.0	12.8	13.5	15.4
2000	8.1	10.2	9.1	13.1	13.8	15.9
2001	8.2	10.3	9.2	13.1	13.9	16.0
2002	8.0	10.0	9.0	12.7	13.4	15.6
2003	7.9	9.8	8.8	12.4	13.0	15.4
		Corrected for the impact of the tax reform of 1998				
1998	7.9	10.0	9.0	12.9	13.7	15.6
1999	7.8	9.7	8.8	12.5	13.2	15.2
2000	7.9	9.9	9.0	12.8	13.5	15.7
2001	8.0	10.0	9.0	12.9	13.6	15.8
2002	7.8	9.7	8.8	12.4	13.1	15.4
2003	7.7	9.5	8.7	12.1	12.8	15.3

Note: percentage points.
Source: elaborations on OECD STAN data.

A.3 Measures for profitability and wage pressure

Labour shares are computed based on value added at current basic prices, correcting for self-employment income at the industry level. This was done by imputing to self-employed workers the same average compensation as for employees working in the same industry.

The rate of return on capital is computed as the ratio of value added at current prices, net of compensation of workers, to the gross capital stock measured at substitution prices.

Real wage per efficiency unit is computed as the index number of the following variable:

$$WE_i = \frac{W_i/D_i}{L_i * e_i}$$

where
W = compensation of employees
L = dependent workers
D = industry value added deflator
$e_i = \exp\left[\sum_t \frac{Solow\,Residual_{t,i}}{\alpha_{t,i}}\right]$
with e equal to 1 at the starting period. It measures the efficiency of labour in industry i.
α = labour share.

Estimating Potential Output with a Production Function for France, Germany and Italy *

Mustapha Baghli, Christophe Cahn, and Jean-Pierre Villetelle

Banque de France, 41-1376 SEPREV, 39 rue Croix des Petits Champs, 75049 Paris Cedex 01. Corresponding author: christophe.cahn@banque-france.fr

Summary. This paper discusses the supply conditions for economic growth in terms of potential GDP estimated by the production function approach for France, Germany and Italy. The aim of this study is twofold: first, we keep a consistent framework as regards national accounts institutional sectors. Second, after defining Total Factor Productivity (TFP) in the so-called productive sector from the Solow residual, we specify it in a general framework for the three countries as a function of a time trend corrected for the effects of the age of equipments and the capacity utilisation rate (CUR). This framework allows to distinguish temporal considerations: in the medium to long term, the variables that could generate short to medium term fluctuations in potential output growth are assumed to be stable at a structural level. This implies modifications of the functional specifications related to the time horizon.

Keywords: potential growth, production function, total factor productivity, age of equipments.
JEL classification: C51, E32, O11, O47.

1 Introduction

Recent developments in Europe have raised several interesting issues. Among them, one of paramount relevance concerns the existence of business cycle asymmetries between the three main countries of the euro area, namely France, Germany and Italy. The weak business cycle synchronization between these three countries is an important topic of concern since the determinants of such a lack of connection in Europe are far from being clearly established. Consequently, this raises the question whether business cycle asymmetries between France, Germany and Italy are temporary or structural.

An interesting approach to determine the causes of the lack of business cycle synchronization between France, Germany and Italy is to focus on the

---

* Useful comments and suggestions by Olivier de Bandt, Gerhard Rünstler and Roberta Zizza are gratefully aknowledged. The usual disclaimer applies.

long run production capacity of the economy and to point out the differences in the estimated potential output among the three countries. Indeed, the identification of factors driving potential growth will allow to structurally explain asymmetries in business cycles from supply-side developments.

In line with Solow's neoclassical model, we use the so-called production function approach in order to estimate potential growth. This methodology relies on an explicit modelling of the production technology such that economic growth is a function of standard factors of production (labour and capital) and an unobservable technological change. The notion of production function seems more appropriate as regards firms than as regards the public sector for instance. Thus, this approach consists in choosing a technical relationship supposed to represent the productive capacity of the economy (productive sector), calibrating key parameters on the basis of the relevant data, determining the level of potential output on the basis of this calibrated function and modelling the resulting Solow residual in order to explain its developments, using econometric techniques. Estimates are extended to the whole economy by introducing, in a second step, the government sector (that we label 'non productive sector'). Nevertheless, it is worth noting that this more sophisticated approach applied to the productive sector implies a higher burden in terms of data requirements. In most cases, several pieces of information are available only for France (*e.g.* productive capital stock, household employment); corresponding series for Germany and Italy have been estimated by introducing assumptions that may be somewhat arbitrary.[2]

Contrary to the standard approach to estimate the long run potential output, we distinguish two horizons, each one being associated with steady-state conditions. First, we consider medium term developments where the contributors to potential growth are the traditionally observed factors (actual capital and labour), as well as Total Factor Productivity (TFP) trend. Second, we analyze the long run steady-path where the economy grows in relation to the evolution of the long term trend of the labour force and the technology and eventually the ratio between value added prices and investment prices. These relative prices are incorporated in order to take into account, that over the sample, the capital intensity is stable in nominal terms rather than in real terms as often assumed. This separation of horizons will provide useful measures of potential output. Thus, we will be able to give a diagnosis about the position of the economy in the business cycle in both the medium term and the long term, and therefore indicators of inflationary pressures in the medium to long term.

The main result of our investigations is that the medium term potential growth for France and Germany appears to be similar in average over the period 1986-2003, amounting to 2.1% per year. As for Italy, it seems to be outperformed by 0.5 percentage point. Focusing on the determinants of potential growth, results show more contrasted contributors. For both Ger-

---

[2] See Appendix Sections for more details.

many and France potential growth is mainly driven by TFP and non productive sectors; for France also the contribution of capital is slighlty significant. As regards Italy, potential growth is largely explained by capital and
the non productive sectors. In the long term, the potential growth of France
remained roughly constant, close to 2.5% over the sample. In Germany, long
run potential growth reached a plateau of about 3% between 1986 and 1998
and strongly declined to around 2% thereafter. For Italy, long run potential
growth gradually decreased over the period 1986-2003, from 1.5% to 1%.

The structure of the paper is as follows. In Section 2, we present the theoretical framework and lay out the method for estimating potential output.
In Section 3, we discuss the results and some concluding remarks are made
in Section 4. A description of the construction of capital stock series and the
database for the three countries is given in the Appendix.

2 Theoretical framework

2.1 General overview

We consider that the production technology in the productive sector of one
economy can be represented by a Cobb-Douglas production function with
constant return to scale on labour and capital. Analytically, the production
function can be expressed in logarithms as follows:

$$q_t = (1 - \alpha)k_t + \alpha l_t + g_t,$$

where q_t, k_t and l_t are, respectively, the real value added, the stock of productive capital and the labour input (measured in hours worked) in the productive sector, α ($0 < \alpha < 1$) represents the wage share in the value added of
the productive sector and g_t is Total Factor Productivity.

The other gross domestic product (GDP) components, namely value added of households, non profit institutions serving households (NPISH), public administrations and institutions and indirect taxes net of subsidies are
smoothed by means of an Hodrick-Prescott (HP) filter and then added to the
potential value added of the productive sector to build up the potential GDP
of the whole economy.

A two-step approach is adopted. First, the labour share is set at its average level over the sample to define the TFP, as the Solow residual of the
neoclassical model:

$$g_t = q_t - (1 - \alpha)k_t - \alpha l_t.$$

Second, following de Bandt and Rousseaux (2002), the impacts of the determinants of TFP, around a time trend, are estimated using the following
specification:

$$g_t = \gamma_0 + \gamma_1 g_{t-1} + \gamma_2 t + \gamma_3(cur_t - \overline{cur}) + \gamma_4(\tau_t - \bar{\tau}) + \gamma_5 \tilde{t} + \varepsilon_t, \qquad (1)$$

where cur_t is the capacity utilisation rate (CUR), in logs, and $\overline{cur}$ is the corresponding average level, τ_t is the age of the capital stock of equipment goods, in logs, and $\bar{\tau}$ is the corresponding average level. ε_t is an error term.

The deterministic trend t is considered assuming that the technical change is exogenous so that TFP grows at a constant rate. The term $\tilde{t} = \mathbb{I}(t > t^*)(t - t^*)$ is introduced in order to capture a possible country-specific break in the rate of change at date t^*.[3] γ_3 measures the cyclical component of the TFP. We expect that TFP grows as the domestic production capacities are used more intensively than usual, so the parameter γ_3 should be positive. Moreover, an ageing stock of capital as compared to its average age, could impact negatively on the TFP such that the parameter γ_4 should be negative. Finally, an autoregressive term is introduced to capture inertia in TFP changes. The break in trend is omitted in the two following subsections ($\gamma_5 = 0$).[4]

2.2 Medium term developments

Total Factor Productivity

Uncovering the TFP trend in the medium run requires two assumptions. First, we assume that the growth rate of the TFP, ρ, is constant. This rate is estimated by the average growth rate over the period. Second, the capacity utilisation rate is assumed to be at its average level so that the gap between cur_t and $\overline{cur}$ is null.

From the first assumption, we can write medium run TFP (in logs) as $\tilde{g}_t = \tilde{g}_{t-1} + \rho$. So,

$$\tilde{g}_t = \tilde{g}_{t-1} + \rho = \gamma_0 + \gamma_1 \tilde{g}_{t-1} + \gamma_2(t - 1 + 1) + \gamma_4(\tau_t - \bar{\tau}),$$

$$(1 - \gamma_1)\tilde{g}_{t-1} = (\gamma_0 - \rho + \gamma_2) + \gamma_2(t - 1) + \gamma_4(\tau_t - \bar{\tau}),$$

which gives the following period:

$$(1 - \gamma_1)\tilde{g}_t = (\gamma_0 - \rho + \gamma_2) + \gamma_2 t + \gamma_4(\tau_{t+1} - \bar{\tau}).$$

This last equation defines the medium term TFP:

$$\tilde{g}_t = \frac{\gamma_0 - \rho + \gamma_2}{1 - \gamma_1} + \frac{\gamma_2}{1 - \gamma_1} t + \frac{\gamma_4}{1 - \gamma_1}(\tau_{t+1} - \bar{\tau}). \tag{2}$$

In the medium run, the TFP evolves around a trend and a measure of capital ageing. We assume that inflexions due to capital stock ageing or replacement sluggishly disappear at a slower pace than those caused by CUR variations. These inflexions impact on TFP and last over the medium term. However, the effect of capital ageing vanishes in the long run.

---

[3] The indicator function $\mathbb{I}(.)$ is defined as $\mathbb{I}(A) = 1$ if A is true and $\mathbb{I}(A) = 0$ otherwise.

[4] See Section 3.

Labour input

After computing the medium term TFP, we have to estimate potential labour input. As we consider labour input in hours worked, we first smooth hours worked, h_t. The potential employment in the productive sector is defined by:

$$N_t^* = \Omega_t^* r_t^* (1 - u_t^*) - (N_t^{H*} + N_t^{P*} + N_t^{\text{NPISH}*}), \tag{3}$$

where N_t^{H*}, N_t^{P*} and $N_t^{\text{NPISH}*}$ are respectively smoothed series of employment in household sector, public sector and NPISH sector. Ω_t^*, r_t^* and u_t^* represent respectively the filtered working age population, the filtered medium term participation rate and the non-accelerating inflation rate of unemployment (NAIRU). In order to derive smoothed components, the HP filter has been always used, with standard value for the smoothing parameter ($\lambda = 1600$, since we are dealing with quarterly data, except for the hours worked – where $\lambda = 20000$ – and the NAIRU (see appendix for sources)).[5]

As regards levels, in the medium term, potential real value added in the productive sector is given by:

$$Q_t^{prod*} = K_t^{(1-\alpha)} (N_t^* h_t^*)^{\alpha} e^{\tilde{g}_t}. \tag{4}$$

Then, we add contributions to GDP from the other sectors as well as net indirect taxes to construct the potential GDP Y_t^* of the whole economy:

$$Y_t^* = Q_t^{prod*} + Q_t^{H*} + Q_t^{P*} + Q_t^{\text{NPISH}*} + T_t^*, \tag{5}$$

where Q_t^{H*}, Q_t^{P*} and $Q_t^{\text{NPISH}*}$ are the filtered value added series respectively of households, of the public sector and of NPISH, and T_t^* the filtered series of net indirect taxes. These series are smoothed with an HP filter ($\lambda = 1600$).

Contributions to potential growth

We first define the quarterly year-on-year growth rate of potential GDP by:

$$g_{Y^*,t} = \frac{Y_t^*}{Y_{t-4}^*} - 1.$$

Then we specify the share of the potential GDP associated to the non-productive sectors and taxation as:

$$\theta_t = \frac{Q_t^{H*} + Q_t^{P*} + Q_t^{\text{NPISH}*} + T_t^*}{Y_t^*}.$$

So, the contribution of the capital stock of the productive sector to whole economy potential GDP growth is given by:

---

[5] We choose a non-standard value for the smoothing parameter related to hours worked in order to eliminate any cyclical evolution of filtered data.

$$\sigma_{K,t} = (1-\alpha)(1-\theta_{t-4})g_K,$$

with g_K the year-on-year growth rate of capital stock.

In the same way, the following equation defines the contribution to potential growth of employment in the productive sector:

$$\sigma_{N^*h^*,t} = \alpha(1-\theta_{t-4})g_{N^*h^*},$$

where g_{N^*} is the growth rate of potential employment in the productive sector.

The contribution of the non-productive sectors can be written as follows:

$$\sigma_{Q^{\text{NPS}},t} = \theta_{t-4}g_{Q^{\text{NPS}}},$$

where $g_{Q^{\text{NPS}}}$ is the growth rate of the value added of the non-productive sectors ($Q^{\text{NPS}} = \theta_t Y_t^*$).

Since changes in the age of the capital stock around its average level are taken into account to model TFP, two terms define the TFP's contribution. The first one consists in the contribution of the time trend as in equation (2):

$$\sigma_{trend} = 4(1-\theta_{t-4})\frac{\gamma_2}{1-\gamma_1}.$$

As original series are expressed on a quarterly frequency, a coefficient 4 is introduced to measure annual contribution. The second term represents the contribution of the age of the capital stock:

$$\sigma_{\tau,t} = (1-\theta_{t-4})g_{\tilde{\tau}},$$

with $g_{\tilde{\tau}}$ the year-on-year growth rate of $\tilde{\tau}$ which is given by:

$$\tilde{\tau} = \exp(\frac{\gamma_4}{1-\gamma_1}(\tau_t - \bar{\tau})).$$

Thus, the total contribution of the TFP can be written as follows:

$$\sigma_{\text{TFP},t} = \sigma_{trend,t} + \sigma_{\tau,t}.$$

Finally, we obtain the following breakdown in contributions to whole economy potential GDP growth, which will be analyzed in section 3.2:

$$g_{Y^*,t} = \sigma_{K,t} + \sigma_{N^*h^*,t} + \sigma_{Q^{\text{NPS}},t} + \sigma_{\text{TFP},t}. \qquad (6)$$

2.3 Long run developments

In the long run, we impose several additional assumptions. First, the age of the capital stock tends towards its average level, leading us to disregard the contribution of age to potential growth.[6] Then, we consider that employment and potential value added of the non-productive sectors grow at the same rate as in the productive sector. Moreover, we set the participation rate r_t^*, NAIRU u_t^* and the worked hours h_t to their average level. Finally, we assume that the output/capital ratio is stable in nominal terms over all the sample.[7] This last assumption drives us to consider the following equation:

$$\frac{p_{q,t} Q_t^{prod}}{p_{I,t} K_t} = \zeta, \tag{7}$$

where $p_{q,t}$ and $p_{I,t}$ are respectively the value added and investment deflators in the productive sector and ζ is a constant. As we can see in Fig. 1, this stylized fact is met for France and Italy but could be less relevant in the case of Germany.

Combining equations (4) in logs and the definition of TFP in (2), we find:[8]

$$\Delta_4 q_t^{prod\,*} = (1 - \alpha)\Delta_4 k_t + \alpha \Delta_4 n_t^* + 4\frac{\gamma_2}{1 - \gamma_1}. \tag{8}$$

Moreover, according to equation (7), we have:

$$\Delta_4 k_t = \Delta_4 q_t^{prod\,*} + \Delta_4 \ln\left(\frac{p_{Q,t}}{p_{I,t}}\right). \tag{9}$$

As productive and non-productive sectors are growing at the same rate, the long term potential GDP growth is given by substituting (9) in (8):

$$g_{Y^*,t}^{lt} = \Delta_4 q_t^{prod\,*} = \frac{(1 - \alpha)}{\alpha}\Delta_4 \ln\left(\frac{p_{Q,t}}{p_{I,t}}\right) + \Delta_4 n_t^{prod\,*} + \frac{1}{\alpha}\frac{4\gamma_2}{1 - \gamma_1}.$$

Furthermore, as the participation rate, the time-varying NAIRU and the worked hours are supposed to be constant in the long run, the annual growth rate of potential employment is given by variations in working age population. As a consequence, the potential GDP growth in the long run is given by:

$$g_{Y^*,t}^{lt} = g_{\Omega^*,t} + \frac{1}{\alpha}\frac{4\gamma_2}{1 - \gamma_1} + \frac{(1 - \alpha)}{\alpha}\Delta_4 \ln\left(\frac{p_{Q,t}}{p_{I,t}}\right). \tag{10}$$

The growth rate of the economy is driven by the growth rate of the population $g_{\Omega^*,t}$, the value of the trend of TFP and the drift in relative prices. It is worthwhile to mention that the TFP trend contributes differently to the potential growth depending on the time horizon: as we assumed that the

---

[6] We can show that on a balanced growth path, the age of the capital stock corresponds to the inverse of the depreciation rate plus the growth rate of the economy.

[7] See Jorgenson and Stiroh (1999), Cette et al. (2005) for more details.

[8] Δ_4 operator is defined by $\Delta_4 x_t = x_t - x_{t-4}$ and corresponds to the year-on-year growth rate of variable X_t.

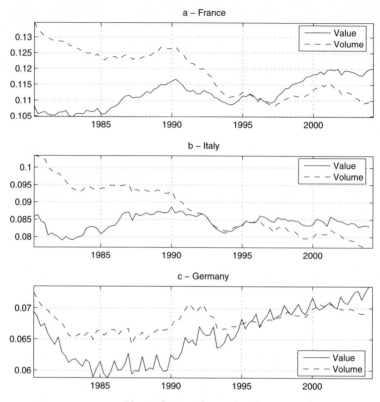

Fig. 1. Output/capital ratio

economy evolves on its steady growth path in the long run, the contribution of TFP corresponds analytically to the trend divided by the share of labour, which is lower than one. As a result, the contribution of TFP appears higher in the long run than in the medium term.[9]

3 Results and comparative estimates

3.1 Estimates for the TFP

Before estimating the TFP components, the parameter α is set to the sample average share of wages in value added for the productive sector. The resulting values of α for France, Germany and Italy are respectively 0.72, 0.74 and 0.65. Fig. 2 represents the resulting estimates of TFP for the three countries.

---

[9] We could have avoided the introduction of α in the expression of the long run GDP growth by considering the TFP as a Harrod-neutral technological change.

One of the advantages of this method lies in its homogeneity that allows to obtain comparable levels of TFP. Taking capital and labour as given, we are therefore able to distinguish the economies according to their productive performance. Furthermore, these first results suggest that during the period 1980-1999, Italy has the higher level of TFP among the three countries, before being caught up by Germany and then France in the last years of the sample.

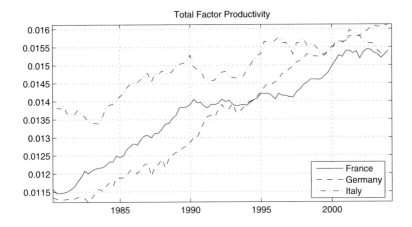

Fig. 2. Estimated level of TFP, $\exp(\tilde{g})$

Estimations by Ordinary Least Squares (OLS) of the TFP parameters of regression (1) are presented in Table 1 for each country.[10] All coefficients are

Table 1. Estimations of the TFP for the three countries

Country	γ_0	γ_1	γ_2	γ_3	γ_4	γ_5
	intercept	g_{t-1}	t	$cur_t - \overline{cur}$	$\tau_t - \bar{\tau}$	$\tilde{t}$
France	-1.6136	0.6365	0.0011	0.1621	-0.1638	-
	(0.3259)	(0.0732)	(0.0002)	(0.0296)	(0.0595)	
Germany	-0.7667	0.8292	0.0007	0.0478	-	-
	(0.2380)	(0.0527)	(0.0002)	(0.0206)		
Italy	-0.6240	0.8531	1.36E-4	0.0991	-	-
	(0.2393)	(0.0561)	(7.81E-5)	(0.0416)		

In parenthesis are given the estimated standard errors.

---

[10] In order to obtain economically meaningful estimated coefficients, the estimation period for France and Germany runs from 1986Q1 to 2003Q4, whereas for Italy it begins in 1980Q1.

significant. The signs of estimated parameters are consistent with our expectations: coefficients are positive for the trend and the capacity utilisation rate, negative for the age-gap. In order to uncover potential breaks in TFP equation (1), we carried out the Bai-Perron (1998) test. This procedure allows both to test the number of multiple unknown structural changes and to estimate the location of the breaks. As a result, no break was found for each of the three countries whatever the variable assumed to have a time-varying impact on TFP, according to the Bai-Perron terminology.

Concerning the estimation of parameter related to age of capital, France only presents a significant contribution of this variable. According to the definition of medium term TFP in equation (2), a one-year younger equipment capital stock, which corresponds to a decrease by about 14.3% for an average of 7 years, leads to an increase of the TFP growth rate by approximatively 6.4 points. This assessment is quite close in terms of magnitude to other estimates in the literature.[11]

As regards the trends, our estimates correspond to medium term growth rate of 1.2%, 1.6% and 0.4%, respectively for France, Germany and Italy. The difference between Italy and the other countries seems to be a potential source of structural gap in productivity.

3.2 Potential growth and contributions in the medium term

The following table (Tab. 2) shows the different contributions resulting from equation (10) of each component of potential output from 1986 to 2003 for France, Germany and Italy. In the period 1986-2003, the average annual growth rate of potential output is 2.1% for France and Germany, and 1.6% for Italy. As regards the results for France, the main contributor to potential growth appears to be related to the non productive sectors (public sector, households and NPISH) and reaches 0.9 percentage point over the period. Contribution of labour in the productive sector is insignificant and the stock of capital and TFP contribute positively by respectively 0.5 percentage point and 0.7 percentage point. Concerning Germany, potential growth is mainly driven by the TFP with 1.3 pp of contribution. The contributions of capital (0.3 percentage point), labour in the productive sector (-0.2 percentage point) and the other sectors (0.6 percentage point) are the lowest among the three countries. For Italy, Tab. 2 shows the large contribution of the non productive sectors (0.8 percentage point) to potential growth. The contribution of capital is the highest among the three countries and amounts to 0.7 percentage point. Labour in the productive sector contributes negatively by -0.1 percentage point to the potential growth. At this stage, TFP appears to be the most striking factor to distinguish between France, Germany and Italy in terms of potential growth. Figure 3 depicts the country-specific time-series profile

---

[11] Based on different approach and samples, Cette and Szpiro (1989) assess this impact to 3.6 points.

Table 2. Contributions to the average potential growth rate from 1986 to 2003 in percentage

Period	pot. growth	capital	labour	others	TFP[(*)]
		France			
1986 to 1989	2.1	0.6	-0.1	0.8	0.8
1990 to 1994	1.9	0.5	-0.2	1.0	0.6
1995 to 1999	1.9	0.4	-0.0	1.0	0.6
2000 to 2003	2.5	0.5	0.3	0.8	1.0
1986 to 2003	2.1	0.5	-0.0	0.9	0.7
		Germany			
1986 to 1989	2.3	0.5	-0.3	0.7	1.4
1990 to 1994	2.4	0.4	-0.0	0.6	1.4
1995 to 1999	1.9	0.2	-0.2	0.5	1.4
2000 to 2003	1.7	0.2	-0.4	0.5	1.4
1986 to 2003	2.1	0.3	-0.2	0.6	1.4
		Italy			
1986 to 1989	1.9	0.8	-0.3	1.1	0.3
1990 to 1994	1.6	0.7	-0.3	0.9	0.3
1995 to 1999	1.7	0.5	-0.0	0.9	0.3
2000 to 2003	1.4	0.7	0.2	0.3	0.3
1986 to 2003	1.6	0.7	-0.1	0.8	0.3

(*) Including age of capital for France.

of the main components of potential growth in the medium term. From this figure, we can also notice that a marked decrease in medium term potential growth took place in the middle of the 1990s. Thus, there remains at this horizon some cyclical patterns, for example the contraction of 1993-1994 in Europe.

3.3 Potential growth and contributions in the long run

Figure 4 presents the country-specific time-series profile of the main components of potential growth in the long run, derived from equation (10).

In the long term, potential growth in France stayed roughly around the level of 2.5% over the sample. The relative price drift explains part of the decrease in potential growth, this effect being of structural nature. In Germany, long run potential growth remained around 3% between 1986 and the sec-

172 Mustapha Baghli, Christophe Cahn, and Jean-Pierre Villetelle

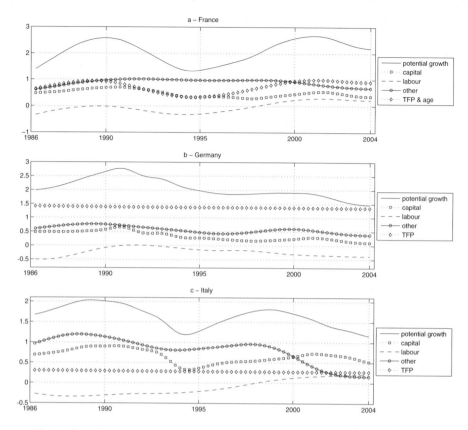

Fig. 3. Contributions to the medium term potential growth, percentage points

ond quarter of 1991, and then gradually diminished until reaching 2.2% in 2003. For Italy, long run potential growth gradually declined over the period 1986-2003, from 1.5% to 1%. This decrease is largely linked to the gradual reduction in potential employment over the period. For this country, the difference with medium term growth is explained by the discrepancy in real value added growth between the productive sector and the non productive sectors.

4 Concluding remarks

The analysis of output growth in the three major euro area economies undertaken in this paper suggests that in the medium term, France and Germany experienced an identical average potential output growth over the last 20 years. Italy stands out as the country witnessing a slower growth. All three countries benefited, albeit to different extents, from the buoyant contribu-

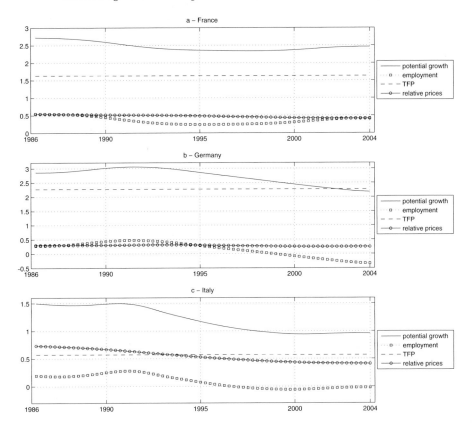

Fig. 4. Contributions to the long run potential growth, percentage points

tion of non-productive sectors over the period. In contrast to Italy, the contribution of TFP to the potential output growth in France and Germany was found clearly significant. In France and Germany, the contribution of capital appears to be weak, whereas in Italy this factor contributes at a higher and steady level over the sample. Over the 2000-2003 period, however, potential growth decreased in Germany and Italy while it increased in France. In the long term, the growth divergences between these economies tend to disappear, especially between France and Germany since the long term pace of growth is estimated at about 2 to 2.5% for both countries. For Italy, the long run potential growth amounts to 1% at the end of the sample and leads to the conclusion that weak Italian output developments over the period as compared to the two other countries comes from structural sources.

An interpretation of these divergent growths which prevail in the three major euro area economies, may be, besides the differences in economic performances, the differing macroeconomic policies. Moreover, although a comprehensive discussion of these mechanisms is out of the scope of the paper, microeconomic studies would potentially allow to evaluate to which extent factors such as the adoption of the information and communication technology, the sector-level labour cost, firm-level tax burden or the impact of R&D intensity affect the engine of economic growth. Moreover, this microeconomic approach should permit to model together the three countries within a panel data framework.

Another interesting way of research would be to focus on the non-productive sectors in order to better distinguish the sources of differences and their impacts on the economy. If some gaps are found, this would be extremely informative for the medium and long term diagnosis on the convergence of European economies.

References

Baghli M., V. Brunhes-Lesage, O. De Bandt, H. Fraisse and J.-P. Villetelle (2004) "Modèle d'Analyse et de préviSion de la COnjoncture TrimesTriellE". NOTE D'ÉTUDES ET DE RECHERCHE DE LA BANQUE DE FRANCE n°106, february 2004 (http://www.banque-france.fr/fr/publi/main.htm).

Bai J. and P. Perron (1998) "Estimating and Testing Linear Models with Multiple Structural Changes". *Econometrica*, 66(1), 47-78, January.

Bandt (de) O. and P. Rousseaux (2002) "Estimation du PIB potentiel et de l'écart par la méthode structurelle". In "PIB potentiel et écart de PIB : quelques évaluations pour la France". NOTE D'ÉTUDES ET DE RECHERCHE DE LA BANQUE DE FRANCE n°89, july 2002 (http://www.banque-france.fr/fr/publi/main.htm).

Cette G., S. Garcia and J.-P. Villetelle (2003) "La croissance potentielle de moyen-long terme de l'économie française". Banque de France, SEMEP, Internal Document No. m04-099.

Cette G., J. Mairesse and Y. Kocoglu (2005) "ICT diffusion and potential output growth". *Economics Letters*, 87(2), 231-234, May.

Cette G. and D. Szpiro (1989) "Une interprétation du ralentissement de la productivité industrielle au moment du second choc pétrolier". *Économie et Prévision*, No. 87, 33-42.

Coen R. (1980) "Depreciation, Profits, and Rates of Return in Manufacturing Industries." *in The Measurement of Capital,Studies in Income and Wealth*, Vol. 45, 121-152, edited by Dan Usher, University of Chicago Press, for the National Bureau of Economic Research.

Fraumeni B.M. (1997) "The Measurement of Depreciation in the U.S. National Income and Product Account", *Survey of Current Business*, No. 77, 7-23.

Giorno C., P. Richardson, D. Roseveare and P. van den Noord (1995) "Potential Output, Output Gaps and Structural Budget Balances". OECD Economics Studies n24, OECD Economics Department.

Jorgenson D. and K. Stiroh (1999) "Productivity Growth: Current Recovery and Longer-Term trend". *The American Economic Review*, 89(2), 109-15, May.

Maddison A. (1993) "Essays on innovation Natural Resources and the International Economy, Standardized Estimates of Fixed Capital Stock: a six country comparison". Innovazione E Materie Prime, April 1993, 1-29.

OECD (2001) "Measuring Capital. A manual on the Measurement of Capital Stocks, Consumption of Fixed Capital and capital Services", September 2001.

Triplett J.E. (1997) "Concepts of Capital for Production Accounts and for Wealth Accounts: The Implications for Statistical Programs." Paper presented at the *International Conference on Capital Stock Statistics*, Canberra, Australia, March 10-14.

Turner D., P. Richardson and S. Rauffet (1996) "Modelling the Supply Side of the Seven Major OECD Economies". Economics Department Working Papers n167, OECD Economics Department.

Villetelle J.-P. (2002) "Construction de séries de capital pour la base de données du modèle réel". Banque de France, SEMEP, note m02-003.

A Appendix : Construction of capital stock time series

Capital stock data are very dependent on the methodology adopted by national statistical institutes and can vary subsequently across countries.

In the framework of this paper, we propose to use capital stock series built according to a methodology elaborated by Villetelle (2002) for France. This methodology, which uses as input only national account data on the average service life of capital goods (equipment and buildings), is easy to implement. Based on the perpetual inventory method (PIM), it requires however long investment time series. In addition to making capital stock data more comparable, this method uses an age-efficiency profile which has the advantage of defining a *productive* capital stock which is more relevant for the estimation of potential growth by a structural approach. This appendix describes the different steps required to get the *underlying* capital stock on the basis of a minimum number of assumptions. The result is nevertheless not easily tractable. In particular the *underlying* capital stock yields a non-constant depreciation rate δ_t.

The approach that we suggest is then based on a geometric approximation of the law of motion of capital:

$$K_t = I_t + (1 - \delta)K_{t-1} = (1 - \delta)^t K_0 + \sum_{j=0}^{t}(1 - \delta)^j I_{t-j}. \tag{11}$$

We calibrate the constant depreciation rate δ that locally better approximates for the best the profile of the *underlying* capital stock.

Table 3 gives the final output. The initial capital stock is estimated by fitting the geometric law of motion to the *underlying* capital stock for the final part of the sample.[12]

Table 3. Average duration of capital and depreciation rate

Equipments		Constr. excl. Housing		Housing	
Deprec. rate (%)	Average duration (years)	Deprec. rate (%)	Average duration (years)	Deprec. rate (%)	Average duration (years)
9.50	10.5	1.50	66.7	1.00	90.9

A.1 Main ingredients

Different definitions of capital stock are possible. We concentrate on the concept of *productive* capital, but define before gross and net capital. The gross capital stock measured at date t is the sum of past investment (from $t = 0$ to $t = T$, *i.e.* until maximum lifetime) weighted by survival probabilities. Each investment flow is valued at *as new* prices regardless of the age and actual condition of the assets:

$$K_t^G = \sum_{i \geq 0} s_i I_{t-i},$$

with K_t^G indicating the gross capital stock at the date t at the base year price, I_t the investment flows between $t - 1$ and t at the base year price and s_i the survival rate at t of past investment made between $t - i - 1$ and $t - i$.

The net capital stock measured at the date t takes into account the *consumption of fixed capital* defined as the decline, during the course of the accounting period, in the current value of the stock of fixed assets as a result of physical deterioration, normal obsolescence or normal accidental damage.

$$K_t^N = \sum_{i \geq 0} \nu_i I_{t-i},$$

with K_t^N indicating the net capital stock t at the base year price and ν_i the valuation of an i-period asset over its remaining duration life valuation at the base year price.

We introduce the concept of *productive* capital which allows us to take into account a decreasing efficiency of surviving assets over the time.

---

[12] Actually, the depreciation rate δ is taken as the average depreciation rate on the period for which the capital stock can be computed, given that data for investment are required for T periods, where T, to be defined thereafter, is the maximum lifetime.

$$K_t^P = \sum_{i \geq 0} s_i e_i I_{t-i}, \tag{12}$$

with K_t^P the productive capital stock t at the base year price, s_i the survival rate at t of a i-period asset and e_i the efficiency of a i-period old asset.

That way, in addition to the survival function used for the gross capital stock, we use an other rule indicating how investment efficiency decreases over age (age-efficiency profile).

A.2 Specific assumptions on mortality and efficiency over time

Mortality function

We use as mortality function a delayed linear function. Delay is arbitrarily set to $1/3$ of the total life duration. The average service life is taken from the national accounts. According to this pattern, the coefficients of the survival function (see Fig. 5a) are:

$$s_i = \begin{cases} 1 & , \ 0 \leq i \leq \frac{T}{3} - 1 \\ 1 - \frac{i - T/3}{T - T/3} & , \ \frac{T}{3} \leq i \leq T \end{cases} ,$$

with T the maximum duration life, defined on the basis of the average duration life M and the above assumptions as the solution of $M = \frac{2}{3}T + \frac{1}{2}$. Figure 5b draws the mortality function, which represents the probability density function of age.

Age-efficiency profile

In line with some statistical offices, we choose for the age-efficiency profile an hyperbolic shape in order to have a decreasing with age and time-invariant function (see Fig. 5c):

$$e_i = \frac{T - 1 - i}{T - 1 - \beta i}.$$

We used $\beta = 0.5$ for machinery and equipments, $\beta = 0.75$ for both buildings and housing. This is relatively standard in the literature.[13] The combination of both the mortality of assets and the decrease in efficiency over their lifetime gives the patterns illustrated by Figure 5d.

---

[13] Same values are used by the US Bureau of Labor Statistics and the Australian Bureau of Statistics for the age-efficiency profile.

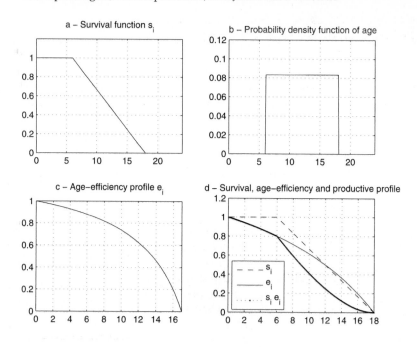

Fig. 5. Specific assumptions on mortality and efficiency

A.3 Computation of capital stock for Germany

For Germany, we computed the capital stock data using the method described above and national accounts series at an annual frequency provided by the Bundesbank. The investment data used are in real terms and correspond to the investments in Machinery and Equipments (ME) and investments in Building excluding Housing (BeH).

In order to construct an investment data set for Germany, we first applied the West German growth rate to the total German investment series (both ME and BeH) from 1990 to 1970 backwards.

Second, for getting longer series on investment, we used the historical series on fixed capital stock (gross stock of non-residential structures and gross stock of ME) constructed by Maddison (1993). We backcasted the two total German investment series (ME and BeH) available from 1970 to 2003 with the preceding series (available respectively from 1920 to 1990 and 1880 to 1990) and obtained two total German investment (BeH and ME) series that runs from 1920 to 2003 and 1880 to 2003 respectively.

Concerning the question of calibrating the PIM, we used the same assumptions as for France. The maximal duration of the capital for ME was set to 18 years and 75 years for BeH. These assumptions are not prejudicial since in a document from the OECD (2001), it appears that the average durations for ME and BeH correspond respectively to 12 and 52 years, *i.e.* to the maximal duration of the capital 17.3 years and 77.3 years. As for the depreciation rate, we selected the ones used for France, at an annual frequency 1.5% and 9.5% respectively for BeH and ME. Following these assumptions, we obtained two stocks of productive capital, one associated to investments in BeH and the other to investments in ME, the sum of these two components gives the stock of productive capital for the productive sector in Germany.

A.4 Computation of capital stock for Italy

For Italy, we could not fully compute the capital stock data using the method suggested in the previous subsections since the data set (national accounts series at an annual frequency) are too short and no investment data set is available for Italy in Maddison (1993). The remaining solution consisted therefore in computing stock of capital from a geometric approximation of the mortality law of capital. In order to calculate this geometric approximation, we used the same assumptions as for France.

Since we had at our disposal an investment series for BeH only from 1970 and an investment series for Total Buildings (TB) from 1951, we constructed an investment series for BeH by taking the average share of BeH in TB from 1970 to 2003 and by applying this average share to TB from 1951 to 1969. We obtained then an investment series for BeH only from 1951 to 2003.

In order to initialize our model, we needed an initial stock of capital $K_{t_0}^P$ (for both BeH and ME). In order to circumvent this concern, we computed this initial stock of capital so that the GDP/capital stock ratio for Italy is identical as the one for France:

$$\frac{K_{t_0}^{P,FR}}{GDP_{t_0}^{FR}} = \frac{K_{t_0}^{P,ITA}}{GDP_{t_0}^{ITA}},$$

with $t_0 = 1950$ and for both investments in BeH and ME.

The GDP figures came from Maddison (1993) ($GDP_{1950}^{ITA} = 164957$ and $GDP_{1950}^{FR} = 220492$ in millions of dollar). Following these assumptions, we obtained two stocks of capital, one associated to investments in BeH and the other to investments in ME, the sum of these two components gives the stock of productive capital for the productive sector in Italy.

B Data appendix

The purpose of this section is to precisely explain how the database used has been built so as to be consistent with the proposed method of estimation.

The productive sector can be identified with the non financial (NFC), financial (FC) and individual (IC) corporations, as defined in the national accounts. It is a distinct concept from the private sector, since the latter is related to the whole economy excluding the public sector. The other sectors of the economy are households, public institutions and NPISH. All available data are taken from the National Statistical Institutes.

Nevertheless, the degree of details varies across countries. In particular, National Accounts in Germany and Italy do not publish the breakdown of macroeconomic indicators (value added, deflators, prices, *etc*...) and production factors (employment, stock of capital, *etc*...) by institutional sector. This breakdown is reconstructed here, based on strong assumptions. It is worthwhile to note that these approximations are necessary in order to keep aggregation consistency.

Before going into the details of the country-specific calculations for France, Germany and Italy, we first present the common calculations performed on the series.

B.1 Common calculations

Households

The series for household employment, N_t^H, is directly available for France, but not for the other countries. An average number of persons employed by French households, $\bar{\nu}_t$ is computed by dividing this series by the number of households H_t^{FRA}:

$$\bar{\nu}_t = \frac{N_t^{H^{\text{FRA}}}}{H_t^{\text{FRA}}}.$$

On a yearly basis, the hypothesis is made that this result also holds for Germany and Italy. Multiplying the average number of persons employed by households by the number of households in each of these countries:

$$N_t^{H^i} = \bar{\nu}_t H_t^i, \quad i \in \{\text{GER,ITA}\},$$

gives an estimate of employment in households' sector for Germany and Italy which is presented in Figure 6a.

This computation requires a long series of annual number of households for each country H_t^i, $i \in \{\text{FRA,GER,ITA}\}$. This is performed by back-dating H_t^i, $i \in \{\text{FRA,GER,ITA}\}$ by means of population series including the number of people between 25 and 64 years. This number stems from the Eurostat website with some official figures as starting points. Still as regards official data, the other sources are the German Federal Ministry of Health and Social Security[14] for Germany and the Mission for Digital Economy of the French Ministry of Finance for Italy and France.[15] Figure 6b shows the calculated number of households for the three countries.

We employ the same method to approximate the households' real value added, Q_t^H. As such data is directly available for France, we used it in order

---

[14] http://www.gbe-bund.de/.

[15] http://www.men.minefi.gouv.fr/webmen/informations/tabord/indi/meth/meth.htm.

to compute a series of value added per household, and is then multiplied by the number of German and Italian households, H_t^i, which is still computed as above. Figure 6c shows the estimated real value added of households in millions of euros.

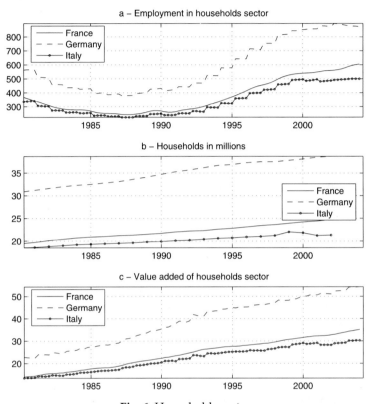

Fig. 6. Households sector

Public sector

Employment in the public sector N_t^P is computed by subtracting the employment in the private sector from total employment. The value added of the public sector, Q_t^P, for Germany and Italy are computed with ratios decomposing the gross value added according to its components as a percentage of GDP. These ratios are taken from the Eurostat website. For the sake of simplicity, the indirect taxes net of subsidies are added to the value added of public sector. Figures 7a and 7b plot, respectively, the value added, including indirect taxes net of subsidies, and the employment in the public sector.

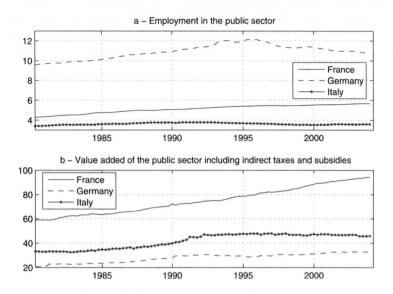

Fig. 7. Public sector

Productive sector

The value added, Q_t^B and the employment N_t^B of the productive sector are obtained by subtracting from the total the public, households, NPISH and fictitious unit[16] components, except for Italy for which data on employment in the productive sector are provided by the Banca d'Italia.

Age of the capital stock

The mean age of the stock of productive capital τ_t is calculated by computing an average age, weighted by the part of each investment I_t, discounted at the corresponding scraping rate δ^{mat}, in the current stock of productive capital[17]. The truncation lag T is chosen so that the rest is negligible:

$$\tau_t = \sum_{i=0}^{T} i \frac{(1 - \delta^{mat})^i I_{t-i}}{K_t}.$$

Labour force, participation rate and NAIRU

To keep the data consistent, the computation of the labour force is based on the whole economy employment and unemployment rate series. Partic-

---

[16] Fictitious unit corresponds to the non-classified sector.

[17] More precisely, τ_t is the age of the stock of productive capital associated to investments in ME.

ipation rate is then calculated with the working age population series. In the medium term, we use the smoothed OECD's measure of time-varying NAIRU (u_t^*) for both Germany and Italy. For France, we used a smoothed version of the NAIRU stemming from the Banque de France's macroeconometric forecasting model for the French economy.[18]

B.2 Country-specific calculations

Germany

Given the lack of data and breaks in time series, mainly due to the reunification, we have performed some simplifications: (i) real value added and employment of German NPISH are supposed to be negligible; (ii) series are back-dated before 1991 using West German data (growth rates); (iii) it turned out that time-series related to employment in the public sector and derived from data in the private sector, presented around 1991 a statistical artefact mainly due to the backdating method. Thus, before 1991, time-series are back-dated with growth rate computed from the difference between employment in the private sector and total employment. After 1991, data are extrapolated by using the growth rate of the ratio $\tilde{N}_t^P = W_t^P / \eta w_t$, where W_t^P is total wages paid by the public sector (available on the Eurostat website), w_t is the compensation per employee for the whole economy and η is a constant. Such a series approximates employment in the public sector.

Italy

The real value added of NPISH is computed with ratios splitting up the gross value added as percentages of GDP. These ratios are taken from the Eurostat website. By assuming that it essentially consists of wages, the employment of NPISH is calculated by dividing the nominal value added by the adjusted compensation per employee.

---

[18] See Baghli et al. (2004).

Part IV

Demand Side

Synchronisation of Cycles: a Demand Side Perspective*

Guido Bulligan

Bank of Italy, Via nazionale 91, Rome, Italy guido.bulligan@bancaditalia.it

Summary. The paper addresses the issue of synchronisation of economic cycles. While the literature has focused on the supply side, we present evidence from a demand side perspective. Using different measures of correlation both in the time and the frequency domain, we find evidence of a high degree of co-movement between GDP national business cycles. Studying the cyclical properties of demand aggregates, we find similar high values of synchronisation only for import and more recently for export variables. Investment series show intermediate values of correlation while consumption cycles are considerably less synchronised. Estimation of unobserved factor models supports these findings. Furthermore, GDP cycles seem to have become more synchronised over time, reflecting a general increase of correlation coefficients among demand components; the uncertainty surrounding point estimates indicates however that results should be taken only as preliminary.

Keywords: euro area business cycles, factor models, spectral analysis.
JEL classification: C22, E32.

1 Introduction

With the introduction of the single European currency, interest has grown on measures of business cycle synchronisation among member countries. On one side, synchronisation of economic fluctuations seems a fundamental prerequisite for an effective Monetary Union. On the other side, interest has grown in understanding the role played by the common monetary policy in harmonising national business cycles. The empirical literature on the subject is vast and varies according to the geographical focus (see for instance, Artis and Zhang (1997), Artis, Krozlig and Toro (1999) for a European focus, Bordo and Helbling (2003) and Canova, Ciccarelli and Ortega (2003) for a wider focus) and the time span. However, common to the literature is the empirical

---

* Useful comments and suggestions by Olivier de Bandt, Sandra Eickmeier, Eric Dubois and Francesco Zollino are gratefully aknowledged. The usual disclaimer applies.

approach: looking at GDP and industrial production series. We think that a deeper understanding of the mechanisms at work in a Monetary Union can be reached by adopting a different point of view which highlights the role played by GDP components. The paper presents, therefore, new evidence on the behaviour of GDP, consumption, private non-residential investment, import, export and inventory over the cycle for the three biggest economies of the Euro area.

The measurement of business cycles is one of the oldest research area in empirical macroeconomics. Since the seminal work by Burns and Mitchell (1946) business cycle analysts have focused on *"expansions occurring at about the same time in many economic activities, followed by similar general recessions, contractions and revivals which merge into the expansion phase of the next cycle; this sequence of changes is recurrent but not periodic..."*. While the NBER approach, stemming from the work of Burns and Mitchell, has drawn attention to fluctuations (expansions and recessions) in the absolute level of economic activity, recent work has proposed a different interpretation of the cycle, defined in terms of deviations of the level of economic activity from its long-term trend. [2] From a methodological point of view, it is this second method, sometimes referred to as "growth-cycle " approach, that is followed in this work. The structure of the paper is as follows: section two presents results based on three different measures of correlation; for each of these, the results for GDP are compared with those for its main components. In section three a common European cycle is estimated and evaluated according to its ability in explaining the variability observed in the data. Section four deals with synchronisation over time. Section five concludes.

2 Synchronisation of cycles

In this section, after a first look at the statistical properties of the data, three measures of synchronisation are presented which highlight different characteristics of the business cycle and represent a robustness check for the results obtained from any single measure.

2.1 Statistical properties of the Data

The data are from quarterly national accounts expressed at constant 1995 prices, converted in euro at fixed parities and cover the period 1970-2004. Consumption (C) refers to households expenditure, Investment (I) refers

---

[2] This approach is better suited than the classical NBER approach to capture the cyclical characteristics of modern economies which often show positive growth rates even during recessions. However one open issue is how to reconcile the differences among cyclical components extracted with different detrending procedures; for a interesting point of view see Canova (1998) and Burnside (1998).

to Private non residential Investment, Import (IMP) (export, EXP) refers to imports (exports) of goods and services to the rest of the world, Inventory (DINV) refers to the contribution of inventory change to GDP growth, net trade (net external demand, NET) to contribution of external demand. German data are backdated before 1991 using West-Germany growth rates. Given a clear upward trend in all series except inventory and net external demand, unit root tests have been performed,[3] to check for non-stationarity. The results do not allow to reject the null hypothesis of non-stationarity; furthermore, the same test indicates that the variables are integrated of order one (Table 1).

Table 1. Unit root test

	Level	1st Difference	O.I.*
Italy			
GDP	-1.9	-7.8	1
C	-1.4	-6.3	1
I	-2.5	-9.7	1
IMP	-3.2	-12.7	1
EXP	-2.2	-15.3	1
France			
GDP	-3.2	-5.4	1
C	-3.1	-5.9	1
I	-2.5	-9.7	1
IMP	-3.2	-7.6	1
EXP	-2.3	-5.8	1
Germany			
GDP	-2.1	-12.1	1
C	-1.6	-14.6	1
I	-1.8	-12.3	1
IMP	-2.1	-12.1	1
EXP	-2.6	-11.8	1

T-Statistics for ADF test. Quarterly data 1970-2004
* Order of Integration

The underlying assumption in the business cycle literature, is that any time series x_t can be expressed as the sum of trend (T), cycle (C), seasonal (S) and irregular (I) (unobserved) components as follows: $x_t = Y + C + S + I$. The trend includes long-term fluctuations both stochastic as well as deterministic,

---

[3] Only GDP, Consumption, Investment, Import and Export series are tested, as contribution to GDP growth from inventory change and net external demand are clearly stationary.

the cycle refers to medium-term systematic fluctuations, the seasonal components refers to oscillations with period shorter than 1.5 year, while the irregular component is the residual of the decomposition. As the components are not observable, to focus on busines cycle fluctuations one needs to assume independence among them and transform the observed series through application of a filter. In this study the above step is accomplished by using different filtering techniques (Baxter and King filter, VAR forecast errors, spectral analysis), which however share the same definition of business cycle as fluctuations with a period between 6 and 32 quarters. Our empirical strategy is the following: first we extract the cyclical component of each series, then we compute different measures of synchronisation. The first one is the correlation coefficient between reference cycles and can be used to assess the length of time two series spend in the same phase (either "expansion" or "recession"): by nature it does not take account of the characteristics of the phase such as duration (time distance between consecutive turning points), and amplitude (gap in the level of activity between peaks and troughs). However, it reflects the similarity in the sequence of turning points. The second one focuses on the role played by shocks affecting the observed correlation among macroeconomic variables. Although no structural interpretation is given to the shocks, this approach allows to measure the correlation at various horizons between them. The third one highlights the role played by waves of similar periodicity in contributing to the variability of the series. It therefore implicitly takes into account all characteristics of the cycle.

2.2 Synchronisation: measure 1. Harding and Pagan (2002)

Given two variable x_t and y_t Harding and Pagan (2002) propose to measure the degree of synchronisation by the correlation coefficient among their respective reference cycle.[4] The reference cycles are represented by two dummy variables S_t^x and S_t^y, which take values one during expansions (defined as the period between troughs and peaks) and values zero during recessions (defined as the period between peaks and troughs in the filtered series). Peaks and troughs can be detected through the turning point algorithm proposed by Bry and Boschan (1971). Having defined the reference cycles, the correlation coefficient can be measured by running the following regression:

$$\sigma_x^{-1} \cdot S_t^x = \alpha_{xy} + \rho_{xy} \cdot S_t^y + \mu_t \tag{1}$$

---

[4] The authors follow the classical NBER approach to business cycle analysis and construct the reference series based on the levels of the variables. Here the series have been previously filtered with the Baxter and King (1994) filter and those fluctuations with period between 6 and 32 quarters retained; the growth-cycle approach is therefore followed. The latter mitigates the problem arising from the fact that only few recessions can be detected when following the NBER approach and therefore tests of synchronisation might be biased in favour of rejecting the null hypothesis of no synchronisation.

where σ_x is the standard deviation of the variable S^x, ρ_{xy} is the estimated correlation coefficient and α_{xy} is a regression constant. Tests for synchronisation can be carried out on the parameter ρ_{xy}. More precisely, a t-test for the null hypothesis that ρ_{xy} equals zero can be performed, provided autocorrelation corrected standard errors are used.[5] Table 2 reports the estimated correlation coefficients obtained by estimating equation (1) for GDP and all demand components for each pair of countries. The correlation coefficient between any GDP pair results positive and significantly different from zero. It ranges from 0.31 between Germany and France to almost the double (0.57) between France and Italy, with that between Italy and Germany in the middle (0.47) (the standard errors indicate however that these differences should not be emphasised[6]). When the main demand components are analysed some differences emerge: correlation is high and significant for import and export series,[7] (non-residential) investment cycles are slightly less (but still positively) correlated, while consumption series are not significantly synchronised.

Table 2. Correlation between reference cycles*

	GDP	C	I	EXP	IMP	NET	DINV
IT-DE	0.5	-0.1	0.3	0.3	0.6	0.1	0.2
	0.1	*0.1*	*0.1*	*0.4*	*0.1*	*0.1*	*0.1*
IT-FR	0.6	0.1	0.4	0.4	0.4	0.1	0.1
	0.1	*0.1*	*0.1*	*0.1*	*0.1*	*0.1*	*0.1*
FR-DE	0.3	0.2	0.3	0.5	0.5	-0.1	0.2
	0.1	*0.1*	*0.1*	*0.1*	*0.1*	*0.1*	*0.1*
Average	**0.5**	**0.1**	**0.4**	**0.4**	**0.5**	**0.0**	**0.2**

Estimates of ρ_{xy} over period 1972:Q1 2002:Q2
*Cycles obtained by using Baxter and King filter
Newey and West (1987) corrected standard deviations in italics

2.3 Synchronisation: measure 2. Engle (1993) and den Haan (2000)

The second measure of synchronisation has been advocated by Engle (1993) in a study of real exchange rates and relative prices as well as by den Haan

---

[5] For instance Newey and West (1987) provide heteroskedasticity and autocorrelation consistent covariance matrix.

[6] To have a feeling for the magnitudes, the same statistic has been calculated with respect to US GDP and the Rest of Euro Area (REA) GDP. On average (average over values for Italy, France and Germany), the correlation with the US reference cycles is zero while that with the Rest of Euro Area (REA) is 0.5.

[7] However when net export are considered the correlation coefficients drop considerably.

(2000) working on price and output dynamics. More recently, Camacho et alii (2004) proposed to study the business cycle properties of industrial production series across different European countries. The measure is the correlation coefficient between pairs of k-step-ahead-forecast errors as determined by estimation of two variable Vector Auto Regressions. The main advantage of such an approach is to distinguish between short-run and long-run correlation coefficients and therefore to evaluate the role played by shocks (or innovations) at different horizons.[8] Formally, let us consider the vector $Z_t(2 \times 1)$ of the variables x_t and y_t and let us assume the following specification:

$$Z_t = c + \sum_{j=1}^{t} A_j \cdot Z_{t-j} + \varepsilon_t \tag{3}$$

where A_j is a (2×2) matrix of regression coefficients, P is the number of lags and ε_t are serially uncorrelated errors. The k-period ahead forecast error (FE_t^k) is

$$FE_t^k = Z_{t+k} - E_t[Z_{t+k}] = \sum_{j=0}^{k-1} \Theta_j \cdot \varepsilon_{t+k-j} \tag{4}$$

where $E_t[Z_{t+k}]$ is the k-period ahead forecast based on information available up to time t and Θ_j may be obtained recursively from

$$\Theta_j = \sum_{i=1}^{P} A_i \cdot \Theta'_{j-1}; \Theta_0 = I; \ \Theta_j = 0 \ j < 0 \tag{5}$$

The covariance matrix of the k-step-ahead forecast errors becomes therefore

$$E_t \left(FE_t^k \cdot FE_t^k \right) = \sum_{j=0}^{k-1} \Theta_j \cdot \Theta'_{j-1} \tag{6}$$

Finally, the correlation between forecast errors will be given by the ratio between element (2,1) of the previous matrix and the product of the two estimated standard deviations (from the diagonal elements (1,1) and (2,2)).

In this application x_t and y_t represent stationary transformations of the series of GDP and its component for each pair of countries (all series have been transformed into percentage rate of growth, except in the case of net

---

[8] Suppose x_t follows a AR(1) process

$$x_t = \alpha x_{t-1} + \varepsilon_t \tag{2}$$

and $y_t = \varepsilon_t$, where ε_t is a iid stochastic disturbance with zero mean and variance σ_ε^2 and $\alpha < 1$. The correlation between 1-period-ahead forecast errors for variables x_t and y_t will be 1, reflecting the fact that both processes share the same innovation; correlation at longer horizon will instead be lower, reflecting the (increasing) role of different autoregressive structures.

trade and inventory changes which are stationary), and a VAR has been estimated where the lag length minimises the AIC criterion. The correlation coefficients among GDP forecast errors (we focus on the 32 quarter-horizon;[9] table 3) are very high and lie in a narrow range between 0.6 and 0.7,[10]. Import and investment cycles are the most synchronised components. Export and consumption are slightly less correlated, in particular when Italy and Germany are considered. Finally, inventory and net external demand series are poorly synchronised between any pair of countries.

Table 3. Correlation between VAR forecast errors*

	GDP	C	I	EXP	IMP	NET	DINV
IT-DE	0.7	0.3	0.4	0.3	0.6	0	0.3
IT-FR	0.7	0.5	0.8	0.4	0.8	0.2	0.2
FR-DE	0.6	0.6	0.6	0.6	0.6	0.2	0.2
Average	**0.7**	**0.5**	**0.6**	**0.4**	**0.7**	**0.1**	**0.2**

32 quarters ahead. Estimates over period 1970:Q1 2004:Q4

It is interesting to compare the results for the 32-quarter-ahead forecast horizon with those for the 1-quarter-ahead horizon (Table 4). The latter coincides with the correlation coefficients between the stochastic components of each variable in the VAR and can tell us the degree of similarity among the various shocks hitting the economies. Correlation values are generally lower than at the business cycle horizon suggesting that, in the very short run national idiosyncratic shocks differ considerably; the role of the transmission mechanism both within and across countries is therefore central in explaining cyclical similarities.

Table 4. Correlation between VAR forecast errors*

	GDP	C	I	EXP	IMP	NET	DINV
IT-DE	0.2	0.1	0.2	0.3	0.3	0	0.3
IT-FR	0.3	0.1	0.2	0.3	0.4	0.2	0.3
FR-DE	0.5	0.3	0.2	0.4	0.2	0.1	0.3
Average	**0.3**	**0.2**	**0.2**	**0.3**	**0.3**	**0.1**	**0.3**

1 quarters ahead. Estimates over period 1970:Q1 2004:Q4

[9] Correlations between 6, 8 and 24 quarter ahead forecast errors have been also computed, obtaining very similar results.

[10] The average correlation coefficient between forecast errors for the three european countries and US is 0.3 that with the Rest of Euro Area is 0.7.

2.4 Synchronisation: measure 3. Croux, Forni and Reichlin (2001)

The final measure of synchronisation is based on the spectral representation of a time series. This allows to assign the variance of a variables to different periodicities. As a preliminary step, spectral analysis requires the series to be stationary, therefore all series have been transformed into rate of growth. Among the various measures of comovement proposed in the literature the so-called dynamic correlation is chosen. Given two stationary variables x_t and y_t, the latter is defined as

$$\rho_{xy}(\lambda) = \frac{Cxy(\lambda)}{\sqrt{S_x(\lambda) \cdot S_y(\lambda)}} \tag{7}$$

where $S_x(\lambda)$ and $S_y(\lambda)$, defined for the frequency space $-\pi \leq \lambda \leq \pi$, are the spectral density functions of x_t and y_t and $Cxy(\lambda)$ is their co-spectrum. Dynamic correlation takes on real values between –1 and +1 and keeps the sign of the relation between the series. When three or more variables are considered a weighted average of pair-wise coefficients is calculated and called cohesion; given n variables x_i with $n > 2$ and weights ω_i with i = 1,...,n cohesion $(coh_x(\lambda))$ is defined as follows

$$coh_x(\lambda) = \frac{\sum_{i \neq j} \omega_i \cdot \omega_j \cdot \rho_{x_i x_j}(\lambda)}{\sum_{i \neq j} \omega_i \cdot \omega_j} \tag{8}$$

Both measure can be calculated over frequency band $[\lambda_1 - \lambda_2]$ in order to isolate the phenomenon of interest (long run cycles, business cycles or short cycles). Figure 1 shows cohesion values for different aggregates over the whole frequency space.[11]

The fact that all variables show lower values of cohesion as the frequency increases, confirms the previous finding that in the short run national idiosyncratic factors play an important role.

Focusing on the band associated with long run movements (λ between 0 and $\frac{\pi}{16}$ corresponding to cycles longer than 8 years), not only GDP but also consumption, investment and import show very high and similar values of cohesion, thus revealing a widespread degree of synchronisation. Surprisingly, unlike import, export cycles do not seem to share similar dynamic properties, mainly because of the low correlation over this band between Italy and Germany.

Over the band associated with business cycle fluctuations (λ between $\frac{\pi}{16}$ and $\frac{\pi}{3}$, corresponding to cycles of one and a half and 8 years), however, while cohesion among GDP series reaches a peak at a frequency associated with cycle of three years and then decreases, consumption and investment show considerably lower level of synchronisation. In fact only import cycles

---

[11] As the economies considered are of similar size, the weights ω_i in (8) are set equal to 1.

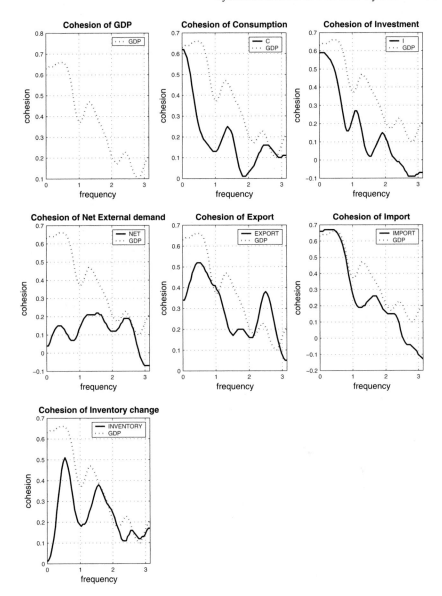

Fig. 1. Cohesion of GDP and demand components

maintain the same high level of cohesion as of GDP. Table 5 shows pair-wise dynamic correlation coefficients for each component over the business cycle band.[12] Pair-wise analysis does not detect significant differences across countries: for instance dynamic correlation coefficients are quite similar across countries for investment, import and, consumption series.

Table 5. Dynamic correlation*

	GDP	C	I	EXP	IMP	NET	DINV
IT-DE	0.2	0.1	0.2	0.3	0.3	0	0.3
IT-FR	0.3	0.1	0.2	0.3	0.4	0.2	0.3
FR-DE	0.5	0.3	0.2	0.4	0.2	0.1	0.3
Cohesion**	**0.3**	**0.2**	**0.2**	**0.3**	**0.3**	**0.1**	**0.3**

* Estimates of $\rho_{xy}(\lambda)$ with λ such that period between 6 and 32 quarters
** Estimates of $coh_x(\lambda)$ where country weights ω_i are set to 1
Estimates over period 1970:Q1 2004:Q4

The evidence from different measures of synchronisation suggests that GDP cycles are well synchronised both in the long run and at business cycle frequencies, while in the short run national differences matter considerably. From a demand side perspective output synchronisation mainly reflects synchronisation in trade (import and to a lesser extent export) and investment cycles. The analysis points to a lower degree of comovement in consumption cycles. This finding adds to the wide international evidence on the consumption puzzle stressed in the international macroeconomics literature (see for instance Backus, Kehoe and Kydland (1992)) which however has not emphasised how such puzzle disappears at longer horizons. Furthermore the results seem fairly similar across countries and correlation measures.

3 Extracting the European cycle: A common factor approach

In this section we aim at identifying the source (factor) of the synchronisation documented so far. The underlying assumption is that the observed pattern in GDP and demand aggregates is affected by a latent variable,[13] which reflects a common "European" cycle. In order to extract such common factor, the dynamic factor model approach introduced by Stock and Watson (1991) is adopted. Accordingly, each national variable is affected, with different weights, by a common component and by a idiosyncratic, specific to each

---

[12] It should be noted, however, that values of cohesion on a given band are not the average of the values taken on by the dynamic correlation index within the band (see expresion (8) in Croux at alii (2001)).

[13] As different models for GDP and the demand component are estimated, a latent common factor for each variable is presented.

country. Given non stationary series and lack of cointegration,[14] the model can be cast in the following form:

$$\Delta y_{it}^J = I_i + \gamma_i \cdot \Delta c_t^J + e_{it} \tag{9}$$

where Δy_{it}^J represents the logarithmic first difference of the variable y_t^J (where J stands for the log tranformation of GDP, Consumption, Investment etc.) at time t and for country i (here Italy, France, Germany and the rest of the euro area, herafter REA); I_i is a country specific constant, Δc_t^J is the change in the common component (specific to the variable J of interest) affecting the left hand side variable in each country with country specific weight γ_i and e_{it} is an idiosyncratic factor affecting country i at time t (for instance in the case of consumption, the interpretation of the common component would be that of a common "European" consumption factor vis a vis a country specific factor in explaining the observed variable across countries).

The common component is assumed to follow an AR(p) process (note that this implies that the level follows an ARIMA(p,1,0) process) so that it can be expressed as

$$\Phi(L)\Delta c_t = \delta + \eta_t \tag{10}$$

where $\Phi(L)$ is a polynomial in the Lag-operator of order p, δ is the mean growth rate and η_t is a normally distributed disturbance with zero mean and variance σ_η^2.

The error term e_{it} is assumed to follow the process,

$$\psi(L)e_{it} = \varepsilon_{it} \tag{11}$$

where $\psi(L)$ is a polynomial in the Lag operator of order k and ε_{it} are normally and independently distributed disturbances with zero mean and variance σ_ε^2.

In order for the model to be identified some restrictions are introduced.[15] Firstly, the parameter σ_ε^2 is normalised to one; secondly, since the long run mean of Δy_{it}^J cannot be separately identified in its determinants I_i and δ, the model is estimated in de-meaned values. The estimation is achieved by casting the model (a system of four country specific equations and one equation describing the dynamics of the common component) in state-space form and using a full information maximum likelihood estimator.

In this application both the common and the idiosyncratic components are assumed to follow a AR(1) process,[16] so that

$$(\Delta c_t - \delta) = \Phi_1 \cdot (\Delta c_{t-1} - \delta) + \eta_t \tag{12}$$

---

[14] Results for the cointegration tests are available from the author.

[15] The identification issues of a coincident economic indicator model are discussed in depth by Stock and Watson (1991) and are therefore just briefly mentioned here.

[16] Several alternative specifications have been tried but the information criteria did not report any significant improvement with respect to the parsimonious specification adopted here.

$$e_{it} = \psi_1 e_{it-1} + \varepsilon_{it} \tag{13}$$

In Fig 2 the comparison between the estimated GDP common component and the Eurocoin indicator (see Altissimo et alii, 2001), a monthly cyclical indicator for the Euro area, suggests that Italy, France and Germany are affected by a set of factors, here represented by the common component, whose effects are best visible at business cycle frequencies. Fig. 3 shows the common components for each demand aggregate: for consumption and investment a cyclical pattern is evident. Table 6 contains the estimates of the autoregressive parameters Φ_1 of the common components (column 2) and the loadings γ_i in each country equation (columns 3 to 6) for each variable (rows).

All parameters are statistically significant at the 1% level (exceptions are the net trade equation and the inventory equation). The common component is quite persistent, as can be inferred from the estimates of its autoregressive parameter Φ_1 (column 2): in the case of GDP, it takes around one year to absorb 90% of the initial shock.

The importance of each common component in explaining national variability is measured by its share of total variance (columns 7 to 10).[17]

For all demand aggregates, this is highest for France (0.66 for GDP, 0.3 for consumption, 0.6 for total investment), Italy and the REA) show intermediate values while Germany appears to be only marginally affected by the common European component.[18] A look at the results across demand aggregates reinforces previous findings: the explanatory power of the common cyclical component is on average higher in the model for GDP (40%) than for any component; among the latter, consumption is the variable where the common component plays the smallest role (20%).

Table 7 reports the estimates of the first autoregressive parameter of the common and the idiosyncratic components for the main demand aggregate. The former show very high and positive values, which is consistent with a discernible cyclical behaviour (Fig. 3). The country specific components are characterised instead by lower and negative values: in order to match the values of autocorrelation observed in the data one has to conclude that in the short run idiosyncratic factors play a significant role.

In conclusion, dynamic factor analysis provides a useful framework to quantitatively measure to what extent countries' business cycles are affected by a single common cycle and to assess existing differences between demand aggregates. The estimated common factors show clear cyclical proper-

---

[17] As the individual series have not been adjusted for their standard deviation, the loadings cannot be directly interpreted as measure of the importance of a common cycle in explaining total variance.

[18] This result does not depend on the particular stationary transformation adopted. Results for GDP series previously band-pass-filtered (Baxter and King filter) confirm that the German cycle is the least affected by the common component (variance ratio is 0.4 versus 0.78 for Italy, 0.81 for France and 0.76 for the rest of Euro Area).

Table 6. Common factor approach

	Φ_1	γ_i				Variance Ratio				
		DE	IT	FR	REA	DE	IT	FR	REA	Average
GDP	0.6	0.3	0.4	0.4	0.3	0.2	0.4	0.7	0.3	0.4
	0.1	*0.1*	*0.2*	*0.2*	*0.1*					
C	0.8	0.2	0.2	0.2	0.2	0.1	0.2	0.3	0.2	0.2
	0.1	*0.1*	*0.1*	*0.1*	*0.1*					
I**	0.8	0.5	0.5	0.8	0.6	0.1	0.2	0.6	0.1	0.3
	0.1	*0.2*	*0.1*	*0.1*	*0.1*					
EXP*	0.4	1.3	1.2	1.3		0.2	0.1	0.5		0.3
	0.1	*0.3*	*0.3*	*0.3*						
IMP*	0.6	0.8	1.6	1.3		0.2	0.2	0.5		0.3
	0.1	*0.1*	*0.3*	*0.2*						
NET*	0.4	0.0	0.2	0.2		0.0	0.0	0.3		0.1
	0.2	*0.1*	*0.1*	*0.1*						
DINV*	0.1	0.2	0.6	0.2		0.1	0.4	0.2		0.2
	0.2	*0.1*	*0.2*	*0.1*						

MLE estimates over period 1970:Q1 2004:Q4. Standard Error in italics

Φ_1 *is the AR coefficient of the common component.* γ_i *is country specific loading of common component*

Variance ratio is $\sigma_\eta^2 \times \sigma_\varepsilon^{-2}$

** *Total Investment is used instead of private non-residential Investment*

* *Only data for Italy, Germany and France are used; REA is euro area minus the three countries*

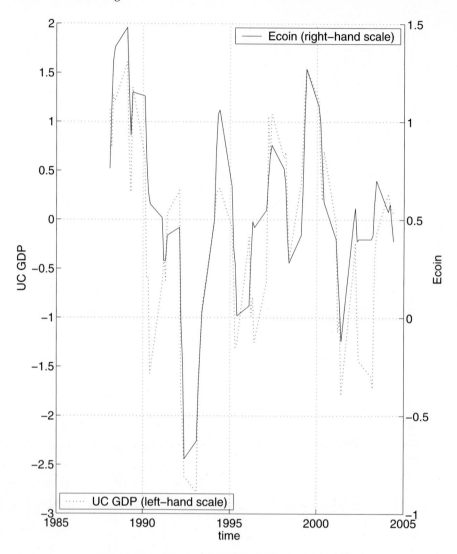

Fig. 2. Common component of GDP and Eurocoin

ties which play quantitatively a significant role and which call for area wide policy measures. The analysis, however does not provide a answer to what phenomena can account for such common forces, nor does clarify to what extent they reflect a wider "world" cycle in economic activity.

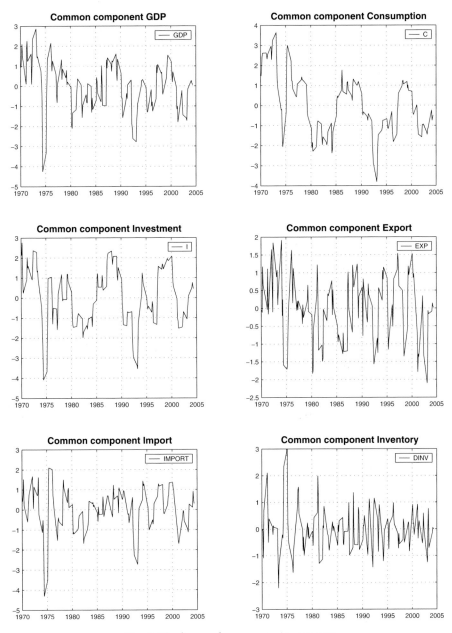

Fig. 3. Unobserved common components

4 Stability of synchronisation

The aim of this section is to evaluate whether synchronisation has remained constant or has changed over time and in what direction. In Europe there

Table 7. Autoregressive coefficients

	GDP	C	I	EXP	IMP
Common*	0.6	0.8	0.8	0.4	0.6
Idiosyncratic factors and observed values/***					
DE	-0.1	-0.3	-0.2	-0.2	-0.2
	0	*-0.2*	*-0.1*	*-0.1*	*-0.1*
IT	0.2	0.4	0.0	-0.3	-0.3
	0.4	*0.5*	*0.1*	*-0.3*	*-0.1*
FR	-0.4	-0.4	-0.3	-0.3	0.1
	0.3	*-0.1*	*0.4*	*0.1*	*0.4*
REA	-0.2	-0.3	-0.4		
	0	*-0.1*	*-0.2*		

* Entries refer to Φ_1; ** entries are ψ_1
*** first order autocorrelaton in italics

have been both institutional and market-driven changes in recent years which might have affected the way national business cycles interact (from the strengthening of trade relationships to the creation of a single currency area, to more integrated financial markets). From a theoretical point of view, Heathcote and Perri (2001) show how increased financial integration may be an endogenous reaction to less correlated real shocks and can in turn further reduce the degree of business cycle synchronisation, Faia (2002) instead argues that the diversity in financial structures is negatively correlated with business cycle synchronisation. More generally it is possible that financial integration, trade openness and sectoral specialisation interact to produce non-obvious effects on business cycle correlation (see Imbs ,2004, for an empirical analysis). In this section we present evidence on the change of correlation at business cycles frequencies, without trying to explain the causes. Among the measures proposed in Section 1 we focus on the cohesion coefficient over three time intervals: 1970-1990; 1993-2004 and 1999-2004. The period between 1990 and 1993 is not included in the analysis as the German reunification might have temporarily blurred the true correlation, the third sub-sample has been chosen to evaluate in a preliminary way to what extent the degree of cyclical synchronisation might have changed since the launch of the European Monetary Union. Figure 4 shows the values of cohesion for the three periods.

Focusing on the frequency range associated with business cycle fluctuations, point estimates of cohesion seems to support the view that an increase in the synchronisation of GDP cycle has been taking place and that it has been relatively stronger since 1999. An increase is also evident among demand components. Table 8 reports the values of cohesion in the three periods. Cohesion among GDP cycles seems to have been relatively constant

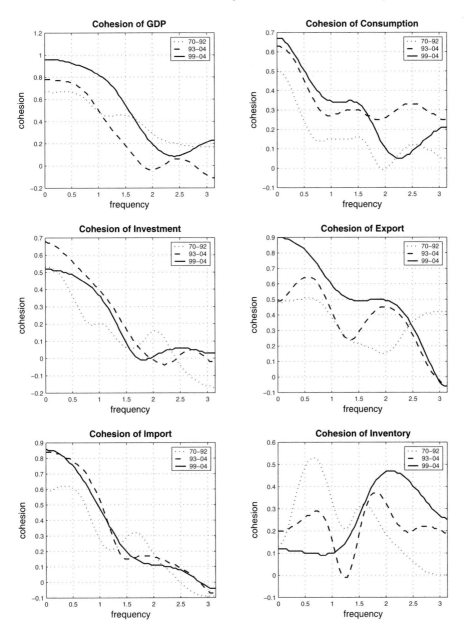

Fig. 4. Stability of synchronisation: cohesion estimates

between the first and second period, but to have increased in the last five years. Among demand aggregates, trade flows have become more synchronised showing values of cohesion similar to those observed for GDP. Investment and consumption cycles remain considerably less synchronised than GDP, suggesting that national differences in labour and financial markets still matter. Finally while net external demand cycles have become more synchronised, inventory cycles have become less so.

Table 8. Cohesion* at business cycle frequencies

	GDP	C	I	IMP	EXP	NET	DINV
1970-1990	0.6	0.2	0.3	0.5	0.5	0.1	0.4
1993-2004	0.7	0.4	0.5	0.7	0.7	0.2	0.1
1999-2004	0.9	0.5	0.5	0.7	0.8	0.5	0.1

* Estimates of $coh_x(\lambda)$ where country weights ω_i are set to 1

While point estimates indicate an increase in synchronisation, one has to bear in mind that they are surrounded by a high degree of uncertainty, especially concerning the very short subsample 1999-2004: for instance looking at the 32 quarter horizon (at the frequency 0.2), the 10-90% confidence band for the cohesion coefficient among GDP cycles ranges between 0.45 and 0.73 in the first subsample (1970-1989) and between 0.6 and 0.8 for the last period (1999-2004), with an overlap of 0.13 percentage points. Figure 5 shows the confidence band (at the business cycle frequencies) for the estimated cohesion coefficient among GDP series: the bands are quite large with some overlap, reflecting the high uncertainty around point estimates and providing therefore only mild evidence in favour of an increase of synchronisation in the last five years.

5 Conclusion

This study uses the growth-cycle approach to evaluate the degree of synchronisation between national cycles; the focus is on the three biggest economies of the Euro area and the analysis considers separately the contribution of the various demand components: consumption, investment, import, export and inventory. Different measures of synchronisation are used, each of them focusing on a specific characteristic of the cycle. The main general finding is that there is a high degree of comovement between GDP cycles. Among demand components, synchronisation is high for import series, intermediate for investment and export, and considerably lower for consumption and inventory. These finding are confirmed by the estimation of unobserved component models through which we are able to extract a common European cyclical factor. The latter is able to explain between 20% (for consumption) and 40% (for GDP) of the variance in the series, suggesting that in the short-term idiosyncratic factors play an important role in determining the growth

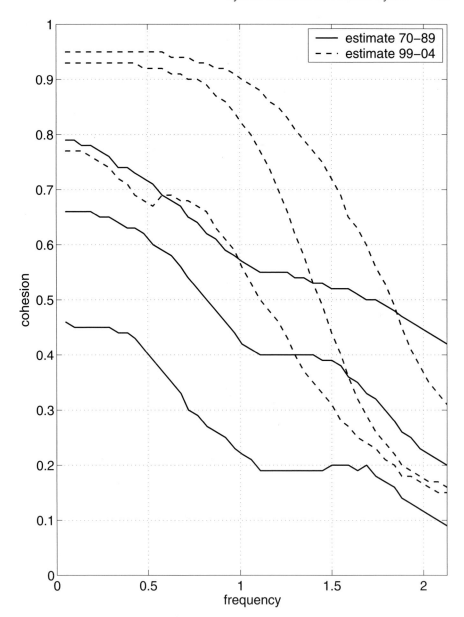

Fig. 5. Stabilisation of synchronisation: cohesion confidence bands

performance of each country. Indeed, in the most recent cycle the differences in GDP growth rates among Italy, France and Germany can be partly explained by the contributions coming from national idiosincratic factors.

These have draggewd down growth in Italy and Germany, while have been neutral in France and the rest of the Ero Area. Finally the analysis finds that synchronisation of output cycles seems to have increased since the introduction of the common monetary policy, probably reflecting increased correlation of trade flows. The persistent lower degree of synchronisation between consumption cycles relative to GDP series, a phenomenon which disappears when longer horizons are considered, suggests however that national differences in labour and financial markets still matter in the medium run.

References

Altissimo, F., Bassanetti, A., Cristadoro, R., Forni, M., Lippi, M. and W. Zahng (1997), Reichlin, L. and G. Veronese, (2001) "A real time coincident indicator of the euro area business cycle", Bank of Italy, Tema di discussione N. 436

Artis, M. and W. Zahng (1997), "International business cycles and the ERM", International Journal of Finance and Economics, Vol.2, N.1

Artis, M., Krolzig, H. and J. Toro (1999), "The European business cycle", European University Institute Working Paper N. 24

Backus, D. K., Kehoe, P. J. And F. E. Kydland (1992), "International Real Business Cycles", The Journal of Political Economy, Vol.100, N. 4, pp. 745-775

Baxter, M. and R. G. King (1994), "Measuring business cycles: approximate band-pass filter for economic time series", NBER Working Paper, N. 5022

Bordo, M. D. and T. Helbling (2003), "Have national business cycles become more synchronized?", NBER Workin Paper N. 10130

Bry, G. and C. Boschan (1971), "Cyclical analysis of time series: selected procedures and computer programs", NBER technical paper, N. 20

Burns, A.F. and W. C. Mitchell (1946), "Measuring business cycles" in NBER (eds.), "Studies in business cycles", New York, Columbia University Press

Burnside, C. (1998), "Detrending and business cycle facts: a comment", Journal of Monetary Economics, Vol. 4, pp. 513-532

Camacho, M., G. Perez-Quiros, L. Saiz (2004), "Are European business cycles close enough to be just one?", www.eabcn.org/workshops/vienna_2004/documents/camacho.pdf

Canova, F., M. Ciccarelli, E. Ortega (2004), "Similarities and convergence in G-7 countries", ECB Working Paper 312

Canova, F. (1998), "Detrending and business cycle facts", Journal of Monetary Economics, Vol. 4, pp. 475-512

Croux, C., Forni, M. and L. Reichlin (2001), "A measure of comovement for economic variables: theory and empirics", The Review of Economics and Statistics, Vol. 83, pp. 232-241

den Haan, W. J. (2000), "The comovement between output and prices", Journal of Monetary Economics, Vol. 45, pp. 3-30

Engle, C. (1993), "Real exchange rates and relative prices", Journal of Monetary Economics, Vol. 32, pp. 35-50

Faia, E. (2002), "Monetary policy in a world with different financial systems, ECB Working paper N. 183

Gregory, A. W., Head, A. C. and Jaques Raynauld (1997), "Measuring world business cycles", International Economic Review, Vol. 38, N. 3, pp. 677-701

Harding, D. and A. Pagan (2002), "Synchronisation of cycles" Melbourne Institute of Applied Economic and Social Research, Mimeo

Heathcote, J. And F. Perri (2001), "Financial globalization and real regionalization", Stern School of Business

Kim, C. J. and C. R. Nelson (1999), "State-space Models with regime switching", MIT University Press

Imbs, Jean (2004), "The real effects of financial integration"

Massmann, M. and J. Mitchell (2002), "Have UK and Eurozone business cycles become more correlated?", National Institute Economic Review, N. 182

Nadal-De Simone, F. (2002), "Common and idiosyncratic components in real output: further international evidence", IMF Working Paper N. 229

Newey, K. and K. West (1987), "A simple positive semi-definite, heteroskedasticity and autocorrelation consistent covariance matrix", Econometrica, Vol. 55, pp. 703-708

Stock, J. H. and M. W. Watson (1991), "A probability model of the coincident economic indicators" in K. Lahiri e G. H. Moore (eds.), "Leading Economic Indicators, Cambridge University Press

Short-Run and Long-Run Comovement of GDP and Some Expenditure Aggregates in Germany, France and Italy*

Thomas A. Knetsch

Deutsche Bundesbank, Economics Department, Wilhelm-Epstein-Strasse 14, D-60431 Frankfurt am Main, Germany thomas.knetsch@bundesbank.de

Summary. The paper presents empirical work on short-run and long-run comovement between the German, French and Italian GDP as well as the aggregates of private consumption, business investment, exports, imports, and changes in inventories. In country-specific data sets, cointegration analyses are carried out both to identify long-run economic relationships and to remove the trend components from the nonstationary series. Analytically, this is done by reparametrizing the vector error correction model in its common trends representation. The resulting (Beveridge-Nelson) trend and cycle components as well as the series of changes in inventories are analyzed with a focus on synchronicity. To measure cross-country comovement at different frequencies, "cohesion", a summary statistic developed by Croux et al. (2001), is applied. Sampling variability and parameter uncertainty are captured by bootstrapped confidence intervals.

Keywords: cointegration, trend-cycle decomposition, cohesion, bootstrap.
JEL classification: C32, E32.

1 Introduction

Since the outset of the European monetary union, the topic of business cycle synchronization within the euro area has been attracting much attention. Empirical research has raised the question whether or not a euro area business cycle exists, and if so, how it can be measured. The existing literature may be decomposed into several branches. Descriptive approaches have been applied to derive stylized facts on the European business cycle(s). Lots of pairwise cross correlations as well as synchronicity or concordance measures are

---

* The author thanks Benoît Mojon for discussing the paper at the JRP conference in Paris. Useful comments and suggestions by Jörg Breitung, Olivier de Bandt, Jörg Döpke, Heinz Herrmann, Karsten Ruth, Christian Schumacher, and Giovanni Veronese are gratefully acknowledged. Of course, the author is fully responsible for all remaining shortcomings. The paper expresses the author's personal opinion which does not necessarily reflect the views of the Deutsche Bundesbank.

documented in this type of examination.[1] Alternatively, econometric systems have been specified and estimated by means of statistical techniques which fit to the scale and the complexity of the respective model structure. When the focus is primarily on measurement, factor models have become very popular. Based on principal components analysis, common cycles can be extracted out of large-scale data sets.[2] In more structural approaches, comovement between European time series has been studied by means of multivariate unobserved components models. This class of models is typically estimated by the Kalman filter technique.[3]

The aim of this paper is to study comovement of economic activity in Germany, France and Italy. This is done not only on the basis of a single measure, say GDP. We will, instead, take a broader position by including some expenditure categories such as private consumption, business investment, exports, imports, and changes in inventories. These aggregates are chosen because they are expected to exert a predominant impact on economic activity in industrialized countries. Within-country and cross-country comovements have to be distinguished conceptually. Furthermore, as all series except changes in inventories are nonstationary, comovements split into a short-run and a long-run aspect (henceforth called "co-cycling" and "co-trending"). This requires an idea about the trend-cycle decomposition to be applied.

The first part of the paper addresses the issue of within-country co-trending in the specific notion of cointegration. In particular, we group the variables country by country and test for cointegration within each set of series. First, the analysis provides insight into the long-run structure of GDP and the expenditure aggregates of each country. Second, the results can be used to decompose the nonstationary series into trend and cycle components. Consequently, synchronicity of economic activity in Germany, France and Italy is studied on the basis of trend-cycle decompositions of the multivariate Beveridge-Nelson (1981) type, i.e. the trend components are modelled as linear combinations of random walks whereas the cycle components describe adjustment processes back to the long-run equilibria. In analytical terms, the estimated vector error correction models (VECMs) are rewritten in their common trends representations.

---

[1] See Artis and Zhang (1995, 1999), Christodoulakis et al. (1995), Dickerson et al. (1998), Altavilla (2004) and Artis et al. (2005) for recent examples. In this volume, such an approach is adopted by Bulligan (2006).

[2] A prominent example is *EuroCoin*, a coincident indicator for the euro area business cycle released monthly by the CEPR; see Altissimo et al. (2001) for details on the construction of this index. The methodological background is the generalized dynamic factor model developed by Forni et al. (2000). A similar modelling strategy which has been often used as an alternative are the large-scale static factor models proposed by Stock and Watson (1989). In this volume, large-scale factor models are applied by de Bandt et al. (2006) and Cristadoro and Veronese (2006).

[3] Recent examples are Luginbuhl and Koopman (2004) and Carvalho and Harvey (2005).

As argued by Canova (1998), business cycle facts are sensitive to the choice of the detrending method. Thus, the trend-cycle decomposition used should be defendable regarding the empirical properties of the time series and the general purpose of the analysis. It is fair to assume the nonstationary series be integrated of order 1 [henceforth I(1)]. Moreover, there are good reasons to believe that cointegrating relations exist between the series of the same country. Provided that changes in inventories do not exhibit a trend, GDP and the expenditure aggregates have to be interrelated as a consequence of the aggregate income identity and of trade balance mechanisms. Within-country cointegration should therefore be fulfilled even if variable-specific growth potentials varied from country to country because of, say, differences in the rate of technical progress or the degree of international trade exposure.

In the second part of the paper, on the basis of the trend and cycle components obtained, the cross-country perspective of comovement is investigated by correlation measures, partly defined in the frequency domain. Precisely, synchronicity is studied by means of the summary statistic "cohesion". In the given context, the measure suggested by Croux et al. (2001) seems appropriate for the following reasons. First, it allows us to examine at which frequency comovement is strongest. Second, in contrast to usual correlation measures, it can be applied to sets of more than two series. Third, in contrast to rank-reduction concepts, it is able to grade synchronicity according to its degree.[4]

The country-specific cointegration analyses provide some interesting results. The long-run comovement of GDP and the expenditure aggregates shows common features in Germany and France while Italy turns out to possess a different structure. Specifically, the same set of restrictions applies to the cointegrating space of the German and the French VECM. This identification scheme implies the existence of two stochastic trends : one drives consumption, investment and output, whereas the other can be assigned to the export and import volumes. In Germany and France, economic activity is therefore characterized by a dichotomy between internal and external sources of growth. From a broader perspective, i.e. when all series are grouped together, cross-country cohesion is significantly positive at business cycle frequencies. For the single aggregates, however, the results lack robustness from a statistical point of view, although point estimates achieve comparably high values for private consumption and, especially, business investment. In the case of cross-country co-trending, however, significant values are found for the single aggregates. In this respect, grouping leads to a

---

[4] Within-country and cross-country comovement are treated asymmetrically. While the latter is regarded as a purely descriptive issue (in the sense that we seek to learn about the degree of synchronicity), the long-run aspect of the former additionally serves a purpose in the modelling exercise needed to perform the trend-cycle decompositions. Hence, cointegration is the appropriate concept in this respect because modelling has to rely on "yes" or "no" decisions.

marked increase of synchronicity. Finally, cross-country comovement seems stronger for trend innovations than for cycle components.

The remainder of the paper is organized as follows. In Sect. 2, we carry out the cointegration analysis separately for the German, French and Italian data sets. The investigation presents the long-run equilibrium relationships found between the variables under investigation and Beveridge-Nelson decompositions which can be derived from them. In Sect. 3, the resulting cycle components are used to study cross-country comovement at business cycle frequencies. A look at cross-country co-trending complements the analysis. Section 4 concludes.

2 Cointegration and trend-cycle decomposition

The econometric analysis is carried out in country-specific samples which start in the first quarter of 1970 and terminate in the fourth quarter of 2004. Most macroeconomic time series under consideration are nonstationary. According to the plots of the series,[5] this property is evident for private consumption, business investment, exports, imports, and GDP in all three countries. Standard unit root tests indicate that these series (transformed in natural logarithms) can be regarded as I(1) processes.[6] The well-known concept of cointegration accounts for the observation that I(1) series may be interrelated in a way that linear combinations between them are stationary. The reason is that cointegrated series share common (stochastic) trend factors.

In the present context, cointegration is a useful concept for three reasons. First, the macroeconomic theory gives several suggestions regarding the long-run comovement of the economic quantities. Second, an overwhelming body of econometric literature exists on how cointegrating relations can be identified and estimated in VECMs. Third, trend components can be obtained by rewriting the estimated VECM in its common trends representation. On the one hand, these features allow to base the trend removal on theoretical considerations which can be empirically tested. On the other hand, the analysis of this section generates an output of its own value.

In Sect. 2.1, the connection between cointegration and the multivariate Beveridge-Nelson decomposition is explained briefly. Sections 2.2 and 2.3 deal with the specification and the estimation of VECMs for the German, French and Italian data sets. The estimated cointegrating vectors and adjustment parameters are discussed in detail. In Sect. 2.4, diagnostic checks on the VECMs are performed. Finally, the properties of the multivariate Beveridge-Nelson decompositions, especially the resulting cycle components, are analyzed.

---

[5] See Figs. 8 through 10 in Appendix A.
[6] The results are reported in Table 3 in Appendix A.

2.1 Some methodological notes

Let y_t be a K-dimensional vector of nonstationary time series. In general, the vector process can be decomposed into:

$$y_t = y_0 + \tau_t + c_t \qquad (1)$$

where τ_t and c_t are the trend and the cycle components, respectively, and y_0 comprises the starting values of the series.

We are interested in investigating comovement on the basis of correlation measures, partly defined in the frequency domain, for which data need to be stationary. If the analysis only stressed the cyclical aspect, the task would be to detrend y_t. Standard approaches proposed in the literature are regression analysis and filtering. Whereas the former assumes that τ_t can be described by a linear combination of known functions in the time index t, differencing, as a prominent example of the latter, uses the property that the q th difference of τ_t will reduce to a constant if τ_t is a q th degree polynomial in t (see e.g. Priestley, 1981, Sect. 7.7).

However, purely statistical methods may bear interpretational problems with respect to the series which have been made stationary. It could well be that one succeeds in finding a transformation so that the resulting series seem to fulfill the conditions of stationarity, although they stem from an economy whose underlying structure comprises structural breaks (see e.g. Granger, 1967). Hence, from an empirical point of view, a theory-based trend-cycle decomposition might be preferable. First, use prior (economic) knowledge to identify the long-run relationships between the series, and second, apply their estimates to annihilate the (stochastic) trends. As a result, the remaining components can be regarded as stationary provided that the imposed structure is correct and does not change over time. Note that the German data set includes an obvious statistical break because the observations prior to 1991 refer to western Germany as the territorial basis.[7] But this shift will be captured within the structure of the model.

As shown by Stock and Watson (1988), a VECM has a common trends representation whose general structure is equivalent to (1). More precisely, a K-dimensional vector autoregressive model with r cointegrating relations possesses $K - r$ common trends which may be described by random walks with or without drifts. Note that the common trends representation is the multivariate extension of the Beveridge-Nelson (1981) decomposition, i.e. the cycle components are stationary sequences representing adjustment processes towards the trend paths modelled as random walks.

To illustrate the formal link between the VECM and the common trends representation, let the data generating process of y_t be described by:

---

[7] More precisely, the structural break is due to the German unification. Until the fourth quarter of 1990, national accounts rely on western Germany. From the first quarter of 1991, the territorial basis switched to Germany as a whole. Further details on the break may be found in Appendix A.

$$y_t = [\mu_0 + \mu_0^b \, \mathsf{S}(t \geq T_B)] + [\mu_1 + \mu_1^b \, \mathsf{S}(t \geq T_B)] \, t + x_t \qquad (2)$$

where μ_0, μ_0^b, μ_1, μ_1^b are K-dimensional parameter vectors and $\mathsf{S}(t \geq T_B)$ is a step dummy variable which is unity for $t \geq T_B$ and zero otherwise. The model allows for a structural break at time T_B, $0 < T_B < T$, which may take a flexible form. In particular, the series might obey a mean shift and a broken trend. The stochastic component x_t is assumed to follow a p th order vector autoregression which can be written in error correction form as:

$$\Delta x_t = \Pi x_{t-1} + \sum_{i=1}^{p-1} \Gamma_i \Delta x_{t-i} + \varepsilon_t \qquad (3)$$

where Π and $\Gamma_1, ..., \Gamma_{p-1}$ are $(K \times K)$ parameter matrices, and ε_t is a K-dimensional Gaussian residual process with zero mean and a nonsingular covariance matrix Ω.[8]

Suppose the cointegration rank be r, $0 < r < K$, which implies that $\Pi = \alpha \beta'$ where α and β are $(K \times r)$ matrices of full column rank. Let the $(K \times (K - r))$ matrices $\alpha_\perp$ and $\beta_\perp$ denote the orthogonal complements of α and β, respectively, and let $\Psi \equiv I_K - \sum_{i=1}^{p-1} \Gamma_i$ where I_K is a K-dimensional identity matrix. According to the Granger representation theorem (Engle and Granger, 1987; Johansen, 1991), x_t can be expressed by:

$$x_t = C(1) \sum_{i=1}^{t} \varepsilon_i + C^*(L) \, \varepsilon_t \qquad (4)$$

where $C(1) = \beta_\perp (\alpha'_\perp \Psi \beta_\perp)^{-1} \alpha'_\perp$ and $C^*(L) \equiv (1 - L)^{-1} [C(L) - C(1)]$ with $C_j^* \equiv -\sum_{i=j+1}^{\infty} C_i$.

As regards the deterministic part of the model, assume $\beta' \mu_1 = \beta' \mu_1^b = 0$. The former condition means that the cointegrating vectors annihilate both the stochastic and the deterministic trends (which is sometimes called "deterministic cointegration"), while the latter additionally imposes "drift cobreaking".[9] Note that μ_1 and μ_1^b have the same left null space as $C(1)$. Consequently, one can write $\mu_1 = C(1)\bar{\mu}_1$ and $\mu_1^b = C(1)\bar{\mu}_1^b$.

By substituting (4) in (2), the observable vector y_t can be represented by[10]

$$y_t = [\mu_0 + \mu_0^b \, \mathsf{S}(t \geq T_B)] + C(1)\left\{ [\bar{\mu}_1 + \bar{\mu}_1^b \, \mathsf{S}(t \geq T_B)] \, t + \sum_{i=1}^{t} \varepsilon_i \right\} + C^*(L) \, \varepsilon_t. \quad (5)$$

---

[8] Note that $\Delta \equiv 1 - L$ denotes the difference operator where L is the lag operator, i.e. $L^k x_t = x_{t-k}$.

[9] For a detailed discussion of different forms of co-breaking, see Clements and Hendry (1999, Chap. 9).

[10] For a proof of the Granger representation theorem in the presence of structural breaks in the deterministic trends, see Johansen et al. (2000, Theorem 2.1).

Following Stock and Watson (1988), let us define $H \equiv [\alpha : \alpha_\perp]$ so that $C(1)H = [0 : \Phi]$ where $\Phi \equiv C(1)\alpha_\perp$ is a $(K \times (K-r))$ matrix of loading parameters. Then, (5) yields the common trends representation:

$$y_t = [\mu_0 + \mu_0^b \, S(t \geq T_B)] + \Phi\zeta_t + C^*(L)\,\varepsilon_t \tag{6}$$

with

$$\Delta\zeta_t = \kappa + \kappa^b S(t \geq T_B) + \nu_t \tag{7}$$

where $\kappa \equiv (\alpha_\perp' \alpha_\perp)^{-1}\alpha_\perp' \bar{\mu}_1$ and $\kappa^b \equiv (\alpha_\perp' \alpha_\perp)^{-1}\alpha_\perp' \bar{\mu}_1^b$ are $(K-r)$-dimensional parameter vectors and $\nu_t \equiv (\alpha_\perp' \alpha_\perp)^{-1}\alpha_\perp' \varepsilon_t$ is a $(K-r)$-dimensional vector white-noise process. Hence, the process ζ_t describes a multivariate random walk.

The (potential) structural break in y_t can be decomposed into mean shifts and broken trends at the same time. Owing to (7), the latter are modelled by a change in the drift parameter vector of the random walk. Furthermore, with $\tau_t = \Phi\zeta_t$ and $c_t = C^*(L)\,\varepsilon_t$, the common trends representation (6) suggests a trend-cycle decomposition of the form (1). For the subsequent empirical application, this implies that the cycle components can be obtained by the following two-step procedure. First, specify and estimate an appropriate VECM specification for y_t, and second, compute the cycle components according to (6) by $\hat{c}_t = y_t - \hat{\tau}_t - y_0$ where $\hat{\tau}_t$ is the estimate of the trend components. In the absence of structural breaks, the initial value y_0 is simply given by μ_0. Otherwise, the model depends on two initial conditions which are related to the parameters μ_0 and μ_0^b.

An estimable VECM specification for y_t is obtained by linking (2) and (3), i.e.:

$$\Delta y_t = \delta D_{t-1} + \Pi y_{t-1} + \sum_{i=1}^{p-1} \Gamma_i \Delta y_{t-i} + \sum_{i=0}^{p-1} \xi_i I_{t-i} + \varepsilon_t \tag{8}$$

where δ is a parameter matrix attached to the intercept term and potentially the step dummy variable, i.e. $D_t \equiv [c : S(t \geq T_B)]$. In the case of a structural break, the model also includes a set of impulse dummy variables I_{t-j} which are unity for $t = T_B + j$ and zero otherwise. Consequently, $\xi_0, \xi_1, ..., \xi_{p-1}$ are K-dimensional parameter vectors which are attached to these additional dummy variables.[11]

---

[11] Note that the coefficients collected in δ and ξ_i, $i = 0, ..., p-1$, are algebraic expressions of the parameters of the data generating process documented in (2) and (3). For the nature of these relations in a similar case, see Saikkonen and Lütkepohl (2000), for instance. If the specification (8) was estimated, a set of restrictions would actually have to be taken into account. As this is not straightforward to do, we decide to estimate the VECM unrestrictedly. In the model specification step, however, the impulse dummies are not regarded as "full" regressors. Compared with the other, they only count for one half in the penalty term of the information criterion.

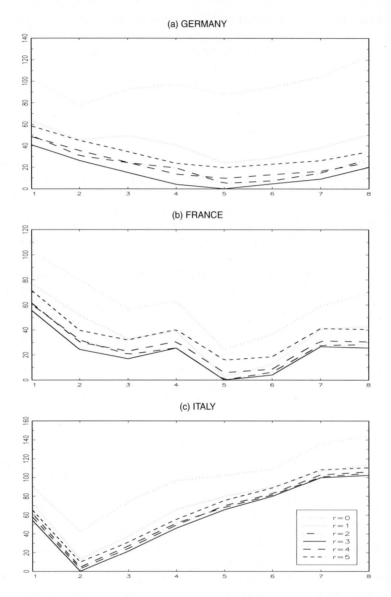

The graphs depict the AIC values resulting from VECM estimations with lag orders $p = 1, ..., 8$ and cointegration ranks $r = 0, ..., 5$. AIC values are adjusted according to the equation $\overline{\text{AIC}}(p, r) = \text{AIC}(p, r) - \text{AIC}^m$, where AIC^m is the (country-specific) minimum.

Fig. 1. Specification search

2.2 Determining the lag order and the cointegration rank

For the first step of the cointegration analysis, we define a (country-specific) vector containing all series but changes in inventories. Requiring this vector to be described by a cointegrated vector autoregression, we have to specify the lag order p and the cointegration rank r. Contrary to the conventional practice where these parameters are selected sequentially,[12] we base our choice on a simultaneous search over the two-dimensional space spanned by $p = 1, ..., 8$ and $r = 0, 1, ..., 5$. In fact, we select the combination (p^*, r^*) minimizing Akaike's information criterion (AIC). This procedure is justified by the fact that a structural break has to be modelled in the case of Germany. Under these circumstances, a cointegration analysis on the basis of the Johansen (1991) LR trace statistic is rather complicated.[13] Alternatively, one could use information criteria to determine the cointegration rank, too. As a matter of consistency, the search for r could then be performed simultaneously with the determination of the lag order p.[14]

Fig. 1 shows the results of the specification search. The first observation is that the lines indicating the various cointegration ranks mostly move in parallel, while the optimal choices for p differ amongst the countries. For the German system, $p = 5$ is optimal. In the case of France, the AIC suggests $p = 5$ as well, and for Italy, the minimum is given by the relatively short lag order 2. The second observation is that, except for the hypothesis of no cointegration at all, the lines are more or less clustered together. However, $r = 3$ minimizes the AIC for all countries at almost all lag orders. Especially in the case of France and Italy, the optimal optimal choice $r = 3$ is closely followed by the hypothesis $r = 2$.

---

[12] Specifically, one chooses first the lag order p by applying an appropriate information criterion (see Lütkepohl, 1993, Chap. 4, for an overview) and then, conditional on p, one tests for the cointegration rank using the multivariate technique proposed by Johansen (1991), for instance.

[13] See Johansen et al. (2000) for the asymptotics of LR trace tests for the cointegration rank in the context of structural breaks. Recall that we generally allow for mean shifts in the cointegrating relations together with broken trends in the series. Especially in this setup, the limiting distributions of the LR trace test statistics are shown to be strongly affected by nuisance parameters.

[14] A simultaneous search for p and r has been discussed in Chao and Phillips (1999). They advocate the Posterior Information Criterion (PIC) which differs from the Schwarz criterion through a twice-as-high penalty term on the parameters of the cointegrating matrix. Despite weaker performance detected in their simulation exercise, we nonetheless use the less parsimonious AIC because, in our investigation, it is important to ensure the whiteness of residuals. A further argument for the use of the AIC is that the lag order selection need not prioritize the limitation of the number of short-run parameters because they will be reduced in a second step. This is done by an automatic procedure which successively imposes zero restrictions on the parameters possessing t-statistics below a threshold in absolute values.

For the VECM specification exercise, we should therefore take into account $r = 2$ and $r = 3$ as possible cointegration ranks. The final choices, however, will be determined in a comprehensive specification process where, in addition to statistical inference, economic intuition plays a role. First, the estimated cointegrating vectors should be consistent with economic theory, and second, the resulting cycle components should fit to basic characteristics which are typically assigned to them in applied business cycle research. But also the chosen lag orders may be questioned during the modelling exercise. One reason is that the series of changes in inventories is not considered here, while it belongs to the vector of endogenous variables later on. Thus, p might be adequate for the nonstationary series but too short for changes in inventories.

2.3 Estimating the parameters of the cointegrating space

In contrast to the previous analysis, the vector to be modelled comprises all six series under consideration, namely:[15]

$$y_t \equiv [\, \mathsf{cons}_t, \ \mathsf{inv}_t, \ \mathsf{exp}_t, \ \mathsf{imp}_t, \ \mathsf{gdp}_t, \ \Delta \mathsf{st}_t \,]'.$$

Given the values pre-selected for the lag order and the cointegration rank, we are going to specify and estimate country-specific VECMs. Although the short-term dynamics represented by the parameter matrices Γ_i, $i = 1, ..., p - 1$, also affect the trend-cycle decompositions, our focus here is on the parameters of the cointegrating space, i.e. the cointegrating matrix β and the matrix of adjustment parameters α. The reason is that implications from economic theory are mostly related to long-run parameters.

The identification and estimation process is structured as follows. First, we try to find an identification scheme for the cointegrating matrix β. Second, zero restrictions are imposed on the adjustment parameter matrix α whenever possible. During this process, the trend-cycle decompositions which are implied by the diverse specifications under review are thoroughly checked in terms of whether the cycle components follow stationary processes and whether these cycles show features which correspond to the conventional wisdom on the cyclical behavior of GDP and the expenditure aggregates in these countries. The specification exercise exhibits the need to reduce the lag order in the case of France. The reason is that the French VECM tends to fail stability for lag orders equal to or greater than 5. Hence, we decide to reduce the lag length to 3 which is found to be a local minimum in Fig. 1(b). In the case of Italy, diagnostics point to a lag augmentation because, with $p = 2$, serial correlation is present in the residual series of changes in inventories.

---

[15] The acronym cons denotes private consumption, inv business investment, exp exports, imp imports, and Δst changes in inventories. More information on the series is given in Appendix A.

The most striking result of the identification exercise is that, under $r = 3$, the same set of restrictions on β can be applied to the German and the French VECM. As regards internal demand, we are able to identify a cointegrating relation between private consumption and GDP as well as between business investment and GDP. Consequently, the cointegrating relations can be labelled as consumption-output and investment-output relation respectively. In both countries, all series but one, namely private consumption for the former and business investment for the latter cointegrating relation, are weakly exogenous. Furthermore, there is a third linear combination in the system which is found to be stationary. Since this involves exports and imports, we call it "external trade relation". The variables bearing the adjustment process back to the third long-run equilibrium relationship are exports in the case of Germany and imports in the case of France.

For the **German data set**, the long-run part of the VECM(5) with $D_t = [\mathsf{c},\ \mathsf{S(91\!:\!1)}]'$ is given by[16]

$$
\hat{\beta}'y_t = \begin{bmatrix} \mathsf{cons}_t - \underset{(0.04)}{0.98}\,\mathsf{gdp}_t \\[4pt] \mathsf{inv}_t - \underset{(0.13)}{1.23}\,\mathsf{gdp}_t \\[4pt] \mathsf{exp}_t - \underset{(0.08)}{1.19}\,\mathsf{imp}_t \end{bmatrix}, \quad
\hat{\alpha} = \begin{bmatrix} \underset{(0.09)}{-0.17} & 0 & 0 \\[4pt] 0 & \underset{(0.06)}{-0.16} & 0 \\[4pt] 0 & 0 & \underset{(0.08)}{-0.12} \\[4pt] 0 & 0 & 0 \\[4pt] 0 & 0 & 0 \\[4pt] 0 & 0 & 0 \end{bmatrix} \cdot
\begin{matrix} \mathsf{cons}_t \\[4pt] \mathsf{inv}_t \\[4pt] \mathsf{exp}_t \\[4pt] \mathsf{imp}_t \\[4pt] \mathsf{gdp}_t \\[4pt] \Delta\mathsf{st}_t \end{matrix}
\tag{9}
$$

For the **French data set**, a VECM(3) with an unrestricted constant is specified. The estimates of the cointegrating space are

$$
\hat{\beta}'y_t = \begin{bmatrix} \mathsf{cons}_t - \underset{(0.03)}{0.92}\,\mathsf{gdp}_t \\[4pt] \mathsf{inv}_t - \underset{(0.07)}{1.43}\,\mathsf{gdp}_t \\[4pt] \mathsf{exp}_t - \underset{(0.05)}{0.93}\,\mathsf{imp}_t \end{bmatrix}, \quad
\hat{\alpha} = \begin{bmatrix} \underset{(0.04)}{-0.07} & 0 & 0 \\[4pt] 0 & \underset{(0.04)}{-0.09} & 0 \\[4pt] 0 & 0 & 0 \\[4pt] 0 & 0 & \underset{(0.04)}{0.06} \\[4pt] 0 & 0 & 0 \\[4pt] 0 & 0 & 0 \end{bmatrix} \cdot
\begin{matrix} \mathsf{cons}_t \\[4pt] \mathsf{inv}_t \\[4pt] \mathsf{exp}_t \\[4pt] \mathsf{imp}_t \\[4pt] \mathsf{gdp}_t \\[4pt] \Delta\mathsf{st}_t \end{matrix}
\tag{10}
$$

Against the hypothesis of just-identification of the cointegrating vectors and no restrictions on the matrix of adjustment parameters, on the 5% level, LR

---

[16] Standard errors are given in parentheses. To the right of the estimated adjustment parameter matrix, we indicate to which left-hand side variable the corresponding row of $\hat{\alpha}$ belongs.

tests do not reject the set of restrictions which are imposed to obtain these estimates.[17]

The estimates of the bulk of cointegrating vectors are theoretically appealing because they are close to $(1, -1)'$, implying that the simple ratio between the respective variables can be given an interpretation in terms of a long-run equilibrium relationship. The sole clear exception is the French investment-output relation. Furthermore, it is an interesting observation that the adjustment parameters are always smaller (in absolute values) in the case of France than in the case of Germany. Consequently, the adjustment processes back to the three long-run equilibrium relationships last longer in France than in Germany, which in turn implies that cycle components are expected to be more persistent.

From an interpretational point of view, the identification scheme of the cointegrating matrices is interesting because it allows us to separate the trend components of GDP and the internal demand aggregates from those driving export and import volumes. Each group is characterized by its specific stochastic trend. In the long run, there is a dichotomy between the internal and the external sides of the economy. The internal trend might be due to technical progress leading to productivity shocks with permanent character.[18] Owing to standard trade balance mechanisms, export and import volumes ought to share a common trend which might be explained by the rising integration of the world economy.

Since the German and the French data possess the same long-run structure, the error correction terms of the respective cointegrating relations can be compared directly. These long-run residual series are plotted in Fig. 2.[19] Although the estimates of the free parameter in the investment-output relation differ somewhat, the long-run residuals implied by the second cointegrating relation show the most similar pattern. The long-run residual series are not only comparable in duration and volatility but also in the timing of cyclical phases. The long-run residuals derived from the consumption-output relation show a looser connection in cyclical terms. In the 1970s and 1980s, private consumption behaved rather similarly in both countries. But whereas the consumption-to-GDP ratio remained more or less stable in Ger-

---

[17] The test statistics are 26.55 and 25.49 for the German and the French data set, respectively. As these LR tests are asymptotically χ^2 distributed with 21 degrees of freedom, the marginal significance levels are 0.186 and 0.227; see Johansen (1995, Chaps. 7 and 8) for hypothesis testing on the parameters of the cointegrating space.

[18] It is worth mentioning that, according to King et al. (1991), standard neoclassical growth models suggest that the consumption-to-output and the investment-to-output ratios (the so-called "great ratios") should be stationary when (exogenous) technical progress is specified by shocks to productivity with permanent character.

[19] The long-run residual series are defined as the residuals obtained from regressing the error correction terms on the set of deterministic regressors relevant to the cointegrating space. In the case of Germany, it consists of a constant and a step dummy. In the case of France, the error correction terms need to be mean-adjusted.

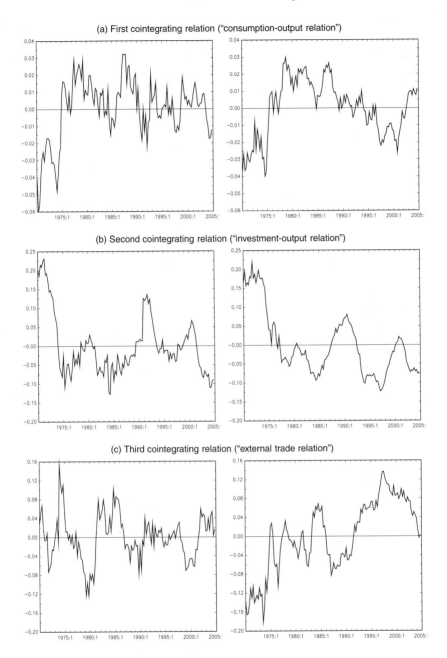

(a) First cointegrating relation ("consumption-output relation")

(b) Second cointegrating relation ("investment-output relation")

(c) Third cointegrating relation ("external trade relation")

The plots depict the long-run residual series (as a percentage) obtained by regressing the cointegrating relation on an intercept and, in the case of Germany, additionally on a step dummy modelling the unification break.

Fig. 2. Cointegrating relations – GERMANY and FRANCE

many since the unification, it was on a downward trend in France during the 1990s before it recovered strongly in the first years of the new millenium. The long-run equilibrium relation between the export and import volumes does not show any commonality between Germany and France. This comes as no surprise taking into account the fact that the two countries are main trading partners for each other. Offsetting forces are likely to be at play. First, the export-to-import ratios should comove when both countries are symmetrically hit by global developments. Second, if external shocks are asymmetric and the domestic parts of the economies are in different shapes, the close trade relations are likely to mitigate the economic consequences in the two countries.

In the model for the Italian economy, it is not possible to identify three cointegrating vectors which are satisfying from the standpoint of economic theory and which lead to reasonable cycle components. The reduction of the cointegration rank to 2, however, yields a better result. Hence, the **Italian data set** is appropriately represented by a VECM(3) including an unrestricted constant where the estimates of the cointegrating space are

$$
\hat{\beta}'y_t = \begin{bmatrix} \text{cons}_t + \underset{(0.03)}{0.11}\,(\exp_t - \text{imp}_t) - \underset{(0.01)}{1.08}\,\text{gdp}_t \\ \text{inv}_t \qquad - \underset{(0.04)}{0.64}\,\text{imp}_t \end{bmatrix}, \quad \hat{\alpha} = \begin{bmatrix} -\underset{(0.03)}{0.13} & 0 \\ 0 & -\underset{(0.03)}{0.10} \\ 0 & 0 \\ 0 & 0 \\ 0 & 0 \\ 0 & 0 \end{bmatrix} \cdot \begin{matrix} \text{cons}_t \\ \text{inv}_t \\ \exp_t \\ \text{imp}_t \\ \text{gdp}_t \\ \Delta\text{st}_t \end{matrix}
$$

$$(11)$$

The set of restrictions which are imposed to obtain these estimates is accepted by an LR test where the alternative hypothesis is just-identification of the cointegrating vectors and an unrestricted matrix of adjustment parameters.[20]

In contrast to Germany and France, the long-run equilibrium relationships do not imply a dichotomy between the internal and external sides of the economy. It is therefore not straightforward to assign an economic meaning to the three common trends in the Italian data set. First, neither private consumption nor business investment is directly cointegrated with GDP. Second, there is no stable long-run relationship between exports and imports. Nonetheless, the second cointegrating relation may be regarded as an investment equation in which, in contrast to the other two countries, the import volume is given a direct impact. This could be explained by the specialization of the Italian industrial sector in consumer goods, which in turn implies that capital goods have to be imported to a large extent. The first cointegrating relation establishes the result that the consumption-to-output ratio and

---

[20] The test statistic is 11.84 implying a marginal significance level of 0.691 on the basis of a χ^2 distribution with 15 degrees of freedom.

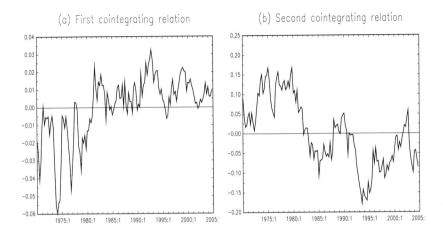

The plots depict the long-run residual series (as a percentage) obtained by regressing the cointegrating relation on an intercept.

Fig. 3. Cointegrating relations – ITALY

the ratio between exports and imports are inter-connected in the long run, although each ratio is nonstationary itself. In economic terms, a surplus in the trade balance coincides with a "consumption sacrifice" of Italian households in the sense that a comparably low consumption-to-output ratio occurs. The long-run residuals resulting from the two cointegrating relations are plotted in Fig. 3.

2.4 Residual checks

To model the German, French and Italian data sets, VECMs are estimated. In this section, some diagnostic checks on the VECM residuals are performed. This is done in order to substantiate that the models are well specified and to ensure that the parametric bootstrap is founded on a sound basis.

Through the parameter matrix Ψ, the trend-cycle decomposition is *inter alia* dependent on the short-term parameters of the model collected in the matrices $\Gamma_1, ..., \Gamma_{p-1}$. In a six-dimensional system, even lag orders of medium size result in an enormous number of coefficients to be estimated. Bootstrap procedures, however, may suffer from distortions if zero restrictions are not imposed, although coefficients are actually zero. Hence, the dimension of the parameter space is reduced by successively eliminating regressors whose t-statistic is lower than a threshold in absolute value. Brüggemann and Lütkepohl (2001) showed that, in single-equation models, this testing procedure is equivalent to a sequential elimination of regressors on the basis of information criteria. In general, the threshold depends on the chosen criterion, the length of the time series, and the number of regressors in each step

Table 1. Diagnostic checks on the residual series

I. GERMANY

Residual test statistic	Series					
	cons$_t$	inv$_t$	exp$_t$	imp$_t$	gdp$_t$	Δst$_t$
AC-LM(1)	0.50 [0.481]	1.59 [0.207]	0.00 [0.976]	0.89 [0.346]	0.98 [0.323]	0.05 [0.815]
AC-LM(4)	4.44 [0.350]	3.25 [0.517]	2.45 [0.654]	3.16 [0.531]	2.39 [0.664]	4.89 [0.299]
ARCH-LM(2)	3.08 [0.215]	10.97** [0.004]	8.40* [0.015]	1.78 [0.411]	1.32 [0.517]	0.79 [0.674]
JB normality	2.34 [0.311]	9.74** [0.008]	12.90** [0.002]	2.47 [0.291]	17.90** [0.000]	6.73* [0.035]

II. FRANCE

Residual test statistic	Series					
	cons$_t$	inv$_t$	exp$_t$	imp$_t$	gdp$_t$	Δst$_t$
AC-LM(1)	0.22 [0.641]	2.52 [0.112]	0.31 [0.579]	2.30 [0.129]	3.09$^{(*)}$ [0.079]	0.31 [0.579]
AC-LM(4)	1.97 [0.741]	2.53 [0.639]	10.82* [0.029]	7.18 [0.127]	5.48 [0.242]	4.46 [0.347]
ARCH-LM(2)	1.42 [0.491]	1.68 [0.431]	1.28 [0.526]	1.09 [0.581]	1.39 [0.499]	8.45* [0.015]
JB normality	1.49 [0.475]	0.348 [0.840]	1.93 [0.381]	0.03 [0.984]	0.78 [0.677]	6.79* [0.033]

III. ITALY

Residual test statistic	Series					
	cons$_t$	inv$_t$	exp$_t$	imp$_t$	gdp$_t$	Δst$_t$
AC-LM(1)	0.17 [0.680]	0.17 [0.682]	1.20 [0.273]	0.73 [0.393]	0.68 [0.408]	0.23 [0.634]
AC-LM(4)	3.76 [0.440]	4.89 [0.299]	3.86 [0.425]	5.11 [0.276]	1.23 [0.874]	5.35 [0.253]
ARCH-LM(2)	14.57** [0.001]	6.95* [0.031]	2.54 [0.280]	7.95* [0.019]	3.32 [0.190]	5.79$^{(*)}$ [0.055]
JB normality	3.29 [0.193]	3.44 [0.179]	1.87 [0.393]	9.10* [0.011]	0.30 [0.860]	1.58 [0.454]

The statistics of the residual tests are asymptotically χ^2 distributed. Marginal significance levels are given in brackets. **,*,$^{(*)}$ mean rejection of the null hypothesis at the 1%, 5% and 10% level respectively.

of the procedure. In system approaches, an exact correspondence cannot be established. In order to mimic the sequential elimination of regressors on the basis of the AIC, we decide to use the constant threshold $\sqrt{2}$ as an approximation.[21] The resulting subset VECMs have substantially smaller numbers of parameters to be estimated.[22]

In Table 1, standard diagnostic checks on the VECM residual series are reported. These include LM tests for remaining autocorrelation (AC-LM) of order 1 and 4, an LM test for autoregressive conditional heteroscedasticity (ARCH-LM) of order 2 and the Jarque-Bera (JB) test for normality. Serial correlation is absent in the residual series of the German system. However, the error terms of the investment and the export equation possess significant conditional heteroscedasticity. Solely the residuals of the consumption and import equation can be regarded as being drawn from a normal distribution. In the case of France, problems with remaining serial correlation of order 4 exist in the residual series of the export equation. The absence of ARCH effects and distributional normality is rejected only for the residuals of changes in inventories. In the case of Italy, autocorrelation does not seem present in any error sequence. ARCH effects are found in the majority of residual series, however. All error terms but those of imports can be taken as drawn from a Gaussian distribution.

In general, residual series which significantly deviate from an identical and independently distributed random draw must be regarded as detrimental. However, taking into account the fact that the chosen lag orders are already large, the benefit from possibly erasing some deficiencies might not outweigh the cost of additional parameters to be estimated if the lag length were augmented in these high-dimensional systems. In the diagnostic checks, the focus is mainly on the avoidance of serial correlated residual terms. The rejection of distributional normality is less severe in this context because the applied estimation techniques, albeit based on the maximum likelihood principle, are robust to potential non-normality and the bootstrap directly draws from the realized residuals so that their specific distribution is preserved.

2.5 The trend-cycle decompositions

As discussed in Sect. 2.1, the VECMs can be rewritten in their common trends representations providing trend-cycle decompositions of the multivariate

---

[21] The threshold value is derived from the formula presented in Brüggemann and Lütkepohl (2001, Prop. 1) by setting $c_T = 2$ (AIC) and assuming $T \gg K + j$ where j is the step of the testing procedure.

[22] Precisely, 100 out of initially 186 coefficients which belong to either the deterministic part or the short-term dynamics of the German VECM need to be estimated in the final subset model. In the case of France and Italy, the numbers are 49 and 39 out of 78.

Beveridge-Nelson type. Evans and Reichlin (1994) argued that the multivariate version typically assigns more volatility to the cycle components than the univariate one.[23] In applied business cycle research, the latter has often been criticized because of the noisy cycles it generates. Along this line of criticism, it may be interesting to know how large the variance of the extracted trends is in comparison with the series itself, i.e. $\mathrm{var}(\Delta\tau_t^k)/\mathrm{var}(\Delta y_t^k)$, $k = 1, ..., K$. Note that this standardized trend variance is lower than unity when the trend component is smoother than the series. With reference to Evans and Reichlin's paper, we also compute the cycle-trend variance ratio, i.e. $\mathrm{var}(\Delta c_t^k)/\mathrm{var}(\Delta\tau_t^k)$, $k = 1, ..., K$. This measure is greater than unity when the volatility of changes in the cycle components exceeds that of trend innovations and vice versa. Moreover, we will analyze the cycle components of the five trending series as well as changes in inventories in mean-adjusted form. Apart from a rough visual assessment, we are going to report some simple descriptive measures in order to describe key characteristics of the cycle components.

Table 2, Panel A, reports the standardized trend variance for the nonstationary series. As expected, it is common to all countries that business investment is clearly more volatile than its trend. Otherwise, the results seems quite different across countries. In the case of Germany, all variables but exports possess trend components which are smoother than the actual series. In the case of France, the standardized trend variance is close to unity for private consumption and the external trade aggregates, while trend output is almost twice as volatile as GDP itself. In the case of Italy, it is private consumption whose estimated trend component is much more volatile than the actual series. While business investment and the trade volumes possess a smooth trend component, the variance of the Italian trend output exceeds that of GDP by about 40 per cent.

With respect to the cycle-trend variance ratios which are reported in Table 2, Panel B, the results obey a more uniform pattern. In all countries, it is found that the cycle changes of business investment are more volatile than the trend innovations, while the opposite holds true for private consumption, exports and GDP. In the case of imports, the French aggregate differs from those of Germany and Italy in the sense that the cycle-trend variance ratio exceeds unity. Extreme values (in either direction) are mostly found for the German aggregates. In the case of business investment, for instance, the variance of cycle changes is five times larger than the variance of trend innovations. In France and Italy, the factor is only about two. Conversely, the

---

[23] Intuitively, this result is explained by the fact that the forecast error variance is typically smaller in multivariate models than in univariate models because the information set upon which the forecasts are conditioned is larger. Better predictability, however, leads to an increase in the variance of the cycle component in a Beveridge-Nelson decomposition.

Table 2. Statistics of the trend-cycle decomposition

Country	$cons_t$	inv_t	exp_t	imp_t	gdp_t	Δst_t
A. standardized trend variance						
GERMANY	0.78	0.13	1.24	0.88	0.80	
FRANCE	0.96	0.32	1.08	1.02	1.89	
ITALY	2.76	0.48	0.56	0.71	1.38	
B. cycle-trend variance ratio						
GERMANY	0.34	5.01	0.59	0.54	0.19	
FRANCE	0.87	2.38	0.17	1.34	0.37	
ITALY	0.77	1.86	0.39	0.55	0.59	
C. cycle variability						
GERMANY	0.017	0.080	0.047	0.028	0.012	3.22
FRANCE	0.021	0.078	0.017	0.078	0.009	1.71
ITALY	0.029	0.082	0.017	0.031	0.013	1.73
D. cycle persistence						
GERMANY	0.840	0.893	0.813	0.830	0.892	0.667
FRANCE	0.929	0.955	0.864	0.930	0.817	0.754
ITALY	0.932	0.939	0.324	0.646	0.810	0.482

The standardized trend variance and the cycle-trend variance ratio are defined in the text. The variability of the cycle components is measured by the standard deviation. Cycle persistence is approximated by the first-order autocorrelation coefficient.

trend-cycle variance ratios reported for GDP and private consumption are markedly lower in Germany than in the other two countries.

Next, it is worth looking at the plots of the cycle components in Fig. 4.[24] Except for Italian exports, the multivariate Beveridge-Nelson cycles of all series under consideration turn out to pass the visual test of possessing a "reasonable" cyclical shape. By conventional standards, the estimates do not exhibit fluctuations that are too noisy. Apart from this general common feature, there are important differences along both the variable-dimension and the country-dimension. Only the cycle components of business investment turn out to show a marked degree of comovement in the cross-country perspective. As regards private consumption and especially GDP, the cyclical relationships between the three countries seem surprisingly loose, although the cycle components look similar in terms of persistence and amplitude. The cyclical factors of the external trade volumes, however, do not even have these characteristics in common. Whereas the cycle component of German exports fluctuates with a considerably greater amplitude than its counterparts, it is the French import series whose cycle component has a compara-

---

[24] Figure 4(f) does not depict a Beveridge-Nelson cycle component. Changes in inventories are only mean-adjusted.

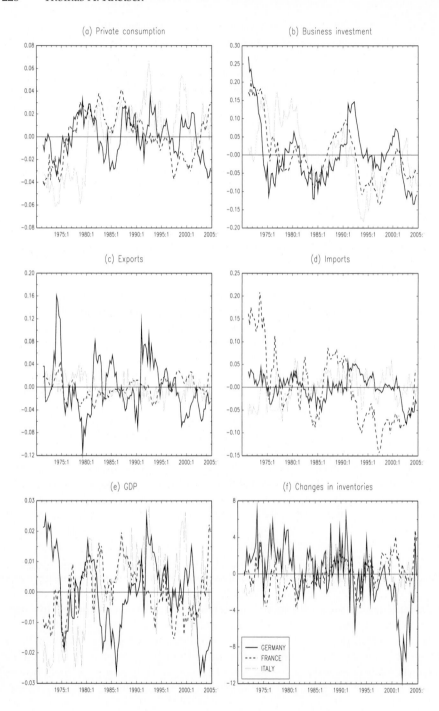

Fig. 4. Plots of the cycle components

bly high variability. This difference is explained by the fact that the large and persistent long-run residuals of the external trade cointegrating relation are "corrected" by exports in the case of Germany and by imports in the case of France. Changes in inventories are too noisy to assess the degree of comovement by a visual check. From the plots in Fig. 4(f), it is obvious that the very negative values observed for German inventory investment since 2000 are exceptional—both in historical terms and in a country comparison.

Further insight into the statistical properties of the cycle components can be gained from some simple descriptive measures which point to the duration and the amplitude of the oscillations. Whereas the variability of the cycle components is measured by the standard deviation, persistence is approximated by the first-order autocorrelation coefficient. The results are found in Table 2, Panels C and D, respectively.[25]

As regards variability, the cycle components can be ordered quite similarly in all countries. It comes as no surprise that business investment is the most volatile aggregate. Furthermore, the output cycles are less volatile than the consumption cycles. In quantitative terms, the cross-country perspective shows no great differences in volatility for private consumption, business investment and GDP. With respect to exports and changes in inventories, the German volumes are markedly more volatile than those of France and Italy, whereas the standard deviation of the French import cycle is more than twice as high as its German and Italian counterparts.

Finally, it is worth mentioning that the cycle components of all nonstationary series but Italian exports are quite persistent. As expected, changes in inventories are less persistent, although the estimated serial correlations are still substantial. In all countries, the highest first-order autocorrelation is observed for business investment. In Germany and Italy, private consumption and GDP are ordered between investment on the one side and the external trade volumes on the other. Surprisingly, in the case of France, the GDP cycle shows the lowest first-order autocorrelation amongst the nonstationary variables under study. But this estimate is still slightly higher than its Italian counterpart. In the cross-country perspective, it is noticeable that the cycle components of the French expenditure aggregates are most persistent. This is particularly valid for private consumption, business investment and imports. This high persistence is a consequence of comparably long-lasting error correction processes implied by the low adjustment parameters documented in (10).

---

[25] Note that, insofar as the standard deviation is concerned, changes in inventories should be taken aside in within-country comparisons because its dimension is billion euro (rather than a percentage as in the case of the other aggregates). Cross-country comparisons, however, are valid, of course.

3 Cross-country comovement

Comovement between nonstationary series has a short-run and a long-run aspect. Long-run comovement between the series of the same country has been studied by the cointegration analysis. However, there are good reasons to believe that co-trending is present in the cross-country dimension, too. This issue will be addressed in Sect. 3.2. First, we are going to study cross-country co-cycling. This analysis uses the Beveridge-Nelson cycle components of the nonstationary series as well as the series of changes in inventories.

3.1 Cross-country co-cycling

In studying the synchronicity of business cycles in Germany, France and Italy, it is of main interest to analyze cross-country correlations of GDP and the expenditure aggregates. If comovement ought to be studied at distinct cycle periodicities, the concept of "dynamic correlation" could be applied in general. This measure translates the simple interpretation of the standard (static) cross correlation into the frequency domain. But as its time-domain counterpart, dynamic correlation is a bivariate concept. Hence, it is not fully appropriate for the present application. A multivariate extension was proposed by Croux et al. (2001), however. This measure called "cohesion" summarizes the dynamic correlations which can be constructed by combining pairwise all series in the set of variables under study.[26] In the context of this summary statistic, a weighting scheme has to be chosen. We decide to give an equal weight to Germany, France and Italy because the countries are comparable in size. An equal-weight cohesion of three series may take values ranging from -0.5 to 1.[27] Negative cohesions would be difficult to interpret in the present context, however.

In Fig. 5, the cross-country cohesions of the cycle components of GDP and the expenditure aggregates are plotted. Let us first look at the point estimates only. At around 0.4, cohesion is found to be highest for business investment. In the range of business cycle frequencies, the cohesion of private consumption amounts to about 0.25. Compared with this level, the cohesion graphs of imports and changes in inventories exhibit higher peaks. But as these are located around the frequency $2\pi/5$, synchronicity is concentrated at cycles with a very short duration, namely below two years. The Beveridge-Nelson cycles of exports and GDP are not synchronized at all. While this does not seem very surprising in the former case, the evidence for GDP runs counter

---

[26] Further details on this measure may be found in Appendix B.

[27] Whenever correlation between series is perfectly positive, cohesion is unity. Whereas the upper limit is fixed, the lower bound depends on the number of series and the weighting scheme. In the current context, the lower bound will be reached if dynamic correlation is perfectly positive between two of them while it is perfectly negative between these two and the third.

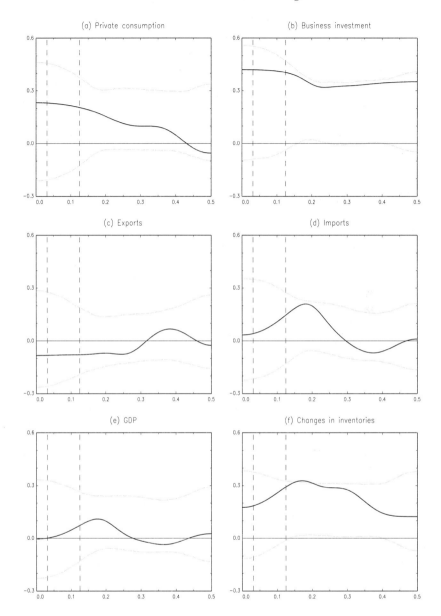

The graphs depict the point estimates of cohesion (solid line) together with the 95% confidence bands resulting from thebootstrap procedure (dotted lines). The abscissa scale is frequency divided by 2π. The dashed vertical lines limit the frequency band attributed to periodicities of two and eight years ("business cycle frequencies").

Fig. 5. Cross-country co-cycling – single aggregates

to economic intuition. In fact, one would actually expect that the output gaps of the three countries should be strongly correlated owing to their close economic connections. However, by looking at the plots in Fig. 4(e), we are able to convince ourselves visually as well that comovement between the output gap estimates is largely absent. In order to interpret the evidence that the cycle components of private consumption and business investment are synchronized across Germany, France and Italy, while the production cycles are not, one has to bear in mind that the three countries are well integrated in international trade, enabling that the economies to specialize in the production of specific goods despite similar consumer preferences and production technologies.

The point estimates of cohesion are informed by bootstrapped 95% confidence intervals. These are rather wide and include the horizontal axis, at least in the range of business cycle frequencies. In a strict statistical sense, cross-country co-cycling cannot be proven to be significant for any single expenditure aggregate under study. This statement is also valid for business investment despite high point estimates and the visual impression in Fig. 4(b). On the one hand, the width of the confidence intervals dashes the hope that cycle components would bear statistically robust common features if they were generated by the multivariate Beveridge-Nelson decomposition, which is based on a number of econometrically demanding test and estimation procedures.[28] On the other hand, the results are nonetheless worth considering because, they are, at least in part, different from those of filter techniques widely used.

It is worth looking at cohesions of groups of aggregates because, from a statistical perspective, grouping might average out sampling variability to some extent. But also from an interpretational point of view, it may also be interesting to study synchronicity on a broader basis. For instance, it is reasonable to summarize private consumption, business investment and changes in inventories as internal demand factors, while export and import volumes logically group together because they both belong to external trade. However, when demand categories with or without GDP are combined, it is a difficult task to find an appropriate weighting scheme. For instance, using the GDP shares of the accounting identity is not a good idea for obvious reasons. Imports would have to be given a negative weight and changes in inventories a very small weight. Apart from these arithmetical problems, the example of inventory investment makes clear that an expenditure aggregate with a marginal proportion of GDP may have an enormous impact on output fluctuations nonetheless. Instead, the impact on output fluctuations would principally be the preferable standard. However, since this is exactly

---

[28] In this respect, neither the careful search for an identification scheme of the cointegrating space nor the data-dependent reduction of the set of short-run parameters has obviously succeeded in sufficiently diminishing the uncertainty surrounding the VECM estimates.

the object of the empirical investigation, we should take a neutral position at the beginning. Otherwise, the results risk being determined by the chosen weights. As a consequence, all series are given the same weight in the variable-dimension as well as in the country-dimension.

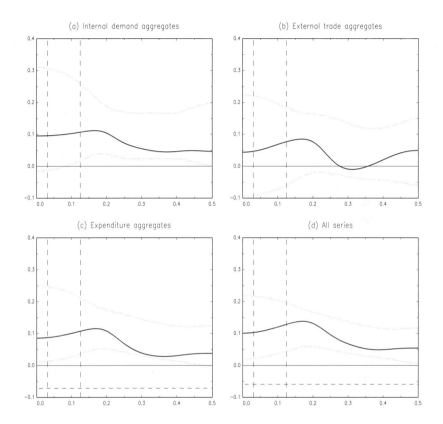

The graphs depict the point estimates of cohesion (solid line) together with the 95% confidence bands resulting from the bootstrap procedure (dotted lines). The abscissa scale is frequency divided by 2π. The dashed-dotted horizontal line shows the lower limit of admissible values. The dashed vertical lines limit the frequency band attributed to periodicities of two and eight years ("business cycle frequencies").

Fig. 6. Cross-country co-cycling – groups of aggregates

Apart from sorting the internal demand and the external trade aggregates, two further groups are formed. They comprise all expenditure categories – the one excluding GDP and the other including GDP. In Fig. 6, the cohesions of these four groups are plotted. A look at the bootstrapped confidence intervals shows that grouping does, in fact, help to reduce the uncertainty surrounding the point estimates. Confidence bands are still large in the case of the internal demand and the external trade aggregates, where cohesion is only based on nine and six series, respectively. However, if 15 or all 18 series of the data set are considered, confidence intervals reduce substantially. Hence, statements on the extent of co-cycling are the more reliable, the larger the set of variables for which cohesion is computed. Moreover, with more series included, the point estimates tend to become more stable, too.

Except for the group of external trade aggregates, the point estimates of cohesion are about 0.1 at business cycle frequencies. All graphs peak slightly outside this range, implying that strongest synchronicity is found for very short-term cycles. Interestingly, in Figs. 6(c) and (d), confidence bands are found to be above the horizontal axis. In a strict statistical sense, this is the only piece of evidence which allows us to conclude that the Beveridge-Nelson cycle components of GDP and the expenditure aggregates in Germany, France and Italy do, in fact, comove in the range of business cycle frequencies. Taking into account the loose synchronicity of the single aggregates in the cross-country dimension, this result actually means that cycle components turn out to be more correlated within countries than across countries.

In sum, there is synchronicity of the cycle components between GDP and the expenditure aggregates in Germany, France and Italy. In terms of statistical significance, however, this conclusion can only be drawn when aggregates are grouped together. Overall, co-cycling at short-term periodicities seems slightly stronger than at long cycle durations. The cycle components of the single aggregates do not show statistically significant cohesion across the three countries, although, at least within the range of business cycle frequencies, the point estimates for private consumption and, especially, business investment exhibit comparably high values. Perhaps the most striking observation is that, regarding output gap synchronicity, even the point estimates are close to zero in the business cycle range.

3.2 Cross-country co-trending

In this section, let us address the cross-country dimension of co-trending. Precisely, we are going to study comovement between the trend components of the nonstationary series. Although generally possible, this issue is not tackled by a cointegration analysis. Instead, we take up the procedure of the previous section by evaluating cross-country cohesions. Two peculiarities of the current approach are worth noting, however. First, owing to the I(1) property, the analysis is based on the first differences of the trend components.[29] Second, since these follow white-noise processes by construction,

---

[29] In these calculations, the structural break in the German data set is considered as follows. The mean shifts are removed from the trend components. The potential change in the drift parameter vector of the random walk component is regarded as part of the trending behavior of the German time series, however.

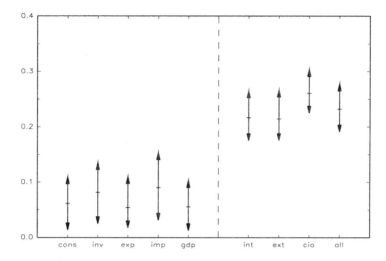

Cross-country co-trending is measured by (static) cohesion of the trend components transformed in first differences. The short horizontal lines indicate the point estimates while the vertical arrows span the 95% confidence intervals resulting from the bootstrap procedure. On the left-hand side, the trend cohesion of the single aggregates are plotted. The right-hand part of the figure comprises four arrows depicting the trend cohesion of groups of aggregates. The acronyms mean the following: int = trending internal demand aggregates, ext = external trade aggregates, cio = the group comprising consumption, investment and GDP, all = all (nonstationary) variables.

Fig. 7. Cross-country co-trending

the cohesion measure can be built on static rather than dynamic correlations. For each set of variables, we therefore obtain only one value which indicates the extent of what we call trend cohesion for brevity. In Fig. 7, the point estimates of trend cohesion are depicted by small horizontal strokes within the vertical arrows indicating the bootstrapped 95% confidence intervals. On the left-hand side, the trend cohesions of the five nonstationary aggregates are depicted. As in the analysis of cross-country co-cycling, grouping may be advantageous. Hence, we also report the estimates of trend cohesion for some groups of aggregates which are found in the right-hand part of the figure.

With some adjustments, the groups formed in the previous section can be adopted in the analysis of co-trending, too. As the series of changes in inventories do not exhibit a trend, the group of internal demand aggregates only consists of private consumption and business investment. The external trade group is taken over unchanged. Of course, with "all", only the trending series are meant in this context. Furthermore, a fourth group (called "cio") is formed which summarizes consumption, investment and output. If exports and imports were equally affected by the external trend factor, GDP would solely be driven by the internal trend factor as a consequence of the accounting identity. Understood as technical progress, for instance, the internal trend should be the driving force behind the upward drift in consumption, investment and output. Cross-country co-trending of this group of variables would therefore imply that the three countries face the same shocks to productivity with permanent character.[30]

The first observation is that all arrows lie entirely in the positive range. Hence, the hypothesis that the trend innovations of all expenditure aggregates are positively correlated across countries cannot be statistically rejected on the 5% level. The second observation is that trend cohesion is substantially lower for the single aggregates than for the groups. Of course, this comes as no surprise in the light of the fact that the trend-cycle decomposition explicitly uses the property that variables of the same country share common trends.

In terms of magnitude, we do not find marked differences when comparing co-trending of the single aggregates. The point estimates are all below 0.1. The highest values are documented for imports and business investment. With respect to the groups, however, the point estimates of trend cohesion are between 0.2 and 0.3. It is conspicuous that co-trending within the "cio"-group is strongest. In particular, its confidence set does not contain the point estimate of trend cohesion of the external trade group. This might be regarded as evidence supporting the view that technical change disseminates rather quickly, whereas the three countries differ with respect to the degree they participate in the dynamic development of international trade integration.

Finally, let us briefly examine whether co-trending is stronger than co-cycling or vice versa. Owing to the large confidence sets documented in Fig. 5, any satisfying answer to this question cannot be derived on the basis of the single aggregates. Taking all series as a group, we find that the confidence set of trend cohesion is mainly located above 0.2. This level, however, is not exceeded by the upper bound of the confidence band in Fig. 6(d), at least when averaging over all frequencies of the business cycle range. Hence, the broad view would suggest that cross-country synchronicity is higher in the very long run than at business cycle frequencies.

4 Conclusion

We have studied short-run and long-run comovement of GDP and some expenditure aggregates in Germany, France and Italy. Economic activity is multidimensional by nature. Thus, it does not seem sufficient to look at a single

---

[30] This is the interpretation of the common trend suggested by the neo-classical growth models of the style documented in King et al. (1991), for instance. See also Footnote 18.

measure such as GDP. Rather, the specific information which can be drawn from private consumption, business investment, exports and imports as well as changes in inventories must not be neglected. As all variables but the latter are nonstationary, a trend-cycle decomposition has been chosen in order to obtain series to which correlation measures can be applied. Concretely, we have applied multivariate Beveridge-Nelson decompositions which result from rewriting the estimated country-specific VECMs into their common trends representations.

The cointegration analysis, necessary to specify the VECMs, is also interesting from an interpretational point of view. We have been able to study the long-run comovement of economic variables within the countries. For instance, the same set of restrictions can be applied to identify the three cointegrating vectors which have been found in the German and the French data sets. More precisely, stable long-run relationships exist between consumption and output, investment and output as well as between exports and imports. With one exception, the estimated cointegrating vectors are close to $(1, -1)'$. The five nonstationary series are thus driven by two common stochastic trends. There is an internal trend forcing consumption, investment and output and an external trend factor driving exports and imports. Hence, we have been able to conclude that, in a long-run perspective, the German and the French expenditure aggregates are dichotomized into an internal and an external part. The results which have been derived from the Italian data set differ from this interpretationally appealing structure in several respects. First, only two cointegrating relations are established. Second, the estimated long-run relationships imply that the export and imports interfere with the internal demand aggregates. Third, there is no straightforward assignment of the three common trends to economic sources.

Except for changes in inventories which have been solely mean-adjusted, the estimated VECMs have been used to extract cycle components from the nonstationary series. The resulting multivariate Beveridge-Nelson cycle components meet many characteristics which are common knowledge in applied business cycle research. But especially with respect to the cross-country dimension, some findings contrast to the results typically found when standard filter techniques are applied for detrending. As regards cross-country comovement, we have distinguished between co-cycling and co-trending. Both aspects have been measured by the concept of cohesion. While the former is based on the estimated cycle components, the latter evaluates the first differences of the trend components. A parametric bootstrap procedure has been applied to construct confidence intervals around the point estimates capturing both sampling variability and parameter uncertainty. In the cross-country dimension, the cycle components exhibit statistically significant synchronicity only if the variables are grouped together. Although high point estimates of cohesion have been found for private consumption and, especially, business investment, in the range of business cycle frequencies, confidence bands are so wide that they all contain the zero axis. Reasons for this are the

238 Thomas A. Knetsch

uncertainty of the VECM estimates and the intrinsically low degree of stability of frequency-domain statistics. Co-trending, however, is statistically significant for the single aggregates, although the point estimates are rather low. For groups of variables, the extent of co-trending rises to higher values. This is affected by the common-trends assumptions which have been imposed on the country-specific data sets. Finally, it has been found that co-trending is stronger than co-cycling.

A Data and unit root tests

In the econometric investigations, we analyze the time series properties of private consumption, business investment, exports, imports, and GDP as well as changes in inventories for Germany, France and Italy. The series are seasonally and working-day adjusted and in real terms (i.e. in billions of 1995 euro). Furthermore, the first five series are taken in natural logarithm. In the remainder, we denote the series by $cons_t$, inv_t, exp_t, imp_t, gdp_t, and Δst_t, $t = 1, ..., T$, respectively. The sample starts in the first quarter of 1970 and ends in the fourth quarter of 2004. The sample size is $T = 140$.

In Figs. 8 through 10, all series under consideration are plotted. At first glance, private consumption, business investment, exports, imports, and GDP appear to be nonstationary, whereas the series of changes in inventories seems to exhibit properties of a stationary process. In all countries, the investment aggregate is most volatile while private consumption turns out to be at least slightly smoother than GDP. Moreover, the export and import volumes seem to be closely connected in terms of both trending and cycling behavior. Finally, in the German case, a statistical break in the first quarter 1991, when the territorial basis changed from western Germany to Germany as a whole, has to be taken into account, although it appears to be visible only in the series of GDP, private consumption, and less obviously, business investment.[31]

In order to obtain more information on the trending behavior of the time series, unit root tests are performed. In Table 3, the results of standard procedures are reported. Namely, we apply the augmented Dickey-Fuller (ADF), the Phillips-Perron (PP),[32] and the test proposed by Kwiatkowski et al. (1992) (KPSS). Whereas the ADF and the PP procedures test for a unit root in the series, the KPSS test assumes (trend-)stationarity under the null hypothesis.

---

[31] The behavior of exports is special around the unification break because, in the run-up of unification, intra-German trade was measured in the west German trade volumes, whereas it logically disappeared in the data for Germany as a whole. Consequently, the enormous flow of goods from western to eastern Germany inflated the export figures in 1990, while the transition to the national accounts statistics for Germany as a whole caused a negative break in this aggregate.

[32] Details on the ADF and the PP test are given in Hamilton (1994, Chap. 17), for instance.

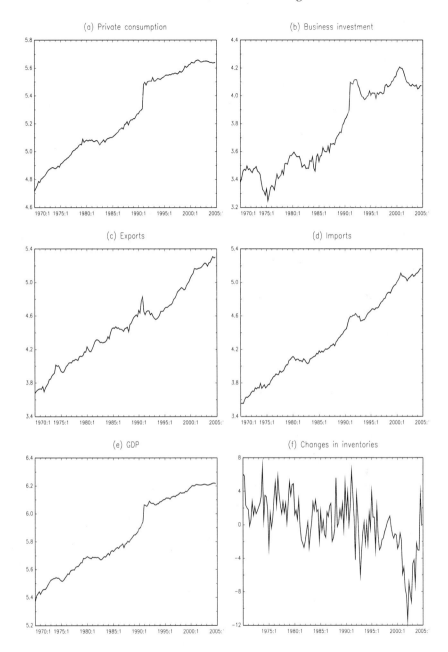

The plots in Charts (a) through (e) depict the series in natural logarithm, while Chart (f) shows the original series. All variables are measured in 1995 euro.

Fig. 8. Series plots – GERMANY

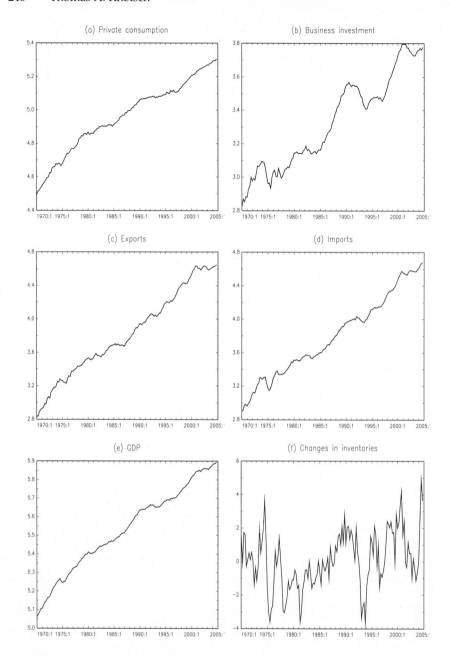

The plots in Charts (a) through (e) depict the series in natural logarithm, while Chart (f) shows the original series. All variables are measured in 1995 euro.

Fig. 9. Series plots – FRANCE

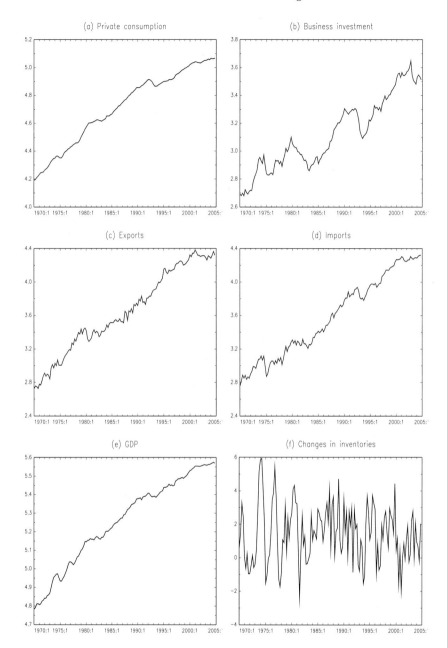

The plots in Charts (a) through (e) depict the series in natural logarithm, while Chart (f) shows the original series. All variables are measured in 1995 euro.

Fig. 10. Series plots – ITALY

Table 3. Unit root tests

I. GERMANY

Series	Deterministic terms	ADF	PP	KPSS	
$cons_t$	c, t, S(91:1), t S(91:1)	(5) -2.77	(14) -3.75	(4) $0.201^{\star\star}$	(14) $0.074^{(\star)}$
inv_t	c, t, S(91:1), t S(91:1)	(5) -3.93	(13) -3.01	(4) $0.162^{\star\star}$	(14) $0.061^{(\star)}$
exp_t	c, t, S(91:1), t S(91:1)	(2) $-4.17^{(\star)}$	(5) -3.83	(4) $0.077^{\star\star}$	(14) 0.039
imp_t	c, t, S(91:1), t S(91:1)	(3) -3.31	(11) -3.21	(4) $0.112^{\star\star}$	(14) 0.045
gdp_t	c, t, S(91:1), t S(91:1)	(0) -3.93	(10) $-4.26^{\star}$	(4) $0.120^{\star\star}$	(14) 0.051
Δst_t	c	(4) $-2.69^{(\star)}$	(15) $-5.96^{\star\star}$	(4) $1.806^{\star\star}$	(14) $0.811^{\star\star}$

II. FRANCE

Series	Deterministic terms	ADF	PP	KPSS	
$cons_t$	c, t	(5) -2.96	(6) $-3.42^{(\star)}$	(4) $0.586^{\star\star}$	(14) $0.228^{\star\star}$
inv_t	c, t	(3) -2.77	(12) -2.63	(4) $0.141^{(\star)}$	(14) 0.059
exp_t	c, t	(4) -2.54	(6) -2.65	(4) $0.319^{\star\star}$	(14) $0.135^{(\star)}$
imp_t	c, t	(9) -2.82	(8) -2.89	(4) $0.306^{\star\star}$	(14) $0.141^{(\star)}$
gdp_t	c, t	(4) $-3.65^{\star}$	(9) $-3.37^{(\star)}$	(4) $0.412^{\star\star}$	(14) $0.174^{\star}$
Δst_t	c	(3) $-4.40^{\star\star}$	(8) $-4.18^{\star\star}$	(4) $0.773^{\star\star}$	(12) $0.478^{\star}$

III. ITALY

Series	Deterministic terms	ADF	PP	KPSS	
$cons_t$	c, t	(1) -1.48	(8) -1.17	(4) $0.796^{\star\star}$	(14) $0.300^{\star\star}$
inv_t	c, t	(4) $-3.33^{(\star)}$	(11) -2.71	(4) $0.218^{\star\star}$	(14) 0.096
exp_t	c, t	(1) -2.28	(13) -3.00	(4) $0.187^{\star}$	(14) 0.081
imp_t	c, t	(0) $-3.26^{(\star)}$	(5) $-3.34^{(\star)}$	(4) $0.226^{\star\star}$	(13) 0.112
gdp_t	c, t	(6) -1.32	(10) -1.45	(4) $0.767^{\star\star}$	(14) $0.300^{\star\star}$
Δst_t	c	(4) $-6.08^{\star\star}$	(6) $-6.93^{\star\star}$	(4) 0.081	(4) 0.081

The numbers in parentheses indicate the lag length in the ADF procedure and the bandwidth parameter in the PP and KPSS procedures. In the version including a deterministic trend, MacKinnon (1991) critical values for the ADF and the PP tests are -4.03, -3.44 and -3.15 for significance at the 1%, 5% and 10% level respectively; in the version with an intercept term only, they are given by -3.48, -2.88 and -2.58. For the KPSS testing the null of trend-stationarity, the asymptotic values are 0.216, 0.146 and 0.119, and 0.739, 0.463 and 0.347 in the test for stationarity. For the ADF and the PP including a structural break, critical values are tabulated in Perron (1989, Table VI.B) which are -4.88, -4.24 and -3.95 in the given setup. For the KPSS including a structural break, they are found in Kurozumi (2002, Table 1d): 0.091, 0.066 and 0.056. **, *, $^{(\star)}$ mean rejection of the null hypothesis at the 1%, 5% and 10% level respectively.

The testing setup for all trending series includes a constant c and a deterministic trend t; for the series of changes in inventories, only an intercept term is included. In the case of Germany, the alternative hypothesis is trend-stationarity including a break in mean and in trend at the (known) date of unification for all series but changes in inventories. Following Perron [1988], the ADF and the PP test can be applied to the residual series resulting from the auxiliary regression on c, t, the step dummy variable S(91:1) and the broken trend dummy t S(91:1) where S(91:1) is unity from the first quarter of 1991 onwards and zero otherwise. Unit root tests have nonstandard limiting distributions. Critical values are taken from MacKinnon (1991) for the ADF and the PP test and from Kwiatkowski et al. [1992] for the KPSS test, respectively. In the case of structural breaks, the Dickey-Fuller distribution is subject to nuisance parameters dependent on the date of the break T_B. Here, we apply the critical values tabulated in Perron (1989, Table VI.B) for $T_B/T = 0.6$. Critical values of the KPSS test for trend-stationarity around a break in mean and in trend are taken from Kurozumi (2002, Table 1d).

For any trending series, the existence of a unit root cannot be rejected by both the ADF and the PP test if we accept the 5% level. For all series but French business investment, nonstationarity is confirmed by the KPSS test results as far as the short lag truncation is regarded as relevant.[33] Although somewhat optimal, with the bandwidth parameter chosen by the automatic procedure suggested by Newey and West (1994), the KPSS test turns out to suffer from considerable power erosion in the samples at hand. In sum, we are able to conclude that private consumption, business investment, export, imports and GDP (all in logs) are described by unit root processes.

With respect to changes in inventories, results are not clear-cut. Only in the case of Italy, we obtain what is expected a priori, namely that the ADF and PP tests reject the presence of a unit root while the two KPSS versions accept the stationarity hypothesis. According to the ADF and PP tests, the French series does not possess a unit root while the KPSS tests tend to reject stationarity at the same time. The signs for nonstationarity are even more accentuated in the case of the German aggregate where both KPSS versions reject stationarity at the 1% level and only the PP test is able to reject the presence of a unit root at the 5% level. In drawing conclusions from these results, however, we should be aware of the fact that, for real time series, it is not always possible to unambiguously answer the question on the degree of integration. There are cases in between, and those are obviously relevant to the German and the French series of changes in inventories. Once again looking at the time series plots, we may find reasons for this. In the German case, a potential source of nonstationarity might be seen in the phase of extraor-

---

[33] The short bandwidth parameter value results from applying the rule of thumb integer$[4(T/100)^{1/4}]$ which was inter alia suggested by Schwert (1989) in his influential Monte Carlo investigation of unit root tests and which was also used by Kwiatkowski et al. (1992).

dinary destocking during the period 2001 through 2003. In the French case, changes in inventories show a marked degree of persistence. Despite these observations, we think that it is fair to conclude that the series of changes in inventories do not contain a unit root. As a working hypothesis for the analysis, they will be consequently taken as I(0) series.

B Cohesion

This appendix introduces cohesion which is a frequency-domain summary statistic developed by Croux et al. (2001). After a brief description of the concept, we are going to show how cohesion can be estimated. This includes an outline of a parametric bootstrap procedure which is used to set up confidence bands around the point estimates.[34]

B.1 Concept

Let c_t^k, $k = 1, ..., K$, denote the cycle component of the nonstationary series k stacked in the K-dimensional vector y_t. The cycle components are assumed to be zero-mean covariance-stationary, and any bivariate pair of them fulfill the condition of stationary correlation: for all $t = 1, ..., T$ and $k, l = 1, ..., K$,

- the mean: $E(c_t^k) = 0$,
- the variance: $\gamma_k(0) \equiv E(c_t^k c_t^k) < \infty$,
- the auto-covariances: $\gamma_k(s) \equiv E(c_t^k c_{t-s}^k) < \infty \; \forall \, s > 0$, and
- the cross-covariances: $\rho_{kl}(s) \equiv E(c_t^k c_{t-s}^l) < \infty \; \forall \, s > 0, \, l \neq k$.

Let $S_k(\omega)$, $-\pi \leq \omega < \pi$, represent the spectral density function of c_t^k. Co-movement between two cycle components, say k and l, can be analyzed by using their cross-spectral density function $S_{kl}(\omega) = C_{kl}(\omega) + iQ_{kl}(\omega)$ where the cospectrum and the quadrature spectrum are denoted by $C_{kl}(\omega)$ and $Q_{kl}(\omega)$, respectively, and $i \equiv \sqrt{-1}$.

In the frequency domain, a standard measure of co-cycling between two series is squared coherency. This statistic is real and symmetric. It measures the degree of linear association, i.e. the proportion of the variance of one series at frequency ω that is accounted for by variation in the other series. However, the squared coherency disregards phase differences between the series, i.e. it takes the same value for c_t^k and c_t^l as for c_t^k and c_{t-j}^l. Croux et al. (2001) therefore doubt its adequacy for measuring correlation at different frequencies. Alternatively, they suggest using the statistic

---

[34] The presentation is aimed to equip the reader with sufficient knowledge to be able to follow the empirical investigation. However, the explanation of these elements is necessarily rather brief. Many details are omitted. The reader who is interested in further information is referred to the cited literature.

$$R_{kl}(\omega) \equiv \frac{C_{kl}(\omega)}{\sqrt{S_k(\omega)\,S_l(\omega)}} \tag{12}$$

which is called "dynamic correlation" between the variables k and l. Notice that the dynamic correlation is nothing else than the correlation coefficient between real waves of frequency ω in the interval $0 \leq \omega < \pi$. In general, it is real and symmetric, and just like a static correlation, it varies between -1 and 1.

To measure the degree of comovement for more than two variables, Croux et al. developed the concept of cohesion, which is a weighted average over the dynamic correlations of all bivariate combinations within the set of variables. In our example, it is interesting to calculate the cohesion of the variable k between $N \geq 2$ countries defined by

$$G_k(\omega) \equiv \frac{\sum_{m \neq n}^{N} w_{m.k} w_{n.k} R_{mn.k}(\omega)}{\sum_{m \neq n}^{N} w_{m.k} w_{n.k}}, \quad m, n = 1, ..., N, \tag{13}$$

where $w_{n.k} \geq 0$ is the weight of country n's variable k. In general, $|G_k(\omega)| \leq 1$ and, if all bivariate pairs of series are perfectly correlated, $G_k(\omega) = 1$. The lower bound, however, depends on the number of variables and the weighting scheme. For $N = 2$ and perfectly negative correlation, $G_k(\omega) = -1$; for $N > 2$, the lower bound lies somewhere between -1 and 0 because pairwise negative correlation between more than two variables cannot exist, of course. In the important case of equal weights, $G_k(\omega)$ cannot fall below $-1/(N-1)$.

B.2 Point estimation

To compute cohesion, we need estimates of $S_k(\omega)$ and $C_{kl}(\omega)$ in the interval $0 \leq \omega \leq \pi$ for all k and $l \neq k$.[35] In general form, consistent estimates are given by

$$\hat{S}_k(\omega) = (2\pi)^{-1} \sum_{s=-M}^{M} \kappa_M(s)\hat{\gamma}_k(s) \cos \omega s \tag{14}$$

$$\hat{C}_{kl}(\omega) = (2\pi)^{-1} \left[\hat{\rho}_{kl}(0) + \sum_{s=1}^{M} \kappa_M(s)\Big(\hat{\rho}_{kl}(s) + \hat{\rho}_{lk}(s)\Big) \cos \omega s \right] \tag{15}$$

where $\hat{\gamma}_k(\cdot)$ and $\hat{\rho}_{kl}(\cdot)$ are consistent estimates of the variances, autocovariances and cross-covariances, respectively, and $\kappa_M(\cdot)$ is a symmetric lag window with $M < T - 1$. In the analysis, we apply the lag window suggested by Parzen (1961), i.e.

---

[35] See, for instance, Priestley (1981) or Brockwell and Davis (1987) for a closer look at the estimation of (cross-)spectral density functions.

$$\kappa_M(s) = \begin{cases} 1 - 6(s/M)^2 + 6(|s|/M)^3, & |s| \le M/2, \\ 2(1 - |s|/M)^3, & M/2 \le |s| \le M, \\ 0, & |s| > M \end{cases} \qquad (16)$$

where M is the number of auto-covariances used.

It is well known that a trade-off exists between the bias and the variance of a spectral estimate. Whereas the estimate becomes more stable as M increases, the bias goes up at the same time because fine characteristics of the spectrum are "smoothed away".[36] In the empirical application, we set $M = 8$, implying a relatively high degree of smoothness. The low value has to be chosen in order to ensure the stability of the point estimates in comparison with the bootstrapped confidence bands.

B.3 Bootstrapped confidence bands

Asymptotic confidence bands may be misleading for two reasons. First, the asymptotic distribution can only approximate the sampling properties of the statistic of interest in finite samples. Second, and perhaps more importantly, the series which are to be analyzed by correlation measures cannot be observed directly. Hence, their estimation is subject to parameter uncertainty which generally affects the width of the confidence bands, too.

Bootstrap methods can be applied to correct for those effects.[37] In fact, the proposed trend removal gives a natural basis for the application of a residual based resampling because the VECM residual series $\hat{\varepsilon}_t$ can be regarded as realizations of vector white-noise processes. From the empirical residuals, bootstrap innovations are generated by resampling with replacement. Pseudo-data for the endogenous vector process y_t is obtained on the basis of the estimated VECM and p initial observations. The pseudo-data is then used to re-estimate the VECM in order to receive the trend-cycle decomposition from the constructed series. Once this procedure is repeated many times,[38] we are finally able to set up confidence bands around the point estimate of the statistic of interest.

In order to provide some details on the bootstrap procedure, denote the statistic of interest by $\hat{\theta}$ and its bootstrap equivalent by $\hat{\theta}^*$. To form bootstrap confidence bands for $\hat{\theta}$, the standard method would simply use the $(a/2)$- and $(1 - a/2)$-quantiles of the bootstrap distribution of $\hat{\theta}^*$, where a

---

[36] The exact expressions for the asymptotic bias and variance of a spectral density estimate are derived in Priestley (1981, Sect. 6.2.4), for instance.

[37] For an overview on bootstrap techniques for time series models, see Li and Maddala (1996) and Berkowitz and Kilian (2000), for instance.

[38] In the application, we run 5,000 replications. In order to preserve the correlation structure within and across countries, the seat of the residuals is randomly chosen in each bootstrap replication.

is the significance level. In the context of vector autoregressions, the standard bootstrap algorithm is usually not optimal because the ordinary least squares estimator of the slope coefficients is systematically biased so that resulting coverage rates are often unsatisfactory.[39] We follow two suggestions proposed in the literature which help to reduce this deficiency.[40] First, the empirical residuals will be corrected for the bias prior to bootrapping. Second, in contrast to the standard method, we are going to use the so-called "percentile method" where the $(a/2)$- and $(1 - a/2)$-quantiles are taken from the distribution of $(\hat{\theta}^* - \hat{\theta})$.

References

Altavilla C (2004) Do EMU Members Share the Same Business Cycle. Journal of Common Market Studies 42: 869-896

Altissimo F, Bassanetti A, Cristadoro R, Forni M, Lippi M, Reichlin L, Veronese G (2001) A Real Time Coincident Indicator of the Euro Area Business Cycle. Temi di Discussione 436, Banca d'Italia

Artis MJ, Zhang W (1995) International Business Cycles and the ERM: Is There a European Business Cycle. International Journal of Finance Economics 2: 1-16

Artis MJ, Zhang W (1999) Further Evidence on the International Business Cycle and the ERM: Is There a European Business Cycle. Oxford Economic Papers 51: 120-132

Artis MJ, Marcellino M, Proietti T (2005) Dating the Euro Area Business Cycle. In: Reichlin L (ed.) The Euro Area Business Cycle: Stylized Facts and Measurement Issues. Centre for Economic Policy Research, London, pp. 7-33

Berkowitz J, Kilian L (2000) Recent Developments in Bootstrapping Time Series. Econometric Reviews 19, 1: 1-48

Beveridge S, Nelson CR (1981) A New Approach to Decomposition of Economic Time Series into Permanent and Transitory Components with Particular Attention to Measurement of the "Business Cycle". Journal of Monetary Economics 7: 151-174

Brockwell PJ, Davis RA (1987) Time Series: Theory and Methods. Springer, New York et al.

Brüggemann R, Lütkepohl H (2001) Lag Selection in Subset VAR Models with an Application to a U.S. Monetary System. In: Friedmann R, Knüppel L, Lütkepohl H (eds.) Econometric Studies—A Festschrift in Honour of Joachim Frohn. LIT, Münster, pp. 107-128

Canova F (1998) Detrending and Business Cycle Facts. Journal of Monetary Economics 41: 475-512

---

[39] See, for instance, Berkowitz and Kilian (2000) for further details and the literature.

[40] Once again, the reader who is interested in more details is referred to the survey articles Li and Maddala (1996) as well as Berkowitz and Kilian (2000), for instance.

Carvalho VM, Harvey AC (2005) Convergence and Cycles in the Euro-Zone. Journal of Applied Econometrics 20, 2: 275-289

Chao JC, Phillips PCB (1999) Model Selection in Partially Nonstationary Vector Autoregressive Processes with Reduced Rank Structure. Journal of Econometrics 91: 227-271

Christodoulakis N, Dimelis SP, Kollintzas T (1995) Comparisons of Business Cycles in the EC: Idiosyncracies and Regularities. Economica 62: 1-27

Clements MP, Hendry DF (1999) Forecasting Non-Stationary Economic Time Series. MIT Press, Cambridge (Ma.) London

Croux C, Forni M, Reichlin L (2001) A Measure of Comovement for Economic Variables: Theory and Empirics. Review of Economics and Statistics 83, 2: 232-141

Dickerson AP, Gibson HD, Tsakalotos E (1998) Business Cycle Correspondence in the European Union. Empirica 25: 51-77

Engle RF, Granger CWJ (1987) Co-Integration and Error Correction: Representation, Estimation, and Testing. Econometrica 55, 2: 251-276

Evans G, Reichlin L (1994) Information, Forecasts, and Measurement of the Business Cycle. Journal of Monetary Economics 33: 233-254

Forni M, Hallin M, Lippi M, Reichlin L (2000) The Generalized Dynamic-Factor Model: Identification and Estimation. Review of Economics and Statistics 82, 4: 540-554

Granger, CWJ (1967) New Techniques for Analyzing Economic Time Series and Their Place in Econometrics. In: Shubik M (ed.) Essays in Mathematical Economics—In Honor of Oskar Morgenstern. Princeton University Press, Princeton New Jersey, pp. 423-442

Hamilton JD (1994) Time Series Analysis. Princeton University Press, Princeton New Jersey

Johansen S (1991) Estimation and Testing of Cointegration Vectors in Gaussian Vector Autoregressive Models. Econometrica 59, 6: 1551-1580

Johansen S (1995) Likelihood-Based Inference in Cointegrated Vector Autoregressive Models. Oxford University Press, Oxford New York

Johansen S, Mosconi R, Nielsen B (2000) Cointegration Analysis in the Presence of Structural Breaks in the Deterministic Trend. Econometrics Journal 3: 216-249

King RG, Plosser CI, Stock JH, Watson MW (1991) Stochastic Trends and Economic Fluctuations. American Economic Review 81, 4: 819-840

Kurozumi E (2002) Testing for Stationarity with a Break. Journal of Econometrics 108: 63-99

Kwiatkowski DA, Phillips PCB, Schmidt P, Shin Y (1992) Testing the Null Hypothesis of Stationarity Against the Alternative of a Unit Root: How Sure Are We That Economic Time Series Have a Unit Root? Journal of Econometrics 54: 154-178

Li H, Maddala GS (1996) Bootstrapping Time Series Models. Econometric Reviews 15, 2: 115-158

Luginbuhl R, Koopman SJ (2004) Convergence in European GDP Series: A Multivariate Common Converging Trend-Cycle Decomposition. Journal of Applied Econometrics 19: 611-636

Lütkepohl H (1993) Introduction to Multiple Time Series Analysis, Second Edition. Springer, Berlin et al.

MacKinnon JG (1991) Critical Values for Cointegration Tests. In: Engle RF, Granger CWJ (eds.) Long-Run Economic Relationships: Readings in Cointegration. Oxford University Press, Oxford, pp. 267-276

Newey WK, West KD (1994) Automatic Lag Selection in Covariance Matrix Estimation. Review of Economic Studies 61: 631-653

Parzen E (1961) Mathematical Considerations in the Estimation of Spectra. Technometrics 3: 167-190

Perron P (1989) The Great Crash, the Oil Price Shock, and the Unit Root Hypothesis. Econometrica 57, 6: 1361-1401

Priestley MB (1981) Spectral Analysis and Time Series. Academic Press, London et al.

Saikkonen P, Lütkepohl H (2000) Testing for the Cointegrating Rank of a VAR Process with Structural Shifts. Journal of Business and Economic Statistics 18: 451-464

Schwert GW (1989) Tests for Unit Roots: A Monte Carlo Investigation. Journal of Business and Economic Statistics 7, 2: 147-159

Stock JH, Watson MW (1988) Testing for Common Trends. Journal of the American Statistical Association 83: 1097-1107

Stock JH, Watson MW (1989) New Indexes of Coincident and Leading Indicators. NBER Macroeconomics Annual 1989: 352-394

Synchronization of Responses to Cyclical Demand Shocks in France, Germany and Italy: Evidence from Central Banks Macro-models*

Andrea Tiseno

Banca d'Italia, via Nazionale 91, 00184 Roma,
andrea.tiseno@bancaditalia.it

Summary. This paper uses the macro-econometric models of the European System of Central Banks to simulate a measure of the extent to which the sources of business cycle of France, Germany and Italy can be traced down to common and/or idiosyncratic factors and to investigate the propagation mechanism of these factors through the various components of aggregate demand. The paper computes responses of GDP and components to hypothetical cyclical shocks that may perturb some of the exogenous factors driving the three economies. Moreover, it shows with couterfactual simulations that over the 1998Q4-2003Q4 period: a) the cycle of world demand could account for up to 35% of the French GDP cycle, 23% of the German and 17% of the Italian; b) the cycle in the Euro exchange rate could account for a large fraction of the German GDP cycle, but only a small fraction of the French and the Italian; and c) taking French government consumption as a benchmark –because the most counter-cyclical– the deviation of government consumption growth with respect to the benchmark could only account for up to 8% of the Italian GDP cycle and only up to 7% of the German.

Keywords: business cycle, macro-econometric models, counterfactual simulation.
JEL classification: E37, E58, E65.

* Special thanks go to Christian Schumacher and Karl-Heinz Toedter of Bundesbank and JP Villetelle of Banque de France for providing calibrated simulation results and precious comments. Thanks also go to Werner Roeger for helpful discussion; to Olivier De Bandt, Heinz Herrmann and Giuseppe Parigi for coordinating the research project of which this paper is part and to Guido Bulligan, Fabio Busetti, Antoine Devulder, Andrea Lamorgese, Alberto Locarno, Libero Monteforte, Stefano Siviero, Daniele Terlizzese, Fabrizio Venditti, Giovanni Veronese and Francesco Zollino for useful comments. The views expressed here are those of the author, who is solely responsible of the remaining errors.

1 Introduction

Against the background of growing disparities among the economic performances of Euro area countries, in particular France, Germany and Italy, one would like to disentangle between possible candidate explanations. A necessary step towards this goal is understanding the role of the exogenous determinants: are the growing disparities mostly due to the fact that idiosyncratic shocks have a larger impact than common ones, or is it rather attributable to a systematic difference in the transmission mechanism of common shocks? This paper is an attempt to investigate such issue from the point of view of aggregate demand. The paper uses the macro-econometric models of the French, Italian and German National Central Banks (NCB) –part of the European System of Central Banks (ESCB)– to simulate the degree of synchronization in the response of the three economies to exogenous shocks. This exercise is part of a joint effort of the three institutions to uncover determinants and obstacles to the synchronization of the business cycle in the three economies.

Macro-econometric models may help study the determinants of synchronization in at least two ways. First of all, they are capable of illustrating and quantifying the synchronization of the economies' responses to exogenous cyclical demand shocks. Secondly, they can be used to measure similarities in the dynamic response to exogenous (counter)-cyclical policy shocks. The paper exploits this explanatory power in two interrelated parts. In the first part, the models of the three economies are counterfactually simulated in order to compute the responses of aggregate demand components to purely hypothetical cyclical shocks. This thought experiment allows to point out, clearly and without the nuisance of high frequency noise, similarities in the dynamic response of the three economies to exogenous shocks at the business cycle frequency. The exercise is performed with three types of shock: a) a cyclical shock to the balanced growth rate of world demand; b) a cyclical shock to the steady state of the Euro exchange rate against all other currencies; and c) a cyclical shock to the growth rate of government consumption.

The second part of the paper performs counterfactual experiments on a historical period of our recent history: the five years between 1998:Q4 and 2003:Q4. The purpose of this experiments is to point out how the history of the three economies would have gone had the world (the history of the exogenous variables) gone differently. This particular time span is the most recent one that has witnessed a full cycle of GDP growth along with a cycle of some of its exogenous determinants. It is obviously controversial that the recovery was already on its way by the end of 2003, however it is probably uncontroversial that this period has witnessed a full cycle in the growth rate of world demand and in the depreciation of the Euro against all other currencies. Full cycles in some of the common exogenous determinants, as well as in the growth rate of GDP of the three economies, make this time period the ideal laboratory for an experiment designed to illustrate the joint dynamics of the three economies, as summarized by their central banks' macro-models.

The experiments of this paper are simulations of counterfactual paths for the growth rate of aggregate demand and components, during the 1998:Q4-2003:Q4 period, under alternative scenarios for the history of the exogenous factors driving the model economies. For each economy, three different scenarios are considered in turn: a) a constant growth rate of world demand at the period average rate of 6.8% per year (1.7% per quarter); b) a zero appreciation of the Euro against all other currencies; and c) a growth rate of government consumption as counter-cyclical as that of France, which was the most accommodating during the period under study. The experiments exploit dynamic multipliers, which summarize the dynamic properties of the three macro-models as delivered by full simulations. Using a linear approximation, dynamic multipliers allow to reconstruct the response of the components of aggregate demand to any arbitrary shock that perturbs the historical path of the exogenous factors. More specifically, the counterfactual experiments of this paper are performed by computing the responses to those arbitrary shocks that would exactly offset the cyclical component of the exogenous factors during the period under study. This methodology allows to reconstruct an approximation of what the history of aggregate demand and components would have been under the three scenarios outlined above. This experiment allows to compare counterfactual histories of GDP and components across the three countries and evaluate how smoother and/or similar their cycles would have been. The multipliers used in this analysis are those used in the context the Eurosystem's Inflation Persistence Network (IPN). They were computed with full simulations of the three models on the basis of harmonized assumptions and shocks.

The paper uses the simulated paths of aggregate demand and components to quantify, with a very simple methodology, the extent to which cycles would have been dampened by a smoother history of each of the exogenous variables in turn. The methodology consists of comparing the differential of average growth rates across phases of the cycle under the two scenarios: the historical and the counterfactual. The main results are that: a) the cycle of world demand may explain up to 35% of the French GDP cycle, 23% of the German and 17% of the Italian one; b) the cycle of the euro exchange rate may explain only a small fraction of the French and Italian GDP cycle, while it may even over-explain the German; and c) taking French government consumption as a benchmark –because the most counter-cyclical– the deviation of government consumption growth with respect to the benchmark could explain only up to 8% of the Italian GDP cycle and only up to 7% of the German. The results on the exchange rate shock must be read with some caution as some recent contributions point out that elasticities might have changed in recent years.

The remaining of the paper is structured as follows. Section 2 outlines the structure of the macro-models of the three central banks. Section 3 explains the methodology of the simulation exercises. Section 4 describes the effect, on the dynamics of GDP and its components, of purely hypothetical cyclical shocks that perturb the exogenous variables. Section 5 is the core of the paper: it describes the counterfactual simulations, outlines the results and provides rough quantitative estimates of the relative importance of each exogenous factor in explaining the cycle. Finally, section 6 draws conclusions from the paper.

2 The econometric models of France, Germany and Italy

As most macro-models, the econometric models used by Banque de France, Bundesbank and Banca d'Italia belong to the same tradition as the generation of models of the eighties, well exemplified by the MPS model of the U.S. economy as described in Brayton and Mauskopf (1985). The salient features of these models are that they integrate the time series results of the literature using error correction specification; they reconstruct the flows and funds representation of the sectors of the economy; they have particular concern for the institutional mechanism of the economy; they integrate demand and supply on each market by explicitly considering the equilibrium mechanism that acts through prices. The macro-models of this tradition are Keynesian in the short-run, with the level of economic activity primarily determined by the behavior of aggregate demand, and neo-classical in the long-run, akin to Solow's model of exogenous growth. Along a steady-state growth path, the dynamics of the models stem solely from capital accumulation, productivity growth, foreign inflation and demographics; in the short-run, a number of additional features matters, namely the stickiness of prices and wages, the putty-clay nature of the production process and inflation surprises. They separate public and private sector and, within the latter, some of them also distinguish among energy, agriculture and the rest of the economy. As to the expectations formation mechanism, some of these models make extensive use of survey data. Most equations in these models are estimated by limited-information techniques, mostly ordinary least squares, while a limited set of parameters are calibrated. The macro-models of this tradition, although lacking the theoretical consistency of more recently developed dynamic general equilibrium models, are more data congruent, hence more useful for the exercise at hand –see Henry and Pagan (2004).

The common feature of the macro-models of Banque de France, Bundesbank and Banca d'Italia is that in equilibrium –*i.e.* once shocks no longer affect the model, expectations are fulfilled and all adjustment processes have come to an end– they describe a full employment economy, in which output, employment and the capital stock are consistent with a constant return to scale aggregate production function, relative prices are constant, inflation equals the exogenous rate of growth of foreign prices and money is neutral –though not super-neutral– so that the model is stable.

The three macro-models serve several purposes, the main one being to provide short and medium-term projections. Since monetary policy affects target variables only with substantial lags, policy actions need to be forward-looking and hence must be based on forecasts of target variables at horizons which are consistent with the delayed response of the economy to monetary policy impulses. These models are also used in policy evaluation exercises, to assess the policy mix which is best suited for raising social welfare, and in counterfactual analysis, in which actual developments in the economy or policy programmes are contrasted with fictitious alternatives so as to gain a better understanding of the costs and benefits inherent in economic actions. For an exhaustive exposition of the econometric models of the Euro-area central banks and an explanation of their use see Fagan and Morgan (2005).

2.1 The Banque de France model

The Banque de France "Mascotte" model of the French economy identifies four agents in the economy: the business sector, the household sector, the public sector and the rest of the world. Firms have price-setting power in a monopolistically competitive regime: they add a "mark-up" to their production costs in order to maximize profits subject to demand and production constraints. First order conditions determine factor demands. The exogenous growth rates of labor productivity and population determine the growth rate of the economy in the long run. In the short run, capacity utilization rate and adjustment lags determine both employment and investment, with the latter also affected by profitability.

The consumption equation specifies the way in which households divide their disposable income between consumption and savings. A long-run unit income elasticity of consumption makes the saving ratio a function of the rate of growth of the real disposable income in the long run and of inflation (the inflation tax). Housing investment is an endogenous variable determined by real disposable income and real long term interest rate. Inventories are function of the change in demand (including total consumption, total investment and exports).

In the trade block nominal exchange rates are exogenous. The main export equation models export of goods as a function of a world demand variable (weighted average of imports of the main trade partners) and price competitiveness. The export deflator is a function of a production price index and a competitors' price index. As regards imports, a distinction is made between energy and non-energy goods and services. The latter are a function of a weighted sum of the components of total demand; this index therefore includes exports. The biggest weights are given to stock-building and investment. The import deflator (excluding energy) is a function of a competitors' price index and a production price index, modified in the short run by the capacity utilization rate. Imports of energy are linked to the overall level of activity and the relative price of imported energy. The latter is a function of the price of oil.

The theoretical structure implies that only relative prices matter in Mascotte. If all nominal variables are changed in the same proportion after a shock, relative prices are unchanged, hence the real equilibrium is unaffected in the long run. In the short run, prices are almost fixed and output is determined by the components of demand. With exogenous exchange rates and in the absence of any reaction function, the mechanism that stabilizes the model after a shock comes primarily from the adjustment in prices. A change in the price level impacts on competitiveness and determines market shares both on the export and import sides and hence the level of activity. The way value added is broken down between wages and profits also impacts on investment and activity. A change in the level of activity modifies in turn the level of employment, alters the unemployment rate and then impacts on wages and prices in return. In the long run, the absence of monetary illusion present in the model, insures the stability of relative prices and, as long as relative prices are unchanged, the nominal side has no impact on real activity. In this respect, a feature of this model is that the wage-price equations is slow to fully adjust after a shock. This stems from the strength of the wage bargaining process. This feature is specified in the equation through the presence of a term of trade effect : a rise in prices leads to upward pressures on wages, on the basis of the consumption deflator on the side of workers, that firms tend to oppose in order to preserve their earnings – on the basis of the value added deflator. This conflict results in a partial adjustment of wages in the short run, and a protracted adjustment thereafter. An additional feature of the response functions of the model is that a nearly homogeneous response in prices is reached well before the full adjustment in the price level. As a consequence, since relative prices are close to what they will be in the long run, even though price levels are not, volumes that respond to relative prices only, can be close to baseline even if the adjustment in the price level is not completed. For a detailed description of the Banque de France model see Villetelle et al. (2005) and Baghli et al. (2004a, 2004b).

2.2 The Bundesbank model

The Bundesbank model of the German economy decomposes aggregate demand among private and government consumption, corporate and government gross investment in machinery/equipment and in construction, imports and exports of goods and services. The private components are almost entirely specified as endogenous variables, except "other investments", which is exogenous. For the government sector, most of the demand components are exogenous. The key exception is government consumption in nominal terms, which is determined by a fiscal rule.

Real private consumption is determined in the long-run by disposable income, private wealth, and an ex-post long-term interest rate. The sum of the coefficients of wealth and disposable income sum to one by restriction in the long run. The short run dynamics include the same determinants as in the long-run but the variables enter in first differences except the cointegration error. Public consumption is specified in nominal terms. The government faces a trade-off between stabilizing the fiscal deficit on the one hand and the output gap on the other. In the long-run equation, government consumption is explained relative to nominal potential output. The deficit is stabilized relative to the fiscal surplus except government consumption, again related to potential output.

In the long run, the key determinant of investment in machinery and equipment are final demand and the ratio between the deflator of final demand - corrected for indirect taxes - and the real user costs of capital. In the short-run, first differences of final demand and an autoregressive term enter the equation. Similar to investment in machinery and equipment, construction investment by the private sector is mainly determined by final demand and relative prices between user costs and the final demand deflator. Real investment in residential construction is determined by real disposable income per capita and a smoothed long-term real interest rate, which is obtained by taking a moving average over six quarters of the long-term interest rate and inflation. Changes in inventories are mainly determined by final demand. If the lagged change in final demand is larger than the change in inventories, contemporaneous inventories increase.

The two key determinants of real exports are world demand and the real effective exchange rate. Real imports are determined by final demand and the relative price ratio between domestic demand prices and import prices. To account for the exceptional strong import growth not explained by these determinants, additional time trends are included in the long-run equation. For a detailed description of the Bundesbank model see Bundesbank (2000), Todter (2002) and Hamburg and Todter (2005).

2.3 The Banca d'Italia model

The theoretical structure underlying the steady-state of the Bank of Italy Quarterly Model (BIQM) of the Italian economy is a traditional one. The supply sector can be thought of as being composed by producers who are price-setters in output market and price-takers in factor markets. Each producer, being endowed with the same Cobb-Douglas constant-returns-to-scale technology, knows the minimum average cost of his competitors and fixes the level of the mark-up so as to keep potential entrants out of business. Along a steady-state growth path, firms decide in each period the cost-minimizing factor mix and the level of domestic activity is then set to generate, given factor demands, a non-accelerating-inflation rate of unemployment. Life-cycle consumers choose the desired addition to the real stock of total wealth, which is then allocated among foreign assets, physical capital and government debt. As consumers compute their life-time resources without anticipating the need for the government to satisfy a long-run solvency condition, the stock of public debt is perceived to be part of total wealth and Ricardian equivalence does not hold. A detailed description of the theoretical underpinnings of the BIQM is in Banca d'Italia (1986) and a good summary is in Busetti et al. (2005). Other useful descriptions of the main features of the model are Galli et al. (1989), Terlizzese (1994) and Siviero (1995).

The BIQM does not distinguish between households and firms; the explanatory variables in the equations modeling consumption accordingly refer to the private sector as a whole. Consumption of non-durables and durables are treated separately. The former is modeled consistently with the life-cycle theory and is driven by permanent income, proxied by a weighted average of disposable income and wealth. Disposable income is computed by adjusting for the capital gains/losses on financial assets engendered by changes in the inflation rate. Since wealth is not measured at market value, the real interest rate is included among the explanatory variables. The demand for durables is driven by total consumption expenditure: its share depends on the relative price of durable goods and on the long-term interest rate.

The investment component of aggregate demand is determined by the optimality of firms' behavior on the supply side. Since capital is non-malleable, the choice of productive factors is limited to the additions to previously existing stocks. In each period, given demand expectations, firms set the desired addition to capacity by solving a cost minimization problem. Given the level of aggregate demand, this determines desired capital accumulation. Since it takes time to produce and deliver capital goods, actual and planned investment differ, with the former being a weighted average of the most recent values of the latter. As typical with models assuming that capital is putty-clay, investments react to changes in demand and changes in relative factor price differently: while in the first instance the shape of the response conforms to the accelerator principle, in the second it is smooth and monotone. The equation for housing investment relies on a variant of Tobin's q model: residential capital depends on the present value of the future streams of profits (proxied by the market price) of an additional unit of capital. Financing constraints are accounted for by using the expected real interest rate as an explanatory variable and a time trend is included to capture demographic effects on the total demand for housing; fiscal factors also play a role in the equation. The interaction between supply and demand for houses, the latter modeled as a portfolio allocation problem, determines the market price.

The modeling of the demand for imports and exports relies on the assumption of imperfect substitutability between foreign and domestic goods. In accordance with demand theory, imports may be viewed as the solution to the maximization problem of a representative consumer, who acts taking into account a budget constraint. Separability and homogeneity of the utility function ensure that the saving decision and consumption allocation - in particular the choice between domestic and foreign goods - can be treated separately. Absence of money illusion is imposed by considering relative prices and real income. The scale variable driving imports is a weighted average of aggregate demand components, with exports and investments in machinery having the largest weights; the degree of utilized capacity is included in the specification so as to capture the fact that sudden changes in domestic demand are initially more than proportionally met by foreign production. Exports are modeled in a similar way: the scale variable is world imports and the degree of utilized capacity is used as a proxy for non-price competitiveness. Both imports and exports have unit elasticity with respect to their respective scale variables.

3 Multipliers and the methodology of the simulation exercise

The simulations of the paper are based on the use of dynamic multipliers computed with full simulations of each of the macro-model. In particular, the approach is based on the methodology used by the ESCB for its IPN exercise. In that context, the effects of exogenous shocks on inflation in the euro area are studied through the aggregation of dynamic responses of the individual country models to common exogenous shocks, with the addition of area-wide policy rules. The aggregation is based on a linear approximation of multipliers that are obtained from non-linear dynamic simulation of the econometric models of the euro area central banks. For a full description of the exercise see Berben et al. (2005). This paper borrows the multipliers of the French, German and Italian models in order to reconstruct a linear approximation of each country's response to exogenous cyclical shocks.

Three limitations must be emphasized with regard to this methodology. First of all, multipliers are provided without standard errors, so that none of our simulations can be bounded within a confidence band. Secondly, the country multipliers are based on the assumption that there is no policy rule at the country level, because policy rules are imposed at the Euro area level after aggregation. Using the country level multipliers –and skipping aggregation– this paper is disregarding the effect of area-wide rules at the country level. As it will be discussed later, this is a source of bias for our estimates of the relative effects of exogenous shocks on each country's cycle: for this reason, results provided here should be seen as upper bounds. Finally, comparisons among countries may not only reflect real differences among countries but also differences in modeling strategies (see Fagan and Morgan, 2005)

Dynamic properties of large-size econometric models of the type used by central banks are customarily investigated by inspection of the dynamic elasticity of endogenous variables with respect to exogenous ones. Labeled as "multipliers", dynamic elasticities are simulated with experiments in which exogenous variables are shocked one at the time around a dynamically simulated path. Typically, properties of a model are summarized with multipliers to permanent shocks, *i.e.* with the elasticity of the future path of endogenous variables to shocks that perturb exogenous variables permanently. We call these "cumulated multipliers". If models were linear, cumulated multipliers would be all that is needed in order to infer the dynamic elasticities to shocks with any arbitrary path –which we call "counterfactual multipliers"– because responses would be independent of the time period in which they were computed. In particular, simple time differentiation of cumulated multipliers would allow to recover "impulse multipliers", *i.e.* the elasticity of the future path of endogenous variables to shocks that perturb exogenous variables only for one period. Counterfactual multipliers could then be inferred as the cumulate of the impulse multipliers corresponding to all the impulse shocks of which the arbitrary shock is composed. In principle, due to the non-linearity (in variables) of large-size econometric models, special care has to be used to infer counterfactual multipliers from the cumulated ones. In practice though, there is considerable evidence that in many of these models non-linearity is quite mild, at least for most of the variables, so that the above type of inference is a good approximation.

In order to illustrate how the methodology works in practice, suppose that K variables of interest $x_t = \left(x_t^1 ... x_t^K\right)$ respond to H exogenous variables $z_t = \left(z_t^1 ... z_t^H\right)$, where $t = 1, 2...T$. For a linear model, the response of x_t to a given path of shocks to the $h - th$ exogenous variable z_t^h can be expressed as

$$dx_t^h = \sum_{s=1}^{T} \alpha_s^h dz_{t-s+1}^h \equiv \beta_t^h; \quad h = 1, ...H \tag{1}$$

where $\alpha_t^h = \partial x_t / \partial z_1^h$ is the $K \times 1$ vector of impulse multipliers at horizon $t = 1, ...T$ –the response to a single impulse after t periods. By construction, the simulation results available from the IPN exercise do not provide dynamic multipliers α_t^h for each shock $h = 1, ... H$ directly, but only the cumulated responses β_t^h to permanent shocks $dz_t^h = dz^h, t = 1, ...T$. Clearly, for linear models the dynamic multipliers could be obtained exactly solving equation (1) recursively, which delivers

$$\alpha_1^h = \beta_1^h / \partial z_1^h$$

$$\alpha_t^h = \left(\beta_t^h - \sum_{s=1}^{t-1} \alpha_s^h dz_{t-s+1}^h \right) / \partial z_1^h; \quad t = 2, ...T.$$

If the model is non-linear these equalities only hold approximately.

If one starts with permanent multipliers –the typical format in which dynamic multipliers of large macro-models are presented– the time series of shocks is a vector of ones, *i.e.* $dz_t^h = dz^h = 1$ for all t. For this case, it follows that $\alpha_t^h = \beta_t^h - \beta_{t-1}^h; t = 2, ...T$. For all $h = 1, ...H$ the linear approximation to counterfactual multipliers can thus be obtained in two steps: first impulse multipliers α_t^h for $t = 1, ...T$ can be recovered by simple differentiation of the series β_t^h for $t = 1, ...T$; then counterfactual multipliers can be re-constructed by iteration of equation (1). If the non-linearities embedded in the models are not extreme, discrepancies between the models' true responses and the linear approximations obtained by this procedure can be regarded as second order effects.

Using the methodology outlined here, this paper exploits cumulated multipliers of the ESCB macro-models to recover the dynamic responses of the French, German and Italian economies to arbitrary shocks. Three types of shocks are considered: a) a permanent shock to world demand; b) a permanent shock to the Euro exchange rate against all currencies; c) a permanent shock to government consumption. The cumulative multipliers of these shocks are used to compute a linear approximation of the counterfactual multipliers of the three model economies. Two thought experiments are performed. In the first one, the economies are perturbed by purely hypothetical cyclical shocks to each of the three exogenous variables in turn. In the second one, the historical path of each of the three exogenous variables is perturbed in turn by a counterfactual shock that exactly cancels out its cyclical pattern during the historical period 1998:Q4-2003:Q4.

It is worth summarizing the main properties of the three model economies by inspecting their cumulated multipliers. Figure 1 displays the cumulated responses of the three economies to a permanent (1%) shock to world demand. The thick lines represent the cumulated responses of GDP, the other lines the cumulated responses of the shares of each aggregate demand component in GDP –i.e. the cumulated responses of each component weighted by its share in GDP. Shares are computed as the average shares during the sample period 1998:Q4-2003:Q4 –which are meant to approximate the steady state shares. As a result of approximation, cumulated responses of the components only approximately add up to the cumulated response of GDP, but with a good degree of precision. Government consumption is held fixed as all policy rules are turned off. The long run elasticity of GDP to world demand eventually reaches approximately 0.2 in all three model economies, although the approach is slower for the Italian one. The contribution of imports and exports to the GDP multiplier is more or less similar in all three model economies, and the same holds true for the contribution of consumption. On the contrary, the reaction of the investment component of GDP is more persistent in the Italian model than in the other two.

Figure 2 plots the cumulated responses of the three model economies to a permanent (1%) appreciation of the Euro exchange rate against all currencies. As before, thick lines represent the cumulated responses of GDP, the other lines the cumulated responses of the shares of each aggregate demand component in GDP; government consumption and all other policy rules are held fixed. The magnitude and speed of responses of the three model economies vary considerably. There is much heterogeneity in the way in which the twelve model economies of the euro area react to this type of shock, with France, Italy and Germany standing at the extremes of the distribution: the

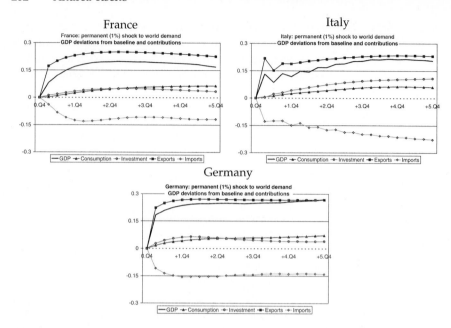

Notes: Dynamic multipliers obtained by simulation of the three models under alternative scenarios for the exogenous variable "world demand": historical versus counterfactual path (1% higher every quarter). The thick line shows the percentage deviation of the counterfactually simulated path of GDP with respect to its history. The other lines represent the contributions of each aggregate demand component to the deviation of GDP. They are computed as deviations weighted by the share in GDP, hence they add up to the deviation of GDP. Notice that a positive deviation in imports contributes negatively to the deviation of GDP, because imports have a negative share.

Fig. 1. Responses of GDP to a permanent 1% shock to world demand and contributions of each aggregate demand component

elasticity of the French GDP to the Euro exchange rate is roughly -0.02% in the short run and dies out quickly, whereas that of the German GDP slowly reaches -0.25% displaying a limited subsequent inversion and that of the Italian GDP drops at an even slower pace. There are also differences in the way in which the different components contribute to the impact on GDP, especially with regard to consumption which grows in Italy and France, after the appreciation of the Euro, while it declines in Germany. These discrepancies partly reflect genuine differences among the three underlying economies and partly differences in the ability of the three models to capture the true dynamic impact of the exchange rate. There are at least three genuine differences among the economies that may explain the larger responsiveness of Germany. First of all, the share of exports in GDP is larger in Germany than in the other two economies. Secondly, the weights of extra Euro area trade in the total is much larger in Germany than in the other two countries. Finally, there

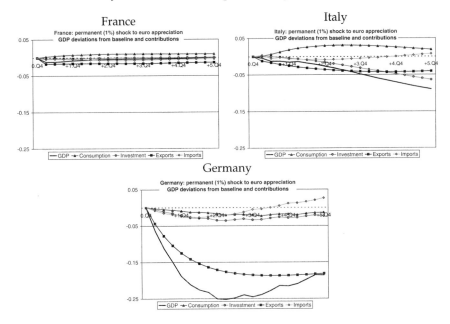

Notes: See notes for figure 1.

Fig. 2. Responses of GDP to a permanent 1% euro appreciation against all currencies and contributions of each aggregate demand component

are structural differences in the mechanism through which shocks are transmitted to the economy, with France and Germany at the two extremes: while in the French model relative prices adjust much more quickly than the price level, so that the effect of the exchange rate shock is smoothed away very quickly, this mechanism is slower in the German model. It must be pointed out that the large difference between the German reactiveness and the French sluggishness to exchange rate shocks may have substantially reduced in recent years. Two contributions of this volume point towards this direction. De Bandt and Villetelle (2006, this volume) report econometric evidence in favor of the idea that the French elasticity of exports to competitiveness may have increased recently. At the same time, Stahn (2006) documents a lower elasticity of German exports to competitiveness. These two developments would substantially reduce the difference in reactiveness, although at this stage it is not possible to quantify to what extent.

Figure 3 plots the cumulated responses of the three model economies to a permanent (1% of beginning of period GDP) shock to government consumption. As before, policy rules are turned off, but a permanent shock to government consumption does not determine a permanent change in its contribution to GDP, as the other components react to the shock. In all three model economies the multiplier is larger than one for some periods before dipping

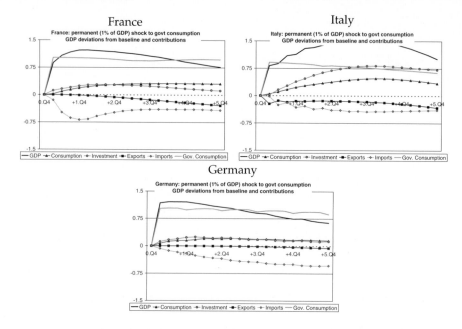

Notes: See notes for figure 1.

Fig. 3. Responses of GDP to a permanent increase in government consumption by 1% of GDP and contributions of each aggregate demand component

below unity. This decay is fastest in Germany and slowest in Italy, where the hump shape of the GDP multiplier is the most pronounced –driven in large part by the strong and slow dynamics of the investment component. Imports –and partly also exports– is the main component that drives the GDP multiplier below unity and this effect is particularly strong in France during the first couple of years.

4 Synchronization of the three economies in response to cyclical demand shocks

This section of the paper describes the effect of purely hypothetical cyclical perturbations of exogenous variables on the dynamics of GDP and its components. The cyclical shocks of this exercise are sine waves that perturb in turn the steady state growth rate of: a) world demand; b) exchange rate; c) government consumption. In all simulations, shocks are perturbations of the growth rate of variables, measured as quarter-on-quarter percentage variation. As already mentioned, unwinding cumulative multipliers to obtain impulse multipliers and rewinding these to obtain counterfactual multipliers –using the methodology outlined in section 3– adds nothing to what cumu-

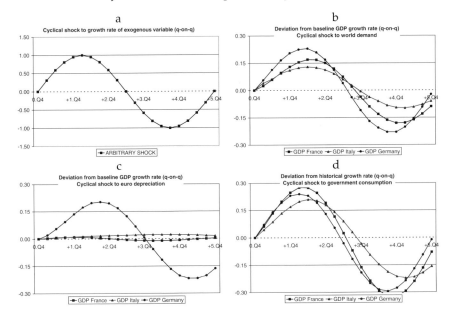

Notes: Panel (a) plots the hypothetical sine-wave shock used to perturb the growth rate of each of the exogenous variables in the three experiments. The other three panels display the effects of the three shocks
on the growth rates of GDP. In panel (b) world demand is perturbed; in panel (c) the euro exchange rate is
depreciated against all currencies; in panel (d) government consumption.

Fig. 4. Responses of GDP growth rates to cyclical shock perturbing the growth rate of
exogenous variables

lative multipliers already say about the dynamics of the model economies.
However, this exercise is useful in order to inspect the synchronicity of the
cyclical responses of GDP components in the three model economies. Each of
the three exogenous variables is perturbed by a shock that over time follows
a sine wave with period of five years and amplitude of 1%. Such a shock generates cyclical responses in the main components of GDP, which are plotted
in Figures 4 through 7. These figures display the counterfactual multipliers
of the three model economies against each other, allowing to measure the
degree of synchronization of responses to exogenous stimuli.

Figure 4 summarizes the synchronization of GDP responses to each of
the three shocks. Panel (a) displays the shock that perturbs the growth rate
of each of the three exogenous factors in the simulations: a sine wave with
period of five years and amplitude of 1% per quarter. Panel (b) shows the
responses to a rise and a fall in the growth rate of world demand. The
three economies respond synchronously, with Germany reacting more than
France, which in turn reacts more than Italy. The growth rate of the German economy experiences a swing of an amplitude of more than 0.2% in the
growth rate of its GDP, while that of the Italian economy of only slightly more

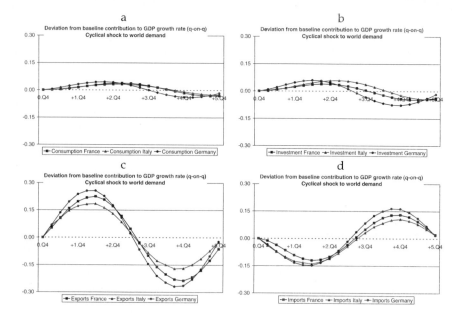

Notes: Panel (a) plots the response of the contribution of consumption to aggregate demand; panel (b) of investment; panel (c) of exports; panel (d) of imports

Fig. 5. Responses of the growth rates of contributions to aggregate demand to a cyclical shock perturbing the growth rate of world demand

than 0.1%. Panel (c) shows the responses to a rise and a fall of the depreciation rate of the Euro against all currencies. Surprisingly, the three economies do not respond synchronously at all. The German economy is by large the most responsive to the exchange rate.[2] Panel (d) shows the responses to a rise and a fall of the growth rate of government consumption. As for world demand, the three economies respond synchronously, this time without much difference in the amplitude of the response. The only slight exception is Italy where the cycle in the growth rate of GDP is delayed with respect to that of the exogenous shock.

Figures 5 to 7 break down the counterfactual multipliers of GDP into the counterfactual multipliers of the contributions of each component –*i. e.* into the multiplier of the components of aggregate demand weighted by their share in GDP. Each figure overlaps the dynamic elasticities of the contributions in the three countries, which together add up to the dynamic elasticities of GDP. Figure 5 illustrates responses of the GDP contributions to an exoge-

---

[2] Comparison with the simulation results of other central bank models shows similar results for other countries. For example, the models of the Austrian and the Finnish economies display similar strong exchange rate effects as the German model, as pointed out in Fagan and Morgan (2005).

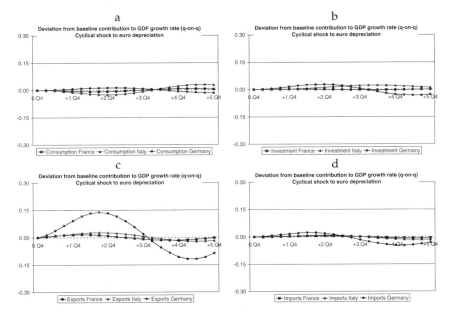

Notes: Panel (a) plots the response of the contribution of consumption to aggregate demand; panel (b) of investment; panel (c) of exports; panel (d) of imports

Fig. 6. Responses of the growth rates of contributions to aggregate demand to a cyclical shock perturbing the Euro depreciation rate

nous shock in the growth rate of world demand. Responses are fairly synchronous across countries, with the exception of the reaction of investment which is fastest in Germany and slowest in Italy . For all three countries, the largest contribution to the GDP growth rate cycle induced by the shock comes from exports, directly activated by world demand, which react at the same frequency in all three economies and are only partially attenuated by imports. As predicted by the life cycle theory of consumption, and confirmed by the cumulative multipliers described in the previous section, the response of consumption is negligible for all three economies.

Multipliers of a negative shock to the euro exchange rate are reported in Figure 6. As reflected in the a-synchronicity in GDP growth responses across the three economies, the contributions of aggregate demand components react with very different strength to the external stimulus. The main contribution to the large swing of the German GDP comes from exports. In the German economy, the cycle in the contribution of exports is even strengthened by the contribution of all other components, that move in parallel fashion. In contrast, the reaction in the contribution of consumption is counter-cyclical in the other two countries and the pro-cyclical contribution of exports is very modest.

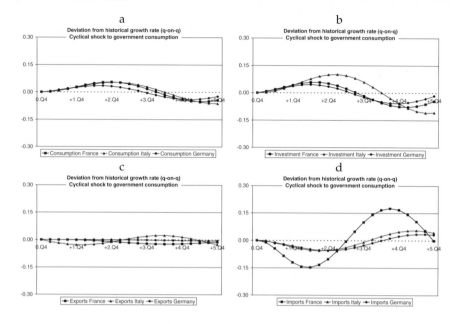

Notes: Panel (a) plots the response of the contribution of consumption to aggregate demand; panel (b) of investment; panel (c) of exports; panel (d) of imports

Fig. 7. Responses of the growth rates of contributions to aggregate demand to a cyclical shock perturbing the growth rate of government consumption

Figure 7 displays multipliers of a shock in the growth rate of government consumption. Three main differences arise from the reaction of GDP components to the shock. First of all, the contribution of investment in Italy is activated at a slower pace than in the other countries, while that of consumption is synchronous across the countries, which partly explains the delay in the response of Italian GDP. Secondly, in Italy the contribution of exports quickly reacts to the shock in government consumption in opposite direction and this too contributes to slow down the cycle in the growth rate of Italian GDP. Lastly, the contribution of imports in contrasting that of government consumption in GDP is larger and faster in France than in the other countries. Overall, similarities in the cyclical response of GDP are obtained, beyond the direct contribution of government consumption, with different contributions of investment, imports and exports across the three countries.

5 Counterfactual simulations

The paper now turns from simulations of hypothetical shocks, which are used to highlight comovements of responses across economies, to counterfactual simulations. We argue that over the recent 5-year period 1998:Q4-

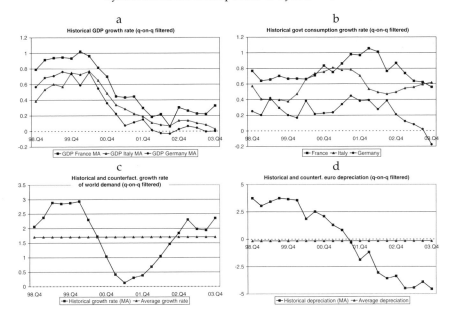

Notes: Panel (a) displays the cycle in the growth rate of GDP of the three economies. Panel (b) the behavior of the three countries' government expenditure during the cycle. Panel (c) shows the cyclical behavior and the average of the growth rate of world demand during the 5-year period. Panel (d) shows the cyclical behavior and the average of the depreciation rate of the Euro during the 5-year period.

Fig. 8. Cyclical history of the growth rates of GDP and the exogenous factors

2003:Q4 the three economies experienced a full cyclical episode in the growth rate of GDP. Disregarding the fact that on average during this period France grew at a slightly faster pace, the time profile of GDP growth rate was parallel in the three countries. We also argue that during the same time span the three economies were hit by two common exogenous cyclical shocks: one in the growth rate of world demand and one in the exchange rate depreciation. These are common factors causing cyclical fluctuations on the demand side. One objective of this section is to determine what fraction of the cycle of the three countries they can account for. Moreover, during the cyclical episode under inspection, government spending followed different growth paths in the three countries –beyond the fact that it was on average growing faster in France. This too is an idiosyncratic factor causing cyclical fluctuations on the demand side. Another objective of this section is to determine what fraction of the cycle of the three countries it can account for.

Evidence in favor of our claim that the 5-year period 1998:Q4-2003:Q4 witnessed a full cyclical episode both in the growth rate of GDP and in the exogenous determinants is illustrated in figure 8. The q-on-q growth rate of GDP in the three economies is plotted in panel (a), after filtering data with a simple moving average (three leads and three lags). The fact that the economies have witnessed a GDP cycle over that period seems an acceptable assumption, although it may be argued that the recovery was not on its way yet by the end of 2003. The shape of the cycle seems identical across the three countries, although there is a constant positive difference between the growth rate of French GDP and the others. Panel (c) and (d) plot the filtered q-on-q growth rates of world demand and Euro exchange rate against the period average. The difference seems to follow a cycle which coincides roughly with the cycle in the growth rate of GDP of the three economies. This evidence should support our claim. Figure 8 also shows, in panel (b), the other exogenous factor that we consider: the growth rate of government consumption in the three countries. Simple eye inspection points out that the growth rate of French government consumption was more counter-cyclical than that of the other two countries.

The counterfactual experiment of this section can be summarized as follows. For each country we reconstruct counterfactual histories for the growth rates of GDP and components, removing the exogenous cyclical sources one at a time. This experiment is performed by first computing counterfactual multipliers for shocks with same magnitude and opposite sign as the cyclical component of the growth rate of the exogenous factors. These multipliers allow to reconstruct counterfactual histories, under the controlled experiment of no cycle in each of the exogenous factors in turn. The counterfactual effect on the cycle of GDP is then compared across the three countries with two methods: a simple graphical method and a simple quantitative method. The graphical comparison is displayed in Figures 9 through 14. For each shock and for each country the figures display historical and counterfactual GDP growth rates (when the exogenous factor is removed) along with a plot of the discrepancy between the two and a plot of the shock to the exogenous factor that was used to perform the experiment. Moreover, the contributions of each component of aggregate demand to the discrepancy between historical and counterfactual GDP grow rates are also displayed.

The quantitative comparisons are reported in Tables 1 through 6. For each shock the results of simulations are reported in two tables. The first table contains historical and counterfactual average growth rates of GDP and components. In the first three columns the components are compared in their average growth rates, with the third column reporting the percentage deviation, whereas in the other three columns they are compared in their average contributions to the growth rate of GDP. The most insightful numbers are the percentage deviations between historical and counterfactual average growth rates. As all these numbers are a few percentage points of small percentage growth rates, these differences are negligible. This reflects and confirms the fact that the counterfactual experiments have been constructed so as to have "zero mean", because all shocks have been demeaned.

In the second table, the 20 quarters under investigation have been split into two sub-periods of 10 quarters each. Average historical and counterfactual growth rates have been computed on each sub-period and the difference across periods is reported in the first two columns. The third column reports the percentage difference between the historical and the counterfactual difference in growth rates across periods. In the first three columns historical and counterfactual components are compared in terms of average difference of growth rates, whereas in the last three they are compared in terms of average difference of their contributions to the GDP growth rate. The most insightful columns are those reporting percentage deviations between historical and counterfactual difference of average growth rates. These are a naive "difference in difference"estimates of the importance of each exogenous shock in explaining the cycle of those years, as they may be interpreted as a measure of the fraction of the 1998:Q4-2003:Q4 cycle that may be accounted for by each exogenous factor. These numbers are the main focus of the paper and they are discussed in the remaining of this section.

A few caveats are worth emphasizing about these experiments. First of all, by construction, the counterfactual simulations of macro-econometric models obtained by perturbation of one exogenous factor at a time assume that all other exogenous factors are constant. While this assumption is reasonable when the exogenous factors under investigation are orthogonal, it might not be fully warranted, because world demand, exchange rate and government consumption are most likely correlated. This implies that our estimates of the importance of each exogenous shock reported in the tables are upward biased and should only be regarded as upper bounds. Secondly, another reason for which our estimates should only be considered as upper bounds is that all simulations are obtained under the assumption that policy rules are turned off. As this is certainly not the case in reality, removing exogenous sources of cyclical variation without removing the counter-cyclical policies that rules would have triggered is likely to overestimate the effects of those shocks. Finally, there is an endemic limitation of the type of experiments carried out in this paper, due to the fact that multipliers are reported by central banks without any standard error. This forces us to measure the relative importance of shocks with point estimates, while confidence bands around them may well be large. In other words, we might be measuring a sizeable effect of an exogenous factor when there is none, or vice versa.

5.1 Counterfactual world demand

The counterfactual experiment of flattening out the growth rate of world demand over the entire 1998:Q4-2003:Q4 period is carried out by perturbing the history of the three economies with an exogenous shock to the growth rate of world demand that coincides with the gap between its actual growth rate and the period average. Such shock is depicted in panel (c) of Figure 9. The rest of Figure 9 illustrates the effects of such experiment on GDP. Panel (a) shows what GDP growth has been for the three countries, panel (b) what it would have been with a counterfactual growth rate of world demand. Al-

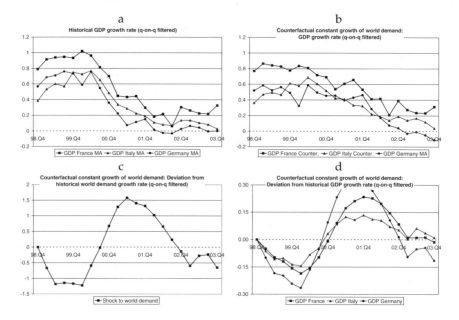

Notes: The four panels illustrate the experiment of a constant growth rate of world demand. Panel (a) and (b) display the historical and counterfactual growth rates of GDP. Panel (c) shows the cyclical shocks to the growth rate of world demand used to perturb the economies in the experiment. Panel (d) the impact of the experiment on the growth rates of GDP.

Fig. 9. Experiment with constant growth rate of world demand: historical and counterfactual GDP growth rates

though the difference is small, the picture shows quite clearly that all three economies would have enjoyed a smoother growth. The actual discrepancies between actual and counterfactual growth rates are plotted in panel (d) which confirms that under the counterfactual exogenous shock the reaction of GDP growth rate would have been counter-cyclical enough to fill at least part of the gap between the average growth rates in the first and second part of the sample, for all three economies.

Figure 10 illustrates the way in which the contributions of each component of aggregate demand would have reacted to this imaginary history. As it may be expected from our analysis of the purely hypothetical case, the contribution of consumption would have not changed much. Investment too would have had a minor role, slightly asymmetrically across countries. On the contrary, the contribution of exports would have obviously accounted for a large part of the difference with similar behaviour across countries. The activation of imports would have partly attenuated the change in contribution of exports, roughly half of it.

Table 2 illustrates what fraction of the 1998:Q4-2003:Q4 cycle could be accounted for, in each of the three countries, by the common factor "world de-

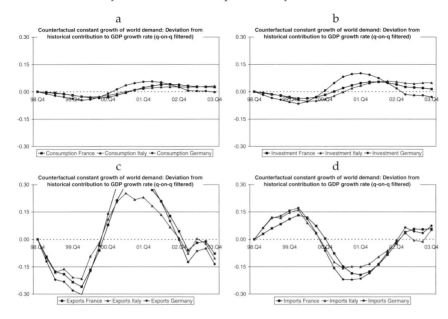

Notes: The four panels illustrate the experiment of a constant growth rate of world demand. Panel (a) shows the impact on the growth rate of consumption's contribution to GDP; panel (b) investment's; panel (c) exports'; panel (d) exports'.

Fig. 10. Experiment with constant growth rate of world demand: impact on the growth rate of each component's contribution to GDP

mand" and how this fraction could be attributed to the contributions of each component of aggregate demand. According to the methodology adopted in this table, up to 35% of the French cycle of those years could be accounted for by the cycle of world demand. This means that if there had been no exogenous shock in world demand, *i.e.* had it continued to grow at the sample average of 1.7% per quarter in every period, the cycle in the growth rate of GDP would have been up to 35% less severe in France. This upper bound drops to 23% for the case of the German cycle and 17% for that of the Italian cycle. With regard to the contributions to the cycle in the growth rate of GDP of each component activated by the common shock in world demand, the net contribution of foreign trade was at most 6% in France, 4% in Germany and almost nil in Italy. Consumption could account for up to 13% of the cycle in France, 10% in Germany and 6% in Italy. Investment could account for up to 16% of the cycle in France, 9% in Germany and 11% in Italy.

5.2 Counterfactual exchange rate

The counterfactual experiment of a flat euro, neither appreciating nor depreciating, over the entire 1998:Q4-2003:Q4 period, is performed by perturbing

Table 1. Impact of world demand shock on average growth rate of demand components (1998:Q4-2003:Q4)

	Average q-on-q growth rates			Average contributions to q-on-q growth rate of GDP		
	Historic.	Counterf.	Diff.	Historic.	Counterf.	%-Diff.
France						
GDP	0.55%	0.57%	0.02%	0.55%	0.57%	4.06%
Consumption	0.60%	0.61%	0.01%	0.31%	0.31%	1.01%
Investment	0.79%	0.83%	0.04%	0.15%	0.16%	1.56%
Govt. Cons.	0.77%	0.77%	0.00%	0.17%	0.17%	0.09%
Exports	0.96%	1.02%	0.06%	0.25%	0.27%	3.23%
Imports	1.31%	1.35%	0.04%	-0.33%	-0.34%	-1.83%
Italy						
GDP	0.37%	0.38%	0.01%	0.37%	0.38%	2.28%
Consumption	0.35%	0.36%	0.01%	0.20%	0.20%	0.42%
Investment	0.59%	0.63%	0.04%	0.11%	0.12%	1.59%
Govt. Cons.	0.57%	0.57%	0.00%	0.09%	0.09%	-0.25%
Exports	0.40%	0.42%	0.02%	0.11%	0.11%	0.84%
Imports	0.54%	0.56%	0.02%	-0.14%	-0.14%	-0.32%
Germany						
GDP	0.31%	0.32%	0.01%	0.31%	0.32%	3.24%
Consumption	0.25%	0.26%	0.01%	0.13%	0.13%	0.98%
Investment	-0.21%	-0.17%	-0.04%	-0.04%	-0.03%	2.25%
Govt. Cons.	0.25%	0.25%	0.00%	0.04%	0.04%	-0.07%
Exports	1.68%	1.71%	0.03%	0.53%	0.53%	2.41%
Imports	1.23%	1.26%	0.03%	-0.35%	-0.36%	-2.33%

Notes: The first column reports averages of historical q-on-q growth rates of GDP and components, for the three countries. The second column displays the averages of counterfactual growth rates when the exogenous cyclical source is removed with the counterfactual experiment. The third column shows the difference between counterfactual and historical growth rates. Columns four and five break down the historical and counterfactual average growth rate of GDP by components of aggregate demand, normalizing the components' growth rate by the share in GDP. The last column reports the percentage difference between historical and counterfactual average growth rate of GDP and how this percentage difference can be decomposed among components of aggregate demand.

the history of the three economies with the gap between the average and the actual euro depreciation rates. This shock is depicted in panel (c) of figure 11 and the whole figure 12 illustrates the effects of this experiment on GDP. It is crucial to recall the point made in section 3, that the large difference between the German reactiveness and the French sluggishness to exchange rate

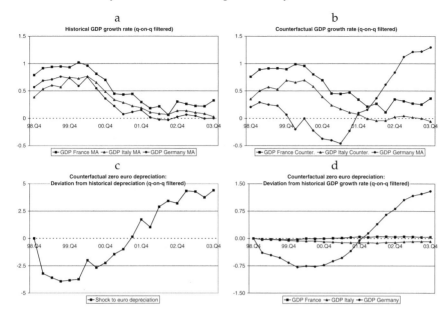

Notes: The four panels illustrate the experiment of a constant (nearly zero) depreciation rate of the Euro against all other currencies. Panel (a) and (b) display the historical and counterfactual growth rates of GDP. Panel (c) shows the cyclical shock to the depreciation rate used to perturb the economies in the experiment. Panel (d) the impact of the experiment on the growth rates of GDP.

Fig. 11. Experiment with constant (nearly zero) depreciation rate of the Euro against all other currencies: historical and counterfactual GDP growth rates

shocks may have substantially reduced in recent years, because export elasticity to competitiveness might have reduced in Germany and increased in France. For this reason, the cross-country comparisons of this section must be read with some caution. Analogously to the previous paragraph, panel (a) shows what GDP growth has been for the three countries, panel (b) what it would have been with the counterfactual Euro depreciation. The cross country difference are quite large. France and Italy would have witnessed more or less the same cycle, while Germany would have gone through a very different history, *i. e.* a significant acceleration of GDP in the second period contrary to what has historically happened. The actual discrepancies in growth rates of GDP between actual and counterfactual are plotted in panel (d) which confirms the fact that with the counterfactual exogenous shock the differential in growth rates would have been very large for Germany and nearly nil for France and Italy. If history had been the counterfactual, GDP growth asymmetries among the three countries would have been even larger than they have actually been.

Figure 12 illustrates the way in which the contributions of each component of aggregate demand would have reacted to this imaginary history. As

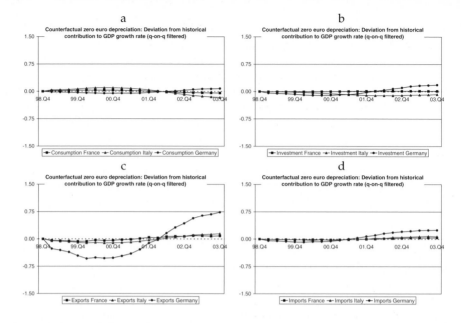

a

b

c

d

Notes: The four panels illustrate the experiment of a zero depreciation of the Euro. Panel (a) shows the impact on the growth rate of consumption's contribution to GDP; panel (b) investment's; panel (c) exports'; panel (d) exports'.

Fig. 12. Experiment with constant (nearly zero) depreciation rate of the Euro against all other currencies: impact on the growth rate of each component's contribution to GDP

expected, it is unequivocally clear that most of the change in German GDP growth rate could be accounted for by the contribution of the growth rate of exports. The change in the contribution of all other components of German aggregate demand appears to be of second order, similar in magnitude to that of other countries as far as consumption and investment are concerned and slightly larger with regard to imports. It is worth noticing though, that in this counterfactual experiment the contribution of consumption and investment in Germany goes in the opposite direction as compared to the other countries.

In Table 4 one can read what fraction of the 1998:Q4-2003:Q4 cycle could be accounted for, in each of the three countries, by the common factor "exchange rate" and how this fraction could be attributed to the contributions of each component of aggregate demand. According to this table, up to 235% of the German cycle of those years could be accounted for by the cycle of euro depreciation. This means that had there been no exogenous shock to the euro depreciation, *i.e.* had the Euro continued to depreciate at the sample average rate of 0.1% per quarter in every period for the entire period, the cycle in the growth rate of GDP would have been up to 235% less severe in

Germany than it actually was. Notice that 100% less severe is equivalent to "no cycle", hence a percentage larger than 100% means an even larger cycle, of the opposite sign. This fraction drops to 11% for the French cycle and -8% for the Italian cycle. A negative percentage means that had there been no exogenous shock to the euro depreciation, the cycle in the growth rate of GDP would have been 8% more –rather than less– severe in Italy than it actually was. With regard to the contributions to the GDP cycle following the euro depreciation, the net contribution of foreign trade was at most 35% in France, 26% in Italy and 283% in Germany. This large figure, net of a negative contribution of 51% of consumption in Germany, accounts for most of the large impact on German GDP. Both in Italy and France the contributions of consumption and investment was at most 20% and 10% respectively.

5.3 Counterfactual government consumption

We have argued that government consumption is one of the idiosyncratic factors underlying the business cycle of the three economies. As a matter of fact, it is a factor that contains both a common and an idiosyncratic component. In order to separate between the two, we take a simple and arbitrary route here: we label as common component the growth rate of government consumption of the country in which it was most counter-cyclical. As we have argued, this seems to have been the growth rate of French government expenditure (it was also the highest on average even though we net out this difference here). Hence we label as idiosyncratic components of the growth rate of German and Italian government expenditure the differences of their growth rate profiles with respect to France, net of the average difference.

The counterfactual experiment that sets the idiosyncratic component to zero in Germany and Italy is a simulation that shocks the growth rate of their government consumption by the difference with respect to the growth rate of the French, net of the average difference. This is a zero mean counter-cyclical shock for each of the two countries and it is depicted in panel (c) of figure 13. The rest of Figure 13 illustrates the effects of this experiment on GDP. Analogously to previous paragraphs, panel (a) shows what GDP growth has been for the three countries, panel (b) what it would have been with the counterfactual growth rate profile of the French government consumption (obviously the counterfactual growth rate in France is identical to its historical rate). The difference is imperceptible by visual inspection. The actual discrepancies in growth rates of GDP between actual and counterfactual are plotted in panel (d) which confirms that, with the counterfactual growth rate of government consumption, Germany and Italy would have experienced a slightly milder cycle in the growth rate of GDP but with an almost unnoticeable difference.

Figure 14 illustrates the way in which contributions of each component of aggregate demand would have reacted to this imaginary history. It confirms the view that the difference between actual and counterfactual growth rates

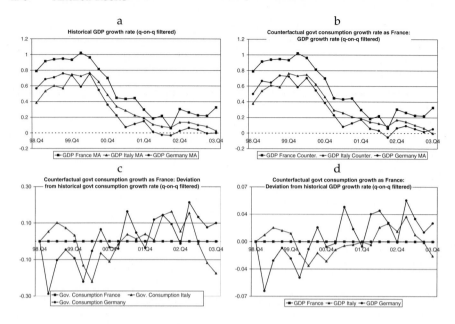

Notes: The four panels illustrate the experiment of a constant growth rate of government consumption. Panel (a) and (b) display the historical and counterfactual growth rates of GDP. Panel (c) shows the cyclical shocks to the growth rate of government consumption used to perturb the economies in the experiment. Panel (d) the impact of the experiment on the growth rates of GDP.

Fig. 13. Experiment with the French profile of growth rate of government consumption, holding the average constant: historical and counterfactual GDP growth rates

of GDP is unnoticeable. It also points to the fact that the main contribution to the difference is that of government consumption itself, as the contribution of other components of aggregate demand is never significantly different from zero. The visual impression is confirmed by Table 6 which reports a quantitative measure of the results of the counterfactual experiment. This table can be read as saying that only up 8% of the cycle of Italian GDP growth rate could be accounted for by the idiosyncratic component of its government consumption, of which up to 7% is attributable to the contribution of government consumption itself. Less than 1% of the cycle of Italian GDP growth rate could be accounted for by the other components of GDP that were not activated by a more aggressive government consumption policy. The table also says that only up 11% of the cycle of German GDP growth rate could be accounted for by the idiosyncratic component of its government consumption, of which up to 7% is attributable to the contribution of government consumption itself. Less than 4% of the cycle of German GDP growth rate could be accounted for by the other components of GDP that were not activated by a more aggressive government consumption policy.

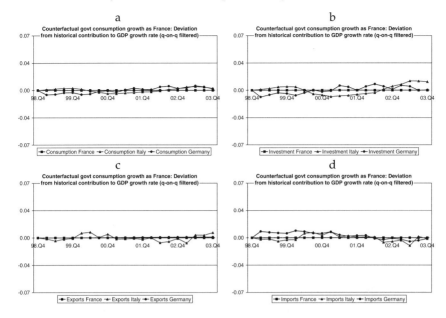

Notes: The four panels illustrate the experiment of a zero depreciation of the Euro. Panel (a) shows the impact on the growth rate of consumption's contribution to GDP; panel (b) investment's; panel (c) exports'; panel (d) exports'.

Fig. 14. Experiment with the French profile of growth rate of government consumption, holding the average constant: impact on the growth rate of each component's contribution to GDP

6 Conclusions

In this paper we have used the macro-econometric models of the ESCB to simulate the extent to which the sources of business cycle of France, Germany and Italy can be traced down to common and idiosyncratic factors. In the first part of the paper, we have computed the responses of GDP and contributions of GDP components to purely hypothetical cyclical shocks perturbing exogenous factors. This thought exercise has allowed to point out, clearly and without the nuisance of high frequency noise, the cyclical response of the three economies to exogenous shocks at the business cycle frequency. This experiment was performed on three types of shocks: a) a cyclical shock to the balanced growth rate of world demand; b) a cyclical shock to the steady state of the Euro exchange rate against all other currencies; and c) a cyclical shock to the growth rate of government consumption.

In the second part of the paper we have analyzed the 5-year period 1998Q4-2003Q4. This period has witnessed a full cycle in the GDP growth of all three economies, as well as a full cycle in the growth rate of world demand and in the depreciation of the Euro against all other currencies. As these were common factors causing cyclical variation on the demand side, we have used counterfactual simulations to determine what fraction of the cycle in the three countries they could account for. This was achieved by counterfactually removing these common sources of cycle one at a time and comparing how smoother the cycle of the three economies would have been. According to the results of the experiment, up to 35% of the French GDP cycle of that period could be explained by the cycle of world demand. This fraction drops to 23% for the case of the German cycle and to 17% for that of the Italian cycle. With regard to the second experiment, up to 235% of the German cycle of those years could be accounted for by the cycle of Euro depreciation. With regard to the second experiment, the cycle of the euro area exchange rate (depreciation, then appreciation) is, according to the simulation, so important in explaining the recent history of the German economy that without it the peak at the end of the 1990s and the trough afterwards would have been roughly the reverse of what was actually observed. On the contrary, only up to 11% of the French GDP cycle could be attributed to the cycle of the euro exchange rate. For the Italian economy, without exogenous shock the cycle in the growth rate of GDP could have been 8% more severe than it actually was. The results on the exchange rate must however be read with some caution as they are subject to the caveats pointed out in section 3.

Moreover, during this cyclical episode, government spending followed different growth paths in the three countries. This was an idiosyncratic factor causing cyclical variation on the demand side. We have assumed that the French government policy was the common policy factor in the three economies, which allowed us to extract idiosyncratic policy factors in the other two countries as difference and to use counterfactual simulations to determine what fraction of the cycle they could account for. According to the results of the experiment, only up 8% of the cycle of Italian GDP growth rate could be accounted for by the idiosyncratic component of its government consumption, of which more than 7% is attributable to the contribution of government consumption itself. As for German GDP growth rate, only up to 11% of its cycle could be accounted for by the idiosyncratic component of its government consumption, of which almost 7% is attributable to the contribution of government consumption itself.

Overall, the conclusion that one may draw from these simple simulations is that, for all three economies, common exogenous demand factors were by far more important than idiosyncratic ones in determining the cyclical episode of the 5-year period 1998Q4-2003Q4. Pushing interpretation a little further, counter-cyclical government consumption policies couldn't have done much to reduce the cyclical episode of those years, even though they would have certainly contributed to worsen the prospects of the stability pact. After all, sticking to the stability pact was not a costly idea in terms of welfare.

References

Baghli M., V. Brunhes-Lesage, O. de Bandt, H. Fraisse and J.-P. Villetelle (2004a), "MASCOTTE, Modèle d'analyse et de prévision de la conjoncture trimestrielle", NER # 106, Banque de France, février.

Baghli M., V. Brunhes-Lesage, O. de Bandt, H. Fraisse and J.-P. Villetelle (2004b), "The Mascotte forecasting model for the French economy : main features and results from variants", Banque de France Bulletin Digest, # 124, April.

Banca d'Italia (1986), "Modello trimestrale dell'economia italiana", Temi di discussione, n. 80.

Berben R.P., R. Mestre, T. Mitrakos, J. Morgan and N. Zonzilos (2005), "Inflation persistence in structural macroeconomic models", ECB working paper.

Brayton and Mauskopf (1985) "The Federal Reserve Board MPS quarterly econometric model of the U.S. economy", Econometric Modelling.

Busetti, F., A. Locarno and L. Monteforte (2005), "The bank of Italy quarterly model", in Fagan, G. and J. Morgan eds, Econometric models of the euro-area central banks, Cheltenham UK, Edward Elgar.

Deutsche Bundesbank (2000), "Macro-econometric multi-country model: MEMMOD", available at http://www.bundesbank.de.

Fagan, G. and J. Morgan (2005), "An overview of the structural economietric models of the euro-area central banks", in Fagan, G. and J. Morgan eds, Econometric models of the euro-area central banks, Cheltenham UK, Edward Elgar.

Fagan, G. and J. Morgan (2005), "Econometric models of the euro-area central banks", Cheltenham UK, Edward Elgar.

Galli, G, D. Terlizzese and I. Visco (1989), "Un modello trimestrale per la previsione e la politica economica: le proprietà di breve e di lungo periodo del modello della Banca d'Italia", Politica Economica, n. 1.

Hamburg B. and K.-H. Todter (2005), "The macroeconometric multi-country model of the Deutsche Bundesbank", in Fagan, G. and J. Morgan eds, Econometric models of the euro-area central banks, Cheltenham UK, Edward Elgar.

Henry, S.G.B. and A.R. Pagan (2004), "The Econometrics of the New Keynesian Policy Model: Introduction", in S.G.B. Henry and A.R. Pagan(eds), The Econometrics of the New Keynesian Policy, Supplement, Oxford Bulletin of Economics and Statistics, 66,581- 607.

Siviero, S. (1995), "Deterministic and stochastic algorithms for stabilisation policies with large-size econometric models", Ph.D. dissertation.

Stahn, K (2006, this volume), "Has the impact of key determinants of German exports changed?".

Terlizzese, D. (1994), "Il modello econometrico della banca d'Italia: una versione in scala 1:15", Ricerche quantitative per la politica economica 1993.

Todter, K.-H. (2002), "Monetary indicators and policy rules in the P-Star model", discussion paper 18/02, Economic Research Centre, Deutsche Bundesbank.

Villetelle, J.P. and O. de Bandt (2006, this volume), "Convergence and divergence in external trade".

Villetelle, J.P., O. de Bandt and V. Brunhes-Lesage (2005), "Mascotte: the Banque de France forecasting model", in Fagan, G. and J. Morgan eds, Econometric models of the euro-area central banks, Cheltenham UK, Edward Elgar.

Table 2. Impact of world demand shock on difference of average growth rates of demand components (1998:Q4-2001:Q2 vs. 2001:Q3-2003:Q4)

	Difference of average q-on-q growth rates			Diff of avg contributions to q-on-q growth rate of GDP		
	Historic.	Counterf.	Diff.	Historic.	Counterf.	%-Diff.
			France			
GDP	0.57%	0.37%	-0.20%	0.57%	0.37%	-34.70%
Consumption	0.29%	0.18%	-0.11%	0.18%	0.11%	-13.07%
Investment	1.58%	1.27%	-0.31%	0.36%	0.27%	-16.16%
Govt. Cons.	-0.27%	-0.27%	0.00%	-0.07%	-0.07%	0.90%
Exports	1.80%	1.24%	-0.56%	0.58%	0.37%	-36.73%
Imports	1.59%	1.10%	-0.49%	-0.49%	-0.31%	30.36%
			Italy			
GDP	0.57%	0.47%	-0.10%	0.57%	0.47%	-17.41%
Consumption	0.37%	0.29%	-0.08%	0.17%	0.13%	-5.86%
Investment	1.39%	0.96%	-0.43%	0.21%	0.14%	-11.04%
Govt. Cons.	0.10%	0.04%	-0.06%	0.01%	0.01%	-1.26%
Exports	2.31%	2.05%	-0.26%	0.49%	0.44%	-8.92%
Imports	1.47%	1.19%	-0.28%	-0.30%	-0.24%	9.67%
			Germany			
GDP	0.58%	0.45%	-0.13%	0.58%	0.45%	-22.80%
Consumption	0.80%	0.71%	-0.09%	0.33%	0.27%	-9.83%
Investment	1.38%	1.09%	-0.29%	0.21%	0.16%	-9.42%
Govt. Cons.	0.00%	0.00%	0.00%	0.00%	0.00%	0.00%
Exports	1.74%	1.40%	-0.34%	0.43%	0.32%	-18.45%
Imports	1.72%	1.43%	-0.29%	-0.39%	-0.30%	14.88%

Notes: The first column reports the difference between the 1998:Q4-2001:Q2 and the 2001:Q3-2003:Q4 averages of historical q-on-q growth rates of GDP and components, for the three countries. This gives a measure of the magnitude of the cycle during the 5-year period. The second column displays the difference between the 1998:Q4-2001:Q2 and the 2001:Q3-2003:Q4 averages of counterfactual q-on-q growth rates when the exogenous cyclical source is removed with the counterfactual experiment. This is a measure of the counterfactual magnitude of the cycle. The difference between these two differences is reported in column three. Columns four and five break down the difference of historical and counterfactual average growth rate of GDP by components of aggregate demand, normalizing the components' growth rate by their share in GDP. The last column reports the percentage difference in the magnitude of GDP cycle, between history and counterfactual experiment, and how this percentage difference can be decomposed among components of aggregate demand.

Table 3. Impact of exchange rate shock on average growth rate of demand components (1998:Q4-2003:Q4)

	Average q-on-q growth rates			Average contributions to q-on-q growth rate of GDP		
	Historic.	Counterf.	Diff.	Historic.	Counterf.	%-Diff.
			France			
GDP	0.55%	0.56%	0.01%	0.55%	0.56%	1.94%
Consumption	0.60%	0.61%	0.01%	0.31%	0.31%	0.30%
Investment	0.79%	0.81%	0.02%	0.15%	0.15%	0.48%
Govt. Cons.	0.77%	0.77%	0.00%	0.17%	0.17%	-0.11%
Exports	0.96%	0.98%	0.02%	0.25%	0.26%	0.86%
Imports	1.31%	1.31%	-0.00%	-0.33%	-0.33%	0.40%
			Italy			
GDP	0.37%	0.28%	-0.11%	0.37%	0.28%	-23.51%
Consumption	0.35%	0.36%	0.01%	0.20%	0.19%	-1.24%
Investment	0.59%	0.26%	-0.33%	0.11%	0.05%	-17.69%
Govt. Cons.	0.57%	0.54%	-0.03%	0.09%	0.08%	-2.56%
Exports	0.40%	0.33%	-0.07%	0.11%	0.08%	-6.24%
Imports	0.54%	0.51%	-0.03%	-0.14%	-0.12%	4.23%
			Germany			
GDP	0.31%	0.31%	-0.00%	0.31%	0.31%	-0.81%
Consumption	0.25%	0.23%	-0.02%	0.13%	0.13%	0.15%
Investment	-0.21%	-0.21%	0.00%	-0.04%	-0.04%	-1.33%
Govt. Cons.	0.25%	0.25%	0.00%	0.04%	0.05%	1.12%
Exports	1.68%	1.47%	-0.21%	0.53%	0.50%	-9.09%
Imports	1.23%	1.05%	-0.18%	-0.35%	-0.33%	8.34%

Notes: See notes for table 1

Table 4. Impact of exchange rate shock on difference of average growth rates of demand components (1998:Q4-2001:Q2 vs. 2001:Q3-2003:Q4)

	Difference of average q-on-q growth rates			Diff of avg contributions to q-on-q growth rate of GDP		
	Historic.	Counterf.	Diff.	Historic.	Counterf.	%-Diff.
France						
GDP	0.57%	0.51%	-0.06%	0.57%	0.51%	-10.61%
Consumption	0.29%	0.38%	0.09%	0.18%	0.28%	17.39%
Investment	1.58%	1.51%	-0.07%	0.36%	0.41%	8.02%
Govt. Cons.	-0.27%	-0.27%	0.00%	-0.07%	-0.08%	-2.27%
Exports	1.80%	1.39%	-0.41%	0.58%	0.53%	-9.05%
Imports	1.59%	1.73%	0.14%	-0.49%	-0.63%	-24.69%
Italy						
GDP	0.57%	0.62%	0.05%	0.57%	0.62%	8.19%
Consumption	0.37%	0.61%	0.24%	0.17%	0.28%	19.66%
Investment	1.39%	1.70%	0.31%	0.21%	0.26%	8.97%
Govt. Cons.	0.10%	0.36%	0.26%	0.01%	0.05%	6.00%
Exports	2.31%	1.76%	0.55%	0.49%	0.38%	-18.81%
Imports	1.47%	1.66%	0.19%	-0.30%	-0.34%	-7.63%
Germany						
GDP	0.58%	-0.78%	-1.36%	0.58%	-0.78%	-235.34%
Consumption	0.80%	0.68%	-0.22%	0.33%	0.63%	51.47%
Investment	1.38%	0.54%	-0.84%	0.21%	0.19%	-4.09%
Govt. Cons.	0.00%	0.00%	-0.00%	0.00%	0.00%	-0.09%
Exports	1.74%	-0.60%	-2.34%	0.43%	-0.33%	-131.05%
Imports	1.72%	2.50%	0.78%	-0.39%	-1.26%	-151.58%

Notes: See notes for table 2

Table 5. Impact of government consumption shock on average growth rate of demand components (1998:Q4-2003:Q4)

	Average q-on-q growth rates			Average contributions to q-on-q growth rate of GDP		
	Historic.	Counterf.	Diff.	Historic.	Counterf.	%-Diff.
			France			
GDP	0.55%	0.55%	0.00%	0.55%	0.55%	0.00%
Consumption	0.60%	0.60%	0.00%	0.31%	0.31%	0.00%
Investment	0.79%	0.79%	0.00%	0.15%	0.15%	0.00%
Govt. Cons.	0.77%	0.77%	0.00%	0.17%	0.17%	0.00%
Exports	0.96%	0.96%	0.00%	0.25%	0.25%	0.00%
Imports	1.31%	1.31%	0.00%	-0.33%	-0.33%	0.00%
			Italy			
GDP	0.37%	0.37%	0.00%	0.37%	0.37%	-0.04%
Consumption	0.35%	0.35%	0.00%	0.20%	0.20%	-0.07%
Investment	0.59%	0.60%	0.01%	0.11%	0.11%	0.10%
Govt. Cons.	0.57%	0.57%	0.00%	0.09%	0.09%	-0.10%
Exports	0.40%	0.40%	0.00%	0.11%	0.11%	-0.04%
Imports	0.54%	0.54%	0.00%	-0.14%	-0.14%	0.07%
			Germany			
GDP	0.31%	0.31%	0.00%	0.31%	0.31%	1.49%
Consumption	0.25%	0.25%	0.00%	0.13%	0.13%	-0.06%
Investment	-0.21%	-0.21%	0.00%	-0.04%	-0.04%	-0.02%
Govt. Cons.	0.25%	0.26%	0.01%	0.04%	0.05%	0.59%
Exports	1.68%	1.68%	0.00%	0.53%	0.53%	0.09%
Imports	1.23%	1.22%	-0.01%	-0.35%	-0.35%	0.90%

Notes: See notes for table 1

Table 6. Impact of govt. consumption shock on difference of average growth rates of demand components (1998:Q4-2001:Q2 vs. 2001:Q3-2003:Q4)

	Difference of average q-on-q growth rates			Diff of avg contributions to q-on-q growth rate of GDP		
	Historic.	Counterf.	Diff.	Historic.	Counterf.	%-Diff.
			France			
GDP	0.57%	0.57%	0.00%	0.57%	0.57%	0.00%
Consumption	0.29%	0.29%	0.00%	0.18%	0.18%	0.00%
Investment	1.58%	1.58%	0.00%	0.36%	0.36%	0.00%
Govt. Cons.	-0.27%	-0.27%	0.00%	-0.07%	-0.07%	0.00%
Exports	1.80%	1.80%	0.00%	0.58%	0.58%	0.00%
Imports	1.59%	1.59%	0.00%	-0.49%	-0.49%	0.00%
			Italy			
GDP	0.57%	0.53%	-0.04%	0.57%	0.53%	-7.97%
Consumption	0.37%	0.37%	0.00%	0.17%	0.16%	-1.00%
Investment	1.39%	1.38%	-0.01%	0.21%	0.20%	-1.19%
Govt. Cons.	0.10%	-0.23%	-0.33%	0.01%	-0.03%	-7.27%
Exports	2.31%	2.34%	0.03%	0.49%	0.48%	-1.25%
Imports	1.47%	1.44%	-0.03%	-0.30%	-0.28%	2.73%
			Germany			
GDP	0.58%	0.51%	-0.07%	0.58%	0.51%	-11.15%
Consumption	0.80%	0.78%	-0.02%	0.33%	0.31%	-3.09%
Investment	1.38%	1.34%	-0.04%	0.21%	0.20%	-2.32%
Govt. Cons.	0.00%	-0.29%	-0.29%	0.00%	-0.04%	-6.69%
Exports	1.74%	1.74%	0.00%	0.43%	0.41%	-2.48%
Imports	1.72%	1.69%	-0.03%	-0.39%	-0.37%	3.44%

Notes: See notes for table 2

Part V

External Side

Market Shares and Trade Specialisation of France, Germany and Italy*

Alberto Felettigh[1], Rémy Lecat[2], Bertrand Pluyaud[2], and Roberto Tedeschi[1]

[1] Banca d'Italia, via Nazionale 91, 00184 Roma
roberto.tedeschi@bancaditalia.it
[2] Banque de France, 46-1405 DAMEP, 39 rue Croix des Petits Champs, 75049 Paris
Cedex 01 remy.lecat@banque-france.fr

Summary. The trade performances of France, Germany and Italy in the 1990s and 2000s have followed heterogeneous national patterns. Contrary to the Italian situation, French and German divergences cannot be explained by relative cost and price developments; geographical specialisation has a limited role in the differences between the three countries. Sectoral specialisation sheds some light to these divergences, emphasising the exposure of Italy to emerging country competition and the limited specialisation of France, while all three countries share a lack of specialisation in ICT products. Non-price competitiveness indicators, such as R&D or education levels, could also contribute to explain the German strength and Italian weakness.

Keywords: market shares, trade specialisation.
JEL classifications: F14, E32.

1 Introduction

Since the year 2000, the euro area external trade performance has resulted from highly heterogeneous national patterns. In Germany, economic activity has been export-led, whereas France and Italy exhibited mediocre export performance. For the three countries, the increase in exports is paralleled or rapidly followed by an increase in imports. Whereas net export contribution has been highly synchronised in the 1990s between France, Germany and to a lesser extent Italy, a large discrepancy has appeared since 2001, with Germany outperforming the other two countries.

---

* The views expressed in this paper are those of the authors and do not necessarily reflect those of their respective central banks. The authors thank Olivier de Bandt, Agnès Bénassy-Quéré , Françoise Drumetz, Axel Jochem and Gilles Moëc for their useful comments, Sophie Garcia for computing the world demand series used in this paper, Claudia Borghese and Anne-Christèle Chavy-Martin for precious research assistance. All errors remain however the authors'.

In the following, a set of indicators of export and import performance for the three countries is presented, in order to assess the link between recent developments over the business cycle and medium term developments, as well as more structural differences (and similarities) between the three economies. No econometric analysis of trade performance is undertaken in this article, the aim rather being at emphasising structural characteristics.

The first part (Section 2) presents stylised facts about the three countries' trade performance through export market share indicators, net export contribution to GDP growth and domestic market shares. Common trends for the three countries, together with their links to the process of globalisation, is emphasised, as well as divergences in trade performance, which were surprisingly large since the beginning of the 2000s.

The following sections address the main determinants of trade performance, that is to say price competitiveness (Section 3), geographical (Section 4) and product specialisation (Section 5) and non price competitiveness (Section 6). Since the establishment of the monetary union, differences in price competitiveness between the three countries have relied mainly on price and cost developments, which are examined in the paper through export prices, unit labour costs and producer prices indicators. Geographical specialisation divergences between the three countries rely first of all on their orientation towards intra versus extra euro area trade; their impact on the business cycle is captured by the contribution of world demand to GDP growth. The analysis of product specialisation tries to assess the impact of the globalisation process, with special attention to information and communication technology products and to the technological intensity of exports. Finally, non price competitiveness is examined through usual indicators of price elasticity, Research and Development intensity and education.

2 Stylised facts about trade performance of France, Germany and Italy

All euro area countries recently experienced losses in market shares in line with the emergence of new world competitors. However, Germany seems to have performed better than the other two countries in the 2000s. Although the three countries share some common trends in their trade performance, diverging patterns have emerged in the last years.

2.1 Common trends in the three countries

The three countries have been commonly affected by the major world trade features of the 1990s, i.e. the emergence of new world trade players and the fast pace of trade expansion.

The emergence of new world trade players has weighed on the export market share of the three countries during the 1990s. In a static world, with given varieties of products and given markets (importers), and well measured and almost stable relative prices, the market share is a good indicator of export (and import) performance.[3]

In the real world, where new participants enter the goods trade with the potential to become important actors, because of a large population, as in the case of China, India, or an initial high GDP per capita, as in the case of the Central and Eastern European Countries, the share of the incumbents can only contract. In Table 1, the market share for goods of the three countries is calculated, to be comparable, as the share of country exports to world imports, in value and volume. [4] Both computations show that the three countries have lower market shares in 2004 than at the beginning of the nineties; such pattern holds true for all advanced economies (IMF definition), whose world market share has decreased in value from 52 per cent in 1990 to 42 per cent in 2004.

Linked with the emergence of new world trade players, the fast pace of trade in the 1990s, relative to GDP growth, has led to a decrease in the domestic market shares of the three countries (cf. Figure 1). Contrary to export market shares (cf. Table 1), which compare trade with trade, here trade is compared with a domestic market size indicator, defined as the share of domestic demand (GDP plus imports minus exports) that is satisfied by domestic production (GDP minus exports). The decreasing trend of the domestic market share indicator in the 1990s comes as no surprise, at a time when, as part of the globalisation process, world trade grew more than in the two former decades and much more than world GDP. Italy and France have shown an almost coincident behaviour since 1997, having identical domestic market shares (about 75 per cent in 2004). The dynamics for Germany, with a lower domestic market share (66 per cent in 2004) due to the higher degree of trade openness of the German economy, was similar to the other two countries until 2000: the decrease in the domestic market share in year 2000 was the largest among the three, and the ensuing recovery was short lived, whereas France and Italy experienced a reversion towards their 1999 levels.

2.2 Recent discrepancies and longer-term diverging trends

Since 2000, the three countries have displayed strongly diverging patterns with respect to trade performance. These divergences seem however to be

---

[3] Below we also consider another indicator, which compares the performance of export growth to that of world demand (cf. Figure 5).

[4] Particular caution in looking at market shares in value is due to the mechanical effect of exchange rate changes on the numerator, as national exports and world trade have to be expressed in a common currency. When the national currency appreciates, national exports in value increase relative to world trade, *ceteris paribus*. The same "relative price" effect applies when oil price peak up (or decrease): the group of non producer countries lose (gain) market shares, despite no change in their exports expressed in volume terms.

Table 1. World market share of total exports

Year	Current exchange rates and prices			Constant 1995 exchange rates and prices		
	France	Germany	Italy	France	Germany	Italy
1990	6.4	12.0	5.0	6.5	12.0	4.4
1991	6.2	11.5	4.8	6.3	11.6	4.2
1992	6.3	11.3	4.8	6.3	11.0	4.2
1993	5.6	10.3	4.6	5.8	10.6	4.4
1994	5.6	10.2	4.5	5.8	10.7	4.5
1995	5.7	10.3	4.6	5.7	10.3	4.6
1996	5.4	9.9	4.7	5.4	10.5	4.3
1997	5.2	9.3	4.4	5.5	10.5	4.0
1998	5.7	10.1	4.6	5.7	10.9	4.0
1999	5.4	9.7	4.2	5.7	11.0	3.6
2000	4.7	8.7	3.8	5.7	11.0	3.5
2001	4.9	9.5	4.1	5.8	11.5	3.5
2002	4.9	9.7	4.0	5.7	11.6	3.3
2003	4.9	10.2	4.1	5.3	11.7	3.1
2004	4.8	10.2	4.0	5.0	11.8	2.9

Notes: exports of goods only - percentage points.
Source: our computations from WEO-IMF, IFS-IMF, national data for Italy.

rooted in trends initiated during the 1990s. The contribution of net exports to GDP growth, a key indicator to assess the final effect of foreign trade on the business cycle, has strongly diverged since 2000, with a high and positive contribution in Germany, compared with negative or weakly positive contributions for Italy and France (cf. Figure 2). A decreasing pattern in the contribution shows up both in Italy and France from 1993 onwards, whereas the tendency has been more favourable in Germany. In both France and Italy, the contribution went from positive to negative during the last decade. After an extraordinary contribution of 4.4 percentage points in 1993, following the devaluation in September 1992 and the 1993 slump, the descent has been steeper for Italy, although a recovery seems to be taking place in 2004. Over the same period, the contribution in France has continued to decline. The German situation is substantially different, with a prevalence of positive contributions (with a peak of 1.9 percentage points in 2002) and an overall positive trend.

The breakdown of the contribution of net exports to GDP growth between exports and imports shows that the three countries displayed very similar patterns for both indicators, especially in the period of stable exchange rates from 1996 onwards. For a given growth of trade, the higher degree of trade openness of the German economy tends to be associated with a larger con-

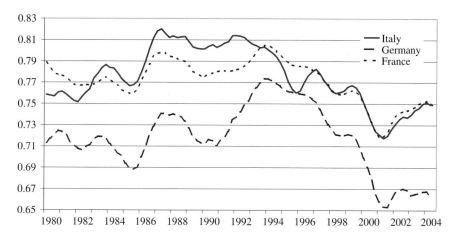

Notes: 4-quarters moving average, ratio of GDP minus exports to GDP plus imports minus exports. Domestic market shares represent the share of domestic demand that is met by domestic output (net of exports): domestic demand is public and private consumption, total investment and stock building (that is, GDP plus imports minus exports).
Source: Eurostat.

Fig. 1. Domestic market share - goods and services

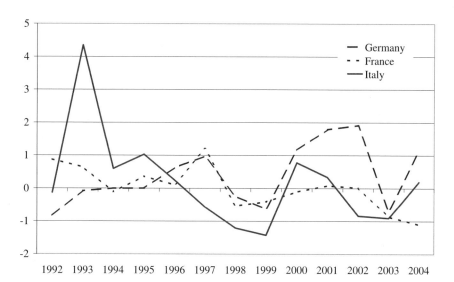

Notes: goods and services - percentage points.
Source: Eurostat.

Fig. 2. Contribution of net exports to GDP growth

tribution of both exports and imports, in absolute value. Moreover, the process of relocation of stages of production, more pronounced in Germany (cf. below), implies that GDP includes a higher content of imports. Import contribution in Germany has been indeed more negative than in Italy since 1998 and than in France in 2003 and 2004 (cf. Figure 3).

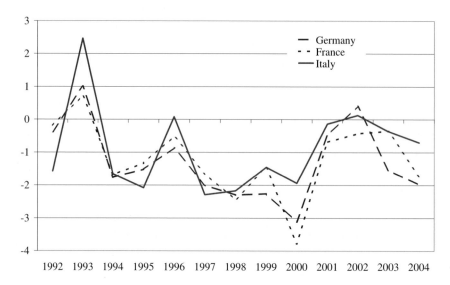

Notes: goods and services - percentage points.
Source: Eurostat.

Fig. 3. Contribution of imports to GDP growth

Similarly, the profile of export contribution to GDP growth is higher in Germany than in the two other countries; the French contribution, which was close to the German one up to 2000, has been decreasing to the Italian level since 2001 (cf. Figure 4). Hence, the divergence in trade performance seems to be rooted first of all in export developments.

Export performance depends on the evolution of both world demand and export market shares. It is instructive to look at the contribution of changes in export market shares to GDP growth, which we define as the difference between the contribution of exports to GDP growth and the contribution of world demand, where the latter is the contribution that exports by the reporting country would have posted if export to each partner country had grown at the same pace as overall imports by the corresponding partner country (a more precise terminology would be contribution of 'world demand addressed to the reporting country'). The decomposition is detailed in Appendix A; Figures 5 and 10 illustrate the results.

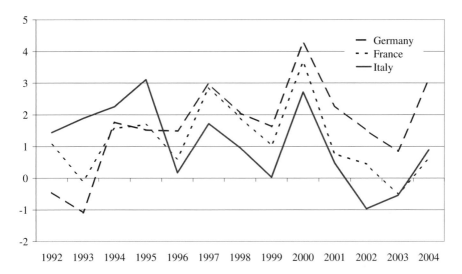

Notes: goods and services - percentage points.
Source: Eurostat.

Fig. 4. Contribution of exports to GDP growth

The contribution of changes in export market shares highlights more precisely trends in trade performance, although it is only under the assumption
that the exporters in the three countries trade in similar products, adopt similar pricing strategies and face similar cost structures, that differences in the
contribution of exports to GDP growth are mainly determined by the evolution of export-market shares.[5] In Germany, the contribution of changes in
market shares is on an upward trend since the mid-nineties, from a negative
contribution at the beginning of the decade to a positive one since 1999. In
France the contribution oscillates around zero until 2002, but becomes significantly negative afterwards (in 2003, the contribution is -1.7 percentage
points). In Italy, the contribution was consistently positive between 1992 and
1995 but has been deeply negative ever since, with an average of -1.2 points
of GDP per year between 1996 and 2004.

These trends translate into the export market shares indicators[6] (cf. Table
1): for Italy, market shares in value and volume tend to decrease strongly

---

[5] In comparison to the indicator in Table 1, such an indicator is weighted, with
weights fixed at a base year (2000 here; again, see Appendix A for the details). As
a consequence, the indicator underestimates the increasing weight of China and
hence the development of trade between China and the rest of the world.

[6] The concept of export market shares used in Table 1, where no weighting has been
used, is however different from the one used in Figure 5. The latter relates export
growth to the growth of an aggregate measure of imports in volume, obtained

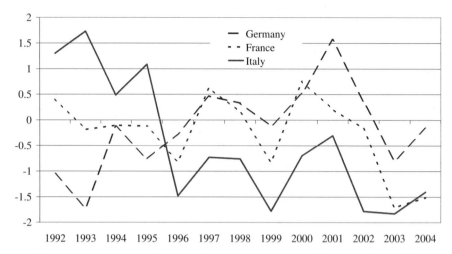

Notes: percentage points. The contribution of market shares to GDP growth is the difference between the contribution of exports to GDP growth and the contribution of world demand addressed to each country.
Source: Banque de France, Eurostat.

Fig. 5. Contribution of changes in market shares to GDP growth

since the mid-nineties; for Germany, markets shares in value and volume decreased strongly after the reunification shock, but have been recovering since the mid-nineties; in France, a declining trend for value and volume indicators has appeared since the beginning of the nineties.

3 Price competitiveness

Different factors may explain the recent divergences in trade performance. Among them are price competitiveness, geographical specialisation, sectoral specialisation and non price competitiveness. Prices depend, in the medium term, on relative cost evolution. Price competitiveness seems to explain a large part of the weaker trade performance of Italy. It might however be insufficient to explain the French performance compared with the German one.

From January 1999 onwards, the bilateral exchange rate between the three countries is irrevocably fixed and it showed only very limited oscillations since the end of 1996. The main cause of variation in relative price competitiveness has disappeared, although the relative nominal effective exchange rate can still change because of differences in the weights of partner countries. Differences in overall relative price competitiveness could also arise

---

by weighting the imports of each partner country by its share in the trade of the reporting country in 2000.

from differing unit labour costs, import prices (raw materials, for example, but also intermediate goods), and pricing behaviour of firms (variable mark-ups). However, when looking at nominal effective exchange rates over the last six years, the cumulated difference between the three countries is less than two percentage points, an irrelevant effect (cf. Figure 6).

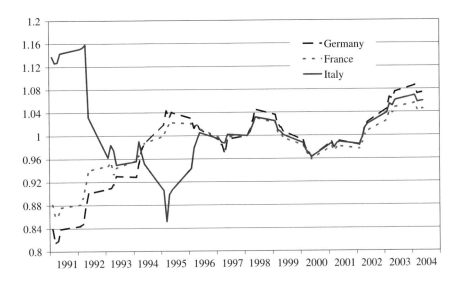

Notes: first quarter 1998=1.
Source: OECD Economic Outlook.

Fig. 6. Nominal effective exchange rate index

International relative price measures only partially reflect different as-pects of the price competitiveness of an economy. It may be also argued that some characteristics of competitiveness are not reflected in prices and may explain differences in export performance (cf. Section 6). However, the first candidates to explain past performance are the prices of traded and tradable goods. Different indicators put more stress on one or the other aspect: export unit values or the deflator of exported goods speak for the price of actively traded goods, whereas producer prices or a total deflator for internal produc-tion can proxy the price of potentially tradable goods. A traditionally used indicator, based on unit labour costs, can represent more closely a long term constraint on prices: in the short run, though, it may have poor explanatory power as a price index.[7] Moreover, it represents only part of the costs, i.e. the labour costs, borne by firms: the relocation of stages of production abroad

---

[7] See the discussion on German competitiveness indicators in the Monthly Report of the Bundesbank, November 1998 issue.

may have lowered the costs of intermediate goods differently from country to country. German large foreign direct investments in Central and Eastern European Countries[8] may have led to a more favourable evolution of its costs for intermediate goods relative to its competitors: such a pattern may be reflected by indicators based on producer prices, contrary to the ones based on unit labour costs or export prices.

Goods and services deflators (national account basis, cf. Figure 7) show that, in the 1997-2003 period, French export prices remained almost constant (in national currency), the German ones grew a few percentage points to decrease somewhat in 2004, while the Italian ones grew by more than 10 per cent. This may be interpreted as a loss of competitiveness for Italy; however, as these goods have eventually been exported, it may also correspond to quality improvement or differentiation phenomena allowing Italian firms to raise their profit margins. De Nardis and Pensa (2004) have shown that Italian exporters of traditional products (textiles, apparel, footwear, leather goods, ceramics and wooden furniture) have been able to apply geographically differentiated mark ups during the 1980s and the 1990s. The apparently good price competitiveness of France that appears from aggregate figures may have been contradicted for some periods by the behaviour in specific sectors. On the basis of detailed data at the sectoral level (5000 products), Cheptea, Gaulier and Zignago (2004) show that countries reacted differently to the appreciation of the dollar in the early 2000: over the 1999-2002 period, whereas German exporters reduced significantly prices in order to increase volumes, French exporters increased their margins.

In terms of the real effective exchange rate based on producer prices (cf. Figure 8) the loss of competitiveness since the launch of the euro is uniformly larger for Italy than for the other two countries. Compounded with lagged effects, this explains part of the last two years' very poor performance of Italian exports.

When we compare competitiveness indicators for the three countries, we see that Italy gained less during the phase of euro depreciation from 1999 to 2001, and lost more afterwards, when the euro appreciated, especially with respect to the US dollar. Germany gained more in the phase of euro depreciation than France, and lost just a few percentage points in the last two years. This moderate gain in competitiveness, however, is unlikely to be the sole explanation for the relatively good performance of German exports.

---

[8] According to ECB, 2005, German FDI to CEEC-8 countries represented, in 2003, 21.5 per cent of the total inward FDI stocks of the latter countries, against 8 per cent for France and 2.8 per cent for Italy.

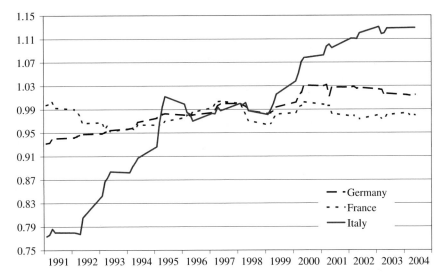

Notes: goods and services deflator - First quarter1998=1.
Source: OECD Economic Outlook.

Fig. 7. Export price index

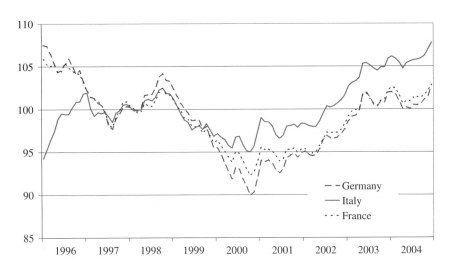

Notes: based on producer price in manufacturing - January 1999=100. An increase indicates a loss in competitiveness.
Source: BIS.

Fig. 8. Real exchange rate

4 Geographical specialisation

Although the geographical specialisations of France, on one side, Italy and Germany, on the other, tend to diverge, their impact on recent evolutions seems to be limited as they remain close to one another.

4.1 Extra versus intra euro area market shares

Historically, focusing on intra euro area trade, the three countries have been commonly affected by the debut in European trade of the new member states of the European Union (Spain, Portugal and Greece from the 1980s onwards; Central and Eastern Europe New Member States from the 1990s onwards), as well as extra euro area competitors such as China (cf. Table 2). The German intra euro area market share in value peaked in 1988 and decreased afterwards until 2000; it peaked in 1995 for France and Italy and decreased ever since, while the Spanish and Portuguese intra euro area market share doubled since their entrance in the European Union (from 2.2 per cent in 1986 to 4.0 per cent at the beginning of the 2000s for Spain and from 0.6 per cent to 0.9 per cent for Portugal), the Chinese one has increased four-fold since 1990 (from 0.9 per cent in 1990 to 4.2 per cent in 2004), and the share of the new EU member states has jumped from 3.0 per cent to 5.5 per cent in the last ten years.

Against the background of globalisation and the rapid increase of world exports, the share of intra euro area exports to total exports for each country (cf. Figure 9) has also declined in comparison with the beginning of the 1990s. The trade integration of countries that entered the European Union in the 1980s (Greece, Portugal and Spain) may have boosted the intra euro area market shares, as their demand grew strongly, while this effect disappeared when the growth of world trade exceeded the pace of intra euro area trade.

As Table 2 and Figure 9 show, there exist marked differences between the three countries. In terms of intra euro area market share, the Italian one declined, especially in the second part of the 1990s and more than what would be expected from the mere effect of the integration of new competitors within the region. Germany regained part of its losses since 2000, while the decline accelerated for France. In terms of the share of the euro area as destination of exports by the three countries (cf. Figure 9), France appears to be much more oriented towards the euro area than Italy and Germany, which increasingly turned towards extra euro area markets in the 1990s and 2000s, while the share of the euro area in French exports has remained stable since the mid-1990s.

Germany and Italy benefited more than France from the fast pace of import growth outside the euro area: from 1994 to 2004, euro area imports grew about 1.5 percentage points less than imports of the non euro area countries, per year. Moreover, the orientation of France towards intra euro area trade may lead, *ceteris paribus*, to a higher sensitivity of exports to competitiveness

Table 2. Market share in Euro area imports of goods

Year	Germany	France	Italy	Spain	Greece	Portugal	China	New 10 EU member states[(*)]
1985	14.5	8.0	6.0	2.0	0.4	0.5		
1986	16.7	8.9	7.0	2.2	0.5	0.6		
1987	17.1	9.2	7.1	2.4	0.5	0.7		
1988	17.1	9.6	7.1	2.4	0.3	0.7		
1989	16.9	9.6	7.0	2.4	0.4	0.7	0.8	
1990	16.2	9.5	7.3	2.7	0.4	0.8	0.9	
1991	15.8	9.6	7.0	2.9	0.4	0.8	1.2	
1992	16.0	9.8	6.9	3.0	0.4	0.9	1.3	
1993	15.3	9.8	7.2	3.1	0.4	0.8	1.6	
1994	14.9	9.8	7.2	3.4	0.4	0.9	1.7	
1995	15.2	9.9	7.4	3.7	0.4	0.9	1.7	3.0
1996	14.6	9.6	7.4	3.9	0.3	1.0	1.8	3.0
1997	13.8	9.3	6.9	3.7	0.3	1.0	2.0	3.2
1998	14.0	9.4	6.8	4.0	0.3	1.0	2.1	3.6
1999	14.0	9.4	6.6	3.6	0.3	1.0	2.3	3.8
2000	13.1	8.8	6.0	3.7	0.2	0.9	2.6	3.9
2001	13.5	8.7	6.1	3.9	0.2	0.9	2.8	4.3
2002	13.8	8.6	6.0	4.0	0.2	0.9	3.1	4.6
2003	14.1	8.7	5.9	4.1	0.2	0.9	3.6	5.0
2004	14.5	8.2	5.7	3.9	0.2	0.9	4.2	5.5

Notes: current exchange rates and prices - percentage points. Denominator is the sum of imports by all Euro area countries from the rest of the world (including the Euro area countries themselves). Numerator is total exports by each of the above countries to the euro area.

Source: Eurostat.

(*) Cyprus, Estonia, Latvia, Lithuania, Malta, Poland, Czech Republic, Slovak Republic, Slovenia, Hungary.

indicators: as both Pluyaud (2006, this volume) and Stahn (2006, this volume) show for France and Germany, the price elasticity of exports is higher for intra euro area trade than for extra euro area trade.[9]

4.2 A similar geographical specialisation

Recently, the geographical specialisation of Germany and Italy has been more favourable than the French one (cf. Appendix C): German and Italian

---

[9] For France, long run coefficients of extra euro area relative export prices are 0.47 and 0.90 for intra euro area relative export prices; for Germany, they amount to 0.63 and 0.92, respectively.

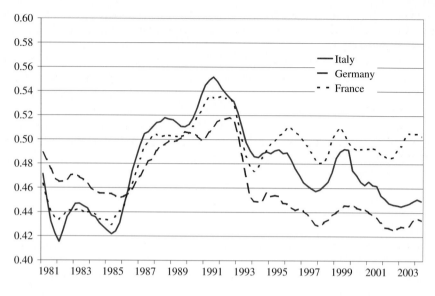

Source: IMF-DOTS.

Fig. 9. Share of intra exports to total exports - value terms

external trade is more oriented towards fast-growing areas such as the Far East, the United States and Central and Eastern Europe, whereas the French one is more turned towards the Euro Area and Africa.

However, what makes the difference in terms of geographical speciali-sation is that, for each of the three countries, the other two taken together are by and large the first commercial partner. From 2000 to 2004, the other two countries accounted for 24 per cent of exports for France, 18 per cent for Germany and 27 per cent for Italy. This implies that the slowdown in do-mestic demand, which affected strongly Germany and Italy at the beginning of the 2000s, played a relevant part in the weak French trade performance, whereas Germany and Italy may have benefited from the relative dynamism of French domestic demand. In fact, imports from euro area countries other than France have grown by an average of 4.0 per cent in volume from 2000-2004; the figure rises to 4.3 per cent when Germany is excluded, and to 4.6 per cent without Italy (cf. Appendix C).

In spite of these considerations, over the last ten years the overall effect of geographical specialisation was almost equivalent across the three coun-tries, as the contribution of world demand to GDP growth shows (cf. Fig-ure 10). This indicator, which takes into account the geographical specialisa-tion in year 2000 for calculating demand as the weighted growth of export markets, confirms the information given by the market shares computed on non-weighted world demand (world imports in volume). The differences between countries in the geographical orientation of external trade do not explain the major differences in export developments, although the contribution of world demand to GDP growth in France has been consistently below the German one. It accounts for a difference of 1.2 points to GDP growth between France and Germany in 2004, which comes partly from the higher share of exports in GDP (0.7 points) and partly from a pure geographical specialisation effect (0.5 points). The difference is similar between Italy and Germany (1.0 points), but the world demand effect is minor (0.2 points) compared to the trade openness effect (0.8 points). A full description of the decomposition between pure geographical specialisation effect and trade openness effect can be found in Appendix A.[10]

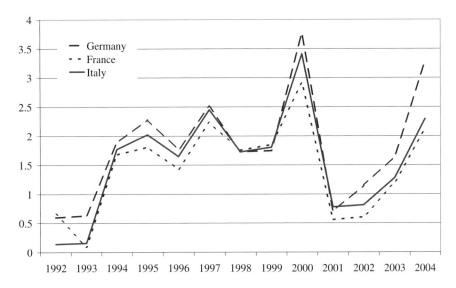

Notes: percentage points.
Source: Banque de France, Eurostat.

Fig. 10. Contribution of world demand to GDP growth

Another explanation of the recent French trade performance may lie in the substitution between French foreign and domestic demand: as domestic demand was dynamic, French producers may have substituted foreign orders for domestic ones. This phenomenon shows up in domestic market shares (cf. Figure 1): from 2000 onwards, domestic market shares have risen for both France and Italy and stopped declining in Germany.

---

[10] See Footnote 5.

5 Sectoral specialisation

The three countries share a weak specialisation in information technology products and suffered from the competition of new world players on labour-intensive goods, although France was affected the least. However, part of the loss in market shares touched the heart of European specialisation products.

5.1 Common weakness in information technology products

A common feature of the three countries is their weak specialisation in infor-mation technology and in energy products.[11] Whereas the information tech-nology trade deficit has been a drag on net exports in volume since the mid-1990s, energy imports have had a major impact on net exports in value only since the recent rise in energy prices.

Sectoral specialisation may be reflected by "revealed comparative advan-tage" indicators (cf. Appendix B), which compare the trade balance for a sector to the balance it would have according to its share in national trade, corrected for relative price evolution. For all three countries, revealed com-parative advantage indicators in 2003 (cf. Appendix D) are negative or close to zero for Computer Equipment (inferior to -5.0 per thousand of GDP), for Consumer Electronics (inferior to -1.0 per thousand of GDP) and Electronic Components (0.5 per thousand for France, -0.3 per thousand for Germany and -0,6 per thousand for Italy). France displays the least unfavourable trade specialisation of the three for all ICT products, which is also true for Telecom-munications Equipment, with a positive revealed comparative advantages indicator for France (1.5 per thousand), close to zero for Germany (-0.3 per thousand) and negative for Italy (-2.4 per thousand). However, recent devel-opments may challenge this feature, as ICT export evolution since 2000 has been less favourable in France (-29.6 per cent in value from 2000 to 2003) than in Germany (+16.8 per cent). In terms of export market shares, ICT products post a negative contribution for all three countries from 2000 to 2003, but it amounts to -0.23 points in France out of a total loss of -0.04 and -0.01 in Ger-many out of a gain of 1.2 points. According to Boulhol and Maillard (2005),

---

[11] Energy prices have a large impact on net exports in value: the 53.2 per cent increase in Brent prices from 2002 to 2004, which was significantly limited by the 31.4 per cent appreciation of the euro against the US dollar over the same period, has nev-ertheless raised the oil deficit from 21.7 to 28.1 billions EUR in France (from -3.4 per cent to -4.1 per cent of total trade or 34 per cent of the increase in the trade deficit) and from 33.7 to 39.6 billions EUR in Germany (from -2.9 per cent to -3.0 per cent of total trade or 20 per cent of the increase in the trade surplus). In Italy, the oil deficit remained stable around 18 billions EUR (from -3.5 per cent to -3.6 per cent of total trade). However, the strong impact of oil prices on the trade deficit in value, which reflects the fact that energy imports are inelastic to prices, is expected to be easily reversible if prices decrease.

who based their analysis on the STAN database, "Radio, television and communication equipment" and "Office machinery and computer" account for more than 40 per cent of the differential in product performance of Germany and France from 1998 to 2003.

As the relative price of these products shows a declining trend, their impact on the trade deficit is growing faster in volume than in value. Over the period 1990 to 2003, the deficit in information technology products in value amounted to 0.3 per cent of GDP for France, for an overall trade deficit in goods of 0.5 per cent, 0.5 per cent in Germany (overall surplus of 3.9 per cent) and 0.5 per cent in Italy (overall surplus of 1.3 per cent).

The analysis in volume terms is based on national data, for which the definition of information technology is not harmonised. In France, the electrical and electronic equipment industry[12] trade deficit increased three-fold from 1996 to 2003 and accounted for -0.9 points over a total of -0.8 points of net exports contribution to GDP growth over the same period. From 1997 and 2003, net exports contribution to GDP growth for Italy was -3.3 points, on which the ICT deficit (same definition as for France) accounted for about -0.6 points. In Germany, net imports in volume of electrical and electronic equipments[13] were multiplied by 2.6 between 1997 and 2003 and accounted for -0.8 points of German net exports contribution to GDP growth.

However, this analysis may be somewhat misleading in terms of overall contribution to GDP growth. Countries which run large surpluses in information technology are developing countries: only the low value-added stages of the production process (assembly of standardised components) may be located in these countries, while research and development or high value-added stages of production may remain in developed countries and post large contribution to GDP growth, although not through the net exports component. Nonetheless, the share of information technology in domestic value added (respectively 0.8 per cent, 0.8 per cent and 0.6 per cent in 2000 for France, Germany and Italy) remains much lower than for the United States (1.8 per cent) or Japan (2.9 per cent), which confirms the weak specialisation in those products.[14]

---

[12] Office machinery and computers; electronic engines, generator and transformer; radio and television apparatus; medical and orthopaedic instruments; measure and control instruments.

[13] Electrical machinery and apparatus, medical, precision and optical instruments watches and clocks as well as office machinery, computers, radio, television and electronic apparatus.

[14] Data are in value, from the STAN database, where IT products include: office, accounting and computing machinery; radio, television and communication equipment.

5.2 Different responses to the entrance of new competitors

The entrance of new world competitors such as China and Central and Eastern European Countries should first impact labour-intensive and low-technology sectors, as these countries have a comparative advantage stemming from the low level of their labour costs.

Competition in low technology sectors

As it can be seen from Appendix D, which presents revealed comparative advantage indicators for the three countries, Italy has specialised mostly in low technology and labour-intensive sectors such as Leather, Yarns fabrics, Furniture, Ceramics, Clothing or Domestic electrical appliances (such as refrigerators). At the lower quality margin, these products suffered competition from (and outsourcing to) developing countries and Eastern European countries. De Nardis and Pensa (2004) studied Italian exporters of traditional goods and showed that emerging or catching-up countries (China, India, Pakistan, Bangladesh but also Spain) exerted significant competitive pressures in some of these sectors (leather goods, footwear, apparel and ceramics) during the 1980s and the 1990s. Nonetheless, in terms of geographical orientation, double trade weights based on imports and exports and capturing domestic competition as well as third market competition effects,[15] show that between 1999 and 2001 Germany was more exposed to competition from CEEC, China, other emerging countries in Asia, Brazil or Mexico than Italy, which was itself more exposed than France (cf. Table 3). However, the computation of these weights relies partly on the export share to emerging countries, which contributes to the positive geographical orientation of German trade and to the negative one of France.

From 1990 to 2003, the contribution of low-technology sectors (except food products, classification based on OECD, 1997) to losses in export market shares has been larger for Italy than for the two other countries: for Italy, it represents 0.5 points out of 1.1 per cent losses in value terms; for Germany, 0.1 points out of 1.5 per cent; for France, 0.3 points out of 1.3 per cent. World market shares of low-technology sectors have decreased by 2.2 points in Italy to 6.8 per cent in 2003; by 2.9 points in Germany to 7.4 per cent; by 1.2 points to 4.0 per cent in France. In the meantime, China's world market shares of these goods have rocketed from 5.1 per cent in 1990 to 17.7 per cent in 2003, while Central and Eastern European Countries market share went from 2.6 per cent to 4.0 per cent and Latin American shares from 3.0 per cent to 5.0 per cent.

In order to take into account the evolution of imports, we may use market position indicators, which relate the trade balance in a sector to world

---

[15] The methodology presented in Buldorini, Makrydakis and Thimann (2002). Only trade in goods is considered.

Table 3. Main competitors as computed from double trade weights

Partner countries	France	Germany	Italy
Central and Eastern European Countries (*)	3.7	9.4	6.6
China	2.7	3.4	3.0
Emerging Asia (**)	6.1	7.3	6.4
Brazil	0.7	0.7	0.9
Mexico	0.5	0.8	0.6

Notes: averages over 1999-2001 - percentage points.
Source: CEPII CHELEM Database, computations by Banque de France.
(*) New Members States of the European Union, Russia, Romania, Bulgaria and Croatia.
(**) South Korea, Hong Kong, Singapore, India, Indonesia, Malaysia, Philippines, Taiwan, Thailand.

trade in that sector: Italy has strongly lost market positions in low-tech products since 1996 (from 5.0 per cent in 1996 to 2.7 per cent in 2003). France and Germany, while starting from very negative market positions in those products (-2.7 per cent for the two countries in 1990), gained over the period (+0.5 points for France and +1.4 points for Germany).

A high product quality in low tech sectors may allow a higher resilience to competition from low-cost countries. Aiginger (2000) ranks countries according to several export quality criteria (export unit value, revealed quality elasticity and position in price segment) and finds that German export quality is the highest, followed by France and Italy; however, according to Fontagné, Freudenberg and Ünal-Kezenci (1999), Italian traditional sectors are characterised by their specialisation in both high and low quality products. In short, the competition from new world players in low-technology sectors has touched all three countries, but Italy has been clearly most affected.

Competition in medium technology sectors

Germany and Italy lost export market shares also in medium technology sectors in which they were highly specialised (cf. Appendix E, where the distinction between medium-high and medium-low technology sectors follows the classification in OECD, 1997): for Germany, their contribution to losses in market shares from 1990 to 2003 amounted to 1.2 points out of 1.5 per cent; for Italy, 0.2 points out of 1.1 per cent. In that period, both countries lost world market shares in those sectors, except for Italy in specialised machines, engines, vehicles components and tubes. When taking into account all medium technology sectors, Germany, Italy and France lost export market shares in both medium-high and medium-low technology sectors,[16] while emerging countries from Asia (China, Asian newly industrialised countries), Latin America (Mexico) and Europe (Spain, Ireland) gained in medium-high technology sectors (cf. Appendix E). As exchange rates movements affect the measurement of market shares in value, the depreciation of European currencies from 1990 to 2003 against the US Dollar may bias this computation.[17]

This analysis needs however to take into account the relocation of stages of production. When an industrialised country shifts part of its production to less developed countries, or shifts from industry to services, its export market shares in goods will decrease (like Japan and the United Kingdom in the last 20 years). If a country shifts (relatively more than similar countries) some intermediate phase of production to third countries, to complete afterwards the process at home, its market share increases, as well as import penetration from third countries. In the case of Germany some of this happened with respect to Eastern European countries, as the large flow of direct investment there seems to confirm: according to ECB (2005), German FDI to CEEC-8 countries represented 21.5 per cent of the total inward FDI stock for the 8 countries in 2003, against 8 per cent for France and 2.8 per cent for Italy, and had a favourable impact on German exports and imports for the low-medium tech and the high tech products (cf. Box 7 in ECB, 2005). Relocation of stages of production increased the import content of exports for the three countries, especially for Germany: the import content increased from 34.7 per cent to 42.8 per cent for Germany, from 34 per cent in 1995 to 40.6 per cent in 2000 for France, and from 31.6 per cent to 35.4 per cent for Italy (ECB, 2005).

France seems to be less affected by competition of new world competitors (cf. Table 3), as it has specialised in food products (beverage and cereals) or high technology products (aeronautics and pharmaceuticals) more than medium technology sectors (cars and cycles, vehicle components). However, sectors accounting for a significant revealed comparative advantage are much scarcer and the corresponding indicator is much lower than in Germany or Italy (cf. Appendix D). One interpretation of this feature may be that French international specialisation is insufficiently developed and may structurally weigh on its export performance. According to Fontagné, Freudenberg and Ünal-Kezenci (1999), which studied high technology specialisation in Europe in year 1996 by building indicators based on high-tech products solely, within high-tech sectors, France has the strongest position in high tech products; however, its specialisation is concentrated in one sector, aeronautics, which is a source of fragility, whereas the German specialisation

---

[16] Italy does not appear in Appendix E for medium-low tech products; its market share went from 3.4 per cent to 3.3 per cent.

[17] The currencies of Germany, France and Italy (the Deutschemark, the French Franc, the Italian Lira and later the Euro) depreciated against the US Dollar over 1990-2003 by 6.8 per cent, 6.3 per cent and 30.1 per cent respectively.

in high tech products is spread across several sectors (transmission apparel, measurement instruments, chemicals, machine-tools). Moreover, high-tech products may be incorporated in medium-tech products, such as cars, to enhance the quality of exports. In that respect, Germany is ahead of France and Italy when it comes to the quality of exports (revealed by export unit values).

A high share of services may have strengthened the resilience of net exports to competition exerted by emerging economies, competition that tends however to develop in that field (consider the case of India for IT services). In that respect, services represent a higher share of exports in Italy (20.2 per cent in 2004, volume terms) and France (17.7 per cent) than in Germany (13.0 per cent).

5.3 Different sensitivity to the world economic cycle

Product specialisation may explain different trade performances in the cycle, as world demand addressed to a country may vary largely according to the product. Revealed comparative advantage indicators (cf. Appendix D) show that France is less specialised in equipment goods than Italy, which is less specialised than Germany. In terms of export composition, the share of equipment goods in France (24.5 per cent in 2002) is higher than in Italy (21.2 per cent) and close to Germany (26.8 per cent). However, this relies heavily on the share of aeronautics: without this sector, equipment goods share is lower in France (18.2 per cent) than in Italy (19.9 per cent) or Germany (25.1 per cent).

The large share of aeronautics in French exports (6.3 per cent) implies a high degree of volatility, as this sector relies on a few large orders. Moreover, due to long lags in the production process, exports of airplanes may lag the cycle: according to French customs data in value, aeronautics, trains, ships and motorbikes exports have decreased in 2002-03 and have stagnated in 2004. Conversely, consumer goods account for a larger share of French exports (27.0 per cent) than Italian (23.1 per cent) or German ones (25.0 per cent).

From Figure 11, which represents a proxy for world demand of equipment and consumption goods,[18] we may see that the geographical orientation has not made a large difference among the three countries; however, demand for equipment goods has been more dynamic, although more volatile, during the 1990s and more precisely during the last upturn.

In conclusion, product specialisation may explain some features of the export performance of the three countries: for Germany, its specialisation in

---

[18] Such proxy weights private consumption and total investment in volume in partner countries by the share in exports by the reporting country (either France, Germany or Italy) in equipment and consumption goods. This is only a proxy for world demand of equipment and consumption goods as the growing propensity to import in the world implies a higher growth rate for imports than for domestic demand.

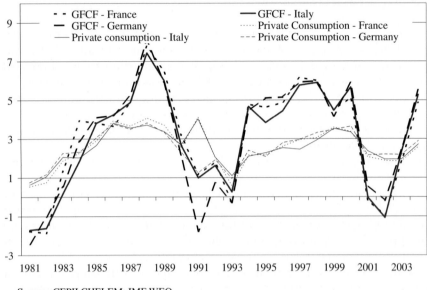

Source: CEPII CHELEM; IMF WEO.

Fig. 11. 69-countries gross fixed capital formation (GFCF) and private consumption weighted by 1999-2001 share in exports of equipment and consumption goods

equipment goods supported the recovery of its exports in the second half of the 1990s and during the recent upturn; for France, the large share of consumption goods may weigh on its long-term export performance and its specialisation in aeronautics may partly explain the weak export performance since 2002; the recent upturn in total investment may have benefited Italian exports. Finally, the lack of specialisation in information technology products, which were strongly affected by the 2001 slowdown, may have supported the export market shares of the three countries at the beginning of the 2000s, as their exports were less affected by this phenomenon than other countries.

However, we may notice that the French and Italian market shares in equipment goods exports towards Emerging Asia or the United States, where demand was dynamic in 2003 and 2004, were stable or declining from 2000 to 2003, whereas they grew for Germany.[19] This shows that product specialisation does not seem sufficient to explain divergent export developments among the three countries.

---

[19] From 2000 to 2003, export market shares in equipment goods towards Emerging Asia were stable for France and Italy and grew by 0.5 points for Germany; towards the United States, they declined by 0.8 points for France, were stable for Italy and increased by 0.4 points for Germany (source: CHELEM).

6 Non price competitiveness

As previously shown, price competitiveness, geographic or sectoral special-isation indicators are insufficient to explain the losses in market shares of France and Italy or the gains in Germany. A recent econometric study (Al-lard, Catalan, Everaert and Sgherri, 2005) confirms that after subtracting the effect of cost competitiveness and geographic specialisation on export per-formance, the unexplained part was positive for Germany and negative for France and Italy. Hence, non price competitiveness factors may be helpful to explain trade performance.

It comes perhaps as no surprise that recent empirical research on export price elasticities (Hooper, Johnson and Marquez, 2000) finds that Italy shows a much higher long run price elasticity for exports (0.9) than France and Ger-many (0.2 and 0.3 respectively). Long run elasticity to foreign income is esti-mated not significantly different from one in the three countries. In fact, the high price elasticity for Italy, in presence of a continuous loss in price com-petitiveness, may be the symptom of a loss in non price competitiveness, or of an increase in competitiveness by new competitors in some of the prod-ucts of Italian specialisation. Non price competitiveness is the name that we give to improved quality and variety of products, not taken into account by the existing product classification. Product quality is, first of all, innovation in the technology of products. Innovation in technology depends on R&D activity and, indirectly, on other structural factors of the economy, like the human capital endowment.

The three countries show a clear and significant ordering in a number of indicators about technological intensity in production and differences in in-vestment on knowledge based activities (in 2002, R&D expenses were about 2.5 per cent of GDP in Germany, 2.2 in France and 1.1 in Italy). The ranking is the same when R&D intensity is measured relative to a weighted average of competitors, with a sharp decrease for France since the end of the 1990s and a slow erosion for Italy (cf. Figure 10). The different specialisation model (in terms of products) of the three countries is important because it is much easier to innovate in the high tech and medium-high tech sector, than in the traditional products. In the latter only innovation in the production process may indirectly improve quality through innovative technology.

In terms of education, another acknowledged determinant of non price competitiveness, the ranking is the same, with Germany leading with 12.95 average years of schooling in 2000, followed by France with 10.73 and Italy with 10.33 (Cohen and Soto, 2003). However, the relative performance in ed-ucation (cf. Figure 13) shows an upward trend in Italy and France and a de-clining one in Germany.

In short, by the measures of non price competitiveness we have consid-ered, the same ordering of the three countries appears, which may shed some light on the reason for the product specialisation of Italy and its strong sen-sitivity to competition from new world players.

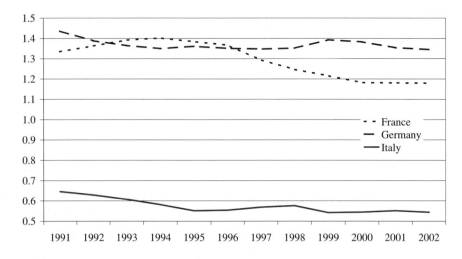

Notes: the relative R&D intensity is the ratio of R&D intensity, i.e. R&D spending over GDP, to 30 competitors' R&D intensity, weighted by double-trade weights. An increase shows a relative improvement in R&D intensity compared to the country's main competitors.
Source: OECD MSTI.

Fig. 12. Relative R & D intensity

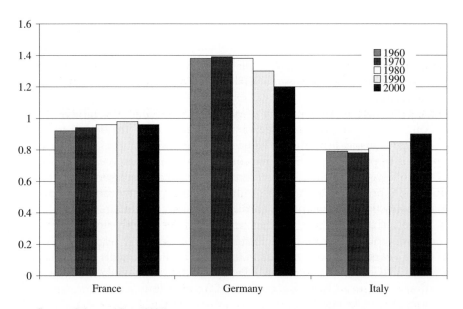

Source: Cohen and Soto (2001).

Fig. 13. Relative average years of schooling

7 Conclusion

In summary, the last upturn of the business cycle, when the exchange rates were irrevocably fixed by the monetary union, showed some puzzling differences. France saw a mixed performance of net exports, which deteriorated strongly in the 2000s, partly because of domestic demand absorbing more imports or more domestic output and, on the other hand, because exports were penalised by the higher share of intra euro area exports and a specialisation on products whose foreign demand is lagging the cycle. Italy was strongly affected by a worsening of price competitiveness: export prices in euro terms went up during the period of euro depreciation, and stayed almost flat during the phase of euro appreciation. The same happened during the 1995-1997 episode of Italian lira depreciation and appreciation. Germany saw an overall improvement of price competitiveness, but not as strong as France: nonetheless, the increase in exports was very strong as demand for investment goods picked up strongly. A lack of specialisation in information technology products and the emergence of new world competitors have weighed on the trade performance of the three countries, although Italy has been more affected than France and Germany. German competitiveness may have benefited from the relocation of stages of production in the new European member States. However, a careful investigation of such an hypothesis is reserved for future research.

References

Aiginger K (2000) Europe's position in quality competition. Background report for "The European competitiveness report 2000", European Commission.

Allard C, Catalan M, Everaert L, Sgherri S (2005) Explaining differences in external sector performance among large euro area countries. IMF Country Report n 05/401, October.

Balassa B (1965) Trade liberalization and revealed comparative advantage. *The Manchester School of Economic and Social Studies*, n 33, May.

Boulhol H, Maillard L (2005) Une analyse descriptive du décrochage récent des exportations francaises. CDC-IXIS, Etude n 2005-02.

Buldorini L, Makrydakis S, Thimann C (2002) The effective exchange rates of the euro. ECB occasional paper n 2.

CHELEM Database (March 2005), CEPII.

Cheptea A, Gaulier G, Zignago S (2004) Marché mondial: Positions acquises et performances. *La lettre du CEPII*, n 231 (février).

Cohen D, Soto M (2003) Growth and human capital: good data, good results. *CEPR Discussion Paper* n 3025.

De Nardis S, Pensa C (2004) How intense is competition in international markets of traditional goods? The case of Italian exporters. ISAE Working Paper n 45.

European Central Bank (2005) Competitiveness and the export performance of the euro area. Occasional Paper Series n 30, June 2005.

Fontagné, L, Freudenberg M, Ünal-Kezenci D (1999) Haute technologie et échelles de qualité: de fortes asymétries en Europe. CEPII Document de Travail 99-08.

Hooper P, Johnson K, Marquez J (2000) Trade Elasticities for the G-7 Countries. *Princeton Studies in International Economics* 87 (August).

OECD (1997) Technology and industrial performance.

OECD (2005) Main Science and Technology Indicators.

Pluyaud B (2006) Modelling imports and exports of goods in France, distinguishing between intra and extra euro area trade. This volume.

Stahn K (2006) Has the impact of price competitiveness on German foreign trade changed? This volume.

A Contribution of world demand and export market shares to GDP growth

We would like to decompose the contribution of external trade to GDP growth between a contribution of changes in export market shares, a contribution of world demand and a contribution of imports, in order to see how gains or losses of market shares have affected external trade and GDP growth over the recent years.

The notations are the following :

X_j corresponds to the exports of the country j (either, Germany, Italy or France) for a given year and $X_j(-1)$ to the exports for the previous year;

M_j corresponds to the imports of the country j for a given year and $M_j(-1)$ to the imports for the previous year;

Y_j corresponds to the GDP of the country j for a given year and $Y_j(-1)$ to the GDP for the previous year.

Typically, we have :
the contribution of external trade to GDP growth :

$$\frac{X_j - X_j(-1)}{X_j(-1)} \times \frac{X_j(-1)}{Y_j(-1)} - \frac{M_j - M_j(-1)}{M_j(-1)} \times \frac{M_j(-1)}{Y_j(-1)} \tag{1}$$

which is the sum of
the contribution of exports:

$$\frac{X_j - X_j(-1)}{X_j(-1)} \times \frac{X_j(-1)}{Y_j(-1)} \tag{2}$$

computed as the export growth rate multiplied by the share of exports in GDP at the previous period,
and
the contribution of imports:

$$-\frac{M_j - M_j(-1)}{M_j(-1)} \times \frac{M_j(-1)}{Y_j(-1)} \tag{3}$$

computed as the opposite of the import growth rate multiplied by the share of imports in GDP at the previous period.

We decompose the contribution of exports (2) between :
a "contribution of changes in world demand":

$$\frac{WD_j - WD_j(-1)}{WD_j(-1)} \times \frac{X_j(-1)}{Y_j(-1)} \tag{4}$$

where WD_j is an index of the world demand addressed to the country j, and :
a "contribution of changes in market shares":

$$\left(\frac{X_j - X_j(-1)}{X_j(-1)} - \frac{WD_j - WD_j(-1)}{WD_j(-1)}\right) \times \frac{X_j(-1)}{Y_j(-1)} \tag{5}$$

What we call "contribution of changes in world demand" to GDP growth (4) corresponds to the contribution that exports would have brought to GDP growth if exports had grown at the same pace as world demand addressed to the country. The difference between the actual contribution of exports to GDP growth and this contribution of world demand is supposed to correspond to changes in market shares.

With a more precise notation, let $WD_{j,t}$ denote the world demand index in period t for country j (either France, Germany or Italy), defined as:

$$WD_{j,t} = \sum_{n=1}^{N} x_{j,T}^n M_t^n \tag{6}$$

where N is the total number of countries in the World, $x_{j,T}^n$ is the market share of the country j in the overall imports of the nth partner country in the base year T (here, T is year 2000), and M_t^n are the overall imports by the nth partner country in period t. The fact that the weights are fixed has an incidence on the calculation, which must therefore be taken as an approximation.

The difference in the "contribution of changes in world demand" between two countries (i and j) can be decomposed between:

a "pure geographical specialisation effect"

$$\left(\frac{WD_i - WD_i(-1)}{WD_i(-1)} - \frac{WD_j - WD_j(-1)}{WD_j(-1)}\right) \times \frac{X_i(-1)}{Y_i(-1)} \tag{7}$$

and

a "trade openness effect":

$$\frac{WD_j - WD_j(-1)}{WD_j(-1)} \times \left(\frac{X_i(-1)}{Y_i(-1)} - \frac{X_j(-1)}{Y_j(-1)}\right) \tag{8}$$

GDP, exports and imports are extracted from ESA accounts. World demand indicators are the ones computed by the Banque de France, based on IMF and OECD.

B CEPII's revealed comparative advantages indicators

CEPII's revealed comparative advantage was based on Balassa 1965 indicator, which is the ratio of the balance of trade for a sector over the total trade of the country:

$$B_i = \frac{X_i - M_i}{X + M} \tag{9}$$

where X_i is exports for products i, M_i is imports for goods i, X and M are respectively total exports and imports.

This indicator is however sensitive to temporary imbalances of net exports, due for example to exchange rate misalignment or lags in the domestic versus world cycle. It was improved by comparing the product balance to a norm representing the contribution of the products if it was proportional to its size in domestic trade:

$$S_i = \frac{X_i - M_i}{X + M} - \frac{(X_i + M_i) \times (X - M)}{(X + M)^2} \tag{10}$$

In order to take into account the evolution of domestic demand, this indicator may be related to GDP instead of total trade:

$$C_i = \frac{1000}{GDP} \times \left[(X_i - M_i) - \frac{(X_i + M_i) \times (X - M)}{(X + M)} \right] \tag{11}$$

Finally, the impact of the evolution of relative prices, which may change the trade balance of a product relative to GDP although the specialisation in volume terms has remained stable, could be corrected by taking into account the evolution of the share of the product into world trade from a base year.

$$M_i = Ci \times \frac{T_0^i}{T_0} \div \frac{T_n^i}{T_n} \tag{12}$$

where T_0 is world trade for the base year; T_n is world trade for the year n; T_t^i is world trade of product i in year t $(t = 0, n)$.

C Geographical specialisation

Trade partners

From / To	France	Germany	Italy
Euro area	51.2	44.0	46.5
United Kingdom	9.9	8.3	6.9
CEEC[1]	2.1	6.5	3.4
Other Europe Industrialised countries[2]	6.2	9.2	5.9
Other Europe Developing Countries[3]	3.3	5.5	7.6
United States	7.3	9.3	8.7
Japan	1.7	2.1	1.8
Far East[4]	5.8	6.8	6.1
Middle East and Africa	8.2	4.0	7.2
America except United States[5]	3.1	3.2	4.6
Australia and New Zealand	0.6	0.7	0.9

Notes: averages between Q1 1995 and Q3 2004 - percentage points.
Source: OECD.

Average growth rate of total imports in volume

	1990-1995	1995-2000	2000-2004
Euro area, France excluded	4.9	8.0	4.0
Euro area, Germany excluded	4.6	8.3	4.3
Euro area, Italy excluded	4.8	8.2	4.6
United Kingdom	2.8	8.5	4.8
CEEC[1]	11.5	14.3	9.5
Other Europe Industrialised countries[2]	2.4	7.2	3.8
Other Europe Developing Countries[3]	8.3	4.7	13.5
United States	6.4	11.1	5.5
Japan	4.0	5.2	5.2
Far East[4]	14.2	8.7	9.9
Middle East and Africa	2.5	4.8	6.1
America except United States[5]	9.4	8.5	3.6
Australia and New Zealand	4.5	7.7	7.6

Notes: percentage points.
Source: OECD.

[1] Czech Republic, Hungary, Poland, Slovak Republic.
[2] Sweden, Denmark, Norway, Switzerland.
[3] CIS, ex-Yugoslavia, Baltic States, Eastern Europe countries (includes: Romania, Bulgaria, Slovenia).
[4] Of which : South Korea, Indonesia, Malaysia, Philippines, Thailand, Singapore, India, Pakistan, China, Taiwan, Hong-Kong.
[5] Latin and Central America, Canada.

D Revealed comparative advantage

First 15 export products by revealed comparative advantage indicators

FRANCE	A	B	C	GERMANY	A	B	C	ITALY	A	B	C
Aeronautics	7.4	-0.01	1.4	Cars and cycles	29.0	0.05	-0.6	Specialized machines	14.3	-0.09	0.7
Beverages	5.7	-0.08	-8.0	Specialized machines	12.5	-0.32	-4.2	Miscellaneous hardware	8.9	-0.03	-0.8
Cars and cycles	5.3	0.00	-0.4	Vehicles components	8.2	-0.16	-5.7	Furniture	7.9	-0.04	-6.5
Toiletries	4.9	0.02	-2.0	Miscellaneous hardware	6.7	-0.13	-4.2	Leather	7.2	-0.14	-4.5
Vehicles components	4.6	-0.02	-0.7	Plastic articles	6.2	-0.12	-5.4	Engines	6.1	0.01	0.2
Pharmaceuticals	4.3	0.15	-1.1	Engines	6.1	-0.10	-3.4	Yarns fabrics	5.4	-0.10	-1.2
Cereals	3.2	-0.01	-3.9	Commercial vehicles	5.8	0.00	0.4	Domestic electrical appliances	4.7	-0.01	-1.9
Electricity	2.5	-0.01	-13.0	Precision instruments	5.5	-0.01	-2.5	Vehicles components	4.6	0.01	0.2
Telecommunications equipment	1.5	0.04	-0.4	Electrical apparatus	3.6	-0.05	-4.2	Jewellery, works of art	4.5	-0.05	-1.2
Fats	1.3	-0.05	-2.9	N.e.s. products	3.6	0.70	14.1	Ceramics	4.5	-0.03	-1.4
Electrical apparatus	1.1	-0.02	-1.5	Construction equipment	3.3	-0.06	-2.4	Clothing	4.1	-0.06	-2.3
Rubber articles (including tyres)	1.0	-0.03	-3.8	Toiletries	2.8	-0.01	-4.9	Beverages	3.7	0.00	0.9
Sugar	0.8	-0.02	0.5	Machine tools	2.8	-0.13	-4.0	Machine tools	3.1	-0.06	-1.0
Engines	0.7	-0.04	-1.6	Paints	2.8	-0.06	-6.0	Knitwear	2.8	-0.09	-8.0
Construction equipment	0.6	-0.03	-1.3	Basic organic chemicals	1.9	-0.11	-5.6	Tubes	2.8	-0.02	1.0

Last 15 export products by revealed comparative advantage indicators

FRANCE	A	B	C	GERMANY	A	B	C	ITALY	A	B	C
Crude oil	-14.1	0.00	0.0	Crude oil	-14	0.00	0.0	Crude oil	-13.5	0.00	0.0
Computer equipment	-5.5	-0.06	-2.5	**Computer equipment**	-7.5	0.02	-1.9	Cars and cycles	-4.4	-0.08	-1.7
Natural gas	-4.3	0.01	0.1	Other edible agricultural products	-7.3	-0.05	-0.1	N.e.s. products	-2.1	0.04	-0.9
Clothing	-3.5	-0.04	-1.9	Natural gas	-6.7	0.00	1.9	**Computer equipment**	-4.4	-0.09	-2.7
Knitwear	-3.0	-0.01	-1.1	Clothing	-4.2	-0.07	-3.2	Non-edible agricultural products	-2.2	0.00	0.7
Miscellaneous manufacturing articles	-2.5	-0.03	-1.3	Knitwear	-4.1	-0.04	-1.2	Meat	-3.2	-0.04	0.4
Leather	-2.5	-0.02	-0.4	Refined petroleum products	-3.9	-0.04	0.2	Basic organic chemicals	-0.9	-0.04	-0.7
Furniture	-2.1	-0.02	-2.5	Leather	-3.1	-0.13	-1.4	Non ferrous metals	-2.5	0.00	0.1
Refined petroleum products	-2.1	-0.01	0.2	**Consumer electronics**	-2.2	-0.04	-2.7	Iron Steel	-2.0	-0.13	-1.0
Paper	-2.1	-0.03	0.1	Meat	-1.8	-0.13	-0.9	Natural gas	-0.1	-0.13	0.1
Plastic articles	-1.9	-0.05	-2.2	Non-edible agricultural products	-1.6	-0.05	-7.3	**Consumer electronics**	-0.5	-0.05	-0.8
Non ferrous metals	-1.7	-0.06	-2.0	Beverages	-1.6	-0.03	0.8	**Telecommunications equipment**	-0.1	0.00	-0.8
Consumer electronics	-1.4	-0.02	-1.1	Carpets	-1.5	0.00	-0.1	Fats	-1.4	0.01	1.2
Meat	-1.4	-0.05	-1.9	Non ferrous ores	-1.3	-0.02	-2.2	Other edible agricultural products	-1.0	-0.03	-0.6
Manufactured tobaccos	-1.4	0.00	1.9	Manufactured tobaccos	-1	-0.01	0.9	Precision instruments	-1.1	-0.01	-0.5

Notes:

A: Revealed comparative advantage, base 2002 (‰ of GDP).

B: Contribution to changes in world export market share from 1990 to 2003 (percentage points).

C: Changes in product market share from 1990 to 2003 (percentage points).

Source: CEPII CHELEM database.

E Medium-technology products

Market shares in medium-technology products

The ten countries[*] which experienced the largest losses in medium-high technology products market shares in the 1990s and 2000s

	Market share in 2003	Changes 1990-2003
Germany	16.8%	-3.0%
Japan	10.7%	-2.7%
United Kingdom	5.1%	-1.3%
Netherlands	2.9%	-1.2%
Switzerland	2.1%	-1.0%
France	6.5%	-0.9%
Italy	5.2%	-0.9%
United States	11.1%	-0.9%
Sweden	1.6%	-0.7%
Norway	0.3%	-0.2%

The ten countries[*] which experienced the largest gains in medium-high technology products market shares in the 1990s and 2000s

	Market share in 2003	Changes 1990-2003
China, People's Rep.	3.2%	2.6%
Mexico	2.5%	1.7%
South Korea	2.4%	1.4%
Ireland	1.5%	1.0%
Spain	3.0%	0.9%
Czech Republic	0.9%	0.9%
Poland	0.8%	0.8%
Russian Federation	0.7%	0.7%
Belgium and Luxembourg	4.6%	0.7%
Hungary	0.7%	0.7%

Notes: percentage points. Products classified according to OECD (1997).
(*) Over the 83 countries/zones of the CEPII CHELEM Database.
Source: CEPII CHELEM.

The ten countries[**] which experienced the largest losses in medium-low technology products market shares in the 1990s and 2000s

	Market share in 2003	Changes 1990-2003
United Kingdom	3.8%	-1.5%
Germany	8.6%	-1.4%
United States	8.1%	-1.3%
Netherlands	4.9%	-1.2%
France	4.2%	-1.1%
Japan	5.4%	-1.0%
Norway	1.0%	-0.9%
Venezuela	0.6%	-0.8%
Singapore	1.7%	-0.8%
Algeria	0.4%	-0.5%

The ten countries[**] which experienced the largest gains in medium-low technology products market shares in the 1990s and 2000s

	Market share in 2003	Changes 1990-2003
China, People's Rep.	7.1%	5.3%
Russian Federation	3.4%	3.4%
South Korea	4.0%	1.9%
Belgium and Luxembourg	5.1%	0.9%
Poland	0.7%	0.7%
Czech Republic	0.5%	0.5%
India	1.0%	0.5%
Thailand	0.8%	0.5%
Ukraine	0.4%	0.4%
Malaysia	0.8%	0.4%

Notes: percentage points. Products classified according to OECD (1997).
(**) Over the 83 countries/zones of the CEPII CHELEM Database.
Source: CEPII CHELEM.

Modelling Imports and Exports of Goods in France, Distinguishing Between Intra and Extra Euro Area Trade[*]

Bertrand Pluyaud

Banque de France, 31 rue Croix des Petits Champs, 75049 Paris Cedex 01
bpluyaud@wanadoo.fr

Summary. This paper presents equations for intra and extra euro area trade for France. Volumes and prices of imports and exports of goods are modelled. Dynamic simulations, residual tests and rolling forecasts indicate that the equations have satisfactory forecasting properties. However, trends and dummy variables are often added and competitiveness effects are not always well captured, probably due to inadequate data. Among other results, we find a stronger long run elasticity to price competitiveness for intra than for extra euro area exports, and positive contributions of price competitiveness to non energy import growth since 1999, probably due to evolutions in costs rather than in exchange rates.

Keywords: intra and extra euro area trade, time series models, France external trade.
JEL classification: C22, C51, F17.

1 Introduction

For the analysis of external trade performance, the introduction of the euro as a single currency, following a long period of exchange rate stability in the ERM since the mid-1990s, represents a major departure from the previous period. Indeed, among the three largest countries, Italy, Germany and France, which account more than 60% of the total, trade is now shielded from exchange rate fluctuations - at least as far as final trade movements are considered. Against this background, it might be useful to investigate whether running a separate analysis on intra and extra trade might improve the fit of trade equations.

This paper presents equations for intra and extra euro area trade for France. By intra euro area trade, we understand exports from France to the other countries of the euro area and imports from these countries. Extra euro

---

[*] Special thanks to Véronique Brunhes-Lesage for providing research assistance and to Olivier de Bandt, Xavier Torres and Jean-Pierre Villetelle for their useful comments.

area trade corresponds to exports from France to the rest of the world and imports from the rest of the world. It is intended to complement MASCOTTE,[2] the Banque de France macro-econometric model of the French Economy, which features only total (intra+extra euro area) trade equations. As it is, most of the modelling choices made here are guided by the necessity to stick to the MASCOTTE model. In particular, intra and extra trade data are compiled consistently in order to ensure that intra and extra trade series add up to the total trade figures of the national account data used in that model. Furthermore, the specifications of equations are, as far as possible, the same.

The modelling strategy relies on error correction equations, which are estimated separately. Imports and exports of goods, but also import and export prices, are modelled for the intra and extra euro area exchanges of France.

Data are consistent with national accounts, but the breakdown between intra and extra trade is constructed with the help of Eurostat's external trade database. Eurostat's trade data mostly begin in 1989, whereas the French National accounts begin in 1978, which implies shorter estimation samples for intra and extra trade than for total trade. Furthermore, Eurostat's database contains unit value indexes, which are not as informative as actual price indexes.

Such limitations, as well as the disparity of data sources, are evident limitations to the quality of estimations. As a consequence, the modelling exercise presented here should be viewed as a calibration exercise "informed" by econometrics. Specification are designed to be consistent with economic theory, but, as it is standard in applied modelling, trends are added when coefficients are not significant or have unexpected signs.

Yet, this exercise is useful, notably because the euro area is becoming the geographical reference to which the French Economy must now be compared. Furthermore, it could help to understand how currency risks affect trade within and outside the euro area. Finally, if this approach were generalized to all countries of the euro area, it could help assessing euro area external trade as a whole.

This paper is divided in five sections. After this introduction (Section 1), the data set is presented (Section 2), then the estimation results (Section 3). Section 4 consists in a short assessment of recent trade evolutions using dynamic contributions of the equations. Finally, Section 5 concludes. Readers interested in the results can directly jump to section 3, without loss of continuity.

---

[2] Wherever MASCOTTE is mentioned in this paper, the full reference is : Baghli M, Brunhes-Lesage V, de Bandt O, Fraisse H, Villetelle J-P (2004) Modèle d'Analyse et de préviSion de la COnjoncture TrimesTriellE. Note d'Etude et de Recherche 106, Banque de France. This paper is available on http://www.banque-france.fr/gb/publi/main.htm.

2 Data

Due to the absence of breakdown between intra and extra euro area in the French national accounts, we compile a new database, using in particular data from Eurostat.

2.1 Trade data

A major problem concerning external trade data is the lack of volume indicators. In the national accounts, volume series are not available for intra and extra trade separately but only for the whole external trade. Nevertheless, Eurostat's External Trade in Goods Statistics database provides volume indexes for the intra and extra euro area trade of goods. These volume indexes are built with unit value indexes, which cannot be truly considered as price indexes, because they do not take into account structure effects, as each category of good merges very different types of products. However, no other volume indicator being available, Eurostats volume indexes are used in this study. They have been seasonally adjusted using Census X12.

In order to obtain volume series, we multiply the volume indexes by the mean of the corresponding value series for a base year (2000 in our database). Eurostat data are then used to compute intra and extra shares for both values and volumes. These shares are multiplied by the total trade series of the quarterly national accounts, for values as well as for volumes. Intra and extra prices are computed afterwards, as ratios between value and volume series. This method allows the intra/extra trade series to be consistent with national accounts total trade series (see Table 1).

As for services, the only sources for intra/extra shares are Balance of Payment statistics. Due to methodological changes, it is difficult to build long time series based on Balance of Payment statistics : current data are not consistent with data prior to 1997. Furthermore, Balance of payment data are only available in value terms. Hence, we prefer to focus on trade in goods in this study.

2.2 Demand indicators

Demand indicator in import equations : import content of domestic demand

The series of import content of domestic demand are used as demand indicators in import equations. They aim at measuring how imports would have evolved if the import content and the demand structure of each product had remained constant as compared to a base year (Villetelle, 2002). The discrepancy between the actual change in imports and the changes in the demand indicator corresponds to competitiveness effects.

Table 1. Method implemented for the construction of trade series

Eurostat value data	$\Rightarrow$	*Intra/extra trade value* **shares**	$\times$	*National accounts trade in value*	$=$	*Intra/extra trade in value*

$$\div$$

Eurostat volume indexes	$\Rightarrow$	*Intra/extra trade volume* **shares**	$\times$	*National accounts trade in volume*	$=$	*Intra/extra trade in volume*

$$=$$

$$Intra/extra\ trade\ deflators$$

National accounts feature a breakdown of domestic demand between different components (households' consumption, public consumption, firms' investment). Input-output tables provide the weight of each sector in these components. In particular, they provide the direct and indirect (i.e. through intermediate consumptions) import content for each sector (or product). From this information, it is possible to compute an import content of each component of domestic demand. The CHELEM database, built by the research institute CEPII, is used to calculate for each sector the share of intra and extra imports. It must be noted that the sectors of the CHELEM database are not fully consistent with the sectors of the national accounts and that approximations must be made. However, the fact that we used the most disaggregated nomenclature of CHELEM to match the main sectors of the national accounts limits the risks of errors: we mapped the 71 categories of products from CHELEM into the 7 main sectors of the national accounts.

For the euro area, the formula is:

$$DI_{euro\ area} = \sum_j \sum_i \alpha_{euro\ area,i}\ \beta_{i,j}\ FD_j$$

with $DI_{euro\ area}$ the Euro area import content of domestic demand, $\alpha_{euro\ area,i}$ the share of euro area in the French exports of the sector i (provided by CHELEM), $\beta_{i,j}$ the content of the jth component of final demand in imports from the sector i (provided by input-output tables) and $FD_j = j^{th}$ component of final demand (households' consumption, public consumption, firms investment...).

For extra euro area trade, the formula is similar:

$$DI_{extra\ euro\ area} = \sum_j \sum_i (1 - \alpha_{euro\ area,i})\ \beta_{i,j}\ FD_j$$

Demand indicators in export equations

Intra and extra euro area demand series are built as geometric averages of imports from the economic partners of France, weighted by the market shares of French exports in these countries (Dauphin, 1999). For a given country, the market share of France is computed as the ratio between the exports of France to this country and the total imports of this country, for a given base year. The discrepancy between these demand series and actual exports correspond to changes in market shares of French exports.

Demand series used in this study are directly derived from those used in MASCOTTE. In particular, they feature the same base year, which is 1996. This choice is convenient because it allows a greater consistency with the previous model. However, strong modifications in the world trade structure have been recorded since 1996, especially with the rise of emerging countries, like China, as major trade partners. This makes these demand indicators less reliable for the assessment of current trade evolutions (see Felletigh et al., 2006, this volume, for indicators based on 2000 weights).

The import series are extracted from the OECD Economic Outlook for OECD countries and from the IMF World Economic Outlook database for developing countries. Until 2004, OECD import series were available for goods, which was convenient for this study. However, as from 2004, data are only available for goods and services, which might deteriorate the quality of equations in the future. Market shares are built using the CHELEM database. The split between intra and extra is directly obtained by separating the country series between euro area members and non-euro area members

In the case of the euro area, the formula is:

$$D_{euro\ area} = \prod_{k \in euro\ area} M_k^{\delta_k}$$

$$\delta_k = \left.\frac{X_{Fr,k}}{M_k}\right|_{t=1996}$$

with $D_{euro\ area}$ the demand addressed by the euro area to France, $X_{Fr,k}$ the French exports to the country k and M_k = Imports of the country k.

Similarly, for extra euro area:

$$D_{extra\ euro\ area} = \prod_{l \in extra\ euro\ area} M_l^{\delta_l}$$

2.3 Competitor prices

Competitor price series correspond to weighted geometric averages of the export prices of France's competitors. As for demand indicators, the base year for weights is 1996 (the remarks concerning the reasons and implications of this choice apply here as well). For practical reasons, the number of countries taken into account has been limited. In particular, no country of Asia excluding Japan has been included, which represents an obvious shortcoming. Export prices of foreign countries are given by OECD International Trade and Competitiveness Indicators. Country weights are computed with CHELEM.

The weighting scheme is different for competitor prices on the import side and on the export side.

On the import side, weights correspond to the market share of each country on the French market, for a given base year (1996 here). Import competitor prices show how import prices would behave if our partners exported to France at their average export prices. (For more details, see Baghli et al., 2004).

For euro area competitor import prices, the formula is the following:

$$P_{M,euro\ area}^* = \prod_{m \in K_I} P_{X,m}{}^{\gamma_m}$$

$$\gamma_m = \left.\frac{X_{m,Fr}}{M_{Fr}}\right|_{t=1996}$$

where $P_{M,euro\ area}^*$ is the euro area competitor import prices, $P_{X,m}$ the export price of the country m, $X_{m,Fr}$ the exports of the country m to France, M_{Fr} the French Imports and K_I is the following set of euro area countries: Germany, Belgium, Spain, Italy, Netherlands.

Similarly, **for extra euro area import prices**, the formula is:

$$P_{M,extra\ euro\ area}^* = \prod_{n \in K_J} P_{X,n}{}^{\gamma_n}$$

$$\gamma_n = \left.\frac{X_{n,Fr}}{M_{Fr}}\right|_{t=1996}$$

where K_J is the following set of extra euro area countries: United States, Japan, United Kingdom, Switzerland.

On the export side, a double weighting system is used. The weight of a given country corresponds to the sum of its market shares in the other countries, weighted by the shares of these countries in the French exports.

Intra euro area competitor export prices are given by the following formula:

$$P_{X,euro\ area}^* = \prod_{q \in K} P_{X,q}{}^{\mu_{q,euro\ area}}$$

where $P^*_{X,euro\ area}$ is the intra euro area competitor export prices, $P_{X,q}$ the export price of the country q, $\mu_{q,euro\ area}$ the weight of the country q as a competitor for exports to euro area and K is the following set of countries: Germany, Belgium, Spain, Italy, Netherlands, United States, Japan, United Kingdom, Switzerland. The weight of the country q as a competitor for exports to the euro area is :

$$\mu_{q,euro\ area} = \sum_{u \in euro\ area} \frac{X_{Fr,u}}{X_{Fr}} \frac{X_{q,u}}{M_u}\bigg|_{t=1996}$$

Extra euro area competitor export prices are computed in the same way:

$$P^*_{X,extra\ euro\ area} = \prod_{q \in K} P_{X,q}{}^{\mu_{q,extra\ euro\ area}}$$

The only difference is in the weight formula. The weight of the country q as a competitor for exports to extra euro area is:

$$\mu_{q,extra\ euro\ area} = \sum_{v \in extra\ euro\ area} \frac{X_{Fr,v}}{X_{Fr}} \frac{X_{q,v}}{M_v}\bigg|_{t=1996}$$

3 Estimation results

3.1 Modelling strategy

Table 2 displays the twenty-four variables that could possibly be modelled. The distinction between energy and non energy is only necessary for imports, as France's energy exports are low.

All variables presented in Table 2 are not modelled by econometric equations. Only real trade and deflator equations are actually estimated. Nominal series are then computed by multiplying real series by the corresponding deflators. Furthermore, total import and export equations have already been estimated in the MASCOTTE model and we focus here on intra/extra equations. The letter "M" in the table indicates the variables which are actually modelled.

Our aim is to estimate equations for intra and extra euro area. However, if one equation is not satisfactory, for example for intra trade, there is still the possibility to use the equations for total trade and extra trade and to compute intra trade with accounting identities.

3.2 Real export equations

Export equations have a very standard form. They are modelled with an error correction mechanism. The long run relationships include a demand indicator and a competitiveness term. Competitiveness is determined by the

Table 2. Trade variables (the variables kept in the modelling strategy are indicated by the letter "M")

$$
\text{Exports}
\begin{cases}
\text{Total}
\begin{cases}
\text{Nominal} \\
\text{Real} \\
\text{Deflator}
\end{cases} \\[2em]
\text{Extra euro area}
\begin{cases}
\text{Nominal} \\
\text{Real} \quad M \\
\text{Deflator } M
\end{cases} \\[2em]
\text{Intra euro area}
\begin{cases}
\text{Nominal} \\
\text{Real} \quad M \\
\text{Deflator } M
\end{cases}
\end{cases}
$$

$$
\text{Imports}
\begin{cases}
\text{Total}
\begin{cases}
\text{Nominal}
\begin{cases}
\text{Non Energy} \\
\text{Energy}
\end{cases} \\
\text{Real}
\begin{cases}
\text{Non Energy} \\
\text{Energy}
\end{cases} \\
\text{Deflator}
\begin{cases}
\text{Non Energy} \\
\text{Energy}
\end{cases}
\end{cases} \\[4em]
\text{Extra euro area}
\begin{cases}
\text{Nominal}
\begin{cases}
\text{Non Energy} \\
\text{Energy}
\end{cases} \\
\text{Real}
\begin{cases}
\text{Non Energy } M \\
\text{Energy} \quad M
\end{cases} \\
\text{Deflator}
\begin{cases}
\text{Non Energy } M \\
\text{Energy} \quad M
\end{cases}
\end{cases} \\[4em]
\text{Intra euro area}
\begin{cases}
\text{Nominal} \\
\text{Real} \quad M \\
\text{Deflator } M
\end{cases}
\end{cases}
$$

ratio between competitor prices on the export side and export prices (expressed in logarithms). The long run elasticity between exports and external demand (intra or extra) is constrained to 1. Hence, in the long run, differences between real exports and demand are supposed to be explained by competitiveness. Linear trends and dummy variables are added. They have no impact on the sign or the magnitude of the coefficients.

In the literature, the introduction of linear trends in exports or imports equations of this form is commonly found. These trends can correspond, for example, to structural changes in the world trade, to sectoral and product line specialisation effects or to non-price competitiveness effects (image, quality, etc.). They might also reflect problems of reliability or consistency of data. It must be noted that a trend might correspond to temporary phenomena, which could lead to errors in forecasting exercises. Hence, the appropriateness of these trends has to be taken with care.

The general form of real export equations is the following:

$$B(L)\Delta x = b_0 + \rho \left(x_{-1} - d_{-1} + \phi \left(px_{-1} - px_{-1}^* \right) \right) + B_1(L)\Delta d$$
$$+ B_2(L)\Delta \left(px - px^* \right) + b_1 t$$

where x, d, px and px^* are the log of, respectively, exports, external demand, export prices and competitor prices on the export side, ϕ is the long run elasticity of exports to competitiveness.

Real extra euro area exports

Table 3 displays the results of the estimation for real extra euro area exports. Student T-stats are given under the coefficients, in parenthesis. The error correction term is very significant and has a correct sign. The long run elasticity of exports to competitiveness is 0.47. However, competitiveness appears to be significant in the long run relationship only when a linear trend is added to the equation. Dummy variables were also introduced to eliminate the residuals with the largest magnitude.

Response functions display uneven patterns, especially for demand (see Fig. 1).[3] This is due to the introduction of lagged variables in the short run dynamics, in order to improve the fitting of the equation. This phenomenon will also appear for most of the other equations. Dynamic simulation seems satisfactory (see Fig. 2). This also holds true for the other equations.

Real intra euro area exports

The error correction term is also very significant in the case of intra euro area exports (see Table 4). The long run elasticity to competitiveness is higher than

---

[3] Dates shown in the response functions figures are only indicative, as the patterns of the responses are independent from the date of the shock

Table 3. Equation for real extra euro area exports

$$\Delta \log(JX) = \underset{(7.92)}{5.215} \underset{(-7.90)}{-0.516} \left(\log(JX_{-1}) - \log(DJX_{-1}) + \underset{(4.53)}{0.472} \log(PJX_{-1}/CPJX_{-1}) \right)$$

$$\underset{(-4.59)}{-0.562} \, \Delta \log(DJX_{-4}) + \underset{(2.57)}{0.328} \, \Delta \log(CPJX_{-4}) + \underset{(3.08)}{0.260} \, \Delta \log(JX_{-1})$$

$$\underset{(-5.47)}{-0.001} \, TREND \underset{(-3.32)}{-0.053} \, DUM19941 + \underset{(3.07)}{0.048} \, DUM19944 + \underset{(3.78)}{0.059} \, DUM19993 + \underset{(3.26)}{0.052} \, DUM20001$$

Sample : 1989Q3 2004Q4			
Degrees of freedom : 51			
JX	Real extra euro area exports		
DJX	Extra euro area demand addressed to France		
PJX	Extra euro area export deflator		
CPJX	Competitor prices on the export side for the extra euro area		
TREND	Linear trend		
R-squared	0.702	Mean dependent var	0.012
Adjusted R-squared	0.644	S.D. dependent var	0.025
S.E. of regression	0.015	Akaike info criterion	-5.380
Sum squared resid	0.012	Schwarz criterion	-5.003
Log likelihood	177.784	Durbin-Watson stat	1.758
Breusch-Godfrey Serial Correlation LM Test:			
F-statistic	0.865	Prob. F(4,47)	0.492
Obs*R-squared	4.250	Prob. Chi-Square(4)	0.373
White Heteroskedasticity Test:			
F-statistic	0.660	Prob. F(22,39)	0.849
Obs*R-squared	16.818	Prob. Chi-Square(22)	0.773
Jarque Bera Normality Test:			
Jarque Bera	2.839	Probability	0.242

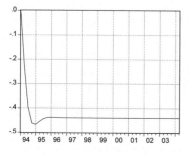 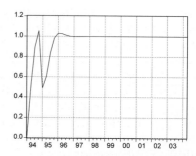

Response to a shock on prices   *Response to a shock on demand*

Fig. 1. Real extra euro area exports: response functions to permanent shocks on prices and demand (elasticity)

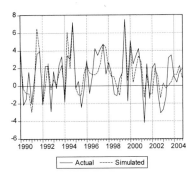

Fig. 2. Real extra euro area exports: dynamic simulation of the equation (quarterly change, in %)

for extra exports (0.90). As in the previous case, a linear trend and dummy variables had to be introduced in the equation.

Long run elasticities to competitiveness turn out to be much higher in this modelling exercise than for aggregate exports of goods: 0.47 for extra exports and 0.90 for intra exports, against 0.18 for total exports. However, they are closer to other estimates found in the literature. For instance, a value of 0.75 was found in MESANGE, the model used at the French Treasury (Allard-Prigent et al., 2001), while Bessone and Heitz (2005) find an elasticity of 0.50[4] (see also Direction de la Prévision, 2001, for an overview of some results found in the literature). Nevertheless, these very different elasticities might induce a problem of consistency if intra/extra equations are used as complements or substitutes to total trade equation.

The elasticities to competitiveness found in this study imply that in the long run French exports to the euro area are more adversely affected by a loss of competitiveness than French exports to the rest of the world. Due to the numerous shortcomings regarding the data, this result is still fragile and has to be confirmed. Nevertheless, it is interesting to note that Stahn (2006, this volume) also find for Germany a higher elasticity to competitiveness for intra euro area exports than for extra euro area exports (0.92 against 0.63).[5] A similar exercise was also implemented on the Spanish economy (Estrada et al., 2004) and led to elasticities of 0.86 for exports to the euro area and 1.08 for exports to the rest of the world. However, competitiveness terms were computed differently, with a mix of competitor prices of exports to the euro area and competitor prices of exports to the rest of the world. This type of specification has not been kept here but reserved for future research.

Negative trends are introduced in both intra and extra euro area export equations, as in the equations of Bessone and Heitz (and also in MESANGE,

---

[4] In the two studies, the long run elasticity of exports to demand is constrained to 1.
[5] However, specifications were different, with no constraint on elasticities to demand, no trend, and longer estimation samples, starting in 1980.

but only until 1988Q4). Negative trends can correspond to a poor sectoral specialisation, to a bad non-price competitiveness, or more obviously, to the emergence of new competitors, especially from Asia.

Finally, when a specification with no trend and no constraint on elasticities to demand is applied, we find elasticities of extra euro area and intra euro area exports to demand of 0.96 and 0.87 respectively, which means that the assumption of unit elasticities can easily be accepted. The fact that, in these cases, elasticities are slightly inferior to 1, is probably linked to the emergence of new competitors, which can be, as mentioned before, taken into account in our equations, at least partly, with negative trends.

Table 4. Equation for real intra euro area exports

$$
\Delta \log(IX) = \underset{(5.46)}{4.162} \underset{(-5.42)}{-0.410} \left(\log(IX_{-1}) - \log(DIX_{-1}) + \underset{(7.26)}{0.898} \log(PIX_{-1}/CPIX_{-1}) \right)
$$

$$
\underset{(-2.88)}{-0.357} \, \Delta \log(PIX/CPIX) + \underset{(6.77)}{0.864} \, \Delta \log(DIX) + \underset{(2.99)}{0.304} \, \Delta \log(DIX_{-1})
$$

$$
\underset{(2.63)}{+0.267} \, \Delta \log(DIX_{-2}) \underset{(-3.41)}{-0.001} \, TREND
$$

$$
\underset{(3.95)}{+0.079} \, DUM19931 + \underset{(2.32)}{0.0354} \, DUM19971 \underset{(-3.25)}{-0.051} \, DUM20014
$$

Sample : 1989Q2 2004Q4			
Degrees of freedom : 52			
IX	Real intra euro area exports		
DIX	Euro area demand addressed to France		
PIX	Intra euro area export deflator		
CPIX	Competitor prices on the export side for the euro area		
TREND Linear trend			
R-squared	0.740	Mean dependent var	0.015
Adjusted R-squared	0.690	S.D. dependent var	0.026
S.E. of regression	0.015	Akaike info criterion	-5.440
Sum squared resid	0.011	Schwarz criterion	-5.066
Log likelihood	182.362	Durbin-Watson stat	2.031
Breusch-Godfrey Serial Correlation LM Test:			
F-statistic	0.449	Prob. F(4,48)	0.773
Obs*R-squared	2.271	Prob. Chi-Square(4)	0.686
White Heteroskedasticity Test:			
F-statistic	1.771	Prob. F(21,41)	0.058
Obs*R-squared	29.963	Prob. Chi-Square(21)	0.093
Jarque Bera Normality Test:			
Jarque Bera	1.095	Probability	0.579

One must notice the strong short run reaction to a shock on demand (see Fig. 3).

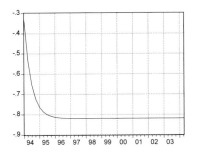 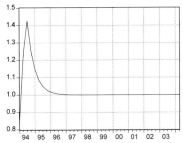

Response to a shock on prices   *Response to a shock on demand*

Fig. 3. Real intra euro area exports: response functions to permanent shocks on prices and demand (elasticity)

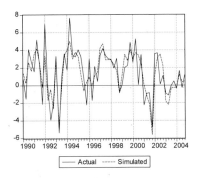

Fig. 4. Real intra euro area exports: dynamic simulation of the equation (quarterly change, in %)

The dynamic simulation does not reveal major instabilities, as in the previous equation (see Fig. 4).

Assessment of the quality of the intra and extra export equations : comparison with the equations for overall exports

The performance of the intra and extra export equations can be compared with the performance of the equations for overall exports.

We compare the addition of rolling forecasts made with the two equations respectively for extra and intra exports on the one hand, with rolling forecasts of the equation for overall exports on the other hand. Equations are first estimated from 1990q1 to 1999q1 and exports are projected h quarter ahead (h= 1 to 4). The estimation sample is then expanded by 1 quarter and a new h quarter ahead projection is made, and so on. Historical data are used for explanatory variables. For each projection and each horizon, intra and extra euro area projected exports are added. Then, for each method (intra/extra trade or aggregated equations) and each horizon, the Root Mean Square Error of the projections are computed, over the period 1999q2-2004q2. In order to have comparable results, we drop from the equations all dummy variables which were included to eliminate the highest residuals.

Table 5. Root Mean Square Errors of rolling forecasts for exports

	Aggregation of intra+extra exports	Overall exports equation	Number of projections
1 quarter ahead	1.67	1.86	21
2 quarters ahead	1.69	1.80	20
3 quarters ahead	1.62	1.69	19
4 quarters ahead	1.65	1.76	18

The aggregation of projections for intra and extra export performs slightly better than the projection for overall exports. Surprisingly, the best performances are obtained for projections 3 and 4 quarter ahead (see Table 5).

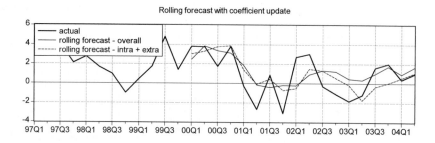

Fig. 5. 4-quarter ahead rolling forecasts for overall and intra+extra exports

3.3 Real import equations

Import equations follow the same scheme as export equations. Hence, imports are also modelled with error correction equations and the long run relationships include a demand indicator and a competitiveness term. The demand indicator is the import content of domestic demand. The long run elasticity between imports and demand is set to 1. Competitiveness is determined by the ratio between French production prices and import prices (expressed in logarithms). Similarly to the case of exports, a linear trend or dummy variables are included when necessary. We tried to introduce, for extra and intra imports, variables corresponding to the difference between the capacity utilisation rate in France and an average of the capacity utilisation rates in France's main competitors. However, these variables did not prove to be significant.

Thus, the real import equations have the following shape:

$$B(L)\Delta m = b_0 + \rho\left(m_{-1} - d_{-1} + \phi\left(pm_{-1} - pq_{-1}\right)\right)$$
$$+ B_1(L)\Delta d + B_2(L)\Delta\left(pm - pq\right) + b_1 t$$

where m, d, pm and pq are the log of, respectively, imports, demand, import prices and production prices, and ϕ the long run elasticity of imports to competitiveness.

Real extra euro area non energy imports

Results for the extra euro area non energy import equation are not very satisfactory. Firstly, competitiveness is significant neither in the long term relationship, nor in the short run dynamics. The elasticity to competitiveness is found to be 1.74, which is much higher than what appears in MASCOTTE for total non-energy imports (0.56), or in MESANGE for total imports of manufactured goods (0.58). Secondly, the long term adjustment of imports on demand is barely significant (with a T-stat of -2.27). For simulations purposes, it is moreover surprisingly low and leads to very slow adjustment processes.

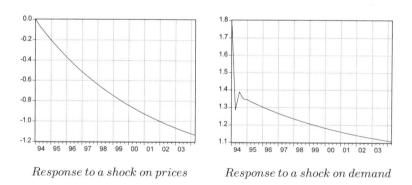

Response to a shock on prices   *Response to a shock on demand*

Fig. 6. Real extra euro area non energy imports: response functions to permanent shocks on prices and demand (elasticity)

Real extra euro area energy imports

The statistical properties of the extra euro area energy import equation are a little bit more satisfactory. There is a significant long term relationship. How-

Table 6. Equation for real extra euro area non energy imports

$$\Delta \log(JMNE) = \underset{(1.89)}{0.008} \underset{(-2.27)}{-0.038} \left(\log(JMNE_{-1}) - \log(DJMNE_{-1}) \underset{(1.90)}{+1.743 \log(PJMNE_{-1}/PPNE_{-1})} \right)$$

$$\underset{(-2.64)}{-0.243} \, \Delta \log(JMNE_{-1}) \underset{(7.53)}{+1.71 \, \Delta \log(DJMNE)}$$

$$\underset{(-2.87)}{-0.046} \, DUM19932 \underset{(-4.01)}{-0.064} \, DUM19961 \underset{(2.96)}{+0.047} \, DUM19971 \underset{(-2.82)}{-0.046} \, DUM20031$$

Sample : 1989Q3 2004Q3			
Degrees of freedom : 52			
JMNE	Real extra euro area non energy imports		
DJMNE	Extra euro area non energy demand indicator		
PJMNE	Extra euro area non energy import deflator		
PPNE	Non energy production prices		
R-squared	0.662	Mean dependent var	0.015
Adjusted R-squared	0.610	S.D. dependent var	0.025
S.E. of regression	0.016	Akaike info criterion	-5.357
Sum squared resid	0.013	Schwarz criterion	-5.045
Log likelihood	172.384	Durbin-Watson stat	2.178
Breusch-Godfrey Serial Correlation LM Test:			
F-statistic		Prob. F(4,48)	0.251
Obs*R-squared		Prob. Chi-Square(4)	0.175
White Heteroskedasticity Test:			
F-statistic		Prob. F(16,44)	0.435
Obs*R-squared		Prob. Chi-Square(16)	0.401
Jarque Bera Normality Test:			
Jarque Bera	0.617	Probability	0.735

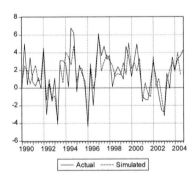

Fig. 7. Real extra euro area non energy imports: dynamic simulation of the equation (quarterly change, in %)

ever, competitiveness is modelled in an unusual way. In fact, the logarithm of the ratio between extra euro area energy import prices and energy production prices did not appear to be significant. Therefore, we chose to replace it by the logarithm of the ratio between extra euro area energy import prices and intra euro area energy import prices. Still, without a linear trend in the equation, competitiveness would not be significant in the long run relationship.

Table 7. Equation for real extra euro area energy imports

$$\Delta \log(JME) = \underset{(1.37)}{+0.042} \underset{(-4.32)}{-0.434} \left(\log(JME_{-1}) - \log(DJME_{-1}) \underset{(2.63)}{+0.119} \log(PJME_{-1}/PIME_{-1}) \right)$$

$$\underset{(3.08)}{+0.259} \Delta \log(JME_{-3}) \underset{(-3.67)}{-0.144} \Delta \log(PJME/PIME)$$

$$\underset{(-1.66)}{-0.001} TREND \underset{(2.39)}{+0.062} DUM19911 \underset{(2.26)}{+0.057} DUM19921 \underset{(3.09)}{+0.074} DUM19964$$

$$\underset{(-2.76)}{-0.067} DUM19984 \underset{(2.45)}{+0.063} DUM20001 \underset{(-2.66)}{-0.067} DUM20013$$

Sample : 1990Q1 2004Q2			
Degrees of freedom : 46			
JME	Real extra euro area energy imports		
DJME	Extra euro area energy demand indicator		
PJME	Extra euro area energy import deflator		
PIME	Intra euro area energy import deflator		
TREND Linear trend			
R-squared	0.712	Mean dependent var	0.005
Adjusted R-squared	0.643	S.D. dependent var	0.040
S.E. of regression	0.024	Akaike info criterion	-4.473
Sum squared resid	0.026	Schwarz criterion	-4.047
Log likelihood	141.729	Durbin-Watson stat	2.105
Breusch-Godfrey Serial Correlation LM Test:			
F-statistic		Prob. F(4,42)	0.534
Obs*R-squared		Prob. Chi-Square(4)	0.394
White Heteroskedasticity Test:			
F-statistic		Prob. F(22,35)	0.880
Obs*R-squared		Prob. Chi-Square(22)	0.802
Jarque Bera Normality Test:			
Jarque Bera	0.827	Probability	0.661

Real intra euro area imports

The long run elasticity of intra euro area imports to competitiveness is quite high (2.15). It is even higher (3.71) without a linear trend in the equation. A

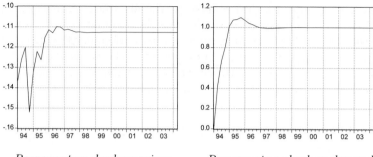

Response to a shock on prices   *Response to a shock on demand*

Fig. 8. Real extra euro area energy imports: response functions to permanent shocks on prices and demand (elasticity)

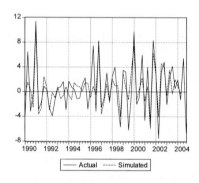

Fig. 9. Real extra euro area energy imports :dynamic simulation of the equation (quarterly change, in %)

similar phenomenon appears for aggregate import equations: the long run elasticity of total non energy imports to competitiveness is estimated at 0.56, but turns out to be 3.29 with no linear trend in the equation.

Still, elasticities of imports to competitiveness are extremely high in this study, for intra euro area imports (2.15) as well as for extra euro area non energy imports (1.74). In comparison, Estrada et al. (2004) found for Spain elasticities of 0.52 for intra euro area imports of goods and 0.48 for extra euro area imports of goods.

If elasticities to demand are not constrainted and no trend is included, we find elasticities of non energy extra euro area and intra euro area imports to competitiveness of 0.83 and 0.68 respectively. However, elasticities of non energy extra euro area and intra euro area imports to demand turn out to be respectively 1.92 and 1.97. This result is pretty standard and corresponds to an increasing openness of the country (see also Direction de la prévision,

2001, for a review of results found in the literature for major industrialized countries). Thus, the constraint of unit elasticity to demand seems hardly viable over the estimation period. However, in equations with constrained unit elasticities to demand, a positive trend, as found in the equation for intra euro area imports, can account at least partly for the increasing openness of the country. In fact, what is surprising here is the absence of a positive trend in the equation for non energy extra euro area imports.

Table 8. Equation for real intra euro area imports

$$\Delta \log(IM) = \underset{(-1.02)}{-0.035} \underset{(-4.17)}{-0.161} \left(\log(IM_{-1}) - \log(DIM_{-1}) + \underset{(3.21)}{2.146} \log(PIM_{-1}/PP_{-1}) \right)$$

$$\underset{(-3.48)}{-0.364} \Delta \log(IM_{-1}) + \underset{(11.17)}{1.881} \Delta \log(DIM) + \underset{(4.24)}{1.255} \Delta \log(DIM_{-1})$$

$$\underset{(-3.39)}{-0.55} \Delta \log(PIM/PP) + \underset{(1.74)}{0.001} TREND \underset{(-3.02)}{-0.038} DUM19933$$

$$\underset{(2.24)}{+0.028} DUM20031 \underset{(-2.14)}{-0.026} DUM20041$$

Sample : 1989Q3 2004Q4			
Degrees of freedom : 51			
IM	Real intra euro area imports		
DIM	Intra euro area demand indicator		
PIM	Intra euro area import deflator		
PP	Production prices		
TREND Linear trend			
R-squared	0.852	Mean dependent var	0.012
Adjusted R-squared	0.822	S.D. dependent var	0.027
S.E. of regression	0.012	Akaike info criterion	-5.919
Sum squared resid	0.007	Schwarz criterion	-5.541
Log likelihood	194.480	Durbin-Watson stat	1.715
Breusch-Godfrey Serial Correlation LM Test:			
F-statistic		Prob. F(4,47)	0.316
Obs*R-squared		Prob. Chi-Square(4)	0.213
White Heteroskedasticity Test:			
F-statistic		Prob. F(21,40)	0.809
Obs*R-squared		Prob. Chi-Square(21)	0.732
Jarque Bera Normality Test:			
Jarque Bera	0.949	Probability	0.622

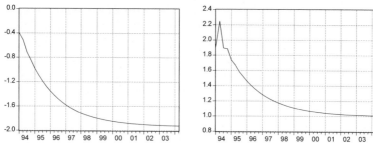

Response to a shock on prices   *Response to a shock on demand*

Fig. 10. Real intra euro area imports: response functions to permanent shocks on prices and demand (elasticity)

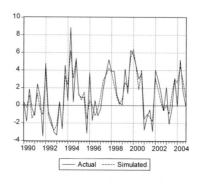

Fig. 11. Real intra euro area imports: dynamic simulation of the equation (quarterly change, in %)

Assessment of the quality of intra and extra import equations : comparison with the equations for overall imports

We implement the same type of exercise than for exports. The performance of the intra and extra import equations are compared with the performance of the equations for overall imports featured in Mascotte.

The addition of the forecasts made with the three equations for intra, extra non-energy and extra energy imports are compared with the sum of the forecasts of the equations for overall non energy and overall energy imports. As in the previous case, we compute rolling forecasts on the period 1999q2-2004q2, and compare the Root Mean Square Errors. The estimations also start in 1990q1. All dummy variables which were included to eliminate the highest residuals are dropped from the equations.

None of the two method appears to be obviously the best : in all cases, the Root Mean Square Errors turn out to be very close (see Table 9).

Table 9. Root Mean Square Errors of rolling forecasts for imports

	Aggregation of intra+extra imports	Overall imports equation	Number of projections
1 quarter ahead	0.81	0.86	21
2 quarters ahead	0.87	0.86	20
3 quarters ahead	0.86	0.87	19
4 quarters ahead	0.85	0.89	18

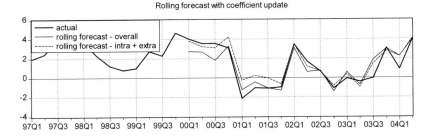

Fig. 12. 4-quarter ahead rolling forecasts for overall and intra+extra imports

4 Assessement of recent trade developments using dynamic contributions

By computing dynamic contributions of each explanatory variable to the estimated variable, it is possible to understand how the recent evolutions of the estimated variable are explained by an equation.

This exercise is implemented for the five real trade equations since 1997. In each case, contributions are divided into categories: demand, price competitiveness and the rest. The contribution of price competitiveness corresponds to the sum of the contributions of domestic and competitor prices. The contributions of residuals, trends and dummy variables are grouped in an item called "rest", which corresponds to what can not be given a clear economic explanation.

4.1 Extra euro area exports

For extra euro area exports, there is a slowdown in the contribution of demand after 2001, corresponding to the world economic slowdown, and a gradual acceleration in 2003 and 2004, along with the worldwide economic recovery (see Fig. 13).

We observe a fall in the contribution of price competitiveness after a peak in 2000. This is certainly due for a large part to the appreciation of the euro, but this might also be due to cost developments.

Finally, the contribution of the "rest" is balanced, and rather strong for some years (1997, 2001, 2003), which challenges the quality of the equation.

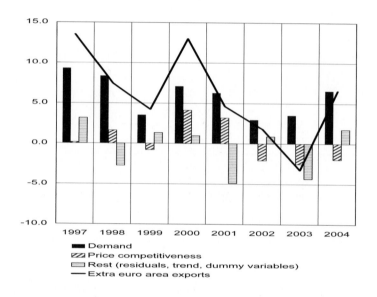

Fig. 13. Extra euro area exports growth and contributions (in %)

4.2 Intra euro area exports

The recent evolutions of intra euro area exports are well explained by demand and price competitiveness over the last three years (see Fig. 14). From 1998 to 2001, intra euro area exports grew less than what can be explained by demand and price competitiveness (negative contribution of the "rest"). The contribution of demand was very strong from 1997 to 2000, due to a robust economic growth in the euro area. After a strong slowdown in 2001 and 2002, there is a significant upturn in 2003 and 2004.

However, this rebound in demand is offset by a negative contribution of price competitiveness. In fact, as in the previous case, there is a peak in the contribution from price competitiveness in 2000 and a decrease afterwards, which can also be partly explained by exchange rates developments (for example, if the exchange rate of the euro against the dollar increases, French exports to the rest of the euro area are getting relatively less competitive than American exports to the rest euro area). The strong negative contribution of price competitiveness in 2003 and 2004, like the strong long run elasticity to competitiveness found for intra euro area exports, is an interesting feature, though it should be investigated further.

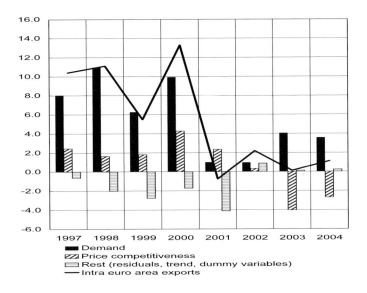

Fig. 14. Intra euro area exports growth and contributions (in %)

4.3 Extra euro area imports

Recent developments for **non energy extra euro area imports** can be mainly explained by the contribution of French demand, which was rather strong from until 2000, but remained close to 0 point in 2001, 2002 and 2003 (see Fig. 15).[6]

The contribution of price competitiveness is rather even and always slightly positive (loss of price competitiveness for France). The smooth pattern of the series contrasts with the strong fluctuations in the contribution

---

[6] Due to a problem of data availability, we were unable to compute extra euro area imports for 2004.

of the competitiveness terms for the export equations. In particular, it seems that extra euro area imports are less affected than exports by exchange rate fluctuations, although the increase in the contribution of price competitiveness is patent in 2002 and 2003, and probably reflects the effect of the appreciation of the euro. The fact that the contribution of competitiveness was also positive in the previous years, even when the euro depreciated, could imply that France was facing problems of price competitiveness not linked to exchange rates, but to costs, for example. It could also be that the variable of price competitiveness captures other effects, like the rise of the emerging countries in the recent years. It would then explain why no positive trend was found in the extra euro area imports equation, as it was the case for the intra euro area import equation.

The strong fall in non energy extra euro imports in 2003 cannot be explained by demand or price competitiveness. The strong negative contribution of the other factors ("rest") in 2003 contrasts with positive contributions for the other years, which seem more consistent with the idea of an increasing demand for products from non euro-area partners, like the emerging countries.

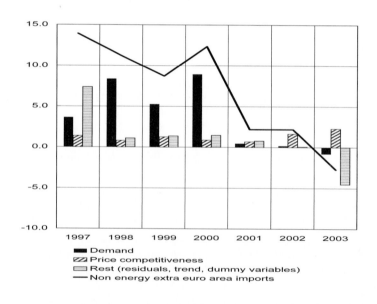

Fig. 15. Non energy extra euro area imports growth and contributions (in %)

It is difficult to infer anything from the contributions to **energy extra euro area import** growth (see Fig. 16). Given the size of the contribution of the "rest", this exercise only underlines the poor quality of the equation.

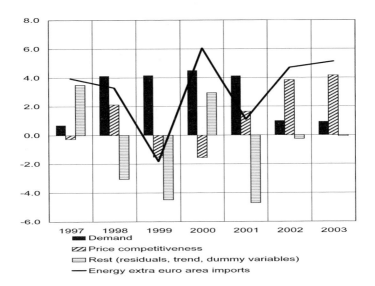

Fig. 16. Energy extra euro area imports growth and contributions (in %)

4.4 Intra euro area imports

For intra euro area imports, the contribution of demand shows the same pattern as in the previous case (see Fig. 17). With a strong contribution until 2000 and a marked slowdown afterwards. In 2004, the economic recovery in France implies a strong rebound in imports.

Furthermore, according to the equation, French imports are fostered by losses of price competitiveness since 1999. Echange rate developments have no direct incidence in this case, as price competitiveness corresponds to a comparison between French production prices and import prices of products from other euro area countries. Hence, in this case, the loss of price competitiveness recorded by France since 1999 could mainly be related to production cost differences between France and its partners.

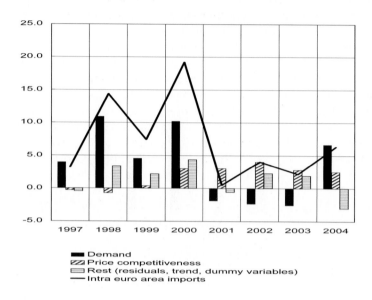

Fig. 17. Intra euro area imports growth and contributions (in %)

5 Conclusion

The objectives of this modelling exercise were to build an intra/extra euro area trade data set and to use it to estimate intra/extra trade equations that can complete aggregated trade equations. Results of the estimations are partly satisfactory. Equations have been computed and intra/extra trade can actually be forecast. Residuals appear to be normal, homoscedastic and independent over time for all equations. On comparable samples, rolling forecasts implemented for intra+extra trade equations prove to be at least as good as for overall trade equations. Furthermore, dynamic contributions showed that trade equations generally give credible explanations of recent trade evolutions.

Some results are interesting and need further investigation. Thus, we find that the long run elasticity of exports to competitiveness is superior for exports to the euro area than for exports to the rest of the world. We also find that the contributions of price competitiveness to euro area import growth are positive since 1999, for non energy extra euro area imports as well as for intra euro area imports, and that they display rather even patterns in spite of strong exchange rate movements, which could imply that evolutions in costs rather than in exchange rates contributed to increase imports over the recent years. Finally, we found that extra euro area non energy import prices and export prices are mainly guided by national prices.

However, there are several shortcomings. Projections can not be guaranteed to be robust. Trends and dummy variables have often been added in order to improve the fitting of the equations or the significance of the variables, although they do not alter the signs or the magnitude of the coefficients. Competitiveness effects are not always clear and well captured. Finally, response functions often display uneven patterns in the short run. These problems might be due to an unsuitable data set. The lack of consistency between data and the lack of actual import and export price indexes have probably had a considerable influence on the results. Furthermore, data samples begin around 1990, which is much shorter than the samples used for overall trade equations. Finally the choice of 1996 as the base year for demand and competitor prices and the absence of emerging countries (especially from Asia) in competitor prices calculations represent serious drawbacks.

Yet this exercise is a first step towards a separate treatment of two parts of trade which are differently affected by currency risks. This type of analysis will certainly become unavoidable, but would probably be greatly improved if the breakdown of intra and extra trade were available in national accounts. It would also certainly be ameliorated with updated and more complete demand and competitor price indicators.

References

Allard-Prigent C, Audenis C, Berger K, Carnot N, Duchêne S, Pesin F (2001) Modèle macroéconomique de prévision Mésange de la Direction de la Prévision. Document de travail de la Direction de la Prévision, Ministère de l'Economie et des Finances

Baghli M, Brunhes-Lesage V, de Bandt O, Fraisse H, Villetelle J-P (2004) Modèle d'Analyse et de préviSion de la COnjoncture TrimesTriellE. Note d'Etude et de Recherche 106, Banque de France

Bessone A-J, Heitz B (2005) Exportations : Allemagne 1 - France 0. In: Note de Conjoncture de juin 2005, INSEE

Dauphin J-F (1999) L'impact de la crise des pays émergents sur le commerce mondial. Bulletin de la Banque de France 72, Banque de France

Deruennes A (2004) Comment expliquer les pertes récentes de parts de marché de la France l'exportation de produits manufacturés? Diagnostics Prévisions et Analyses Economiques 32, Ministère de l'Economie et des Finances

Deruennes A (2005) Quelle lecture faire de l'évolution récente des exportations franaises ? Diagnostics Prévisions et Analyses Economiques 70, Ministère de l'Economie et des Finances

Direction de la prévision (2001) La modélisation macroéconomique des flux de commerce extérieur des principaux pays industriels, In: Note de Conjoncture Internationale de juin 2001, Direction de la Prévision, Ministère de l'Economie et des Finances

Estrada A, Fernandez J-L, Moral E, Regil AV (2004) A quarterly macroeconometric model of the Spanish economy. Documentos de Trabajo 0413, Banco de Espana

Eurostat (2002) Statistiques sur les échanges de biens, Guide de l'utilisateur. Méthodes et Nomenclatures, thème 6, commerce extérieur, Eurostat

Gaulier G, Lahrèche-Révil A, Méjean I (2005) Dynamique des exportations: une comparaison France-Allemagne, La lettre du CEPII 249, CEPII

Girard E (2004) Comment expliquer l'évolution récente du compte courant de la France ? Diagnostics Prévisions et Analyses Economiques 56, Ministère de l'Economie et des Finances

Villetelle J-P (2002), Calcul du contenu en importations des postes de la demande finale. note SEMEP m02-045z, Banque de France

A Export deflator equations

After having modelled trade volumes, we now turn to prices. Error correction equations are also used for deflators.

Long run homogeneity is imposed : the long run elasticities of export prices to domestic prices and to competitor prices sum to 1. This means that an increase by 1% in both domestic and competitor prices implies in turn an increase by 1% in export prices. Hence, the long run relationship can be written as follow:

$$\ln Px = \alpha \ln Pq + (1 - \alpha) \ln Px^*$$

with Px the export prices, Pq the production prices, Px^* the competitor prices on the export side and $0 \leq \alpha \leq 1$. In other words, in the long run, export prices are supposed to be a weighted average between domestic prices and competitor prices on the export side. The long run relationship can also be rewritten as follow:

$$\ln (Px/Px^*) = \alpha \ln (Pq/Px^*)$$

Hence, equations will have the following form:

$$B(L)\Delta px = b_0 + \rho \left((px_{-1} - px^*_{-1}) - \alpha \left(pq_{-1} - px^*_{-1} \right) \right) + B_1(L)\Delta pq + B_2(L)\Delta px^* + b_1 t$$

where px, pq and px^* are the log of, respectively, export prices, production prices and competitor prices on the export side.

Table 10. Equation for extra euro area export deflator

$$\Delta \log(PJX) = \begin{matrix} -0.014 \\ (-2.68) \end{matrix} \begin{matrix} -0.189 \\ (-3.64) \end{matrix} \left(\begin{matrix} \log(PJX_{-1}/CPJX_{-1}) \\ \end{matrix} \begin{matrix} -0.771 \\ (-5.29) \end{matrix} \log(PP_{-1}/CPJX_{-1}) \right)$$

$$\begin{matrix} +0.327 \\ (4.2) \end{matrix} \Delta \log(CPJX) \begin{matrix} +0.176 \\ (2.2) \end{matrix} \Delta \log(CPJX_{-1}) \begin{matrix} +0.231 \\ (2.35) \end{matrix} \Delta \log(PJX_{-4})$$

$$\begin{matrix} -0.024 \\ (-2.08) \end{matrix} DUM19934 \begin{matrix} +0.024 \\ (2.25) \end{matrix} DUM19962$$

$$\begin{matrix} +0.027 \\ (2.35) \end{matrix} DUM19972 \begin{matrix} +0.023 \\ (2.11) \end{matrix} DUM19992$$

Sample : 1990Q2 2004Q4			
Degrees of freedom : 49			
PJX Extra euro area export deflator			
CPJX Extra euro area competitor prices on the export side			
PP Production prices			
R-squared	0.562	Mean dependent var	0.000
Adjusted R-squared	0.482	S.D. dependent var	0.015
S.E. of regression	0.011	Akaike info criterion	-6.097
Sum squared resid	0.006	Schwarz criterion	-5.745
Log likelihood	189.852	Durbin-Watson stat	2.230
Breusch-Godfrey Serial Correlation LM Test:			
F-statistic		Prob. F(4,45)	0.841
Obs*R-squared		Prob. Chi-Square(4)	0.774
White Heteroskedasticity Test:			
F-statistic		Prob. F(18,40)	0.320
Obs*R-squared		Prob. Chi-Square(18)	0.306
Jarque Bera Normality Test:			
Jarque Bera	1.331	Probability	0.514

A.1 Extra euro area export deflator

The long run elasticity of export prices to national producer prices is 0.77. Incidentally, exactly the same value was found for total non energy good export prices. This result implies that French exporters have a low "pricing to market" and make margin adjustments when international supply conditions change, with exchange rates movements, for instance. In comparison, Gaulier *et alii* (2005) found that French exporters absorb 34% of exchange rate movements in their margins.

Intra euro area export deflator

When the general form of the equation is applied to the intra euro area export deflator, we find inconsistent results. Therefore, we decide to calibrate the long run elasticity of export prices to domestic prices to 0.77. As mentioned above, the same elasticity was found for extra euro area export prices

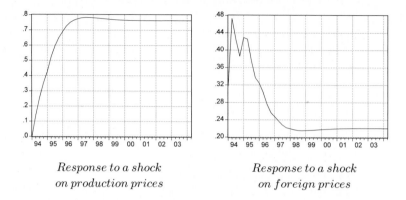

Response to a shock
on production prices   Response to a shock
on foreign prices

Fig. 18. Extra euro area export deflator: response functions to permanent shocks on prices (elasticity)

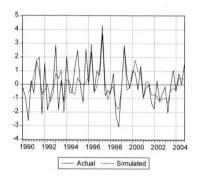

Fig. 19. Extra euro area export deflator: dynamic simulation of the equation (quarterly change, in %)

and total export prices. The error correction term is still very significant. The adjusted R^2 of the regression is equal to 0.56, which is not very high, but quite close to that of the unconstrained equation (0.60).

B Import deflator equations

The modelling strategy is exactly the same as for export prices. Hence, the general form of the equations is as follows:

$$B(L)\Delta pm = b_0 + \rho\left((pm_{-1} - pm^*_{-1}) - \alpha\left(pq_{-1} - pm^*_{-1}\right)\right)$$
$$+ B_1(L)\Delta pq + B_2(L)\Delta pm^* + b_1 t$$

where pm, pq and pm^* are the log of, respectively, import prices, production prices and competitor prices on the import side.

Table 11. Equation for intra euro area export deflator

$$\Delta \log(PIX) = \underset{(1.01)}{0.002} \ \underset{(-5.03)}{-0.083} \left(\log(PIX_{-1}/CPIX_{-1}) - 0.77 * \log(PP_{-1}/CPIX_{-1}) \right)$$

$$+ \underset{(5.09)}{1.117} \ \Delta \log(PP) \ \underset{(-3.53)}{-0.336} \ \Delta \log(PIX_{-1}) \ \underset{(-2.81)}{-0.257} \ \Delta \log(PIX_{-2})$$

$$+ \underset{(2.36)}{0.022} \ DUM19902 \ \underset{(-2.79)}{-0.026} \ DUM19931$$

$$\underset{(-3.33)}{-0.03} \ DUM19951 \ \underset{(-2.85)}{-0.026} \ DUM19992$$

Sample : 1989Q4 2004Q4	
Degrees of freedom : 52	

PIX Intra euro area export deflator	
CPIX Intra euro area competitor prices on the export side	
PP Production prices	

R-squared	0.620	Mean dependent var	-0.003
Adjusted R-squared	0.562	S.D. dependent var	0.013
S.E. of regression	0.009	Akaike info criterion	-6.496
Sum squared resid	0.004	Schwarz criterion	-6.185
Log likelihood	207.142	Durbin-Watson stat	2.423

Breusch-Godfrey Serial Correlation LM Test:			
F-statistic		Prob. F(4,48)	0.178
Obs*R-squared		Prob. Chi-Square(4)	0.118

White Heteroskedasticity Test:			
F-statistic		Prob. F(16,44)	0.531
Obs*R-squared		Prob. Chi-Square(16)	0.484

Jarque Bera Normality Test:			
Jarque Bera		1.214 Probability	0.545

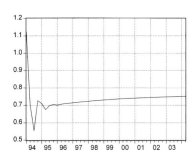

Response to a shock
on production prices

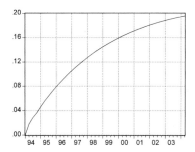

Response to a shock
on foreign prices

Fig. 20. Intra euro area export deflator: response functions to permanent shocks on prices (elasticity)

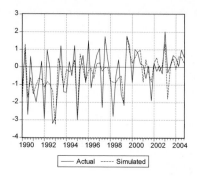

Fig. 21. Intra euro area export deflator: dynamic simulation of the equation (quarterly change, in %)

Extra euro area non energy import deflator

The error correction term is significant. The long run elasticity of import prices to national producer prices is 0.68, which implies that import prices mostly stick to national prices when competitor prices change. In contrast, the elasticity for total non-energy imports was estimated at only 0.43.

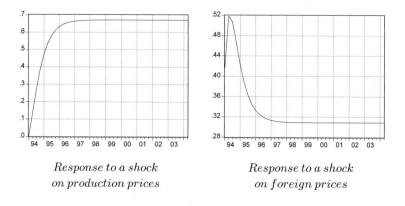

*Response to a shock
on production prices*

*Response to a shock
on foreign prices*

Fig. 22. Extra euro area non energy import deflator: response functions to permanent shocks on prices (elasticity)

B.1 Extra euro area energy import deflator

Energy import prices are modelled differently from other prices. The equation features an error correction on oil prices in euros. Unsurprisingly, the

Table 12. Equation for extra euro area non energy import deflator

$$\Delta \log(PJMNE) = \underset{(2.53)}{0.035} \underset{(-3.8)}{-0.193} \left(\log(PJMNE_{-1}/CPJM_{-1}) \underset{(-5.87)}{-0.681} \log(PPNE_{-1}/CPJM_{-1}) \right)$$

$$\underset{(3.83)}{+0.29} \Delta \log(PJMNE_{-1}) \underset{(9.59)}{+0.427} \Delta \log(CPJM)$$

$$\underset{(-2.92)}{-0.001} \ TREND \underset{(2.39)}{+0.024} \ DUM19901$$

$$\underset{(-3.54)}{-0.032} \ DUM19914 \underset{(-3.11)}{-0.028} \ DUM19932$$

Sample : 1989Q3 2004Q2

Degrees of freedom : 51

PJMNE	Extra euro area non energy import deflator
CPJM	Extra euro area competitor prices on the import side
PPNE	Non energy production prices
TREND	Linear trend

R-squared	0.754 Mean dependent var	-0.005
Adjusted R-squared	0.716 S.D. dependent var	0.017
S.E. of regression	0.009 Akaike info criterion	-6.487
Sum squared resid	0.004 Schwarz criterion	-6.173
Log likelihood	203.618 Durbin-Watson stat	2.106
Breusch-Godfrey Serial Correlation LM Test:		
F-statistic	Prob. F(4,47)	0.160
Obs*R-squared	Prob. Chi-Square(4)	0.104
White Heteroskedasticity Test:		
F-statistic	Prob. F(13,46)	0.916
Obs*R-squared	Prob. Chi-Square(13)	0.882
Jarque Bera Normality Test:		
Jarque Bera	0.317 Probability	0.853

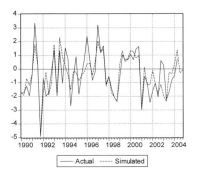

Fig. 23. Extra euro area non energy import deflator: dynamic simulation of the equation (quarterly change, in %)

long run relationship is very significant, and the R^2 is quite high (0.94). However, this does not imply good performance when used in forecasting, as the explanatory variable (oil price) is largely unpredictable. The dummy variable takes into account of a methodological break in the data.

Table 13. Equation for extra euro area energy import deflator

$$\Delta \log(PJME) = \underset{(-12.47)}{-1.817} \underset{(-11.74)}{-0.902} \left(\log(PJME_{-1}) \underset{(-51.42)}{-0.779} \log(BRENTEURO_{-1}) \right)$$
$$+ \underset{(22.73)}{0.543} \Delta \log(BRENTEURO) \underset{(-3.54)}{-0.084} \Delta \log(BRENTEURO_{-2}) \underset{(-6.85)}{-0.072} DUM021FIN$$

Sample : 1989Q2 2004Q2		
Degrees of freedom : 55		
PJME	Extra euro area energy import deflator	
BRENTEURO	Oil price in euros	
DUM021FIN	Dummy variable, equal to 0 until 2001Q4 and 1 after	
R-squared	0.940 Mean dependent var	0.007
Adjusted R-squared	0.934 S.D. dependent var	0.096
S.E. of regression	0.025 Akaike info criterion	-4.484
Sum squared resid	0.033 Schwarz criterion	-4.276
Log likelihood	142.747 Durbin-Watson stat	2.006
Breusch-Godfrey Serial Correlation LM Test:		
F-statistic	Prob. F(4,51)	0.193
Obs*R-squared	Prob. Chi-Square(4)	0.151
White Heteroskedasticity Test:		
F-statistic	Prob. F(11,49)	0.909
Obs*R-squared	Prob. Chi-Square(11)	0.881
Jarque Bera Normality Test:		
Jarque Bera	0.425 Probability	0.809

B.2 Intra euro area import deflator

No satisfying equation was found for this variable. In particular, no long term relationship was uncovered. Once again, this is probably due to the inadequacy of the data set. As a consequence, this variable will have to be modelled indirectly, with the extra euro area import price equations presented above and the total import price equations, by using accounting identities.

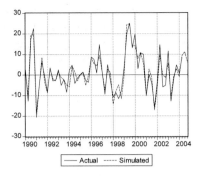

Fig. 24. Extra euro area energy import deflator: dynamic simulation of the equation (quarterly change, in %)

Has the Impact of Key Determinants of German Exports Changed?*

Kerstin Stahn

Deutsche Bundesbank, Economics Department, Wilhelm-Epstein-Strasse 14, D-60431 Frankfurt am Main, Germany kerstin.stahn@bundesbank.de

Summary. The question as to whether changes in the external environment may have caused the importance of key determinants of German exports to shift since the 1990s is addressed by estimating Germany's exports to EMU partner countries (intra exports) and to countries outside the euro area (extra exports). Analytically, this is done first by estimating error correction models across different samples. Second, it is tested whether the long-run export behaviour of intra and extra exports has changed since the 1990s. As an initial and tentative result, the impact of price competitiveness on both intra and extra exports appears to have decreased. Finally, simulations are conducted to reconstruct the adjustment process of both intra and extra exports following demand and price shocks.

Keywords: intra and extra euro-area exports, export demand, price competitiveness, error correction model.
JEL classification: C22, F41.

1 Introduction

The latest appreciation of the euro seems to have had so far relatively little adverse impact on German exports – which has come as a surprise to many observers. This raises the question as to whether the influence of price competitiveness on exports may have changed over time. It can be assumed that changes in the external environment, particularly those that have come about since the 1990s through increasing globalisation, the elimination of the "Iron Curtain" in Eastern Europe, EU enlargement or the establishment of European monetary union, have also had an impact on German exports. To answer this question, Germany's exports are estimated over different periods.

* The paper represents the author's personal opinion and does not necessarily reflect the views of the Deutsche Bundesbank. The author would like to thank Jörg Breitung, Olivier de Bandt, Ulrich Grosch, Heinz Herrmann, Hubert Strauß and Karl-Heinz Tödter for valuable suggestions and comments. All remaining errors are the author's alone.

A further estimation is carried out to assess whether export behaviour has changed since the 1990s. Moreover, Germany's exports are analysed broken down by region. As the changes in the external environment involve both trade with EMU partners and the exchange of goods with non-euro-area countries, the regional analysis focuses on Germany's exports to all euro-area partner countries combined (intra exports) and to "third countries", the aggregate of the countries outside the euro area (extra exports). Finally, simulations are conducted in order to reconstruct the adjustment process of both intra and extra exports following demand and price shocks.

2 Overview of the literature

In the literature, numerous empirical analyses are available for Germany's exports: for total exports, for an aggregate of selected countries, on a bilateral trade basis, or in a sectoral breakdown. In all cases, the key determinants are economic activity in export markets and an indicator of price competitiveness. An increase in economic activity or an improvement in price competitiveness is expected to lead to an increase in exports. Price competitiveness can be improved, *ceteris paribus*, by a decrease in export prices or domestic prices, an increase in foreign prices or a nominal depreciation of the domestic currency. Since the sign of the estimated coefficient of the relative price elasticity depends on how the competitive indicator is defined, the focus here is on absolute price elasticities. Disaggregated analyses are preferable because goods with relatively low price elasticities can dominate the estimation of the aggregated exports, thereby distorting it downwards.[1] Consequently, it would also be possible for exports of largely less price-elastic goods into given regions to put downward pressure on the price elasticity of total exports.

In the following table-form overview of the literature, estimation results for overall exports are presented first. Then empirical findings for exports by region and by sector will be given. The overview will focus on the impact of price competitiveness on exports, since my estimation results show that the most important change in the influence of key determinants of German exports since the 1990s can be found for this variable.

To summarise, the authors generally attempt to use as long a sample as possible. This gives a perceptible weight to pre-German unification economic developments. Moreover, a long sample has the advantage that potential data problems owing to a small number of data points can be avoided.[2] Therefore, in line with most studies, the regressions in this paper are car-

---

[1] See Goldstein and Khan (1985), p 1070.

[2] However, scant mention is made of the possibility of parameter instability at the time of German unification in the literature. Hooper et al (1998) are a notable exception.

ried out first for a *long* sample, including the pre-German unification period. However, changes in the external environment, eg the elimination of the "Iron Curtain" in Eastern Europe and the enlargement or establishment of unified economic or currency areas, mostly occurred in the 1990s. Even in recent studies, a change in the export behaviour for this period is not yet examined. Therefore, in this paper the regressions are subsequently run for a *short* sample which exclusively covers the post-1990 period. Thirdly, a further estimation is carried out to assess whether *changes* in the export behaviour occurred in the 1990s.

Table 1: Overview of estimation results for German exports

Authors	Estimation period	Estimation model	Export region or sector	Indicator of relative prices	Relative price elasticity
Overall exports:					
Döpke & Fischer (1994, pp 59–60)	1970–1992	VECM Trend, capacity utilisation		REER[3] (consumer prices)	./.[4]
Lapp et al (1995, pp 6–7 and p 13 ff)		ECM Export demand		REER (export unit values)	0.9
Clostermann (1996, pp 28–29)	1975–1995	ECM Export demand		Export prices/ foreign deflator of total sales	0.9
				Export prices/ foreign producer prices	0.8
Deutsche Bundesbank (1997, p 58)	1975–1995	ECM Export demand		Export prices/ foreign deflator of total sales	0.9
Deutsche Bundesbank (1998a, p 57)	1975–1997	ECM Export demand		REER (deflators of total sales against	
				18 countries	0.7
				EU competitors	0.4
				non-EU competitors	0.3
Deutsche Bundesbank (1998b, p 49)	1975–1996	ECM Export demand		REER (consumer prices,	0.7
				deflators of total sales,	0.7
				producer prices,	1.0
				unit labour costs,	0.9
				terms of trade)	0.7

Continued on next page

---

[3] REER stands for "real effective exchange rate".

[4] Indicates that a cointegrating relationship between exports and the relative price variable could not be found.

Table 1 – continued from previous page

Authors	Estimation period	Estimation model	Export region or sector	Indicator of relative prices	Relative price elasticity
Strauß (2003, p 186 ff)	1974–1999	ECM Export demand, real global exports/real global GDP		REER (consumer prices)	1.0
		VECM Export demand, real global exports/real global GDP		REER (consumer prices)	1.1
Strauß (2004, pp 118–119)	1975–2000	VECM Export demand		Foreign producer prices (domestic currency units)	0.8
				Export prices	0.3
		Export supply		Foreign producer prices (domestic currency units)	0.4
				Domestic producer prices	1.0
Meurers (2004, p 547)	1975–1999	VECM Export demand		Foreign export prices/foreign consumer prices	0.7
		Export supply		REER	0.8
Camarero & Tamarit (2004, p 362)	1981–1998	Panel 12 OECD countries		Export prices/ trade-weighted export prices	0.8
Hooper et al (1998, pp 47–48)	1970–1996/97	VECM Export demand		Export prices/ foreign deflator of total sales	0.2–0.3
				REER (unit labour costs)	0.9–1.1
Exports by region:					
Hooper et al (1998, p 106)	1970–1996/97	VECM Export demand	Non-EU		0.4
			USA		1.2
			France		2.1
Stephan (2002, p 14)	1985–2001	ECM Export demand, trend	Euro area	REER against euro area (consumer prices)	1.0
Kappler & Radowski (2003, p 189 ff)	1974–2001	ECM Export demand	France	REER	0.7
			Italy		./.
			UK		1.4
			USA		0.7
Exports by sector:					
Milton (1999, p 237 and 242)	1982–1997	Distributed lags, annual percentage changes, cycl. gap	8 sectors machinery clothing	Sectoral REER (sectoral producer prices)	range: 0.0 −1.1
	1988–1997		chemicals clothing		0.5 −2.4

Most studies analyse German overall or bilateral exports. However, some of the most important changes in the external environment since the 1990s have exclusively affected the euro-area countries – eg the establishment of EMU - whereas other changes – eg the elimination of the "Iron Curtain" in Eastern Europe or the catching-up process of Asian emerging market economies – impacted solely on non-euro area countries. As a consequence, German exports to both EMU member countries and countries outside the euro area, as well as the corresponding key determinants, may have developed differently. Therefore, in this paper German exports to euro-area countries and to countries outside the euro-area are estimated. However, empirical analyses focusing on export aggregates broken down by region are still rare. For instance, Hooper et al (1998) examine exports to non-EU countries taken together, while Stephan (2002) focuses on exports to euro-area partner countries.

In their methodology, many authors exclusively estimate export demand equations.[5] They often use single-equation error correction models which capture both long-run and short-run influences of the determinants. This approach is also applied here.

Economic activity in importing countries is usually measured by the volume of world trade, real GDP or manufacturing output, as well as, in some isolated cases,[6] the demand for investment. By contrast, this paper uses export market trends within and outside of the euro area, calculated on the basis of countries' imports of goods and services. This measure has the advantage that the estimated elasticity indicates whether German exports have grown to the same extent as export markets.

In contrast to the foreign economic activity variable, various indicators of price competitiveness are chosen in the literature (terms of trade, indicators based on consumer prices, deflators of total sales, producer prices, unit labour costs, export prices, wholesale prices or export unit values). The estimation results for the impact of price competitiveness on overall exports appear to be, for the most part, influenced less by the methodology applied and more by how the indicator of price competitiveness is constructed. Most studies find that price competitiveness has a noticeable influence on exports, with a coefficient having an absolute value of just under 1.0. By contrast, estimates broken down by region or sector often reveal coefficients for the

---

[5] See Lapp et al (1995), Clostermann (1996), Deutsche Bundesbank (1997), (1998a), (1998b), Strauß (2003), Kappler and Radowski (2003). This corresponds with the assumption that German exporters are "price takers" on the global market. See Sawyer and Sprinkle (1999), pp 10–11. Other papers supplement the factors influencing export demand with export supply determinants. See Döpke and Fischer (1994) or Milton (1999). Some papers also simultaneously estimate export demand and export supply functions. See Strauß (2004) and Meurers (2004).

[6] See Stephan (2002).

relative price variable that are noticeably smaller or larger than one or even insignificant.[7]

An important question is which indicator of price competitiveness appears to be the most appropriate. Deutsche Bundesbank (1998b) compares the suitability of various indicators of price competitiveness (based on consumer prices, deflators of total sales, producer prices, unit labour costs and terms of trade). The absolute values of the estimation coefficients range from 0.7 to 1.0. A comparison of pairs of indicators in the estimation made it possible to demonstrate that the external value based on the deflators of total sales was superior to the competing real external value concepts.[8] For this reason, the indicators of price competitiveness vis-à-vis the euro-area partner countries and vis-à-vis non-euro-area countries, calculated on the basis of deflators of total sales, are used as relative price variables in this paper.

The following analysis begins by explaining the underlying data and the regression models. Then estimation results for intra and extra exports are presented, first for a *long* and a *short* sample and then for *changes* in the export behaviour. Finally simulations are carried out to examine the adjustment processes undergone by intra and extra exports after a positive demand shock and a negative price shock.

---

[7] The estimation period chosen or the methodology applied might lead to fairly sizeable differences among the sectoral estimation results. See Milton (1999), p 237 and p 242. See also Krakowski et al (1993), p 64. They choose a double logarithmic approach, and detect a large exchange rate influence for machinery (absolute value of 1.0) for a somewhat shorter sample period (1980–1992). Döhrn (1993), p 112, finds a similarly high elasticity of the export volume with respect to the real sectoral exchange rate for this sector (0.8 in absolute terms for the 1978–1992 period). However, it must be noted for sectoral estimates that, especially in the case of capital goods, the time span between the receipt of the order and delivery can be considerable. Long estimation periods could therefore indicate changes in the lag structure, which would mean that the exchange rate elasticity of exports might, under some circumstances, be underestimated. For instance, estimating incoming foreign orders received by machinery manufacturers instead of their exports shows that they, too, react sharply to exchange rate changes: the exchange rate influence for the 1978–1992 period is 1.3 in absolute terms and, for a 1985–1994 sample, as high as 1.6. See Döhrn (1993), p 110, and Döhrn and Milton (1998), p 80.

[8] It was tested bilaterally whether the respective competing indicators are able to contribute additional information to the external value indicator specified. To determine this, another indicator variable was added to the export equation. As a result, the real external value based on the deflator of total sales was the only indicator that contributed additional information to explaining German export trends to each of the alternative indicators. At the same time, none of the other indicators contained any information which was not already included in this variable. See Deutsche Bundesbank (1998b), pp 50–51.

3 Data and estimation approaches

Exports are regressed on their key determinants: real demand in export markets and an indicator of price competitiveness. Estimations are performed for exports to euro-area partner countries (intra exports) and to non-euro-area countries (extra exports). Moreover, individual estimates of exports to the Unites States are cited for purposes of comparison. Seasonally adjusted quarterly data are used.

The time series for market growth within and outside of the euro area were calculated on the basis of OECD data. The seasonally adjusted volume of individual countries' imports of goods and services, denominated in US dollars and in 2000 prices, was used. They were weighted by the shares of Germany's exports to each respective region in total exports for 2000. The US import volume was used for the demand trend for German products in the United States.

The indicators of the German economy's price competitiveness against euro-area partners and non-euro-area countries were calculated on the basis of deflators of total sales. Throughout the sample, the 11 other euro-area countries are included as euro-area partners (Germany is not included).[9] The non-euro-area aggregate is composed of Canada, Denmark, Japan, Norway, Sweden, Switzerland, the United Kingdom and the United States.[10] The 1995–1997 period was used for weighting the countries, which includes both exports and imports. The weighting includes not only bilateral trade relations between the German economy and its respective trading partners but also competition in non-euro-area markets.

The regressions are performed for each region across two time periods: a *long* estimation period (from 1980) and a *short* sample (from 1993). The *short* sample includes neither immediate unification effects[11] nor changes in the method of recording EU foreign trade data.[12] Changes in the external environment, eg the elimination of the "Iron Curtain" in Eastern Europe or

---

[9] They are: Austria, Belgium/Luxembourg, Finland, France, Greece, Ireland, Italy, the Netherlands, Portugal and Spain.

[10] These 8 non-euro-area countries and the 11 euro-area partners form the group of participating countries in calculating the indicator of the German economy's price competitiveness, which is published in the Bundesbank's Monthly Reports.

[11] German unification seems to have a distinct impact on regressions for the period following 1991. The intra-export estimation results resemble those of the *long* estimation period, whereas the extra-export regressions are comparable with the results of the *short* sample. In keeping with this result, Hooper et al (1998), p 13 and pp 47 ff, detected considerable parameter instability at the time of unification while estimating overall exports.

[12] Prior to 1 January 1993, goods exchanged with EC countries for values in excess of DM 1,000 were recorded by customs on the day they crossed the border. Since that date, enterprises have been required to report these goods transactions to the Federal Statistical Office whenever their value exceeds DM 200,000; the transactions are assigned to the invoicing month. See Deutsche Bundesbank (1993), p 64.

the establishment of EMU, occurred mostly in the 1990s and therefore have a greater impact on the history of the *short* sample than on the *long* estimation period.

As the trace test rejects the hypothesis that no cointegrating relationship exists for the systems of regionally disaggregated variables, single-equation error correction models can be used to estimate German exports.[13]

Two estimation approaches for the error correction model are presented. In the first approach, the long-run relationship and the short-run adjustment process are estimated simultaneously:

$$\Delta x_t^r = \alpha \cdot (x_{t-1}^r - \beta_0 - \beta_1 y_{t-1}^r - \beta_2 w_{t-1}^r - \beta_3 d_{93-1}) \tag{1}$$

$$+ \gamma \Delta d_{93} + \sum_{i=1}^{4} \lambda_i \Delta x_{t-i}^r + \sum_{j=0}^{4} \mu_j \Delta y_{t-j}^r + \sum_{k=0}^{4} \nu_k \Delta w_{t-k}^r + u_t.$$

x^r denotes Germany's real exports to region r. Here, nominal goods exports (from the balance of payments statistics) are deflated with the respective regional export prices.[14] β_0 is a constant, y^r the real demand in region r addressed to Germany, w^r the price competitiveness of the German economy in relation to its competitors in region r, d_{93} a dummy variable that is zero prior to 1993 Q1 and one otherwise, Δ the first difference of the logarithmic system variables or the shift dummy and u the residual.[15]

The regional estimation approaches across the *long* estimation period differ in the fact that, in the cointegrating relationship of intra exports, a shift dummy for 1993 Q1 is included, as well as the corresponding impulse dummy as an additional short-run determinant. This way, changes in the method of recording EU trade at that point in time are captured.[16]

---

[13] Tests for cointegration are presented in the appendix.

[14] The prices of exports to euro-area partners include, from 2000, the current 11 euro-area countries and, before 2000, the EU/EC countries in their respective borders. Accordingly, the prices of exports to non-euro-area countries contain non-euro-area countries from 2000 and, prior to 2000, the non-EU/non-EC countries in their respective borders. Since prices for exports to the USA are not available, these exports are deflated with export prices for non-euro-area countries as a proxy.

[15] The estimation approach is restricted such that intra and extra exports are estimated completely independent of one another. Neither substitution effects caused by the relative price competitiveness between competitors within and outside of the euro area nor those caused by differences in export market trends between these two areas – enterprises in the euro area might seek to make up for flagging demand in this area through exports to third countries and vice versa – are included. These aspects may be worth analysing in future research.

[16] East German exports, which are added to West German exports from 1990 Q3 onwards, had been so small that a structural break at that point in time could not be detected.

In the second approach, a two-step procedure is applied to the error correction model. In the first step, the long-run relationship is estimated following the asymptotically efficient approach of Saikkonen.[17] The inclusion of the leads and lags of the regressors' first differences overcomes the problem of endogeneity, which – according to the Johansen test – evidently plays a role for the *short* sample estimations of extra exports. The number of the leads and lags is restricted to two. Using the Newey-West covariance estimator, the regressions are adjusted for autocorrelation and heteroscedasticity. In the second step, the short-run adjustment process is estimated, the long-run relationship being given. The two-step estimation has two advantages over the one-step error correction model. First, it overcomes the possibility of endogeneity in the cointegrating relationship. Second, the estimation of the short-run determinants does not have any impact on the elasticities of the long-run relationship.

The estimation approach for the two-step procedure is:

$$\Delta x_t^r = \alpha \cdot ect_{t-1}^r \tag{2}$$

$$+\gamma \Delta d_{93} + \sum_{i=1}^{4} \lambda_i \Delta x_{t-i}^r + \sum_{j=0}^{4} \mu_j \Delta y_{t-j}^r + \sum_{k=0}^{4} \nu_k \Delta w_{t-k}^r + u_t,$$

with the long-run elasticities in the error correction term $ect_t^r = x_t^r - \beta_0 - \beta_1 y_t^r - \beta_2 w_t^r - \beta_3 d_{93}$ stemming from the following equation:

$$x_t^r = \beta_0 + \beta_1 y_t^r + \beta_2 w_t^r + \beta_3 d_{93} \tag{3}$$

$$+ \sum_{m=-2}^{2} \left(\eta_{1m} \Delta y_{t+m}^r + \eta_{2m} \Delta w_{t+m}^r + \eta_{3m} \Delta d_{93+m} \right) + v_t,$$

where v denotes the residual.

To assess whether changes in the external environment in the 1990s have had an impact on the supply behaviour of German exporters or the demand of foreign buyers for German products, a further estimation is carried out using the Saikkonen approach. The case that the influence of the constant

---

[17] See Saikkonen (1991). In contrast to other studies – see eg Döpke and Fischer (1994), Strauß (2003), Hooper et al (1998) – the long-run relationship between exports and its determinants is not estimated by applying a VECM, since this model provides implausible results for the *short* sample period because of the reduced number of data points. However, Strauß (2003), p 186 ff, finds that the long-run influence of the relative price variable is only slightly higher if a VECM is applied than if an ECM is applied.

and each regressor in the sub-samples 1980–1992 Q4 and 1993 Q1–2004 may have changed will be examined. The estimation is therefore conducted across the entire 1980–2004 period, and a dummy variable (which is zero prior to 1993 Q1 and one from that point in time on) is included for each regressor and the constant. Expressed in this way, the elasticities of the dummy variables illustrate how the influence of the respective regressor has changed in the sub-sample 1993 Q1–2004 compared with the earlier sub-sample 1980–1992 Q4.

The estimation approach is:

$$x_t^r = \beta_0' + \beta_1' y_t^r + \beta_2' w_t^r + \sum_{m=-2}^{2} \left(\eta_{1m}' \Delta y_{t+m}^r + \eta_{2m}' \Delta w_{t+m}^r \right) \tag{4}$$

$$+ \left[\beta_0^* + \beta_1^* y_t^r + \beta_2^* w_t^r + \sum_{m=-2}^{2} \left(\eta_{1m}^* \Delta y_{t+m}^r + \eta_{2m}^* \Delta w_{t+m}^r \right) \right] \cdot d_{93} + v_t.$$

It holds:

$$\beta_0' + \beta_0^* = \beta_0, \ \beta_1' + \beta_1^* = \beta_1, \ \beta_2' + \beta_2^* = \beta_2$$

with β_0, β_1, β_2 from equation (3) for the *short* sample.

4 Estimation results

First, estimation results for both the *long* and the *short* sample are presented. Then the estimation results of a *change* in the elasticities of the key determinants of exports are analysed.

4.1 Estimation of intra and extra exports for a *long* and a *short* sample

The following Tables 2 and 3 list the estimation results of the error correction models. The numbers in square brackets denote the t-values and those in round brackets the marginal significance level. The asterisks * on the estimation coefficients indicate a significance level of 1% (***) /5% (**) /10% (*). Moreover, the adjusted R^2 and the standard error (SE) are given. The Breusch-Godfrey-LM test for autocorrelation up to the fourth order (LM(4)), the normality test using the Jarque-Bera criterion (JB) and the White test for heteroscedasticity (without cross terms) are conducted. Regressions labelled with a hash ♯ were estimated using White's heteroscedasticity-consistent procedure.

In addition, two coefficient tests are carried out. A Wald test is run to examine whether the long-run impact of foreign demand is significantly different from one. A second test for omitted variables (OV) is carried out to

Table 2. Estimation results for German exports to the euro-area

Region	Euro-area			
Sample	1980 Q3–2004 Q3		1993 Q1–2004 Q3	
Equation	(1)	(2), (3)	(1)♯	(2)♯, (3)
β_1	0.88 *** [22.79]	**0.91** *** [35.07]	0.98 *** [14.67]	**0.91** *** [12.37]
β_2	0.92*** [3.23]	**0.58*** [3.06]**	0.32 [1.02]	**0.50** [1.17]
β_3	−0.09** [−2.69]	**−0.13*** [−5.36]**	−	−
β_0	4.11*** [2.92]	**2.45** [2.59]**	0.78 [0.47]	**1.95** [0.85]
α	−0.37*** [−3.54]	**−0.38*** [−3.80]**	−0.44*** [−3.54]	**−0.48*** [−3.64]**
Δd_{93}	−0.06** [−2.40]	**−0.07*** [−3.20]**	−	−
Δx^r_{t-1}	−0.30*** [−3.09]	**−0.28*** [−3.02]**	−	−
Δx^r_{t-4}	−	−	−	−
Δy^r_t	0.93*** [5.38]	**0.93*** [6.01]**	0.85*** [4.00]	**0.79*** [4.57]**
Δy^r_{t-1}	0.46** [2.57]	**0.42** [2.62]**	−	−
Δw^r_t	0.48* [1.99]	**0.49* [2.07]**	−	**0.53* [1.86]**
Δw^r_{t-1}	−	−	−	−
Δw^r_{t-3}	−	−	−	−
Adj. R^2	0.48	**0.49**	0.54	**0.56**
SE	0.02	**0.02**	0.02	**0.02**
LM(4)	(0.87)	**(0.84)**	(0.70)	**(0.48)**
JB	(0.24)	**(0.14)**	(0.35)	**(0.54)**
White	(0.15)	**(0.25)**	(0.05)	**(0.06)**
Wald(β_1)	(0.00)	**(0.00)**	(0.86)	**(0.22)**
OV	(0.99)	**(0.97)**	(0.28)	**(0.28)**

find out whether the short-term regressors up to the fourth lag, which are individually insignificant and were therefore eliminated from the error correction model, have a joint significant impact on the change in exports.

The residuals are normally distributed at a 1% significance level according to the Jarque-Bera criterion, homoscedastic according to the White test and not autocorrelated up to the fourth order according to the Breusch-Godfrey LM test. The signs of the estimation coefficients are plausible. The joint influence of the eliminated short-run determinants up to the fourth lag is insignificant in all regressions.

Table 3. Estimation results for German exports to the non-euro-area

Region	Non-euro-area			
Sample	1980 Q2–2004 Q3		1993 Q1–2004 Q3	
Equation	(1)	(2), (3)	(1)	(2), (3)
β_1	0.81 *** [22.22]	**0.79** *** [32.62]	0.99 *** [17.72]	**1.05** *** [30.54]
β_2	0.63*** [3.72]	**0.71*** [8.61]	0.30* [1.91]	**0.01** [0.07]
β_3	—	—	—	—
β_0	3.28*** [4.06]	**3.72*** [9.83]	0.88 [0.93]	**−0.77** [−1.09]
α	−0.23*** [−3.72]	**−0.21*** [−3.54]	−0.37*** [−3.72]	**−0.34*** [−3.56]
Δd_{93}	—	—	—	—
Δx^r_{t-1}	—	**−0.18** [−2.09]	−0.24* [−2.12]	**−0.23** [−2.02]
Δx^r_{t-4}	0.18* [1.95]	**0.18** [2.20]	—	—
Δy^r_t	0.48** [2.40]	**0.55*** [3.49]	0.53* [1.96]	**0.51** [2.29]
Δy^r_{t-1}	—	—	—	—
Δw^r_t	—	—	—	—
Δw^r_{t-1}	0.24* [2.02]	**0.27** [2.33]	—	—
Δw^r_{t-3}	—	—	—	**0.23* [1.89]**
Adj. R^2	0.26	**0.30**	0.36	**0.37**
SE	0.03	**0.03**	0.02	**0.02**
LM(4)	(0.12)	**(0.84)**	(0.49)	**(0.65)**
JB	(0.10)	**(0.03)**	(0.57)	**(0.94)**
White	(0.21)	**(0.14)**	(0.29)	**(0.54)**
Wald(β_1)	(0.00)	**(0.00)**	(0.90)	**(0.12)**
OV	(0.33)	**(0.22)**	(0.90)	**(0.88)**

For both estimation periods, first the effects of export market trends on intra exports and extra exports are interpreted, and then the impact of price competitiveness is analysed (see Table 2 and 3 for the results).

Impact of export market trends

The results from equations (1) and (3) for estimating the long-run impact of *export market trends* on regionally disaggregated exports are nearly identical for both the *long* and the *short* sample. For the *long* estimation period, the elasticity value is 0.9 for intra exports and 0.8 for extra exports.[18]

---

[18] These results are in line with the estimations of overall exports with the world trade volume as variable of foreign economic activity, as conducted by Closter-

By contrast, the regressions across the *short* sample show an elasticity of around one. Moreover, the hypothesis that the elasticity is one cannot be rejected at a significance level of 1%. A look at the period from 1993 on shows that this elasticity means Germany was able to hold its position on the market. This is also borne out by calculations of Germany's share of real world exports based on IMF data.[19]

Furthermore, the short-run impact of current export market growth is significant for both the *long* and the *short* analysis period. This makes the development in German export markets the dominant regressor over the short term, too.[20]

Impact of price competitiveness

By contrast, the long-run influence of *price competitiveness* on regionally disaggregated exports is dependent on the estimation period.

For the *longer* period, the regressions indicate that price competitiveness has a substantial long-run influence: The elasticities assume values of 0.9/0.6 for intra exports and of 0.6/0.7 for extra exports and are highly significant.[21] The estimation results for equations (1) and (3) are again very similar. Apparently, for this estimation period the long-run impact of price competitiveness is nearly as strong as the influence of export market growth.[22]

For the *short* sample, the competitiveness effect is distinctly lower (the elasticities are 0.3/0.5 for intra exports and 0.3/0.0 for extra exports). Moreover, the long-run impact of price competitiveness on both intra and extra

---

mann (1996), p 28, Deutsche Bundesbank (1997), p 58, (1998a), p 57 and (1998b), p 49 (see the case of the real external value on the basis of the deflators of total sales).

[19] See Deutsche Bundesbank (2003), p 21, and Sachverständigenrat (2004), p 355, para 460.

[20] However, this cyclical factor has a somewhat stronger impact on intra exports than on extra exports.

[21] The elasticity of 1.0 in absolute value for intra exports obtained by Stephan (2003), p 14, who uses the real effective exchange rate on the basis of consumer prices as relative price variable, is only slightly higher. Hooper et al (1998), who estimate exports to the non-EU countries taken together – which are comparable with extra euro-area estimations – also obtain slightly sharper elasticities when applying the real effective exchange on the basis of unit labour costs (0.9–1.1 in absolute terms). In contrast, the elasticities of the ratio of German export prices to the foreign deflator of total sales as relative price variable are considerably smaller (0.2–0.3 in absolute terms).

[22] It is striking, however, that the regressions of intra exports for the *long* analysis period (from 1980) are not robust: shortening the estimation period at the current end clearly reduces the long-run influence of price competitiveness. This is further evidence that, in the 1990s, euro-area export market growth was the dominant influence on German intra exports. By contrast, no such effect for extra exports can be detected.

Kerstin Stahn

exports is statistically insignificant at a significance level of 5%.[23] Both estimation approaches show that the long-run impact of export market trends is now perceptibly stronger than the impact of price competitiveness.[24] This is consistent with observations from a continuous analysis of foreign trade, namely that, in the past few years, the influence of trading partners' economic activity on German exports has far outweighed the effects of price competitiveness. Here, too, the intra-export estimation results of equations (1) and (3) are quite similar. For extra exports, the differences between the two estimation approaches regarding the value and significance level of elasticities might be due to the problem of endogeneity in the cointegrating relationship, which is overcome by equation (3), but not taken account of by equation (1).

The estimation results for the short-run effect of competitiveness are in line with those for its long-run influence. For the *long* sample, changes in price competitiveness have a lesser impact on exports than short-run cyclical effects. Moreover, in most regressions the impact is only weakly significant. For the *short* estimation period, hardly any short-run effect of relative prices can be detected empirically.[25]

4.2 Estimation of *changes* in the behaviour of intra and extra exports

In Table 4 below, the elasticities of export market trends and price competitiveness for the sub-sample 1980–1992 and the changes in the elasticities in the sub-sample 1993–2004 compared with the previous sub-sample 1980–1992 are presented. In addition, Wald tests are carried out on the elasticity of foreign demand for both the first sub-sample (Wald(β_1')) and the second sub-sample (Wald($\beta_1' + \beta_1^*$)) to assess whether the long-run impact of foreign demand is significantly different from one.

The impact of export market trends on both intra and extra exports is first examined, then the effects of price competitiveness.

---

[23] Intra-export regressions were also performed with an indicator of price competitiveness which is composed of the ratio between German export prices and euro-area partner countries' producer prices – converted into domestic currency at the nominal effective exchange rate. The estimations also result in the long-run influence of the competitive position on the *short* sample being much lower than that on the *long* analysis period and being, in addition, insignificant.

[24] For the *short* sample, regressions are also performed using export values deflated with regionally disaggregated unit values. They, too, show that, in the long run, the influence of competitiveness is much smaller than the impact of export market developments. For the *long* estimation period, not enough data points are available for this specification.

[25] Menu costs or hedging against exchange rate fluctuations could be the reason why the short-run effect of the competitive position is, on the whole, weak or insignificant.

Table 4. Estimation results for changes in the key determinants of German exports

Region	Euro-area	Non-euro-area	United States
Sample	1980 Q4–2004 Q1	1980 Q4–2004 Q1	1980 Q1–2004 Q1
Equation	(4)	(4)	(4)
y_t^r	0.88 *** [50.70]	0.57 *** [13.36]	0.75*** [9.21]
$d_{93}y_t^r$	0.03 [0.41]	0.49*** [8.88]	0.23** [2.40]
w_t^r	0.81*** [3.94]	0.57*** [8.23]	0.90*** [7.55]
$d_{93}w_t^r$	−0.32 [−0.68]	−0.57*** [−4.00]	−0.19 [−1.31]
Constant	3.62*** [3.85]	4.02 *** [14.73]	2.86*** [5.32]
d_{93}	−1.67 [−0.68]	−4.79*** [−6.31]	−2.01 [−2.44]
Wald(β_1')	(0.00)	(0.00)	(0.00)
Wald$(\beta_1' + \beta_1^*)$	(0.20)	(0.11)	(0.71)

Changes in the impact of export market trends

For the sub-sample 1980–1992, the long-run impact of export market trends on intra exports takes a value of 0.9, whereas for extra exports this elasticity is somewhat lower (0.6). However, both elasticities are significantly less than one. The fact that Germany's exports grew somewhat more slowly during this period than the regional export markets may be interpreted as a loss of market share.[26]

The test for *changes* in the long-run export behaviour indicates that, for the sub-sample 1993–2004, the long-run impact of foreign demand on extra exports rose statistically significantly by 0.5. By contrast, this elasticity remained unchanged for intra exports.

The sharp increase in the long-run impact of foreign demand on extra exports could be explained by changes in the external environment since the 1990s, which affected non-euro-area countries in particular, eg the elimination of the "Iron Curtain" in Eastern europe or the emerging markets' efforts to catch up to the developed world. For instance, German exports, which contain a large share of capital goods, might have benefited in particular from the rising import demand resulting from central and eastern European transition countries' and Asian emerging market economies' efforts to catch up. Furthermore, German enterprises might have gained a better foothold in countries outside the euro area through large infusions of foreign direct investment (FDI).

---

[26] This result is consistent with the pattern of Germany's share of real world exports. See Deutsche Bundesbank (2003), p 21, and Sachverständigenrat (2004), p 355, para 460.

Changes in the impact of price competitiveness

For the sub-sample 1980–1992 the long-run impact of price competitiveness on intra exports assumes a value of 0.8, whereas for extra exports this elasticity is a little lower (0.6). Obviously, across this estimation period for both intra and extra exports the long-run impact of price competitiveness is roughly as strong as the impact of export market trends. This result is similar to that for the *long* estimation period. This statement also holds for the estimation of exports to the United States, where for the first sub-sample the elasticities of foreign demand and competitiveness amount to 0.8 and 0.9.[27]

The test for *changes* in the long-run export behaviour from 1993 on indicates a statistically significant decrease in the long-run impact of price competitiveness on extra exports. Also for intra exports, the influence of competitiveness declined (by 0.3), although this fall was slightly smaller and statistically insignificant. For exports to the United States, too, a decrease in the impact of competitiveness – of 0.2, and thus likewise statistically insignificant – was found.

Thus, for all three regions under review, price competitiveness appears to have been exerting a weaker influence on exports since 1993. There are various possible supply-side and demand-side reasons for this. Supply of or demand for export goods could have shifted in favour of less price-elastic products, for instance. The fact that the share of capital goods in German exports is large may contribute to a dampening of price competition effects. Furthermore, on account of the elimination of fluctuations in the nominal effective exchange rate through the establishment of EMU and the convergence of inflation rates in EMU member states, changes in price competitiveness vis-à-vis suppliers from the (future) euro area, especially since the mid-1990s, have remained quite slight. A further reason might be that the measured changes in price competitiveness are not reflected in suppliers' prices since the pricing behaviour of German exporters might have changed. It is possible that enterprises cushion a larger share of the (relative) fluctuations in prices and exchange rates by adjusting their margins. Increasing intra-firm trade may have led to a reduction in exchange rate pass-through. The advance of globalisation, the establishment of monetary union and EU enlargements may have contributed to pricing-to-market becoming increasingly important for German exporters.[28]

---

[27] See the appendix for the estimation results of exports to the USA across the *long* and the *short* sample.

[28] Estimations based on the aggregated export price index have shown that, in the past few years, the long-run effects of pricing-to-market have been continuously on the rise, with exchange rate pass-through declining at the same time. These findings are in line with results from estimating the export pricing behaviour of German enterprises for eleven categories of goods. The regressions provide evidence that, in the 1990s, exchange rate pass-through effects declined significantly for five product groups, which in 2004 accounted for 25% of German overall export

However, the decline in the relative price sensitivity of extra exports, which is the strongest within the three regions and, moreover, highly significant, might also be due, at least in part, to the construction of the indicator of relative price competitiveness vis-à-vis third-country suppliers, which does not include all non-euro-area countries. For instance, Germany's exports to the United States react sharply to changes in bilateral price competitiveness for both the first sub-sample (the elasticity takes the value of 0.9) and the second sub-sample (elasticity of 0.7). Moreover, since, notably, some Asian emerging markets peg their currencies *de facto* to the US dollar, the US dollar's weight within this indicator, which is fixed at the 1995–1997 period, is probably too small.[29]

To summarise, the test for long-run *changes* in the impact of key determinants of German exports reveals a decrease in the influence of price competitiveness for all three regions under review. Although this decline is statistically significant only for extra exports, these results – taking into account the small size of the sub-samples and the possibility of parameter instability at the time of German unification – might be taken as initial and tentative evidence that, since the 1990s, a decline in the relative price sensitivity not merely of extra exports, but also of both intra exports and exports to the United States has occurred.

5 Simulations

In this section, simulations are performed to follow the adjustment process for exports after shocks. First a permanent 10% increase in demand on the relevant regional export market is analysed. The second shock is a permanent 10% deterioration in the German economy's price competitiveness against competitors in the region under review caused by shifts in the relative price or exchange rate framework. The simulations are based on the error correction model (1).

Table 5 gives the percentage change in exports relative to the *baseline*, ie the development in the absence of the shock, for both the *long* and the *short* sample period. Shocks occur at the beginning of the period t = 0. Figures 1 and 2 of sections 5.1 and 5.2 give a graphic representation of the corresponding adjustment processes.

---

volume. At the same time, pricing-to-market behaviour increased significantly for four categories of goods, which made up 47% of German export volume. See Stahn (2006).

[29] Furthermore, the high aggregation of "third countries" conceals diverging trends in individual countries outside the euro area. This fact might have contributed at least partly to the minor impact of competitiveness on extra exports across the *short* sample if these divergences have increased since the 1990s.

Table 5. Reaction of exports to permanent shocks

Reaction in % at/after	$t = 0$	Q1	Y1	Y2	Y3	∞
10% export market growth						
Intra exports: long sample	9.3	11.0	9.4	9.0	8.8	8.8
short sample	8.5	9.1	9.7	9.8	9.8	9.8
Extra exports: long sample	4.7	5.4	7.7	8.3	8.2	8.1
short sample	5.2	5.7	8.4	9.5	9.8	9.9
10% deterioration in competitiveness						
Intra exports: long sample	−4.9	−5.1	−7.8	−8.8	−9.1	−9.2
short sample	0.0	−1.5	−3.0	−3.3	−3.3	−3.2
Extra exports: long sample	0.0	−3.9	−5.3	−6.5	−6.6	−6.3
short sample	0.0	−1.2	−2.4	−2.9	−3.1	−3.0

5.1 Reaction to increased export market growth

Figure 1 shows that, given a positive demand shock (in $t = 0$), both intra exports and extra exports – irrespective of the estimation period chosen – increase immediately. For the *long* sample, intra exports rise somewhat more sharply than extra exports over the long run. In the short run, by contrast, intra exports rise distinctly more sharply than extra exports. Moreover, in the second quarter after the shock, intra exports considerably exceed their long-term rate of change as they react to export market growth with an additional one-period time-lag. On the other hand, the adjustment process for extra exports is largely monotonic. For both intra exports and extra exports, the adjustment to their demand shock-induced long-term change has largely run its course after three years.

For the *short*-sample simulations, intra exports and extra exports react nearly equally strongly to the export market shock over the long run and somewhat more strongly than for the *long* estimation period. Moreover, both responses adjust monotonically. A large percentage of the reaction of intra exports already transpires immediately after the shock occurs. All in all, intra exports already complete the adjustment process to their long-term change after 1 1/2 years and hence earlier than extra exports (roughly three years).

5.2 Reaction to deteriorating price competitiveness

In response to a deterioration in price competitiveness, intra exports decrease more strongly in the long run for the *long* estimation period than extra exports. Moreover, intra exports are already adversely impacted immediately after the shock occurs (in $t = 0$). By contrast, extra exports react to a deterioration in the competitive position only after a one-period time-lag. In addition, the adjustment process for both intra and extra exports is monotonic.

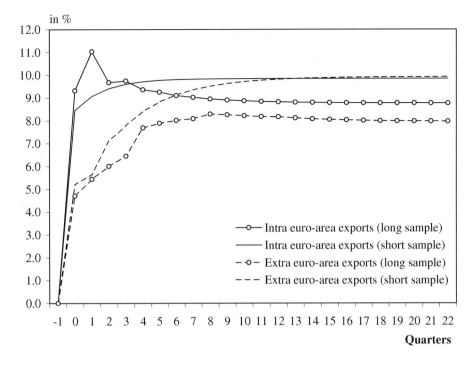

Fig. 1. Reaction of exports to a permanent 10% increase in foreign demand

Intra exports' adjustment to their price shock-induced long-term change is largely completed after three years, and half a year later for extra exports.

In the simulations across the *short* analysis period, intra exports and extra exports decrease nearly equally, but less strongly, than for the *long* sample (see also section 4.1). For both intra exports and extra exports alike, the adjustment process is monotonic. As already determined for the export market shock, after as early as roughly 1 1/2 years the intra exports have nearly completely adjusted to the new long-run change whereas extra exports need around one year longer.

6 Conclusion

Estimations of German exports to euro-area partners (intra exports) and to non-euro-area countries (extra exports) for a *short* sample (from 1993) indicate that both intra and extra euro area exports have grown in line with Germany's export markets. In contrast, the impact of price competitiveness is considerably smaller. This result is consistent with observations from a continuous analysis of foreign trade, namely that, in the past few years, the

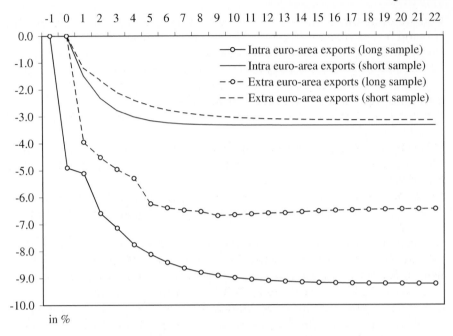

Fig. 2. Reaction of exports to a permanent 10% deterioration in price competitiveness

influence of trading partners' economic activity on German exports has far outweighed the effects of price competitiveness.

Further estimation of *changes* in the impact of German exports' key determinants in the 1993–2004 sample compared to the previous period of 1980–1992 provides evidence that the long-run relative price sensitivity of German exports has declined for both intra and extra exports. Export supply or export demand shifts in favour of less price-elastic products, the possibility that the pricing behaviour of German exporters may have changed – eg through increasing intra-firm trade or the advancing globalisation and the establishment or enlargement of unified currency or economic areas – as well as the quite slight changes in price competitiveness vis-à-vis suppliers from the (future) euro-area – since the mid-1990s – all may have contributed to this. However, the estimation results for extra exports may also be due at least in part to the fact that the corresponding indicator of price competitiveness does not capture all non-euro area countries.

References

Camarero, M and C Tamarit (2004). Estimating the export and import demand for manufactured goods: The role of FDI. *Review of World Economics (Weltwirtschaftliches Archiv)* 140/3, 347–375.

Clostermann, J (1996). The impact of the exchange rate on Germany's balance of trade. Discussion Paper No 7/96, Deutsche Bundesbank.

Deutsche Bundesbank (1993). *Monthly Report* June.

Deutsche Bundesbank (1997). Exchange rate and foreign trade. *Monthly Report* January, 41–59.

Deutsche Bundesbank (1998a). Effects of exchange rates on German foreign trade. Prospects under the conditions of European monetary union. *Monthly Report* January, 49–58.

Deutsche Bundesbank (1998b). The indicator quality of different definitions of the real external value of the Deutsche Mark. *Monthly Report* November, 39–52.

Deutsche Bundesbank (2003). Germany's competitive position and foreign trade within the euro area. *Monthly Report* October, 15–27.

Döhrn, R (1993). Zur Wechselkursempfindlichkeit bedeutender Exportsektoren der deutschen Wirtschaft. RWI-Mitteilungen 44/2, 103–116.

Döhrn, R and A–R Milton (1998). Marktpreise, reale Wechselkurse und internationale Wettbewerbsfähigkeit. Untersuchungen des RWI 24, RWI, Essen.

Döpke, J and M Fischer (1994). Was bestimmt die deutschen Exporte? *Die Weltwirtschaft*, H. 1, 54–66.

Goldstein, M and M S Khan (1985). Income and price effects in foreign trade. In R W Jones and P B Kenen (eds). *Handbook of International Economics* 2, Amsterdam, 1041–1105.

Hooper, P, K Johnson and J Marquez (1998). Trade elasticities for G-7 countries. Board of Governors of the Federal Reserve System, International Finance Discussion Papers, No 609, April.

Judge, G G, R Carter Hill, W E Griffiths, H Lütkepohl and T–C Lee (1988). Introduction to the theory and practice of econometrics. 2nd edition. New York et al: Wiley.

Kappler, M and D Radowski (2003). Der Außenhandelskanal. In M Schröder and P Westerheide (eds): Finanzmärkte, Unternehmen und Vertrauen. Neue Wege der internationalen Konjunkturübertragung. ZEW Wirtschaftsanalysen 64,181–205.

Krakowski, M, D Keller, D Lau, A Lux, C Wacker–Theodorakopoulos and E Wohlers (1993). Strukturelle und konjunkturelle Einflüsse auf die Entwicklung der deutschen Ausfuhr. HWWA Report No 133, HWWA, Hamburg.

Lapp, S, J Scheide and R Solveen (1995). Determinants of exports in the G7-Countries. Kiel Working Paper No 707, Kiel Institute for World Economics, September.

Meurers, M (2004). Estimating supply and demand functions in international trade: A multivariate cointegration analysis for Germany. *Journal of Economics and Statistics (Jahrbücher für Nationalökonomie und Statistik)* 224/5, 530–556.

Milton, A–R (1999). Erhöhung der Wechselkursreagibilität deutscher Ausfuhren? – Eine sektorale Analyse. RWI-Mitteilungen 50/4, Oct/Dec, 223–246.

Sachverständigenrat zur Begutachtung der gesamtwirtschaftlichen Entwicklung (Council of Economic Advisers) 2004. Jahresgutachten 2004/2005.

Saikkonen, P (1991). Asymptotically efficient estimation in cointegrated regressions. *Econometric Theory* 7, 1–21.

Sawyer, W C and R L Sprinkle (1999). The demand for exports and imports in the world economy. Brookfield/USA.

Stahn, K (2006). Has the export pricing behaviour of German enterprises changed? Empirical evidence from German sectoral export prices. Discussion Paper, Deutsche Bundesbank, forthcoming.

Stephan, S (2002). German exports to the euro area. German Institute for Economic Research, Discussion Papers No 286, June.

Strauß, H (2003). Globalisierung und die Prognose des deutschen Außenhandels. *Journal of Economics and Statistics (Jahrbücher für Nationalökonomie und Statistik)* 223/2, 176–203.

Strauß, H (2004). Demand and supply of aggregate exports of goods and services. Multivariate cointegration analyses for the United States, Canada and Germany. Kiel Studies No 329, Kiel Institute for World Economics, Berlin et al.

A Tests for cointegration

To apply the Johansen procedure for cointegration tests, VECMs with four regionally disaggregated system variables (real exports to region r, real demand in region r addressed to Germany, the numerator – the German deflator of total sales – and the denominator – the deflator of total sales in region r, converted into domestic currency units by the nominal external value against the corresponding circle of trading partners – of the indicator of Germany's price competitiveness against trading partners in region r) are set up. In each model the cointegrating relationship includes a constant. Furthermore, for intra exports the shift dummy is restricted to the cointegrating relationship, and the corresponding impulse dummy is factored in the model. Table 6 below maps the trace test statistic under the null hypothesis that the system's rank is zero and the corresponding critical values for a significance level of 5%.[30] It is shown that the null hypothesis is rejected in each model.

Table 6. Tests for cointegration

System	Estimation period	Lags (1st diff.)	Trace test stat. rank = 0	Critic. val. (5%) rank = 0
Intra	1980 Q1–2004 Q3	0	210.62	59.50
euro-area	**1993 Q1–2004 Q3**	**0**	**61.25**	**48.52**
Extra	1980 Q1–2004 Q3	0	84.32	50.81
euro-area	**1993 Q1–2004 Q3**	**0**	**59.48**	**48.52**
United	1980 Q1–2004 Q3	0	144.67	50.81
States	**1993 Q1–2004 Q3**	**0**	**60.36**	**48.52**

---

[30] The critical values were generated using Johansen's DisCo routines.

B Bilateral estimation results

Table 7. Estimation results for German exports to the United States

Region	United States			
Sample	1980 Q1–2004 Q3		1993 Q1–2004 Q3	
Equation	(1)	(2), (3)	(1)	(2), (3)
β_1	0.80 *** [25.57]	**0.80** *** [43.69]	1.00 *** [27.98]	**0.98** *** [20.50]
β_2	1.02*** [9.85]	**0.94** *** [15.30]	0.59*** [7.66]	**0.71***** [8.11]
β_3	—	—	—	—
β_0	3.17*** [6.71]	**2.82** *** [10.04]	0.26 [0.52]	**0.85** [1.37]
α	−0.31*** [−5.38]	**−0.32***** [−5.79]	−0.59*** [−5.11]	**−0.53***** [−4.81]
Δd_{93}	—	—	—	—
Δx^r_{t-1}	−0.34*** [−4.14]	**−0.32***** [−3.97]	−0.25** [−2.48]	—
Δx^r_{t-2}	—	—	—	**0.29***** [3.17]
Δy^r_t	0.73*** [3.55]	**0.63***** [3.28]	0.70** [2.72]	**0.90***** [5.66]
Δy^r_{t-1}	0.64** [2.88]	**0.53**** [2.53]	—	—
Δw^r_t	0.20* [1.92]	**0.19*** [1.82]	0.20* [1.87]	—
Δw^r_{t-3}	—	—	0.38** [3.56]	**0.23**** [2.34]
Adj. R^2	0.48	**0.48**	0.63	**0.61**
SE	0.05	**0.05**	0.03	**0.03**
LM(4)	(0.28)	**(0.49)**	(0.82)	**(0.94)**
JB	(0.16)	**(0.60)**	(0.47)	**(0.59)**
White	(0.53)	**(0.50)**	(0.58)	**(0.52)**
Wald (β_1)	(0.00)	**(0.00)**	(1.00)	**(0.72)**
OV	(0.71)	**(0.73)**	(0.24)	**(0.14)**

Printing: Krips bv, Meppel
Binding: Stürtz, Würzburg